PEOPLE OF THE BODY

SUNY Series, the Body in Culture, History, and Religion

Howard Eilberg-Schwartz, editor

PEOPLE OF THE BODY

JEWS AND JUDAISM FROM AN EMBODIED PERSPECTIVE

EDITED BY
HOWARD EILBERG-SCHWARTZ

STATE UNIVERSITY OF NEW YORK PRESS

Cover photo © 1992 C. Herscovici/ARS, N.Y.
Acknowledgment is also given to Phaidon Press Ltd. for permission to use *Entracte* from the publication *Magritte* by Richard Calvocoressi.

Published by
State University of New York Press, Albany

Printed in the United States of America

For information, address State University of New York
Press, State University Plaza, Albany, N.Y. 12246

Production by Diane Ganeles
Marketing by Fran Keneston

Library of Congress Cataloging-in-Publication Data

People of the body : Jews and Judaism from an embodied perspective / edited by Howard Eilberg-Schwartz.
p. cm.—(SUNY series, the body in culture, history, and religion)
Includes bibliographical references and index.
ISBN 0-7914-1169-9 (CH : acid-free). —ISBN 0-7914-1170-2 (PB : acid-free)
1. Sex—Religious aspects—Judaism. 2. Body, Human—Religious aspect—Judaism. 3. Purity, Ritual—Judaism. 4. Women in Judaism. 5. Judaism—Doctrines. I. Eilberg-Schwartz, Howard, 1956- II. Series.
BM720.S4P46 1992
296.3'2—dc20 91–35081
CIP

10 9 8 7 6 5 4 3 2 1

To
Louis, Rivie, Marty and Paul
friends in-deed
and to
Ann
for the courage to heal

Contents

Acknowledgments ix

Introduction: People of the Body 1

1. The Problem of the Body for the People of the Book 17
Howard Eilberg-Schwartz

2. The Garden of Eden and Sexuality in Early Judaism 47
Gary Anderson

3. The Great Fat Massacre: Sex, Death, and the Grotesque Body in the Talmud 69
Daniel Boyarin

4. *Miẓvot* Built into the Body: *Tkhines* for *Niddah*, Pregnancy, and Childbirth 101
Chava Weissler

5. Purifying the Body in the Name of the Soul: The Problem of the Body in Sixteenth-Century Kabbalah 117
Lawrence Fine

6. Images of God's Feet: Some Observations on the Divine Body in Judaism 143
Elliot R. Wolfson

7. God's Body: Theological and Ritual Roles of *Shi'ur Komah* 183
Naomi Janowitz

8. The Body Never Lies: The Body in Medieval Jewish Folk Narratives 203
Eli Yasif

9. The Jewish Body: A Foot-note 223
Sander Gilman

10. (G)nos(e)ology: The Cultural Construction of the Other 243
Jay Geller

11. Zionism as an Erotic Revolution 283
David Biale

12. Menstruation and Identity: The Meaning of Niddah for Moroccan Women Immigrants to Israel 309
Rahel Wasserfall

13. Why Jewish Princesses Don't Sweat: Desire and Consumption in Postwar American Jewish Culture 329
Riv-Ellen Prell

14. Challenging Male/Female Complementarity: Jewish Lesbians and the Jewish Tradition 361
Rebecca Alpert

Contributors 379

Index 383

Acknowledgments

Several of the essays in this book have been reprinted with permission.

Howard Eilberg-Schwartz's essay (chapter 1) was originally published under the title "People of the Body: The Problem of the Body for the People of the Book" in the *Journal of the History of Sexuality* 2 (1) (1991): 1–24 published by the University of Chicago Press.

Gary Anderson's essay (chapter 2) is an adaptation of his essay "Celibacy or Consummation in the Garden: Reflections on Early Jewish and Christian Interpretations of the Garden of Eden," which appeared in *Harvard Theological Review* 82:2 (1989). Copyright 1989 by the President and Fellows of Harvard College. Reprinted by permission.

"Zionism as an Erotic Revolution" is from *Eros and the Jews* by David Biale. To be published by Basic Books in 1992. Reprinted by permission of Basic Books, a division of HarperCollins Publishers.

My thanks to The Program in Jewish Studies for helping to subsidize the production of the cover.

Introduction: People of the Body

Howard Eilberg-Schwartz

"People of the Book" is one of the most popular characterizations of the Jews in the modern period. But like all characterizations, it masks as much as it reveals. It defines the Jews as a textual community, as a people that has remained committed to their Book (the Torah) always seeking new ways of making it speak to the distinctive circumstances of each generation. This image of the Jews, of course, does grasp certain significant features of Jewish experience and history. But it also distorts that history by privileging certain dimensions of Jewish experience at the expense of others. The purpose of this introduction is to unsettle this excessively disembodied image of the Jews in order to make possible alternative ways of thinking about Judaism and describing Jewish experience.

The designation "People of the Book" implicitly specifies the kind of Jew who should be taken seriously, that is, who should serve as a symbol for what it means to be a Jew. It defines Jews as those people who participate in the activity of learning and interpreting Scripture. But, of course, not all Jews have engaged in such activities. Illiterate or non learned Jewish men and Jewish women, who generally were not encouraged or allowed to study, do not qualify as "People of the Book" and hence seemingly fall outside the category "Jews." This image thus stands in an interesting tension with the way in which Jews actually learn to define themselves and others as Jews. With the exception of converts who do in fact become Jews through a process of learning, Jews are products of genealogy. Certain kinds of sexual unions produce Jewish children; others do not. For much of Jewish history, a Jew was defined as anyone born to a Jewish mother. Recently the Reform movement has opted for bilateral descent; a child is Jewish if either parent is Jewish. But even this recent contestation, as radical as it seems to some, has not challenged the basic underlying mechanism that treats genealogy as the definitive criterion: A Jew is a person born a Jew.

Yet the characterization of Jews as a "People of the Book" defines Jews, not in terms of a genealogy of seed, but in terms of what I have elsewhere called a "genealogy of knowledge."[1] Jews are designated as those people who have been involved in studying and interpreting texts, or to put it another way, who have participated in the reproduction and dissemination of Torah. Intercourse with texts serves as a definitive marker of Jewish identity. There is a danger, then, that the description "People of the Book" will enable the issue of bodily reproduction and sexual intercourse to slide out of sight behind the symbol of the Jew pouring over the text. This elision is particularly ironic in the modern period when proportionately fewer and fewer Jews are knowledgeable about their texts than in the past. If anything has defined Jews in the past three centuries, it has been the commitment to producing children with a Jewish spouse. During the period when Jewishness has become dependent almost entirely on the choice of sexual partners, Jews are preferring to imagine themselves as a textual community. "People of the Book" is thus a romantic image that idealizes a past that it helps to create. And that imagined past in turn helps to sustain a community in which traditional texts are relatively forgotten or ignored. Yet it would be a mistake to understand the ideas of a textual community and a community of seed to be completely antithetical. The two representations of Jews are and may always be deeply entangled in one another. Ideas about how Jews reproduce themselves physically have always provided ways of thinking about how Jews remake themselves culturally. "Disseminating knowledge" and "textual intercourse" are thus much more than playful metaphors. They remind us of the ways in which ideas about knowledge are shaped by ideas about bodies and vice versa.

There is a second and for the present purposes more important distortion encouraged by the image of Jews as a "People of the Book." Since the content of "the Book" is not specified, what Jews study is treated as less significant than the fact that they are committed to books generally. One would never know, for example, that those books, which were of such obsessive interest to Jews, were deeply concerned with the body and bodily processes. Nor would one suspect that these books talk at length and in rich detail about matters such as bodily emissions, skin diseases, circumcision, proper positions for sexual intercourse, how to urinate, how to empty one's bowels, and so forth. This substantive evacuation of the tradition, permitted by the image of "the book," creates an empty space which encourages other associations to be imported, specifically, all the modern connotations that normally trail along behind the image of the book.

The book is not a neutral image in the post-Enlightenment period. Like Rodein's "The Thinker," it is evocative of wisdom and the pursuit of knowledge. In this way, the image of the Jew (who is always male) pouring over a book is misleading. He appears to be involved in an elevated, spiritual pursuit. But if we could peer over his shoulder and see what his text says, he may in fact be reading about matters as mundane as which hand to use in cleaning himself or as erotic as what positions to use during sexual intercourse. The pages, in other words, are not blank and a glance at their subject matter puts a different slant on the activity of reading and study. What is going on in "the thinker's" head or perhaps more interestingly in his loins? "People of the Book" is thus a deceptive image. It directs the gaze to the thinker but not to the subject that is tantalizing his imagination. One might reasonably object that to emphasize the "grosser" side of the tradition is also to misrepresent it since the tradition also deals with ethical or spiritual matters. That of course is true. But no one would be surprised to learn that "the thinker" is studying such elevated matters. It is the other sorts of subjects that raise suspicions about this powerful image of the thinker.

The designation "People of the Book" is thus one of the visible expressions of a larger modern strategy that attempts to disembody Jews and Judaism in hopes of spiritualizing them. In another context, I have explored how important strands of modern discourses on Judaism exhibit nervousness and anxiety over issues related to the body.[2] In the modern period, the majority of Jews came to regard various parts of Judaism, particularly those having to do with the body and sexuality, as primitive and embarrassing. These sorts of feelings and judgments partially explain why Jews have been so enthralled with the designation "People of the Book" in the post-Enlightenment period. Since the late eighteenth century when Jews were able to join European intellectual life, there has been an embarrassment over parts of Jewish tradition dealing with the body, despite the importance of such matters in Jewish sources. Texts dealing with bodily emissions, circumcision, rules for defecation and urination, rules about how to perform sexual intercourse, and so forth evoked embarrassment and shame.

These feelings have to be understood against the background of European discussions of primitive religion. From the eighteenth century onward, there was a consistent attempt to differentiate primitive and higher forms of religion, a pressing intellectual, moral and political problem given the discovery of and continuing European encounter with the peoples of the Americas, among other peoples. Unfortunately for Jews, the definition of savage or primitive religion developed as a contrast for Enlightenment views of a "Religion of Reason" or "Natural Religion," which has in turn been influenced by Protestant views of ritual and law as well as European aesthetic tastes that emerged after the breakdown of feudal society.[3] According to these criteria, much of Judaism appeared to fall into the category of primitive.

It is against the background of this discussion that the emerging Jewish disgust with certain central dimensions of Judaism must be understood. Jews found themselves in the position of trying to explain why Judaism was not a primitive religion and why it was as reasonable as Christianity, the absolute religion. In order to make that claim, however, Jews had to hide, jettison, or explain away the texts and practices that fell into those categories already defined as primitive. It would be a mistake to understand these Jewish responses as simply an intellectual exercise if we fail to grasp the ways in which Jews internalized new aesthetic tastes that fundamentally changed not just their minds, but their whole persons, including what they experienced as disgusting and what kinds of matters evoked shame and embarrassment. Jews would learn to react viscerally to certain dimensions of Jewish tradition. The desire to spiritualize Judaism, to rid it of lower practices and texts, was an attempt to make Judaism palatable to Christian and rationalist tastes, which Jews had made their own. I have recently traced out the effects of this changed aesthetic on how Jews interpreted their past in my book, *The Savage in Judaism*.

This story is further complicated by the fact that in Christian and subsequently secular European discourse, Jews were often stigmatized by various bodily characterizations, as Sander Gilman and Jay Geller show in this book. In European imagination, Jews smelled; they had long noses and big feet; Jewish men menstruated; Jewish women were sexually alluring, etc. The Jew, along with the woman and black, was regarded as closer to nature, more animal-like, and hence more embodied than the white, Protestant, male European. Geller, for example, shows these kinds of associations operating within the stereotype of long Jewish noses. The extended Jewish snout signified that Jews could smell better and depended more heavily on that sense than Europeans. Since humans had by and large superseded the use of smell in the transition from animal to human, and since men had traveled a greater distance in this development than women, the Jewish nose simultaneously feminized the Jew and signified a closer relationship between Jews and animals. But it was not just Jewish noses that were subject to stereotype. The Jewish foot was physically inferior in European imagination, being much more prone to being flatfooted and to various other medical ailments and diseases. Gilman explores how these images of Jewish feet were intimately linked to European discussions about whether Jews could and would participate in the armed forces of developing nations.

Jewish bodies, therefore, were doubly damned. On the one hand, Jews were told that they were inadequately embodied since their bodies had inherent defects which made them inferior to other kinds of peoples. Yet, on the other hand, Jews were accused of being too embodied, too close to nature, too reliant on gross bodily sense. And this overabundance of embodiment was evident in their carnal tradition as well, a tradition with overly concrete modes of thought, embodied in ritual practices, and focusing too much on matters of the flesh. The representation of the Jews as a carnal people had a long history to it, extending back to Patristic ideas of the Jews as a people of the flesh.[4]

Two different strategies emerged for dealing with these contradictory charges. The first, already mentioned, was to flee embodiment through the spiritualization of the tradition and, by extension, Jews themselves. This sort of strategy, with its roots in and nourished by earlier philosophical writings, led Jews to adopt the image of themselves as a "People of the Book" and to suppress those aspects of the tradition that dealt with bodily concerns. Issues of the body were thus relegated to marginalized Jews in the modern period. Orthodox Jews, for example, have been less embarrassed about such topics since they have been more resistant to the aesthetics of secular culture.

The second strategy was to pursue embodiment, exemplified most obviously among some Zionist thinkers such as Max Nordau (1903), but also among other reformers as well.[5] These thinkers agreed with European charges that Jewish bodies were in fact weaker than those of their European counterparts. But in their judgment, this sad state of Jewish bodies was not inherent or irreversible; it was the consequence of contingent historical circumstances that could be corrected. Jewish bodies were weak because Jews had not been permitted to own property and work the soil. Moreover, living in ghettos had produced anemic bodies that paled in comparison with peoples who lived on and worked the land. Nor could the emaciated Jewish body be blamed exclusively on external causes, for the undeveloped and frail body of Jewish men was often produced by the experience of studying in a yeshiva (a rabbinical seminary). For Nordau among others, returning to the land of Israel and becoming involved in agriculture would restore the health of Jewish bodies. In looking back on Jewish history and tradition, therefore, these modern reformers believed Jews and Judaism had been far too spiritual. The fact that learning was the highest form of Jewish activity, an activity that was essentially disembodied, contributed to the weakness of the Jewish body. Muscle-bound bodies thus became a symbol of Jewish hopes for this worldly redemption.[6] These themes are very much at the heart of David Biale's essay "Zionism as an Erotic Revolution." Biale explores the various ways in which Zionism was understood as a kind of erotic revolution that was to free Jews, particularly Jewish bodies, from the emaciated impotence of exile. Yet Biale also explores the inner conflicts in this ideology, showing how these ideas, as well as the actual sexual relationships, were beset with tensions that never were and never could be completely resolved.

In one sense, this Jewish view of history which desired to emancipate the body and sexuality obviously differed from that of other Jewish reformers and intellectuals who believed Jews and Judaism had not been spiritual enough. But in another sense, these two groups of reformers were talking past one another. Zionists wanted to subject Jewish bodies to physical labor while other reformers labored to free Judaism of the subject of the body. It is beyond the scope of this introduction to sort out the similarities and differences of various sorts of modernizers on these matters, a topic that is certainly ripe for further study.

The point I wish to make is that the Jewish struggle to find and create a place in the modern world is very much entangled in a larger project of thinking about the status and character of Jewish bodies. It would be a mistake to think that this project has or ever can be terminated. Riv-Ellen Prell's "Why Jewish Princesses Don't Sweat?" and Rebecca Alpert's "Challenging Male/Female Complementarity: Jewish Lesbians and the Jewish Tradition" show just how central the issue of human bodies remains in contemporary constructions of Judaism and Jewish experience. Prell's chapter explores the image of Jewish women in "Jewish American Princess" jokes, a form of humor that portrays Jewish American women as passive, sexless creatures who do not labor or sweat. Resisting the temptation to treat such jokes as simply misogynist or anti-Semitic humor, Prell enables us to see how representations of the female Jewish body articulate the Jewish experience of entering the affluent middle class in the post–World War II period.

Rebecca Albert in turn explores the dilemmas facing Jewish lesbians struggling to make a place for themselves in a tradition that assumes a complementarity between men and women. Alpert argues against the widespread assumption that it is their sexual relationships which pose the greatest obstacle to the lesbian's acceptance in Jewish communities. Rather, it is the relationship between women generally that poses a difficulty, for such relationships disenfranchise males and thus disrupt the complementarity between men and women which Judaism both assumes and helps to produce.

As is now evident, this book has both historical and constructive motivations, motivations that are inextricably tied to one another. As a constructive project, this book attempts to describe, renew, and participate in this complex and ongoing modern discussion about Jewish bodies and the place of bodies in Judaism. At the most general level, it seeks to unsettle the longstanding and excessively spiritual image of the Jews as a "People of the Book" and to explore in its place an image of the Jews as a "People of the Body." In this sense, it is a reminder that Jews do not simply read and write books. Like other people, they have bodies. And because they have bodies, they worry about what those bodies mean and how they should be handled. By shifting attention from the image of the Jews as a textual community to the ways Jews understand and manage their bodies—for example, to their concerns with reproduction and sexuality, marriage and death—we hope to contribute to the emergence of a different picture of what Jews and Judaism are and have been.

At the same time, this rethinking of Jewish experience and tradition also represents an attempt to bring the study of Jews and Judaism into contact with the questions of the age. There has been a recent explosion of interest in human bodies stemming from a convergence of critical developments since the sixties, including the emergence of gender as a fundamental concern, the philosophical challenges to Cartesian dualism of mind and body, the corresponding challenge to the theory/practice distinction, the emphasis on the "person" and "self" in poststructuralist anthropology, and the rediscovery of Freud. Central to this theorizing has been the work of numerous feminist writers who have explored the way in which female bodies are culturally represented and how those representations contribute to the control of women's bodies and lives. The body, particularly the reproductive female body, has been central to the early feminist writings, such as Millet (1969); Rich (1976), to more recent theorists such as Bynum (1987) and Martin (1987) as well as to French feminists such as Kristeva, Irigaray, Wittig and Cixous, who desire to find a language in which to express feminine desires.[7] The work of Foucault has also been important in exploring how the rational disciplines of modernity developed by exercising increasing control over the body through diffuse power systems that were concretized in micro-practices which regulated human subjects.[8] In the wake of Foucault's work, the human body has become a central issue in social theory.[9]

These theoretical issues, coupled with a variety of social developments, including the women's and gay rights movements, advances in reproductive technology, the development of a holistic health movement, the recognition of eating disorders, and the development of AIDs have made human bodies a site where a variety of social and disciplinary concerns meet.

The constructive project of re-membering the Jewish body is necessarily linked to a historical project of memory. The images that Jews have of themselves and the stories they tell about who they are and whom they wish to be presuppose and produce a memory of who they were and what Judaism had been once upon a time. History at its best, therefore, is a constructive enterprise that simultaneously describes the past even as it critiques and challenges the present.

At issue in this historical revisioning described here is the way in which the Jews in different times and places have situated their bodies as well as the bodies of others in the larger project of making sense of what it means to be and to live as Jews. My own work, *The Savage in Judaism,* was in part an attempt to begin thinking of Jews as a people whose religious culture pondered the dilemmas of embodiment. This book carries that project forward. Judaism, as construed here, is an unfolding religious culture that provides various answers to the questions What does it mean to have and to be a body? and How should bodies be handled? These questions, in turn, engender a host of others: What are bodies for? How should bodily processes (such as defecation and urination) and bodily experiences (such as hunger and sexual need) be treated? In what ways is the body incorporated as a metaphor into the larger religious cosmology and in what ways does the later "organ-ize" the body? What sorts of factors (e.g., historical, social, cultural, symbolic) shape the treatment of the body in given formations of Judaism? These questions cannot be answered without also attending to the ways in which differences in bodies are constructed and construed (such as the differences between male and female bodies, old and young bodies, hermaphrodites and bodies that have traits of both sexes, Jewish and gentile bodies) and the ways in which the body may figure in the making of differences (such as that between humans and God, humans and animals, Jews and gentiles, etc.). As these questions suggest, the description of Jews as a "People of the Body" carries within it its own distortion since "the body" is itself a reification which hides the fact that there is no single body but many different kinds of Jewish bodies.

It is within this matrix of questions that the following chapters all find their place. These chapters do not begin to exhaust the subject of Jewish bodies. But they are intended as a stimulating and provocative conversation starter, a conversation, that already includes interlocutors whose voices could not be present in this book, a conversation which we hope will continue to expand and pique the interest of others.[10]

The chapters that follow are all interested in some respect in why Jewish bodies are represented as they are. The chapters are loosely organized in historical sequence, beginning with Israelite religion and the Hebrew Bible and ending with issues relevant to American Jews. But a great deal would be lost if these chapters were read simply as an unfolding sequence of unrelated windows into the history of Jews and Judaism. For there are also multiple intersecting issues that create subconversations, circulating like eddies around the edges of a larger stream. In some cases, therefore, I have departed from a historical sequence so as to put into the foreground certain issues that emerge in the juxtaposition of these chapters. By far the largest recurring theoretical issue, which cuts across almost all of these chapters, is the place of human bodies in the making and sustaining of difference or otherness. There are two specific forms of difference that draw attention: differences between various groupings of people (men and women, Jews and non Jews, heterosexuals and gays, dead and living people) and differences between humans and God. As previously mentioned, Geller and Gilman deal with European stereotypes of Jewish bodies. Prell's essay on JAPS takes a somewhat different tact, looking at how an internal differentiation within the Jewish community (men's views of women's bodies) becomes the vehicle for expressing changing Jewish (male?) experiences in the larger culture. Rahel Wasserfall explores the ways in which ideas and practices concerning menstruation figure in Moroccan, Jewish women's understandings of what makes them distinctively Jewish in contrast to their Muslim neighbors. Daniel Boyarin's chapter explores the representations of the grotesque rabbinic body. Focusing on stories about sages with huge bodies, Boyarin explores the ways in which ideas about cultural and physical reproduction intersect and conflict in the tales of these big men.

Boyarin's discussion of these grotesque bodies dovetails in interesting ways with a second major issue in the subject of bodies and difference: namely, the relationship between human bodies and divinity. In the modern period, as a legacy of medieval Jewish philosophy and under the spiritualizing tendencies in modern Jewish discourse, Jews have generally come to regard their deity as disembodied. Finkelstein is typical in arguing that "man differs from all other creatures in that he is made 'in the image of God.' Because Judaism denies that God has any physical form, the image of God in this passage refers to man's mind, unduplicated self, individuality."[11] But in fact, there is a representative number of texts that do imagine God as having or at least taking a humanlike form, as has been pointed out by numerous interpreters.[12] Three chapters in this book ponder the scope and meaning of this idea for human embodiment.

In my chapter, I discuss the biblical idea that humans are made in the image of God (Genesis 1:26–28). Interpreters debate the meaning of this claim. Some assume that it refers to various qualitative similarities between God and humans. Others argue that it assumes the human form is made in the divine image. By contrast, I argue that the whole debate about whether God has a humanlike form actually masks a deeper and more problematic issue, namely, the problem of talking about the sex of God. I suggest that the dilemma of representing the sex of God generates a series of cultural conflicts that is partly responsible for turning the human body into a problem which needs to be reckoned with.

Both Elliot Wolfson and Naomi Janowitz take up this issue of God's body. Wolfson explores the theological and symbolic associations of the image of God's feet. Tracing the image from its biblical and rabbinic roots, Wolfson shows how the mystical tradition of imagining the deity's feet is both in continuity with the earlier tradition but develops it in unpredictable ways.

Naomi Janowitz takes up a discussion of God's body as represented in the *Shi'ur Komah,* a medieval mystical text that describes the dimensions of the deity's limbs. Taking a very different tact, Janowitz argues that the question of whether God has a body is beside the point. In her judgment, *any* form of theophany posed a problem in late antique Judaism. The idea of God's body was no more or less problematic in her judgment than the notion of hearing God speak. In her view, the modern debate about whether God has a human form or not improperly introduces our concerns into our reading of the past.

Larry Fine's chapter begins with the ways in which bodily metaphors are co-opted in mystical descriptions of God. The "Sefirot" or emanations of God are both described in metaphors drawn from human bodies and bodily experiences. Fine then goes on to explore the ways in which this metaphorical organ-izing of divinity is contradictory since what is imagined as going on in the body of God is not always acceptable at the level of human experience. Sex in the divine realm is less fraught with ambivalence than in the human realm.

From this major theme of body and difference emerge a number of other recurring subjects, especially the reproductive and sexual body. Sexual intercourse, marriage, reproduction, menstruation repeatedly figure in these chapters. The chapters by myself, Anderson, Boyarin, Biale, Prell, and Alpert explore the ways in which marriage and sexuality are imagined and the ways in which images of those cultural activities become symbolic of other cultural values and experiences. The chapters by Anderson, Biale, Prell, and myself intersect in particularly interesting ways around the issue of sexuality. I argue that sexuality is rendered particularly problematic by the claim that humans are made in the image of a monotheistic God. Since God cannot have anything but a metaphorical sexual experience, sexuality at the divine level is necessary disembodied. Anderson's chapter, by contrast, suggests a much more positive attitude toward sexuality, as is evident in Jewish interpretations of the Garden of Eden story. Whereas Christian interpreters generally regarded sexual intercourse as a result of the Fall, Anderson shows how Jewish interpretations regard consummation as having taken place in the garden of Eden before Adam and Eve's sin. Biale and Prell both show how the issue of marriage and sexuality is simultaneously central and problematic in Jews' representations of themselves in the modern period.

As noted above, the body is in many ways a problematic abstraction. In fact, different kinds of bodies are often recognized within cultural systems, and they are symbolized in diverse ways. It is thus important to remember that male and female bodies are often represented quite differently. For this reason, several of the chapters in this book deal with the representation of women's bodies and women's experience. Whereas many of these chapters explore such images from the hegemonic perspective of masculine culture, the chapters by Weissler and Wasserfall explore the meanings of women's bodies for women. Weissler's chapter in particular considers the extent to which women's own self-representations resist the hegemony of elitist male culture. It thus provides a very interesting contrast to Boyarin's, which focuses primarily on the male rabbinic body. Wasserfall, for her part, is more concerned with how one group of women (Jewish Moroccan) understand their own bodily practices as differentiating them from other women (non-Jewish Moroccan women).

A sensitive and playful reader of this book will also notice how the Jewish speculation about God's feet, analyzed in Wolfson's chapter, sets the stage for Gilman's discussion of the way in which Jewish feet are symbolized in European imagination. These chapters, as well as Geller's on the nose, Weissler's and Wasserfall's on menstruation, Prell's on sweating JAPS, show that the human body is in many ways a misleading abstraction. All cultures contain a multiplicity of assumptions and practices with regard to specific organs, parts, or processes of the body. These pockets of assumptions and practices may or may not be coordinated with one another into larger complexes of coherent meanings or practices. The notion of the body is thus an abstraction that, if reached at all, is constantly in dialectical tension with lower-order concepts and practices that potentially threaten the hegemony of the abstraction. The current fascination with "the body" is in danger of reifying an entity that is in reality constructed piecemeal, organ by organ. There is often no coherent theory of the body, but a multiplicity of competing assumptions about different body organs, parts, and processes and a variety of practices that more or less successfully incorporate these assumptions.

This fragmentation of the body thus leads away from a discussion of the body as such toward a cultural history of specific organs, parts, and processes. Various organs of the body are often endowed with specific cultural messages. The handling of these various organs is thus an engagement of these larger values. When people relate to discrete organs of their bodies, they are not just relating to themselves but to symbols of their culture. The symbolic investment of body organs is the outcome of complex cultural, social, and historical processes.

Methodologically, these chapters are quite diverse. While all of them are innovative in making Jewish bodies and desires a focus of inquiry, there are also methodological innovations as well. My chapter, Boyarin's, Prell's, and Geller's are most representative of the new impulses in cultural studies. These chapters grapple quite explicitly with the nature of symbols and images and are most directly engaged with interlocutors outside the context of Jewish studies. Each, in its own way, takes as its problem to understand how representations of Jewish bodies come about, how and why they are sustained, and what kinds of effects they may have. Each is attentive to the multiplicity of interlocking and sometimes contradictory meanings represented in a symbol. In a sense, each of these chapters attempts to think through what a symbol is and how it works.

Several chapters are important for moving the discussion of the body away from what are traditionally defined as classic sources of Judaism. Weissler, as noted above, turns to prayers of women as a way of looking behind the veil of the elitist masculine culture. In an analogous vein, Yasif argues that the folk traditions of medieval Jews are an important source for understanding how Jews other than the elite came to terms with their bodies. Images of the body in these sources are much more graphic and explicit than in elite sources, which tended to repress certain kinds of imaginative speculation about the body. Yasif asks interpreters of Judaism to consider what unusual tales about the body say about the experience of Jews. Prell, for her part, turns to popular culture as a critical index of how Jewish images of female bodies point to larger cultural dilemmas. Finally, Wasserfall's chapter points to a bias that this book has not overcome. The majority of chapters in this book remain text-focused. That is, the subject of the body is developed through an analysis of texts. Wasserfall's chapter, by contrast, is based on an ethnography, an embodied practice of interpretation. This book, therefore, fails to unsettle the image of the "People of the Book" in one important respect. While it challenges the spiritualizing tendencies that eclipse matters of the body within the tradition, it does not challenge the centrality of texts in representing Jewish history or experience, a challenge, which has been made by others and needs to be repeated.

Indeed, this criticism points to one of the contradictions inherent in the academic practice of writing about the body. As I sit here at my computer, aware of the strain on my back and eyes, I know that a remembering of the body can only begin in the academy but it cannot culminate there. It is not just our minds that we must change: it is our practices as well.

Notes

1. See Eilberg-Schwartz 1990, 217–240.

2. Eilberg-Schwartz 1990, 31–86. See also Eisen's (1987, 283–316) discussion of the idea of Spirit in the strategies of modern Jewish faith.

3. See Elias 1982, 1983.

4. See Daniel Boyarin's forthcoming book *Carnal Israel: Sex and Gender in Late Antique Judaism* (University of California Press) which argues that Judaism, at least in certain of its varieties, did resist the sharp polarities of Hellenistic thought and hence dwelled in the ambiguities and contradictions of the body.

5. I would like to thank Steven Zipperstein for his help in understanding the way this impulse was part of broader stream of reform than I originally thought.

6. See the informative discussion of Luz (1987, 371–401) on the tension between spirituality and earthliness in Zionism. Breines (1990) discusses similar impulses in other contexts.

7. For a review of these French thinker's work, see Jones 1981 and now Butler 1990.

8. See especially Foucault 1979, 1980.

9. See, for example, B. Turner 1984.

10. In seeking contributors for this book, I found that many more people were working on the subject than I had originally known about, including Michael Wyschograd, Shaye Cohen, Marsha Falk, Susan Sered, Ivan Marcus, Alon Goshein Gottstein, among others. In addition, several of the contributors to the present book are working on larger projects of related interest, including myself, David Biale, Daniel Boyarin, Sander Gilman, Riv-Ellen Prell, Rahel Wasserfall, and Chava Weissler. The idea for this book originally grew out of my own earlier work on related matters (Eilberg-Schwartz 1990).

11. Finkelstein 1949, 1338.

12. For references to this literature see my chapter in this book.

References

Breines, Paul
1990 *Tough Jews*. New York: Basic Books.

Butler, Judith
1990 *Gender Trouble*. New York: Routledge and Kegan Paul.

Bynum, Caroline Walker
1987 *Holy Feast and Holy Fast*. Berkeley: University of California Press.

Eilberg-Schwartz, Howard

1990 *The Savage in Judaism: An Anthropology of Israelite Religion and Ancient Judaism.* Bloomington: Indiana University Press.

Eisen, Arnold

1987 "Secularization, 'Spirit,' and the Strategies of Modern Jewish Faith." In *Jewish Spirituality,* 283–316. Vol. 2. Ed. Arthur Green. New York: Crossroad.

Elias, Norbert

1982 *The History of Manners: The Civilizing Process. Vol. 1.* Trans. Edmund Jephcott. Pantheon.

1983 *Power and Civility: The Civilizing Process Vol. 2.* Trans. Edmund Jephcott. Pantheon.

Finkelstein, Louis

1949 "Jewish Religion: Its Beliefs and Practices." In *The Jews.* Ed. Louis Finkelstein. Philadelphia: Jewish Publication Society.

Foucault, Michel

1979 *Discipline and Punish.* Trans. Alan Sheridan. New York: Vintage.

1980 *The History of Sexuality.* Vol. 1. New York: Vintage.

Jones, Ann Rosalind

1981 "Writing the Body: Toward An Understanding of *L'Ecriture Féminine.*" *Feminist Studies* 7 (2):247–263.

Luz, Ehud

1987 "Spiritual and Anti-Spiritual Trends in Zionism." In *Jewish Spirituality,* 371–401. Vol. 2. Ed. Arthur Green. New York: Crossroad.

Martin, Emily

1987 *The Woman in the Body.* Boston: Beacon Press.

Millet, Kate

1969 *Sexual Politics.* Garden City: Doubleday.

Nordau, Max

1903 "Muskeljudentum." *Juedische Turnzeitung* (June 1903). Partially trans. as "Jewry of Muscle" by J. Hessing in *The Jew in the Modern World,* 434, Ed. Paul R. Mendes-Flohr and Jehuda Reinharz. New York: Oxford.

O'Brien, Mary

1981 *The Politics of Reproduction.* Boston: Routledge & Kegan Paul.

Rich, Adrienne

1976 *Of Woman Born.* New York: W. W. Norton.

Turner, Bryan S.

1984 *The Body and Society.* Oxford: Basil Blackwell.

1

The Problem of the Body for the People of the Book

Howard Eilberg-Schwartz

> Perhaps all social systems are built on contradiction, in some sense at war with themselves. (Douglas 1966, 140).

While many cultures are preoccupied with the body, there are specific, local reasons why the body emerges as problematic in any given cultural formation.[1] This chapter explores factors indigenous to ancient Judaism that turned the human body into a problem. To anticipate, I shall argue that the human body was the object around which conflicting cultural representations met and clashed. Like other religious cultures, ancient Judaism was not a tidy entity. Tidiness is a characteristic of philosophic systems, not cultures. Each culture has its own set of conflicting impulses that struggle against one another for hegemony. In the case of ancient Judaism, at least in one of its formations, it was the human body that was caught between contradictory impulses. To cite two of the more important examples: 1) humans are understood as created in the image of God, yet God has "no-body"—neither others with whom to interact nor a fully conceptualized body with which to do it, and 2) procreation is enjoined as a mandate from God, yet semen is considered polluting, even when discharged during intercourse. These contradictions, which first surface in one form of Israelite religion, are inherited by the rabbis (200–600 C.E.), who continue to find the body a source of conflict.

In relying on the idea of cultural contradictions, I depart from the general tendency to think of Judaism as "a system" or series of systems, a metaphor that implicitly and often explicitly guides research on Judaism. This metaphor induces interpreters to produce a coherence that does not always exist; the result is that one impulse of the culture is selected as exemplary at the expense of others. The idea of cultural contradictions allows interpreters to explore the full "dispersion" of cultural assertions (Foucault 1972).

The idea of cultural contradictions has intrigued many theorists of society and culture, including Marx, Freud, Lévi-Strauss, Gluckman, Spiro, B. Turner, V. Turner, Girard and others. Contradictions operate at various levels and in various ways. For Marx, they are part of a complex social process such as capitalism that produces a conflict between the technological level and social condition of technological progress (Kolakowski 1978, 299). Contradictions are also a phenomenon of culture. The *Mythologies* of Lévi-Strauss (1969, 1975, 1978) show how myths are generated by and attempt to solve or hide logical contradictions that trouble the mind. Other theorists have examined how individuals are caught between competing demands emanating from various sources. Freud and his followers are particularly interested in the ways in which conflicts between physiological drives and cultural demands are handled. Spiro (1987, 59–60), for example, notes the intolerable contradiction in which pubescent boys and girls were placed in the early years of the Israeli kibbutz movement. In their attempt to create a sexual equality, in which sexual differences would assume little more importance than other anatomical differences, the kibbutz pioneers established a practice in which boys and girls would be routinely exposed to each other's bodies in lavatories, showers, and sleeping quarters. But at the age of puberty, the kibbutz severely prohibited any sexual contact between the sexes. "Here," writes Spiro (1987, 80–81), "is a classic example of incompatible demands. Such a contradiction can only result in intolerable conflict and unbearable frustration." In this case, Spiro argues, the contradiction seems to be generated by an attempt of culture to override biological impulses. Other theorists, such as Max Gluckman (1955), Mary Douglas (1966, 140–158) and Victor Turner (1967, 1–92), have noted how such conflicts may arise from competing social commitments or competing claims of the social system. For example, Ndembu women experience a conflict between patrilocal marriage and matrilineal descent. Women live with their husband's family yet feel the pulls of their matrilineal kin. Fathers want their sons to remain with them. But the mother's kin want her and her child to return to them. This culturally produced conflict manifests itself in a variety of physical ailments that are attributed to the attacks of deceased matrilineal ancestors. A similar sort of cultural conflict explains the disorder of anorexia nervosa. Young women afflicted with this disorder experience psychic conflict generated by irreconcilable cultural expectations (B. Turner 1984, 192–197). On this point, I find myself in agreement with Girard (1977, 147) who writes that, "far from being restricted to a limited number of pathological cases . . . the double bind a contradictory double imperative, or rather a whole network of contradictory imperatives—is an extremely common phenomenon."

Expanding on the ideas of these theorists, I suggest that the idea of cultural conflicts explain why certain objects arrest more attention than others. Vast cultural and symbolic resources are invested in those objects around which conflicting representations revolve. The symbolic elaboration that occurs around such "conflicted objects" is both a consequence of and strategy for dealing with the conflict in question. Objects that are caught between incompatible impulses are evocative, puzzling, and dangerous. The multiplication of rules that often occurs around such objects has the effect both of mastering a threatening object and of glossing the generative conflict. Under the sheer weight of legal minutiae, the original contradiction is lost from view. These conflicted objects make valuable symbolic resources. Caught between conflicting cultural processes, these objects are volatile; their power or energy can be transferred by association to other more stable cultural meanings. Consequently, these charged objects are often used to symbolize and hence empower a variety of cultural messages.[2] In turn, the established cultural messages, now associated with a potential source of conflict, help to control an otherwise unruly object.

In ancient Judaism, cultural conflicts of this sort developed around the human body, generating an intense preoccupation with the body and its processes. Ancient Jews multiplied rules that both regulated the body and turned the body into a symbol of other significant religious concerns. It is to the conflicted Jewish body that our attention now turns.

The Problem of the Body for the People of the Book

To some it may come as a surprise that Judaism is a tradition that is preoccupied with the body. Judaism is often depicted as having a predominantly favorable attitude toward the body. As evidence of this positive tendency, interpreters point out that Jews are enjoined to procreate with the result that sexuality has a positive regard within the tradition (e.g., Feldman 1968, 21–71; P. Brown 1988, 63; Gordis 1978, 98–109; Pagels 1988, 12–13). Consequently, one generally does not find the tendency toward sexual asceticism within Judaism as in other traditions such as Christianity. Nor does the Hebrew Bible or subsequent rabbinic tradition treat sexuality as a consequence of "a fall" (Sapp 1977; Anderson, this volume). Sexuality is regarded as a natural human act that is part of what it means to be human; the sexual asceticism evidenced among the Jews at Qumran is thus regarded as a deviation. In addition, the sharp dualism of body and soul, characteristic of Greek philosophical traditions, is absent in the Hebrew Scriptures and is resisted in classic rabbinic sources (Urbach 1987, 241; Rubin 1988).

While these characterizations are true, they are also misleading.[3] They ignore the way in which the government of the body has always been a central preoccupation within Judaism.[4] Despite any sharp antithesis between body and soul, and despite the importance of procreation, certain bodily processes are regarded as problematic.

The problem of the body in Judaism is already evident in those very writings that made the Jews a "People of the Book." It is in the Hebrew Scriptures, particularly that strand contributed by the Israelite priests, that the body first appears as a central issue of control. This part of Scripture, which is generally designated as "P" (after its priestly origin), includes narratives and laws, which were generally thought to be written sometime in the sixth to fifth centuries.[5] It is in the writings of the priests, especially the book of Leviticus, but also in the writings of the prophet Ezekiel (who was also of priestly descent), that the boundaries and integrity of the body arouse sustained interest.[6] Leviticus pays particular attention to what passes in and out of the orifices, particularly the mouth and the genitals. Certain kinds of food may not be taken into the body (Lev. 11). Various genital emissions, such as menstrual blood, semen, and other irregular discharges, create pollution (Lev. 12; 15). Concern with the body's integrity expresses itself in elaborate rules concerning skin diseases that are contaminating (Lev. 13–14) as well as interest in congenital or accidental disfigurations of the body (Lev. 21:16–23), which disqualify a priest from serving in the Temple. Leviticus also proscribes intentional disfigurations of the body such as shaving the corners of the face or acts of mutilation associated with mourning (Lev. 19:27; 21:5). In addition to these concerns about bodily boundaries and integrity, Leviticus strictly regulates the use to which persons put their bodies in sexual alliances (Lev. 18; 20:10–21).

This government of the body has both prophylactic and moral motivations. Many of the bodily regulations are intended to protect the sacrificial cult from contamination (Milgrom 1976, 390–99). A priest with a disfiguration or with a discharge cannot perform the sacrifices that must be done in a state of purity and wholeness. Furthermore, contamination that occurs among Israelites who are not priests can jeopardize the purity of the cult. "You shall put the Israelites on guard against their uncleanness, lest they die through their uncleanness by defiling My Tabernacle which is among them" (Lev. 15:30).[7]

But the concern with purity is not exclusively a cultic matter. Israel is enjoined to be holy, just as God is holy. Being holy includes observing the regulations governing what goes in and out of the body (Douglas 1966, 51–52; Wenham 1979). "You shall not eat, among all things that swarm upon the earth, anything that crawls on its belly . . . you shall not make yourselves unclean therewith and thus become unclean. For I the Lord am your God: you shall sanctify yourselves and be holy for I am holy" (Lev. 11:42–44). While being impure is not considered a sin, the state of uncleanness does signify an alienation from God. Furthermore, the violation of certain rules governing the body, particularly those related to sexuality, does constitute an offense against God (Lev. 20:10–26).

It is from the priestly writings that the concern with the government of the body first enters Judaism. Subsequent groups of Jews, including those at Qumran (second and first centuries B.C.E.) and the rabbis (200–600 C.E.) take up and elaborate upon the levitical rules governing the body. The Dead Sea Scrolls and the rabbinic writings both reflect a preoccupation with many of the concerns established in Leviticus. To be sure, this is not a passive acquiescence to tradition since these groups transform the rules in sometimes radical ways. I have explored some of these transformations in another context (Eilberg-Schwartz 1990, 195–216). Nonetheless, had it not been for Leviticus, the problem of governing the body would not have had the prominence it does within subsequent forms of Judaism. What follows, then, is an attempt to understand why the government of the body so preoccupied the priestly community.

The Conflicted Body

Mary Douglas has already speculated about why the body so preoccupied ancient Jews. The body, she argues, is frequently a symbol of society and thus the dangers and concerns of the social structure are reproduced on the human body. "The Israelites were always in their history a hard-pressed minority. In their beliefs all the bodily issues were polluting, blood, pus, excreta, semen, etc. The threatened boundaries of their body politics would be well mirrored in their care for the integrity, unity and purity of the physical body" (Douglas 1966, 124). Douglas also suggests that the levitical restrictions on the body stem from a concern with wholeness. Body emissions, skin-disease, and defects are threats to the integrity of the body and like other things that violate notions of wholeness, they are deemed impure (Douglas 1966, 51–52). Douglas's argument has now been canonized in commentaries to Leviticus (e.g. Wenham 1979, 222–23).

But Douglas's arguments are not entirely satisfying. To begin with, Douglas fails to explain why the body became particularly problematic to one specific group of ancient Jews, namely the Israelite priests. If the external pressures on Israel induced a preoccupation with the body, why are the same sorts of concerns not visible in all genres of Israelite literature? Why is this preoccupation located principally in the writings of the priests? Furthermore, Douglas fails to explain why body emissions would be considered a threat to notions of wholeness. Why was wholeness defined in this and not some other way? The answer to these questions emerges when we consider the distinctive religious formation of the Israelite priests.

Within this religious culture, conflicting and to some extent incompatible representations crystallized around the human body. On the one hand, the priests celebrated procreation. They not only believed that God commanded humans to be fruitful and multiply (Gen. 1:27), but regarded reproduction as a central dimension of the covenant between God and Abraham (Gen. 17). But this impulse, which sprung from the social organization and self-understanding of the priestly community, came into conflict with an important religious conception, namely, that humans are made in the image of God (Gen. 1:26–7). There is a fundamental tension between being made in God's image and being obliged to reproduce. The dilemma arises because Israelite religion places certain limitations on the representation of God. To oversimplify for a moment, God has "nobody," neither others with whom to interact nor a body, or at least a fully conceptualized body, with which to do it. Thus the dual expectations of being like God and being obliged to reproduce pulled in opposite directions. There was no escape for the body. Pressed between these conflicting impulses, the body became an object of cultural elaboration. Let me unravel this conflict in more detail.

Be Fruitful and Multiply

Of all the Israelites who contributed to the Hebrew Bible, the priestly community is by far the most concerned with human reproduction. Procreation is regarded as a central human quality and responsibility. In the priestly myth of creation, for example, the command to reproduce immediately follows the creation of man and woman (Gen. 1:28). In fact, "be fruitful and multiply" are the first words that God addresses directly to humanity. According to the priestly writings, God twice reiterates this instruction to the survivors of the flood (Gen. 9:1, 7). The importance of human fertility is underscored by its close and frequent association with divine blessing (Bird 1981, 157; Sapp 1977, 10; Cohen 1989, 13–24). In both the myths of creation and the flood, the command to procreate is immediately preceded by the statement that God conferred a blessing (Gen. 9:1).

It is not surprising then that the priestly writings regard this blessing as central to the covenant that God makes with Abraham and his descendants.

> As for Me, this is My covenant with you: You shall be the father of a multitude of nations. And you shall no longer be called Abram, but your name shall be Abraham, for I make you the father of a multitude of nations. I will make you exceedingly fertile and make nations of you and kings shall come forth from you. (Gen. 17:4–6)

As I have argued elsewhere (Eilberg-Schwartz 1990, 141–177), the priests regard the rite of circumcision as the physical inscription of God's promise of genealogical proliferation on the body of all Abraham's male descendants. In the priestly understanding, circumcision is not an arbitrary sign of the covenant, as many interpreters construe it, but a symbol that alludes directly to the substance of God's promise to Abraham, namely to multiply Abraham's seed. It is no accident that the symbol of the covenant is impressed on the penis. The penis is the male organ through which the genealogy of Israel is perpetuated. The removal of the foreskin has the effect of giving the penis the appearance it has when erect thus symbolizing great things to come. Furthermore, the priestly writings suggest an analogy between an uncircumcised male organ and an immature fruit tree. They thus associate the circumcision of the male with pruning juvenile fruit trees; like the latter, circumcision symbolically readies the stem for producing fruit.

The priestly writings trace the fate of this blessing. When Isaac gives Jacob his final blessing, he prays that God "bless you, make you fertile and numerous, so that you become an assembly of peoples. May God grant the blessing of Abraham to you and your offspring, that you may possess the land where you are sojourning, which God gave to Abraham" (Gen. 28:3). This wish is subsequently fulfilled upon Jacob's return to Canaan when God blesses him with fertility (Gen. 35:11). As his death approaches, Jacob recalls this blessing when he adopts Joseph's sons, Jacob's grandchildren, into his patrilineage (Gen. 48:3–5). The book of Exodus begins by noting that this blessing has been fulfilled. "The Israelites were fertile and prolific; they multiplied and increased very greatly, so that the land was filled with them" (Exod. 1:6).

As is now evident, the preoccupation with procreation is intimately tied to the issue of descent. The priestly writings are interested in reproduction as the means through which the genealogy of Abraham and then Jacob (Israel) is perpetuated and expanded (Eilberg-Schwartz 1990, 163–176; Sapp, 1977, 12). In particular it is the patriline, that is, the line of male descendants, that evokes interest within the priestly writings. This interest is evident by the fact that the priestly genealogies generally list only male names; the names of wives and daughters are absent (Bird 1981, 134–37; Jay 1985, 283–309, 1988, 52–70; Eilberg-Schwartz 1990, 171–73). The rite of circumcision also serves as a token of this symbolic link between masculinity, genealogy, and reproduction. Impressing a symbol of fertility on the male organ of reproduction establishes a connection between procreation and masculinity and creates a community of men who are linked to one another through a similar mark on their male members. By contrast, the potential connection between women and procreation is symbolically undermined: menstrual blood and blood of birth, which could easily symbolize procreative capacities, are instead associated with death.[8] There is a tension, therefore, between genealogy and reproduction. For the purposes of genealogical reckoning, wives and hence sexual intercourse cannot exist. But the presence of women is always necessary because men cannot reproduce alone.

The preoccupation with these twin themes of procreation and genealogy makes sense given the historical situation and social organization of the priestly community. Israelite priests were an elite community who presided over the sacrificial cult during the Israelite monarchy (tenth to sixth centuries B.C.E.). During this time, they regulated the sacrificial system in the Jerusalem Temple as well as in local sanctuaries outside Jerusalem. In the late seventh century, the cult was centralized in Jerusalem and priests continued to preside over the animal sacrifices in the Jerusalem Temple.

Scholars frequently date the priestly writings to the period during or shortly after the Babylonian exile, when pressures to increase the population may have been particularly acute. But there are other reasons, springing from the self-understanding and organization of priestly community, that would also explain the concern with procreation. The priesthood was inherited patrilineally, from father to son. All priests were purportedly descended from Levi or one of his descendants, such as Aaron. The priesthood, therefore, legitimated itself with a kinship idiom. This idiom shaped the larger interests of the priestly community and accounts for the obsessive interest in detailing genealogies. The "begats" of the Genesis narratives are primarily the work of the priests. The interest in genealogy and reproduction are obviously linked. Since lineages are replenished through the reproduction of its members, societies that define themselves through a kinship idiom frequently focus intense interest on human fecundity and clear lines of descent.[9] To put it another way, without procreation there would be no genealogy and thus no priestly community.

It is for these reasons that the priestly community could not have produced a myth of creation such as Genesis 2 in which the first person is initially created alone (Gen. 2:7).[10] It is true that in this other myth God eventually creates a human partner for Adam, authorizes marriage and apparently sexuality (von Rad 1976, 84–5; Sapp 1977, 12–16).[11] But here God's original intention does not explicitly include sexuality or human companionship. The decision to create a human partner is the result of a process. After creating the first person, God unilaterally decides that it is not good for the first person to be alone and decides to make a fitting partner for the earthling (Gen. 2:18). It is at this point that God creates the animals, as if they might be a fitting partner for the first person. It is only when the animals turn out to be inadequate companions that God fashions a second person from part of the first person. In this myth, then, the first act of reproduction is a kind of fission: a second person is split off from the body of the first. The first act of reproduction thus does not involve sexuality. With the creation of the second person emerges the difference between man and woman, and this provides the basis for the institution of marriage, and presumably sexual intercourse and reproduction. While the authorization of marriage is regarded as the climax of the story by some interpreters (Trible 1978, 102; Sapp 1977, 12–16), another reading is also possible, namely, that sexual intercourse and reproduction are not part of the human essence. After all, God originally created the first person alone; human companionship, intercourse, and reproduction were divine afterthoughts. Thus it is possible to construe this myth as suggesting that the human is most like God when sexual relations are renounced.

It is with these sorts of conclusions, if not this particular myth, that the priestly story of creation takes exception.[12] By synchronizing the creation of man and woman, the priestly myth avoids the otherwise possible conclusion that the sexual division of humanity and hence sexual intercourse and reproduction are not part of God's original intention in creating humanity. By locating authority for procreation not only in the creation account, but at the very moment of human origins, the priestly myth makes reproduction an essential human trait (see Sapp 1977, 10; Otwell 1977, 16).

But the synchronization of man's and woman's creation while solving one problem, generates another in its wake. Specifically, this notion of creation creates a strain with another important conviction of the priestly writer, namely, that God created humanity in the divine image. In what sense can a sexually divided humanity, one that is expected to reproduce, be made in the image of a monotheistic God, who has no partners? It is to this problem that we now turn.

In the Image of God

> And God said, "Let us make Man (*adam*) in our image, after our likeness . . . They shall rule the fish of the sea, the birds of the sky, the cattle, the whole earth, and all the creeping things that creep on earth." And God created Man in His image, in the image of God He created him; male and female He created them. God blessed them and God said to them, "Be fertile and increase, fill the earth and master it; and rule the fish of the sea, the birds of the sky, and all the living things that creep on earth. (Gen. 1:26–28)

There are a number of conflicting interpretations of what it means to say God made humanity in the divine image. It is not my intention to decide which of these interpretations is correct, a hopeless task for reasons I shall suggest. Rather, I explore the implications of each interpretation *on the presumption* that it is correct. In other words, assuming that each interpretation is valid, what implications does it have for human embodiment and sexuality? To anticipate, I shall argue that no matter how the priestly community may originally have construed this passage, if indeed there ever was an original meaning, it must have experienced tension around the human body.

The conflict in question springs from certain limitations that Israelite culture imposed on the representation and conceptualization of God. These limitations made it difficult, if not impossible, to reconcile aspects of human embodiment, particularly human sexual relations, with the idea of being made in the divine image. If these religious convictions had gained the upper hand, they might have generated either a renunciation of the body in general or sexuality in particular. But these impulses in Israelite religion came in conflict with the priests' equally strong commitment to the importance of human sexuality as the vehicle for reproduction. I will sometimes refer to these tensions as the "contradictions of monotheism." But it is important to bear in mind that these tensions appear most forcefully in one particular formation of monotheism, that of the Israelite priests. It is when the conviction that humans are made in the image of God appears in the same cultural formation which exalts human reproduction and sexuality that these tensions emerge most powerfully.

Despite the voluminous literature on the "image of God" passage, the interpretations can be categorized into three major groupings. There are a variety of technical historical and linguistic arguments that support or discount each of these interpretations. These do not bear on the present argument which attempts to show that the body is rendered problematic regardless of which of these interpretations is correct.

A Bodiless God

Certain strands within Israelite literature suggest that God has no form, at least no form that humans can see or imagine:

> The Lord spoke to you out of the fire; you heard the sound of words but perceived no shape—nothing but a voice. . . . For your own sake, therefore, be most careful—since you saw no shape when the Lord your God spoke to you at Horeb out of the fire—not to act wickedly and make for yourselves a sculptured image in any likeness whatever: the form of a man or a woman, the form of any

> beast on the earth. . . . Take care, then, not to forget the covenant that the Lord your God concluded with you and not to make for yourselves a sculptured image in any likeness, against which the Lord your God has enjoined you. For the Lord your God is a consuming fire, an impassioned God. (Deut. 4:12–24)

This passage, dating to the late seventh century B.C.E., asserts that Israelites heard a voice but did not see any divine form during the revelation on Horeb. This is given as the reason for the prohibitions on depicting the deity in plastic art, a prohibition with roots in a much older tradition (Exod. 20:4, 20:23, 34:17; Deut. 5:8, 27:15) (von Rad 1966, 49; Childs 1974, 405–06).[13] What the original motivation for this prohibition is, is debatable.[14] Archaeological evidence confirms that Israelite art did not represent God sitting on the divine throne (Hendel 1988), a proscription that may originally have stemmed from an Israelite ambivalence toward the institution of kingship. The representation of a god on the throne was one means through which ancient Near Eastern cultures legitimated royal authority. The prohibitions of such depictions in Israelite religion may reflect a desire to delegitimize the institution of kingship, a desire that developed during the Israelite tribal league when there were no kings in Israel (Hendel 1988). Below, I will suggest another possible reason for this prohibition. But whatever its prime motivation, the effect of the proscription is clearly to place restrictions on the visualization of God.

Many interpreters reasonably assume that these Israelite impulses to "de-form" God provide the background for the priestly claim that humans are made in the image of God. (e.g. Cassuto 1978, 34–35; Barr 1968–69; Bird 1981).[15] In other words, humans resemble God in some qualitative sense only. Being made in God's image implies no resemblance between the human and divine forms. Interpreters disagree as to the particular qualities humans and God share.[16] But generally they include the "spiritual" or "higher" human functions. Nahum Sarna (1970, 15–16) is representative of this trend when he writes "the idea of man 'in the image of God' must inevitably include within the scope of its meaning all those faculties and gifts of character that distinguish man from the beast and that are needed for the fulfillment of his task on earth, namely, intellect, free will, self-awareness, consciousness of the existence of others, conscience, responsibility and self-control." Other interpreters suggest that humans are like God in ruling over creation. Indeed, the idea that humanity is made in the image of God who is king of the universe slides easily into the idea that humans rule the earth: "They shall rule the fish of the sea, the birds of the sky, the cattle, the whole earth, and all the creeping things that creep on earth" (Gen. 1:26). This line of interpretation is supported by ancient Near Eastern parallels in which the King is said to be the image of God (Bird 1981, 140; Cohen 1989, 16; Miller 1972, 289–304; von Rad 1976, 59; Westermann 1984, 150ff).[17] In addition, the priests considered God's activity at creation paradigmatic in establishing an order that Israelites were responsible for maintaining. Israelites were expected to preserve those classifications that God had implanted at creation (Douglas 1966, 29–57; Eilberg-Schwartz 1990, 217–225).

According to these qualitative interpretations, the priests understood humans to be made in the image of a disembodied and sexless God. "The Creator in Genesis is uniquely without any female counterpart and the very association of sex with God is utterly alien to the religion of the Bible" (Sarna 1970, 13). Embodiment and sexuality are thus traits that humans share with animals "*Unlike* God, but *like* the other creatures, *adam* is characterized by sexual differentiation" (Bird 1981, 148).[18] On this reading, the image of God does not parallel the human differentiation into male and female. It is "generic Man" that is the image of God, but not humankind as sexually differentiated. The "image of God refers to neither Adam alone nor to Eve, but only to the two of them together" (Sapp 1977, 10). "Man's procreative ability is not here understood as an emanation or manifestation of his creation in God's image" (von Rad 1976, 60).

We must be careful not to assume that because biblical writers associated reproduction with animals they therefore regarded sexual intercourse as a "beastly" activity. On the contrary, the command to be fruitful and multiply is considered a blessing that humans share with animals (Gen. 1:21–22) (Bird 1981, 157; Sapp 1977, 10). Indeed, Israel is metaphorically identified with the herds and flocks (Eilberg-Schwartz 1990, 115–140) and multiplying like animals is regarded as a positive image. "I will increase Israel with men as a flock of sheep," says God (Ezekiel 34:31).

Nonetheless, these interpretations leave the human body caught between contradictory expectations. On the one hand, human embodiment and sexuality are considered good; but they are good because God said so (Gen. 1:31), and because they are products of God's creative activity. Yet at the same time they are the very symbols of human difference from God. That is, it is the nonsexual and nonembodied part of the human person that is made in God's image. For this reason, there is a tension between obeying God and being like God. A person who wishes to obey God should be fruitful and multiply. But in doing so, one engages precisely that dimension of human experience that denies one's similarity to God. In fact, sexual intercourse contaminates a couple, alienating them from the sacred and hence from God. These dilemmas arise on any of the strictly qualitative or spiritual interpretations.

But not all strands of Israelite religion deny that God has a form or body, as many interpreters have observed (Barr 1959; Kaufman 1972, 236–37; von Rad 1976, 58; Westermann 1984, 149ff; Mopsik 1989; Boyarin 1990). Indeed, several sources make it clear that some Israelites imagined that God has or at least assumes a human appearance (e.g. Exod. 24:9–11; 33:17; 1 Kings 22:19; Amos 9:1; Isa. 6:1; Ezek. 1:26–28; Dan. 7:9). "Then Moses and Aaron, Nadab and Abihu, and seventy elders of Israel ascended and they saw the God of Israel: under His feet there was a likeness of a pavement of sapphire, like the very sky of purity. Yet He did not raise His hand against the leaders of the Israelites; they beheld God and they ate and drank" (Exod. 24:9).

> And the Lord said [to Moses], "See, there is a place near Me. Station yourself on the rock and, as My presence passes by, I will put you in a cleft of the rock and shield you with My hand until I have passed by. Then I will take My hand away and you will see My back; but My face must not be seen." (Exod. 33:23)

The most detailed description of God is given in the book of Ezekiel. Ezekiel sees "a semblance of a human form. From what appeared as his loins up, I saw a gleam as of amber . . . and from what appeared as his loins down, I saw what looked like fire. There was a radiance all about him . . . That was the appearance of the semblance of the Presence of the Lord" (Ezek. 1:26–28). Since Ezekiel is a priest, it is possible that Ezekiel's image of God was shared by the priestly author of Genesis 1.

There is, then, an important impulse in Israelite religion that does ascribe a human form to God and assumes that, under certain conditions, the divine form is visible. Given this impulse within Israelite religion, an alternative understanding emerges of what it means to be made in God's image, namely, that the human body resembles the divine form.[19] Support for this view comes from the use of the word "image" (*ṣelem*), which most interpreters construe to mean a physical likeness.[20] Furthermore, in Gen. 5:1–3, the terms "image" and "likeness" are used to describe the resemblance between Adam and his son Seth. The repetition of the same terminology here suggests that humanity resembles God in the same way that Seth resembles Adam, which includes a physical resemblance (Sapp 1977, 8; Mopsik 1989, 52).[21] This latter interpretation of the "image of God" passage is compatible with the qualitative interpretations given above. Humans can be like God both in their appearance and qualities (Westermann 1984, 151ff; von Rad 1976, 58; Sapp 1977, 7).

Advocates of the second interpretation, which "re-forms" God, believe this reading rehabilitates the human body in important ways. And to some extent they are right. Since the human form mirrors the divine appearance, having a body is part of what it means for humans to be made in the image of God. The form of the body ceases to be a sign of human and divine difference. But on further reflection, it becomes clear that even the ascription of a human form to God does not completely solve the problem of human embodiment since having the form of a body does not mean that God is materially embodied. From those sources that depict God's body, it is impossible to determine whether it is substantive. Indeed, one can make the argument that God's materialization takes other forms, such as fire (Exod. 3:2; Deut. 4:11–12). If God's body is immaterial, one that does not die, have emissions, require sexual intercourse, and so forth, then it is only the form of the human body that is legitimated but not the experience of embodiment itself.

Furthermore, Israelite sources are extremely reticent about describing the divine body. Indeed, seeing God is considered dangerous and consequently appears to be the privilege of certain qualified leaders (Barr 1959; Boyarin 1990). According to one passage, God tells Moses you "cannot see My face, for no person may see Me and live" (Exod. 33:17–23). Even those sources that suggest that the full body of God is visible avoid any descriptions. When Moses, Aaron, and the elders reportedly see God, the text only describes what is under God's feet. Even Ezekiel is careful to qualify his description of God in fundamental ways. He sees only "the appearance of the semblance of the Presence of the Lord." This circumspection about God's body—about describing and representing it—is also evident in the way Israelite literature avoids *certain* kinds of anthropomorphisms. While God does a variety of humanlike things, including speaking, walking, and laughing, God does not perform "baser" human functions, such as eating, digesting, urinating, or defecating.[22]

In the official conceptions of Israelite religion, then, God's body is only partially conceptualized. This reticence has the effect and may indeed be partially motivated by the desire to veil the divine sex.[23] Ezekiel's description of God, for example, does not make clear whether God's lower regions are human in form: "from what appeared as his loins down, I saw what looked like fire."[24]

A similar concern may be present in the story in which God only allows Moses to see the divine back. Indeed, this incident (which is from the J source) is reminiscent of another story recounted by the same author (Gen. 9:20–27): when Noah is drunk, his son Ham (which means "hot"), sees his father's nakedness. This is purportedly the sin for which Canaan, Ham's son, is subsequently cursed. When Ham tells his brothers, Shem and Japheth, what he has seen, they take a cloth, place it against both their backs and walking backward, cover their father's nakedness; "their faces were turned the other way, so that they did not see their father's nakedness." The similarities between these two accounts are too striking to be passed over. Noah's sons walk backward and divert their gaze so they cannot see their father's nakedness, while God turns away so that Moses can only see the divine behind.[25] It is as if God is being modest about disclosing the divine sex.

Does God have genitals and, if so, of which sex? It is interesting that interpreters have generally avoided this question. This seems a particularly important lacuna for interpreters who understand Gen. 1:26–27 to mean that the human body is made in the image of deity. By avoiding the question of God's sex, they skirt a fundamental question: how can male and female bodies both resemble the divine form? Since God's sex is veiled, however, any conclusions have to be inferred indirectly from statements about God's gender. But however this question is answered poses a problem for human embodiment generally and sexuality in particular. If God is asexual, as many interpreters would have it, then only part of the human body is made in the image of God.

But suppose Israelites did imagine that God had a sex. Given the preponderance of masculine imagery for God (e.g., as man of war, king, father), Israelites would presumably have assumed that God had a penis, if they had bothered to think about it.[26] The story about the sons of God taking wives from daughters of men (Gen. 6:1–4, by the J writer) gives support to the assumption that the divine is considered male. And the parallel between the story of

Noah's nakedness and the story of Moses seeing God's back might also suggest that what God is hiding is a phallus.

While the assumption of a divine phallus may legitimate the male body, it nonetheless leaves human sexuality problematic. To put it bluntly, what would a monotheistic God do with a reproductive organ? In official Israelite monotheism, God had no divine partners with whom to consort. Thus, in contrast to other ancient Near Eastern creation myths in which the gods copulate, Israelite creation stories depict God as creating the world alone (Sarna 1970, 12–13; Sapp 1977, 2–3; von Rad 1976, 58–60). And in the priestly story, God creates the world by speaking (Sapp 1977, 1; Scarry 1985, 181–210).[27] Feminists have emphasized the way that an image of a male God creates a problem for being a woman. If God has the physical likeness of a male, the female body is by definition problematic. But what is emphasized much less frequently is how a monotheistic, male God also leaves males in conflict with their own bodies. If males are to be like God, then their penises are only for show; they should not be used for reproduction. The form of reproduction that can most easily be reconciled with a monotheistic God is fission, as in the second story of creation. Thus even on the interpretation that treats the human form as made in the image of God, the body remains a problem in certain fundamental ways. If God has no sex, then the reproductive organs of both males and females are rendered problematic. And if God does have a sex, whether male or female, God's reproductive organs are useless.[28]

These religious convictions, of course, could easily generate a sexual asceticism. But it is important to remember that the priests could not entertain this option. The theme of reproduction was so deeply embedded in their self-understanding and organization as a patrilineally defined community that to reject these themes would have been tantamount to dismantling their community. So even if the priests had imagined an embodied God, the human body would have been left facing fundamental and irresolvable tensions. But these tensions are generally not visible. And they are not visible because the debate about the image of God passage generally revolves around the question of whether that passage implies a similarity between the human body and the divine form. That debate draws attention away from deepest contradiction of all: namely, the purpose of reproductive organs on the body of a monotheistic God. And it is perhaps this dilemma that contributes to the prohibition on representing God in material form, which is another way of hiding the problem of God's sex.

The Sexuality of God

If the attempt to embody God does so at the expense of God's sexuality (a monotheistic God can have no sexual experience), the obverse is also true: sexuality can only be predicated of God at the cost of divine embodiment. In other words, a monotheistic God cannot have both a body and a sexual experience. This second form of incompatibility is evident in the attempt by some interpreters to reconcile the sexual division of humanity with the image of God. After all, it is reasonable to read Gen. 1:26–28 as suggesting that men and women are both made in the image of God. Phyllis Trible's *God and the Rhetoric of Sexuality* is one of the most articulate expositions of this argument.[29] In Trible's view, the division into male and female is what distinguishes humans from animals. "Procreation is shared by humankind with the animal world . . . sexuality is not" (Trible 1978, 15). That is, although Genesis 1 says that both animals and humans reproduce, the attributes of male and female are exclusively human characteristics, at least in Gen. 1.[30] Animals, by contrast, are divided "according to their kinds," a form of categorization that does not apply to humans. Through a literary analysis, Trible goes on to suggest that "male" and "female" correspond structurally to "the image of God." That is not to say that sexual differentiation can be applied to God (Trible 1978, 21). But sexuality is one of the human experiences that points toward an understanding of Israel's transcendent deity. Trible develops her argument by exploring the metaphors used to depict God. Not only is God metaphorically a father, husband, king, and warrior but also a woman who conceives, gets pregnant, gives birth, nurses, and mothers children.

Trible's interpretation is self-consciously an attempt to recover female imagery and motifs within the Hebrew Scriptures. As suggested by the title of her book, her project includes the attempt to redeem human embodiment and sexuality. Her interpretation thus goes a long way toward reconciling human sexuality with the conviction that humans are made in the image of God.

But in crucial ways this interpretation also leaves the experience of embodiment and sexuality problematic. It is striking that Trible completely ignores the interpretation that ascribes a form or body to God. This omission is interesting in a book that seeks to redeem sexuality. Upon reflection, however, it is clear that this omission is a necessary precondition for any interpretation that seeks a reconciliation between the sexual division of humanity and the image of God. Since there are no other gods, God's act of copulation *can only be metaphoric*. Ezekiel, for example, invokes the metaphor of sexual intercourse to depict the covenant between God and Israel (Ezek. 16:8). While these metaphors do validate human sexuality in important ways, they still leave something to be desired. God cannot have an embodied sexual experience. If God has a penis, it plays no role in the divine relationship with Israel. From this perspective, the metaphor of God having intercourse with Israel actually devalues human copulation in one significant way. If the relation of God to Israel is analogous to that of husband and wife, then what parallels the human act of intercourse is revelation, the insemination of Israel with God's will. Divine intercourse with Israel is mediated through speech. This substitution of speech for sexual intercourse is evident in Ezekiel's depiction of God's intercourse with Israel. Thus God says, "I spread My robe over you and covered your nakedness and I entered into a covenant with you *by oath*" (Ezek. 16:8). Israel is inseminated with the divine will. It is even less clear how the analogy works when God is metaphorically a woman who is impregnated and conceives. Who is Israel's metaphorical father? So when the metaphor of human copulation is projected onto the relationship between God and Israel, it effects only a partial reconciliation between human sexuality and the conviction that humans are made in the divine image. The rehabilitation of human sexuality must take place at the expense of God's body. It is impossible to simultaneously embrace the idea that God has a body with a sex and is a sexual being. As soon as one of these ideas is grasped, the other slides into obscurity. In order for God to have sex, God must not have a body, and to have a body, God can have no sex.

Myth, Contradiction, and Ambiguity

I have consciously avoided favoring any interpretation of "the image of God" passage in order to show that on any of the interpretations, the priests are left with their bodies caught in a morass of fundamental tensions. It is impossible to affirm both the conviction that human sexuality and reproduction are divinely authorized aspects of human experience and the assertion that humans are made in God's image without at the same time rendering the human body or sexuality problematic in some aspect or another. To push this line of thinking further, it is possible that the "image of God" passage never had a single meaning. James Barr (1968–69, 13) anticipates me in writing that "there is no reason to believe that this writer had in his mind any definite idea about the content or the location of the image of God." But according to Barr, this hesitation stemmed from a "delicacy and questionability . . . of any idea of analogies to God." But another possible explanation is now obvious. The ambiguity of the image of God passage may attempt to hide the fundamental dilemmas implicit in the religious formation of the priests. If so, then none of the contemporary interpretations of Gen. 1:26–28 can be construed as the original meaning of this passage. Rather, the wide range of interpretations testify to the power of this myth to simultaneously hold together what are radically different possibilities and thus gloss irresolvable tensions in the priestly religious culture. Indeed, it seems that the passage is carefully formulated so as to obscure, as much as is possible, these various problems.

The shift between plural and singular nouns and verb tenses is one means by which this myth negotiates the conflict between a monotheistic God and a humanity that is sexually divided. The plural "Let us create" has always been puzzling to interpreters. Is the plural referring to other divine beings (von Rad 1976, 58; Sawyer 1974, 423–4) or is it a royal "we" (Speiser 1964, 7)? However this question is answered, it is clear that this construction glosses the problematic fact that there is only one God but two sexes of human beings. Phyllis Bird (1981, 148) writes that " 'Let us' cannot be a slip . . . it appears also to have been selected by P as a means of breaking the direct identification between *adam* and God suggested by the metaphor of image, a way of blurring or obscuring the referent of *ṣelem.*" A similar obfuscation is accomplished by the shift from singular to plural in speaking of humanity (He created *him,* male and female he created *them*). The use of two nouns "image" (*ṣelem*) and "likeness" (*dĕmût*), the former which seems to imply a plastic representation and the later a more abstract, qualitative similarity (Miller 1972, 291), also contributes to the confusion.[31] Furthermore, interpretations of the "image of God" passages differ depending on which of these terms is taken as primary and which secondary. For example, most interpreters argue that the priestly writer introduced the more abstract term "likeness" to qualify the more graphic term "image" so as to avoid any suggestion that the human appearance resembles the divine form (Sawyer 1974, 420).[32] Miller, by contrast, argues that the term "likeness" (*dĕmût*), which has linguistic affinity with the word for "blood" (dām), was original and goes back to Mesopotamian myths that conceive of humans as made from the blood of the gods. The introduction of the term "image" was intended to rule out this sort of interpretation by substituting a word for resemblance that did not have associations to blood.

The second image of God passage only adds to the confusion. This passage employs the term "likeness" to describe the similarity between God and humanity: "This is the record of Adam's line—When God created man, He made him in the likeness of God; male and female He created them." But the passage then goes on to use the terms "likeness" and "image" to describe the similarity of Adam and his son Seth: "When Adam had lived 130 years, he begot a son in his likeness after his image, and he named him Seth" (Gen. 5:1–3). If Gen. 5:1–3 is read by itself, it seems to suggest that the likeness between God and humanity is of a different order than the likeness between a father and son. The resemblance between God and humanity is described by the word "likeness" only. But Adam begets a son who is both in his likeness and image. But if Gen. 5:1–3 is read as a supplement to Gen. 1:26–28, the opposite is the case: the same terms are used to describe the resemblance between Seth and Adam (Gen. 5:3) and between God and humanity (Gen. 1:26–27). The point of these myths, then, may be to hide the basic tensions through a screen of confusion. To be sure, these maneuvers do not entirely hide the problem. But given an impossible task, these myths rise to the occasion.

It is important to realize that the tensions that I am describing were not characteristic of all Israelite writers. As long as humans were understood as different from God, the impulse toward monotheism and the impoverished conceptualization of God's body need not have rendered human embodiment or sexuality problematic. The asexual or formless nature of God would pose less of a problem to the human body on the assumption that humans are made from the dust of the earth (Gen. 2:7). As an earthly substance, humans would be expected to have functions and needs that God does not. Neither the impulse toward monotheism nor toward a disembodied God by themselves necessarily creates a problem for the human body. It is only when these tendencies are coupled with the conviction that humans are created in the likeness and image of God, as the priests suggest (Gen. 1:26–7), that human bodies become problematic.

For these reasons, it is in the priestly writings in particular, and not in Israelite religion as a whole, that the boundaries and integrity of the body become such an intense preoccupation. This cultural obsession, I have suggested, springs from the fact that the human body is caught between contending cultural impulses. This higher order contradiction is reproduced at a lower level in rules governing sexuality. While the priests regard reproduction as one of the most important religious injunctions, semen is contaminating, even if ejaculated during a legitimate act of intercourse (Lev. 15:16–18). One might say that for the priests, therefore, one is "damned if one does and damned if one doesn't." In the very act of carrying out God's will, one alienates oneself from God by becoming contaminated.

These tensions help explain the obsessive interest in the human body in priestly culture. The elaboration of the rules around the body was in part an attempt to control a puzzling object. But these rules did more than control a "foreign body." The absorption in legal regulations also diverted attention from the fundamental conflicts that surrounded the body. Absorbed by the legal particularities surrounding ejaculation, menstruation, and skin disease, those inside and outside the priestly community would have lost sight of the larger dilemmas that inhered in the priests' religious culture. It is for this reason too that the body became one of the richest sources of symbols in the priestly community. As I have shown elsewhere, the circumcised penis is a symbol of the covenant, procreation, and patrilineal descent. In addition, distinctions among body fluids are associated with other symbolic meanings, such as that between life and death, control and lack of control, themes embedded in the larger cultural system of ancient Israel (Eilberg-Schwartz 1990, 141–194). The superimposing of such themes on bodily processes and organs effects a transfer of energy from the conflicted object to the theme symbolized and thus heightens the power of the later. The human body, then, was the site at which conflicting cultural impulses met and clashed. It was that conflict that made the Jews more than just a People of the Book. They also became a People of the Body.

Notes

1. I would like to thank Robert Cohn, Ronald Hendel, Martin Jaffee, Louis Newman, and Riv-Ellen Prell who all made helpful suggestions on an earlier draft. I also profited greatly from conversations with Tikvah Frymer-Kensky.

2. This idea has an affinity with Victor Turner's (1967, 54–55) insight that physiological processes are often symbolic of more abstract cultural

messages because they lend those messages a power that they otherwise would not have. The present argument differs from Turner's in seeing that power as deriving, not from physiological processes, but from contradictions in a cultural formation.

3. See also Biale (forthcoming) who is attempting to correct this overly apologetic presentation of Judaism.

4. I am indebted to B. Turner for the concept and term "government of the body."

5. Some scholars following Yehezkel Kaufman defend a pre-exilic date for P. A review of this issue can be found in G. Wenham 1979, 9–13. See also Richard E. Friedman 1989, 161ff. This debate is not crucial for the present argument, which does not depend on pinpointing the historical context in which the priestly writings were produced.

6. I am not making any claims about any specific *literary* relationship between the book of Ezekiel and the P source in the Hebrew Bible, a problem that has exercised a great deal of biblical scholarship. Rather, I am suggesting that Ezekiel's priestly origin may have contributed to his concern with the government of the body.

7. All quotations of the Hebrew Bible are taken from the translations of the Jewish Publication Society (1962, 1978, 1982).

8. See my discussion of circumcision, menstruation, and the issues of genealogy (Eilberg-Schwartz 1990, 141–195).

9. See my survey of ethnographic studies of circumcision in Africa, which show a recurring linkage between issues of genealogy, virility, and reproduction (Eilberg-Schwartz 1990, 141–177).

10. Most interpreters regard Adam in this story as male and Eve as being separated from a male body. See, however, Phyllis Trible 1978, 72–105 and Bal 1987, 104–131, who argue that the original Adam is neuter and that sexual differentiation occurs only when a split is introduced. To avoid attributing a sex to the first human creation, I refer to Adam as "the first person."

11. Gerhard von Rad, *Genesis,* trans. John H. Marks (Philadelphia, 1976), 84–5, and Sapp, 12–16.

12. See Frank Cross 1973, 293–325, who argues that the priestly writer did not write a complete narrative paralleling the JE narrative, but rather expanded and supplemented it. If so, then the priestly writer felt compelled to supplement the creation story as told in Gen. 2.

13. See von Rad and Childs for the possible connection between the prohibition on images of God and the deuteronomic idea that Israel only heard

but did not see God at Horeb. The latter idea is very likely a later interpretation of the already existing prohibition.

14. Childs (1974, 407–408) summarizes various attempts to explain this prohibition. Von Rad, for example, argues that images were prohibited because they failed to deal adequately with the nature of God. Similarly, Zimmerli argues that the prohibition reflects the idea that God has chosen to be revealed not in a static image, but in ambiguity of dynamic history. Below, I will suggest an additional reason for the prohibition: the representation of God would require defining the sex of God, which would force to the surface the complex tensions surrounding gender and sexuality that are implicit in Israelite monotheism.

15. James Barr (1959, 31–38) originally suggested that the "image of God" passage presupposes the resemblance between the human and divine forms. But he (1968–69, 11–26) subsequently retracted that view based on historical and linguistic analysis.

16. Westermann (1984, 147) provides a review of interpreters who hold this position.

17. For a review of the relevant arguments and the ancient Near Eastern evidence, see especially Westermann 1984, 150ff.

18. It is interesting to compare Bird and Trible on this issue. Bird notes that in other contexts the priestly writer treats the categories of "male" and "female" as applicable to animals. Trible, for her part, argues that in Gen. 1 the division into "male" and "female" is unique to humankind since the animals are divided "according to their kinds," a type of categorization that does not apply to humans. According to Trible (1978, 15), "Procreation is shared by humankind with the animal world . . . sexuality is not."

19. Barr (1959) originally suggests this possibility and then changes his mind. For a history of this interpretation see Miller 1972, 292 and Westermann 1984, 149ff.

20. Not all interpreters agree with this interpretation of *ṣelem*. For a different reading, see Barr 1968–69. Furthermore, most interpreters argue that the other term, "likeness" (*dĕmût*), qualifies the term "image" and is intended to rule out the idea that the human and divine forms are similar.

21. This is not the only reading of the relation between Gen. 1:28 and 5:1–3. I discuss an alternative below.

22. Sexual intercourse is one exception that I shall take up below.

23. In a subsequent context, I hope to consider this whole issue from the vantage point of Lacan's argument that the phallus must be veiled (Lacan 1977, 281–291).

24. I would like to thank my colleague Tikvah Frymer-Kensky for pointing this out to me.

25. The text suggests that God's modesty is motivated by a desire to hide the divine face "for man may not see my face and live" (Exod. 33:20). In another context, I hope to explore how God's face, or more specifically the divine mouth, is treated as a genital organ because of its generative role in creation.

26. Some feminist writers have assumed that God's sex is male on this basis. For example, in *Beyond God the Father,* Mary Daly, in a section entitled "Castrating 'God,' " writes that "I have already suggested that if God is male, then the male is God. . . . The process of cutting away the Supreme Phallus can hardly be a merely 'rational' affair."

Trible and others have noted the feminine images of God. But none of these writers have argued that Israelites would have imagined God as being female, that is, as having a body with breasts, vagina, and womb. For a possible interesting exception, see Biale (1982). Biale argues that the priests thought of God as a "God of Breasts." This is reflected in the priests use of the term "El Shaddai" to describe God, a term that traditionally has been interpreted as "God Almighty." But the word *shaddai* also refers to "breasts," enabling the expression "El Shaddai" to be read as "God of Breasts." To strengthen his interpretation, Biale shows that this association is explicit in one early biblical passage and that the priestly writings use the term "El Shaddai" precisely in those contexts dealing with promises of fertility.

27. Scarry offers a provocative reading of biblical texts in the context of her larger argument about the relationship of voice, body, and pain. She sees a dialectic set in play by the fact that God is imagined as disembodied, as only a voice, whereas humans are embodied. This distance is frequently transversed by a weapon, which mirrors the relationship between a torturer, who magnifies a regime's voice through torture, and the victim, who loses his or her voice through the magnification of bodily pain. Scarry's reading is illuminating in many ways. But her theory needs to be nuanced since it does not deal with those texts that imagine God in human form, an idea that confounds the sharp dichotomies with which she is working.

28. The only remaining possibility is that God is androgynous, an idea that does develop in late antique religions. On this view, male and female bodies are both partially made in God's image. Moreover, it is in the act of sexual intercourse, in the joining of male and female bodies together, that the human achieves the most complete reflection of the androgynous deity. This interpretation comes the closest to reconciling the division of the sexes with the image of God. But there does not seem to be any biblical evidence to support it. Moreover, a hermaphroditic God is a kind of hybrid, and the

priestly writers generally find hybrids and other anomalies abhorrent. Finally, an androgynous deity does not procreate or have a sexual experience, thus still leaving an important difference between humans and the deity.

29. Trible's interpretation has been dismissed by some as a feminist reading that does not pay sufficient attention to the place of Gen. 1 in the larger context of the priestly writings (see, for example, Bird). To a certain extent, this criticism is valid. To read Gen. 1 as an example of incipient egalitarianism ignores the fact that the priestly writings generally privilege the male over the female. As noted previously, the priestly genealogies do not even mention the presence of wives. But Trible's reading cannot be dismissed out of hand. As I have suggested, the simultaneous creation of male and female is motivated by a desire to legitimate procreation. But in order to do so, the priests had to tolerate the seeming implication that both male and female are made in the image of God. To reformulate Trible's question, then, it is interesting to ask how and why the priests managed to tolerate the association of "the female" with the image of God.

30. As noted earlier, Bird points out that the categorization of male and female is used elsewhere in the priestly writings to talk about animals.

31. See, however, Barr (1968–69), who argues that *ṣelem* was the term most apt for avoiding the suggestion of resemblance of the human body and divine form.

32. See Miller 1972, 293 for other references to this argument.

References

Bal, Mieke

1987 *Lethal Love: Feminist Literary Readings of Biblical Love Stories.* Bloomington: Indiana University.

Barr, James

1959 "Theophany and Anthropomorphism in the Old Testament." In *Vetus Testamentum, Supplements* 7:31–38.

1968–69 "The Image of God in the Book of Genesis—A Study of Terminology." *Bulletin of the John Rylands Library* 51:11–26.

Biale, David

1982 "The God With Breasts: El Shaddai in the Bible." In *History of Religions* 21:3, 240–256.

forthcoming *Eros and the Jews*. New York: Basic Books

Bird, Phyllis

1981 " 'Male and Female He Created Them': Gen 1:27b in the Context of the Priestly Account of Creation." *Harvard Theological Review* 74 (2):129–159.

Boyarin, Daniel
1990 "The Eye in the Torah: Ocular Desire in Midrashic Hermeneutic." *Critical Inquiry* 16 (3):532–550.

Brown, Peter
1988 *The Body and Society: Sexual Renunciation in Early Christianity.* New York: Columbia.

Cassuto, U.
1978 *A Commentary on The Book of Genesis* [Heb.]. Pt. 1. Jerusalem: Magnes.

Childs, Brevard S.
1974 *The Book of Exodus.* Philadelphia: Westminster.

Cohen, Jeremy
1989 *Be Fertile and Increase, Fill the Earth and Master It.* Ithaca: Cornell University.

Cross Frank
1973 *Canaanite Myth and Hebrew Epic.* Cambridge: Harvard University.

Daly, Mary
1973 *Beyond God the Father.* Boston: Beacon Press.

Douglas, Mary
1966 *Purity and Danger.* London: Routledge and Kegan Paul.

Eilberg-Schwartz, Howard
1990 *The Savage in Judaism: An Anthropology of Israelite Religion and Ancient Judaism.* Bloomington: Indiana University.
forthcoming, "Damned If You Do and Damned If You Don't: Rabbinic Ambivalence Towards Sex and Body." In *Center for Hermeneutical Studies Protocol Series.* Vol. 61. Berkeley.

Feldman, David M.
1968 *Marital Relations, Birth Control and Abortion in Jewish Law.* New York: Schocken Books.

Friedman, Richard E.
1987 *Who Wrote the Bible?* New York: Harper and Row.

Foucault, Michel
1972 *The Archaeology of Knowledge.* Trans. A. M. Sheridan Smith.

Girard, René
1977 *Violence and the Sacred.* Trans. Patrick Gregory. Baltimore: Johns Hopkins University.

Gluckman, Max
1955 *Custom and Conflict in Africa.* Oxford: Blackwells.

Gordis, Robert

1978 *Love and Sex: A Modern Jewish Perspective*. New York: Hippocrene Books.

Hendel, Ronald

1988 "The Social Origins of the Aniconic Tradition in Early Israel." *Catholic Biblical Quarterly* 50 (3):365–82.

Jay, Nancy

1985 "Sacrifice as Remedy for Having Been Born of Woman." In *Immaculate and Powerful*. ed. C. W. Atkinson et al., 283–309. Boston: Beacon.

1988 "Sacrifice, Descent, and the Patriarchs." In *Vetus Testamentum* 38 (1):52–70.

Jewish Publication Society

1962 *The Torah*. Philadelphia: The Jewish Publication Society of America.

1978 *The Prophets*. Philadelphia: The Jewish Publication Society of America.

1982 *The Writings*. Philadelphia: The Jewish Publication Society of America.

Kaufman, Yehezkel

1972 *The Religion of Israel*. Trans. and abdg. Moshe Greenberg. New York: Schocken.

Kolakowski, Leszek

1978 *Main Currents of Marxism*. Vol. 1. Oxford: Oxford University.

Lacan, Jacques

1977 "The Signification of the Phallus." *Ecrits*. Trans. by Alan Sheridan. New York: Norton.

Lévi-Strauss, Claude

1969 *The Raw and the Cooked*. Trans. John and Doreen Weightman. New York: Harper and Row.

1973 *From Honey to Ashes*. Trans. John and Doreen Weightman. New York: Harper and Row.

1978 *The Origin of Table Manners*. Trans. John and Doreen Weightman. New York: Harper and Row.

Milgrom, Jacob

1976 "Israel's Sanctuary: The Priestly Picture of Dorian Gray." *Revue Biblique* 83:390–99.

Miller, J. Maxwell

1972 "In the 'Image' and 'Likeness' of God." *Journal of Biblical Literature* 91:289–304.

Mopsik, Charles
1989 "The Body of Engenderment in the Hebrew Bible, the Rabbinic Tradition and the Kabbalah." In *Zone: Fragments for a History of the Human Body.* Pt. 1. Ed. Michael Feher with Ramona Naddoff and Nadia Tazi. New York: Ozone.

Otwell, John H.
1977 *And Sarah Laughed: The Status of Woman in the Old Testament.* Philadelphia: The Westminster Press.

Pagels, Elaine
1988 *Adam, Eve and the Serpent.* New York.

Rubin, Nisan
1988 "Body and Soul in Talmudic and Mishnaic Sources." *Koroth.* 9:151–164.

Sapp, Stephen
1977 *Sexuality, the Bible and Science.* Fortress: Philadelphia.

Sarna, Nahum
1970 *Understanding Genesis.* New York: Schocken.

Sawyer, John F. A.
1974 "The Meaning of 'In the Image of God' in Genesis I–XI." *Journal of Theological Studies* (ns) 25:418–26.

Scarry, Elaine
1985 *The Body in Pain.* New York: Oxford University.

Speiser, E. A.
1964 *Genesis.* The Anchor Bible. Garden City: Doubleday.

Spiro, Melford
1987 *Culture and Human Nature.* Ed. Benjamin Kilborne and L. L. Langness. Chicago: The University of Chicago Press.

Trible, Phyllis
1978 *God and the Rhetoric of Sexuality.* Philadelphia: Fortress.

Turner, Bryan
1984 *The Body and Society: Explorations in Social Theory.* Oxford: Oxford University Press.

Turner, Victor
1967 *The Forest of Symbols.* Ithaca, N.Y.: Cornell University.

Urbach, Ephraim E.
1987 *The Sages: Their Concepts and Beliefs.* Boston: Harvard University.

von Rad, Gerhard
1976 *Genesis.* Trans. John H. Marks. Philadelphia: Westminster.
1966 *Deuteronomy.* Trans. Dorothea Barton. Philadelphia: Westminster.

Wenham, G. J.
1979 *The Book of Leviticus.* The New International Commentary on the Old Testament. Grand Rapids, Mich.: William B. Eerdmans.

Westermann, Claus
1984 *Genesis 1–11.* Trans. John J. Scullion. Minneapolis: Augsburg Publishing House.

2

The Garden of Eden and Sexuality in Early Judaism

Gary Anderson

The interpretation of Adam and Eve's sexual life was a matter of some concern for early Jewish and Christian exegetes. As Ginzberg observed (Ginzberg, 1908–38, 5:134 n. 4), several Jewish pseudepigraphical works as well as the writings of many of the early Church Fathers "presuppose that not only the birth of the children of Adam and Eve took place after the expulsion from paradise (Gen. 4: 1ff), but that the first "human pair" lived in paradise without sexual intercourse."[1] The reasons for such an exegesis are not difficult to discern. The Garden of Eden was not simply a story about the primeval world; it could also function as a metaphor for the world-to-come.[2] Hence, the Garden was a paradigm for the ideal world of the eschaton, a world one should attempt to actualize or bring into existence now. Because Christians believed that the next world was devoid of marriage (Luke 20:27–40), it followed that Garden was as well. In addition to this reason, Christians were also exhorted to abstain from marriage as a concession to the apocalyptic ferment of the present world (1 Cor. 7).

Rabbinic Judaism, on the other hand, did not have a high regard for the celibate condition. One midrashic text compares the celibate individual to one who impairs God's image and, even worse, to a murderer.[3] The act of human procreation was not simply an acceptable act, it was a *commanded* act. It is the subject of the very first command God gives men and women: "be fruitful and multiply" (Gen. 1:28). It should come as no surprise, then, that in rabbinic exegesis, the Garden was the location of humankind's first sexual encounter.

The disagreement between Jews and Christians over the theological value of the celibate state was not limited to intellectuals. As Aphrahat's *Demonstrations* show, the issue was an important one among common Jews and Christians as well. Aphrahat describes the ridicule Christians often received from Jews in regard to this issue. As he describes it, the Jews argue that divine blessing and procreation are inseparable themes in the Bible (*Demonstration* 18.1)[4] To abstain from procreation is to live in isolation from divine blessing. God blessed Adam (Gen. 1:28), Noah (9:7), and Abraham (15:5), and in each case, the blessing resulted in progeny. Moreover, one of the prominent features of the promised land is its fertility. As the Torah promises, there shall be no barren women in Israel (Exod. 23:26, Deut. 7:14). The association of the themes land, blessing, and fertility in this text of Aphrahat sounds like an authentic Jewish position. In our discussion below we will see these themes all come together in the Babylonian Talmud, tractate *Ketubot* 8a. In another section of his polemic against the Jews, Aphrahat declares that one Jew has asserted that Christians are unclean because they do not take wives (18.12). He writes:

> I have written to you, my beloved, concerning virginity and holiness (*qaddîšûtâ'*) because I heard about a Jewish man who has reviled one of our brethren, the members of the church (*bnay ʿi(d)tâ'*). He said to him: "You are impure (*ṭamm'în*) for you don't take wives. But we are holy (*qaddîšîn*) and more virtuous for we bear children and multiply seed in the world."[5]

Aphrahat's understanding of holiness (*qaddîšîn*) is significant. He correctly distinguishes the Jewish understanding of the term, as reflected in rabbinic documentation, from the Christian. Jews understood the term to refer to the state of marriage.[6] Syriac Christians understood the term to refer to sexual continence. Aphrahat's identification of sexual abstinence with uncleanness might seem unusual. The rabbis never placed the sexually abstinent individual in the legal category of unclean.[7] Perhaps the usage of uncleanness here reflects an extended metaphorical definition rather than a technical legal designation. In summary, the issues Aphrahat raises in regard to the Jewish position appear authentic and anticipate the issues to be discussed below.

As one would expect, both the rabbis and the early Christians attempted to establish their views about the role of sexual experience in the Garden on the basis of a close reading of the biblical narrative. The questions with which we are concerned are these: on what exegetical bases were these decisions made, are the exegetical processes at all related, and can one date one particular exegetical result as earlier than another? The last concern was treated by Ginzberg. He argued that in the earliest evidence of Jewish exegetical reflection, Adam and Eve lived in paradise without sexual experience. Indeed, this view can be found in some prerabbinic Jewish works. For example in *2 Baruch* 56:5–6, it is said that the conception of children and the passion of parents only came about as a result of the transgression of Adam. This position, originally of Jewish origin, was adopted by Christians according to Ginzberg. Christians took this position because it understands sexual knowledge to be a result of human sin. Once this position became an identifiably Christian one, rabbinic thinkers reacted and opposed this position by creating a tradition of marriage in the Garden.[8] For Ginzberg, the central concern in the history of the exegesis is the sin of Adam and Eve and their consequent expulsion, a sequence of events Christians identify as the 'Fall'. Our intention is to: 1) determine if Ginzberg is right as to the relatively late date of the rabbinic concept of sexual relations in the Garden and 2) to ascertain whether the sin of Adam is the dominant exegetical concern regarding sexual relations in the Garden.

Sexual Consummation in the Garden

Rabbinic materials presume that Adam and Eve are married and consummate their marriage in the Garden of Eden. But the rabbinic materials do not make this exegetical claim in a general manner. As Heinemann has shown (Heinemann 1974), exegetical themes like this one usually develop around a particular text or pair of texts that for some reason or another, appear as problematic to the reader of the Bible. The solution to this problem or problems is usually accomplished by the creation of an aggadic narrative that fills in some 'implied' background information within the text. Though aggada often begins with this type of close reading, the textual origin of a particular aggada can be forgotten and 'erroneously' reattached to new texts or be assumed in the exegesis of other texts. In tracing the tradition history of a piece of aggada, one must not only collect all the examples of it, but one must also attempt to locate the particular verse or set of verses in which it originates.[9]

In order to clarify the point of origin for this motif, it will be helpful to mention several exegetical texts that presume the sexual union of Adam and Even in the Garden.

> "And the woman said unto the serpent . . ." (Gen. 3:2). Now where was Adam during this conversation? Abba Halfon b. Qoriah said: "He had engaged in sex and then fell asleep." (*Genesis Rabbah* 19:3)

> "And they were both naked (*ʿarummîm*) . . . Now the serpent was the most subtle (*ʿarûm*) . . . (Gen. 2:24–3:1). [why is the snake interpolated here and why are the Hebrew words naked and subtle the subject of a world play?] They indicate for what sinful purpose the snake was anxious to do this thing. He had seen them engaging in sex and developed a passion for her. (*Genesis Rabbah* 19:6)

The verse "he built the rib . . . into a woman and led her to him" (Gen. 2:22) is understood as a description of the first marriage ceremony. The act of 'building' is understood as God's adornment of the bride (*Genesis Rabbah* 18.1),[10] and the act of leading is understood as God's acting as Adam's groomsman or *šôšbîn* (*Genesis Rabbah* 18:3). The precious stones of Eden (Ezek. 28:13) are described as the extraordinary *ḥuppâ* under which Adam and Eve were married. There is a definite logical progression implied in these midrashim. In Gen. 2:22, God adorns Eve, prepares the ḥ*uppâ,* and presents the bride to Adam. By the time the snake arrives, just a couple of verses later, Adam and Eve have made love, and Adam has gone to sleep (Gen. 3:1–2). On the basis of what lies before us, we can see that this union must have occurred before the encounter with the snake and (obviously!) after the presentation of Eve to Adam.

This leads to the text in question. In Gen. 2:23–24, we read the following response of Adam to his new wife Eve:

> 23Then God brought her to Adam and he said: "*zōʾt happaʿam,* bone of my bones, flesh of my flesh, she shall be called woman because she was taken out of a man." 24Therefore a man leaves his father . . ."

Modern translations of the phrase *zōʾt happaʿam* are very similar. The *RSV* and *JB* read, "this, at last," the *NEB* "now this, at last" and the *JPS,* "this one, at last." But these similar translations mask several interpretive problems. Just how are *zōʾt* and *happaʿam* related, what antecedent act do they refer to, and how are they related to the following etiology of marriage (v. 24)? Modern translators and commentators have understood *happaʿam* as a reference to something that has happened after a long period of expectation, so the emphasis on the 'at-lastness' of the event. Such a usage can be paralleled in Gen. 29:34,35; 30:20; and 46:30. In fact, the first three texts involve acts of successful procreation. In these cases, the expression is simply *happ'am* with the article *ha-* having the force of the demonstrative pronoun 'this.' Gen. 2:23 is a more emphatic rendering of this idea because it also appends the demonstrative pronoun (somewhat redundantly?) to the phrase.

The Targumim translated the *zō't* as though it were used attributively, *hādâ zimnâ,* "this time." Targum Neophyti and Ps. Jonathon clarify what is so emphatically important and novel about this occasion.

> This time *and never again will a woman be created from a man as* this one *was created from me* (italics = midrashic explanation).

This understanding is also found in the *Abbot de Rabbi Nathan* (B) (hereafter, *ARNB*):

> When Adam saw Eve he said: "This is my mate." As scripture says, "And Adam said: "This at last is bone of my bones (Gen. 2:23). [Meaning] this one time, woman was created from man; from now on a man takes the daughter of his fellow and is commanded to be fruitful and multiply. [Another interpretation:] This one time God acted as groomsman for Adam; from now on he must get one for himself.[11]

Both the Targumim and *ARNB* understand *happa'am* as an act of singular importance, an act that occurred just once and will not be repeated. This interpretation is not without biblical parallels. The term *happa'am* can have exactly this force in Gen. 18:32, Exod. 10:17, and Ju. 6:39 and 16:28. The midrash is clarifying just what was so singular about this presentation of Eve to Adam in the Garden. (This text also solves the problem of *when* God commanded Adam to be fruitful and multiply.)

One other exegetical tradition does focus on the 'at-lastness' of the phrase. This tradition is found in BT *Yebamot* 63a and was adopted by Rashi as the most sensible reading of the text.

> *zō't happa'am.* This teaches that Adam attempted to have sex with all the beasts and animals but his sexual desire ("knowledge") was not cooled off by them.

Behind this midrash is a juxtaposition of Gen. 2:18–20 and Gen. 2:23–24. The latter verses describe Adam's reaction to his mate while the former describe the rather peculiar circumstances that brought about her creation. These circumstances need to be cited.

> [18]And the Lord God said: "It is not good for Adam to be alone, I will make a helper like him. [19]Thereupon the Lord God formed from the ground every beast of the field and bird of the skies and brought them to Adam to see what he would name them. Every name Adam gave a living thing, that was its name. [20]And Adam named all the cattle, the birds of the skies and the beasts of the field. But in respect to Adam himself, he did not find a helper like him.

The important sequence is that of 18–19a and 20b. In 18, God makes the observation that Adam is alone and needs a helper. Then, as if in response to this mental intention, God creates the animals! In the end, Adam still is alone. The subject of the verb "to find" in 20b is somewhat ambiguous. Most modern translators have understood it as an impersonal 3 m.s.: "and a helper was not found for Adam." But an equally probable subject, especially in light of God's stated intention in 18a, is God: "and God did not find a helper for him." One theological problem with this translation is that it makes God look less than perfect in the work of creation. Another problem is that it does not help illuminate Adam's cry in 2:23, "this one, at last." This cry presumes that *Adam* is the one in search of a mate *not God.* In order for that cry to make sense, Adam must come to learn of his need for a mate in 2:20, and so Adam must be made the subject of the verb "to find." Once Adam is understood as the subject, then the presentation of the animals in verses 19–20a can be understood in a fashion that does justice to the Godhead. No longer is God creating the animals in an attempt to find a mate for Adam, rather by way of this creation, Adam will learn on his own of this need. This 'education of Adam' is brought out in the following midrash:

> "And Adam named all the cattle . . ." [This verse teaches that] while he was calling each one by its proper name, he noticed them copulating each with its mate and he couldn't figure out what they were doing because the feeling of erotic attraction had as yet no power over him for scripture says: "But Adam himself did not find a mate like himself."[12]
>
> Then he paraded [the animals] again [after the naming] before him in pairs. Adam said: "Everyone has a mate except me!" (*Genesis Rabbah* 17.4)

The understanding of *zōʾt happaʿam* as a reference to Adam's finally finding a sexual partner and 'knowing' her explains the chronology of marriage in the Garden as it develops in the other midrashic stories about Eden. If this exegesis of *zōʾt happaʿam* was ancient, then the rest of the aggadic developments we traced above would all follow quite logically as an elaboration of this sexual scene. The verses that precede would describe the preparations for marriage (adornment of Eve, God as groomsman, description of *ḥuppâh*), and the verses that follow would describe its consequences (Adam's absence in 3:2, Satan's jealousy). One problem with this reconstruction is that *Genesis Rabbah* does not seem to know this exegetical tradition even though it presumes sexual relations in the Garden. But this is not an insoluble problem. Heinemann has provided many examples of how a specific exegetical source for an aggadic narrative can be forgotten in the subsequent elaboration of a particular narrative theme.[13]

In order to prove decisively the antiquity of this tradition, we must turn to the book of *Jubilees*.

> And Adam named all of [the animals], each one according to its name, and whatever he called them became their names. And during these five days Adam was observing all of these, male and female according to every kind which was on the earth, but he was alone and there was none whom he found for himself, who was like himself, who would help him. And the Lord said to us, "It is not good that the man should be alone. Let us make a helper who is like him." And the Lord God cast a deep sleep upon him and he slept . . .
>
> And [God] brought her to him *and he knew her* and said to her, "This is now bone of my bones and flesh of my flesh. This one will be called by wife because she was taken from her husband."[14] (*Jubilees* 3:2–5a,6, italics indicate significant additions to the biblical text)

This text is remarkable in several ways. It places the act of sexual consummation exactly where *Yebamot* put it, and like *Yebamot,* it also understands Gen. 2:19c–20 to be a narrative wherein Adam learns of his need for a sex partner. God's creation of the animals is not a mistaken attempt at finding a partner for Adam, rather it is an instructive event that informs Adam of his incompleteness and need for a mate. The instructive quality of the event is made quite clear by the lengthy interpolation put into this sequence. For five days, Adam observes the animals in pairs; only then does he (not God!) see his need for a mate. Thereupon God steps forward to provide this mate. As a result of this interpretation, 2:18 is moved down and placed before 2:21. This solves the problem of God setting the animals before Adam as a though they were to be his helper. Adam's recognition of his need and then the provisionment of this need leads to his own sexual union ("and he knew her") and the logical explanation of the cry, "this time, at long last!" Thus the text of *Jubilees,* which is generally dated to the second century B.C.E., shows the antiquity of this exegetical motif.

The concept of sexual relations before the expulsion from the Garden is a very ancient theme that originated as an exegetical solution to Adam's problematic explanation. But the movement from *Jubilees* to rabbinic midrash is not as simple as it may appear. For the rabbis took this piece of exegesis concerning Adam's exclamation and made it the basis for a larger narrative concerning marriage rite *within* the Garden. *Jubilees* does something much different. The book of Jubilees has Adam and Eve meeting one another before their entry into the Garden. Thus, their initial sexual encounter occurs *outside* the Garden. Only after 40 days can Adam enter the Garden, and Eve must wait 80 days. These numbers reflect the days of purification that Lev. 12 requires for those who have just given birth to children. The situation in *Jubilees* does not quite fit the model of Lev. 12., for Adam and Eve have had no children yet and will not have any until they are expelled from the Garden. But their own creation has become a model for the rite of purification enjoined on all subsequent parents.

Garden and Temple

The point of the *Jubilees* narrative is this: Eden is conceived of as a holy site—indeed, it is more holy than any other spot—and those who enter its environs must be pure. Though Eden is not said to be a Temple in this particular narrative, its Temple attributes are clear from the description of Eden in Jubilees 4:23–26. In this section, Eden is the location to which Enoch is taken so that he might survive the flood. Eden is conceived of as a cosmic mountain that the flood waters were not able to overcome. Jubilees ascribes the reason for this as due to the purity of Enoch. He was unique among his generation in not consorting with the Watchers, thus his pure condition made him worthy of reentry into Eden. While in Eden, Enoch offered incense and so provides ample evidence that Eden was thought of in terms of Temple images. With respect to Adam's knowing Eve, it should now be clear why it had to occur outside of Eden. Sexual emissions rendered the person the unclean (Lev. 15:18) and unfit to eat the sacred food of the Temple (Lev. 22:4–7). In rabbinic literature, the danger of sexual impurity necessitated the sequestering of the high priest from his spouse for the week before Yom-Kippur (*M. Yoma* 1:1). For the author of *Jubilees,* it was not an esteem for the celibate state, nor an extreme form of ascetical piety which required that sex not take place in the Garden. Rather, the author is simply building on the biblical motif of purity within the Temple.

Temple and Sabbath

The book of *Jubilees* also outlaws sexual experience on the Sabbath as well (50:8). This is certainly no accident. The creation of Sabbath, in the description of the P writer (Gen. 2:1–3), was comparable to the creation of the Tent-shrine/Temple.[15] The similarities between the Sabbath and Temple were further developed in postbiblical literature. Like the Temple, the Sabbath day was characterized by rest; only the work required for Temple sacrifices was allowable on it. *Jubilees* emphasizes these dimensions as well. By concluding the work with a lengthy peroration on the meaning of the Sabbath and its legal requirements, the writer not only emphasizes its importance, he highlights its eschatological significance. The Sabbath is said to be "a day of the holy kingdom for all Israel" (50:9). This particular phrase calls to mind the image of a restored political Israel; the term "holy kingdom" in sectarian Jewish literature was not a spiritual concept.[16] This phrase portrays the Sabbath as a foretaste of the eschatological era when Israel would return to her status as a world empire. *Jubilees* also raises the Sabbath to the rank of a (Temple-) festival, and like those festivals, all Israel is commanded to eat and drink on that day (50:9–10). Fasting is strictly forbidden, just as it was on feast days of the Temple (50:12–13). And sexual relations, because they are forbidden within the Temple, are also forbidden on the Sabbath. The Sabbath is a means of actualizing, in a non-Temple environment, the requirements of Temple existence.[17]

Rabbinic literature diverges from the strict legal prescriptions found in *Jubilees* just as it diverges from *Jubilees'* treatment of Eden. In contrast to the law of sexual continence in *Jubilees,* rabbinic law enthusiastically enjoined marital relations on the Sabbath.[18] What is curious is that the rabbis, like the author of *Jubilees,* articulated the rules for Sabbath purity in terms of a model that pertains to the (Temple-) feast day.[19] But the rabbis diverge strikingly from the model found in Jubilees by not generalizing the strict norms for existence within the sacred space of the Temple itself (where a recent sexual emission would render one impure) to the Sabbath. The discussion of what constitutes purity on the festival day or Sabbath is framed in different terms altogether: the laws that pertain to the mourner. The mourner is a suitable model for comparison because the discrete ritual activities that define the mourner are also actions which render one unclean. Thus priests, who must be available for service within the Temple, are restricted as to whom they can mourn for (Lev. 21:1–6). Moreover, the high priest was not allowed to mourn for anyone, presumably so that he would always be available for cultic service (Lev. 21:10–12). The impure state of the mourner is not simply a biblical idea. As Huntington and Metcalf illustrate, the mourning period is a time of impurity in many cultures (Huntington and Metcalf 1979). The ritual movement from mourning to joy in the Bible or in rabbinic materials was also a movement from an impure state to a pure one. The Talmud, in fact, explicitly compares the state of the impure leper to that of the mourner (BT *M. Qatan* 15b). There is one peculiarity about the movement from impurity to purity in the case of the mourner. The movement from mourning to joy allows for the *resumption* of sexual relations as part of the ritual process.[20] The resumption of sexual relations as a symbolic action denoting the end of mourning can be seen in numerous Semitic materials.[21]

Eden and the Age of Eschatological Joy

In the restoration literature of the postexilic and post-70 periods, the awaited New Age was described as one of joy while the present age was described as one of mourning. These images of joy in the *Endzeit* soon become images of the primordial *Urzeit*. We begin our investigation of the joyous Edenic state with the list of the six benedictions spoken over the bride and groom in the rabbinic wedding rite. They are found in the Babylonian Talmud, tractate

Ketubot. The literary context in which they are found is a *baraita,* which states that a set of blessings must be said before ten people during the seven days of the marriage celebration. Rab Judah then recites his own formulation of these blessings. As Heinemann has shown, the form of these blessings could vary from one recital to another and some variant formulations have survived (Heinemann, 1977).[22] But the variants are variants in detail, not in gross structure. Because of the conservative tendencies in the oral transmission of these forms of prayer, it is safe to assume that the six blessings Rab Judah, a third-century Amora, cites had a long prehistory.

1. Blessed are you O Lord Our God, King of the Universe, who has created everything for his glory.

2. [Blessed are you O Lord Our God, King of the Universe,] creator of humankind.

3. [Blessed are you O Lord Our God, King of the Universe,] who created humankind in his image, in the image of the likeness of his form. And has prepared for him from his very own person an eternal 'building' (*binyan*), blessed are you O Lord creator of man.

4. May you be glad and exultant O barren one when her children are gathered to her with joy. Blessed are you Lord who makes Zion joyful with her children.

5. May you make joyful these beloved companions just as you made your creatures in the Garden of Eden in primordial times (*miqqedem,* see Gen. 2:8). Blessed are you O Lord, who makes bridegroom and bride rejoice.

6. Blessed are you O Lord Our God, King of the Universe, who created mirth and joy, bridegroom and bride, gladness, jubilation, dancing and delight, love and brotherhood, peace and fellowship. Quickly, O Lord Our God, may the sound of mirth and joy be heard in the streets of Judah and Jerusalem, the voice of bridegroom and bride, jubilant voices of bridegrooms from their canopies and youths from the feasts of song. Blessed are you O Lord who makes the bridegroom rejoice with the bride.

Rashi attempts to discern what is the difference between the two formulations of joy in the fifth and sixth benedictions. He believes the phrase "who makes the bridegroom *and* bride rejoice" (fifth benediction) refers to general rejoicing apart from the wedding itself (*śimḥat bĕrakâh hā-rīšônâh lô' bĕ-śimḥat ḥătunnâh*), while the phrase "who made the bridegroom rejoice *with* the bride" (sixth benediction) refers to the specific pleasures of the wedding event, one of which would include the moment of "marital coupling" (*ḥătunnat dîbbûq*). The commentator R. Isaiah de Trani (early thirteenth century) paraphrases the sixth benediction as "he who created the joy of coupling." Both of these commentators are drawing on a meaning of the term 'joy' that is found throughout the rabbinic literature as well as in other the Semitic languages of the ancient Near East (Hebrew, Jewish, Aramaic, Syriac, and Akkadian).[23] In these languages, the term 'joy' is not so much a general term of emotional pleasure, but rather a term that connotes particular pleasures associated with the observation of specific rituals. In particular, the pleasures that are most characteristic of the experience of joy are those which stood in typological contrast to those of mourning. Thus, just as mourning consists of fasting, rending the garments, putting dust on the head, and sexual continence, so the experience of joy included eating and drinking, putting on festal attire, anointing oneself with oil and bathing, and sexual union. Many restoration texts speak of the inbreaking of joy in the New Age and so convey the idea that this joy will mark the end of the present period of grief and mourning.[24] One particularly prominent display of joy was the marriage ceremony because of the presence of great feasting and dancing as well a the sexual union of the couple.

Many Semitic texts presume this understanding of the term. For example, when Gilgamesh is exhorted by the Alewife to stop his mourning over Enkidu, she commands him "to rejoice in the lap/groin of his wife."[25] A close structural parallel to this can be found in *Jubilees*. In one text, after Adam and Eve have completed their mourning over Abel, it said that "they rejoiced and then Adam knew Eve" (*Jub* 4:7). One should note that both these texts understand the experience of sexual joy to be a ritual marker of the end of mourning. This may illuminate why the Rabbis chose the concerns of the mourner as the means by which they would articulate the requirement for purity on the feast day and Sabbath. The mourner's movement from impurity to purity included the unexpected movement from sexual abstinence to sexual joy.[26]

One should keep in mind the technical sense of the term 'joy' when reading the blessings in *Ketubot* 8a. As can be seen from *B. Bathra,* the joy which is present at the wedding includes both the eating and drinking by the wedding guests, but also the sexual consummation of the marriage. Both types of marital joy are associated with the Garden of Eden. The fifth blessing compares the marital joy of the present age with that of Eden. The second half of the blessing employs vocabulary from the biblical narratives about Eden. The Hebrew word for creatures, *yĕṣîr,* recalls the role of God as creator (Gen. 2:7), and the mention of the Garden existing in primordial times (*miqqedem*) is also an illusion to the diction of the Eden narrative (Gen. 2:8). The third benediction uses imagery from Gen. 1 to describe the creation of man, but it also alludes to the creation of woman in Gen. 2. The benediction says that God prepared for Adam "an eternal building" (*binyān ʿădê ʿad*). The obvious referent here is the creation of Eve. This prayer builds upon a midrashic interpretation of Gen. 2:22: "And the Lord God *built* (*bānâh*) the rib . . . into a woman." This midrash understands the verb to connote not simply the divine act of creation but also the nature of that creation. Eve is to become more than a partner to Adam; she is to be a propagator, a provider of children.[27] *The emphasis of the blessing rests on the procreative act.* It would be an exaggeration to claim that the prayers for joy in *Ketubot* necessarily entail sexual consummation, but the semantic horizon of this term, as well as the general concern of these blessings with the themes of procreation and fertility, makes this understanding a possible, if not, probable one.

The benedictions also portray marriage as having an eschatological significance. In the sixth blessing, the imagery of Jeremiah is used. He had characterized the era of mourning, or divine curse that was to follow the destruction of the Temple and land, as a time when the sounds of mirth and joy, bridegroom and bride, would cease from the cities of Judah and the streets of Jerusalem (Jer. 7:34, 16:9, 25:6). By contrast the era of restoration would be characterized by the return of these joyful sounds (Jer. 33:10–11). So also the sixth benediction characterizes the end times as one of great marital joy. This theme of marriage was also used by early Christian writers, but there was one major difference: they did not share this enthusiasm for real human marriage in the New Age (Murray 1975, 137–42). The image was spiritualized and thought to convey only the mystical marriage of the redeemed to their Savior. The Jewish interest in real human marriage in the New Age is consonant with their perspective that the eschaton would entail a return to a *real* land and a *real* Temple. Also prominent in the eschatology of this sixth benediction is the movement from barrenness (curse) to fertility or ingathering (blessing) in the New Age.

This is reflected in the fourth benediction. The concept of ingathering is very prominent in restoration texts of the Bible (Isa. 54:7, 56:8, Jer. 31:10; Ezek. 37:21; Zech. 10:8).

Eden and the Theological Image of Divine Blessing

The depiction of Eden as a spot of marital bliss derives, in part, from the movement of the joy of the *Endzeit* to the *Urzeit*. But there is more here than a simple transference. The very motif of a Garden of Eden, on its own terms, conjured up the imagery of sexuality and procreation. As the recent discovery of the Tel Fekharyeh materials shows, the verbal root *ʿ-d-n* has a very prominent association in Northwest Semitic religion with the storm-god Baal/Hadad (Greenfield 1984). The verbal root refers to *the provisionment of fertility and blessing* by this god. Late biblical texts make the very same association. In Isa. 51:3 and Joel 2:3 the phrase 'Garden of Eden' refers to the marvelous fertility of the land that divine blessing brings about. Ezekiel also characterizes the repopulated fertile landscape of a restored Israel as an Edenic garden (36:35).

The association of blessing and fertility is not unique to the root *ʿ-d-n*. The linkage between these two themes exists everywhere in Northwest Semitic religion. It is the very backbone of two of the largest Ugaritic epics (Aqhat and Kirta) as well as the patriarchal materials in the Bible. Moreover, curse and blessing lists in the Bible and extrabiblical sources always highlight the imagery of sexual fertility.[28]

Up to this point we have described the relationship of the root *ʿ-d-n* to the general theological concepts of fertility and blessing. The root *ʿ-d-n* can also be used to specify the act of sexual union. The term is used in this fashion in the antediluvian section of the Genesis Apocryphon. The text describes the birth of Noah as a rather fantastic event (2:1–3). Evidently the child has an awesome appearance, and his father, Lamech, worries as to whether he is the true father of this child or if his wife, Bitenosh, has had an adulterous encounter with the Watchers who descended from Heaven. He goes to his wife and implores her to speak truthfully about the matter (2:4–18). Bitenosh begins to address her husband quite vehemently and assures him that he is the true father. Noah's remarkable appearance is due to divine intervention, not to an adulterous realtionship with the angelic Watchers. She implores her husband to "recall my pleasure [. . .] my panting within my body" (2:9–10, cf.

2:13–14). The last phrase could be literally rendered "my breath within its sheath." As Fitzmyer noted (Fitzmyer 1971, 87) "the body is described as a sheath and the panting breath is like a sword moving back and forth within it." This image is quite appropriate for a description of sexual intercourse. More important for our purposes is the phrase, "recall my pleasure." The Aramaic term for "my pleasure" is *ʿdynty,* assuming the root to be *ʿ-d-n.*[29] Some have translated this phrase "recall my pregnancy" as though the root of *ʿdynty* were *ʿdy.* But this cannot be correct. As Fitzmyer observes, though philologically possible, this translation would be logically absurd. Bitenosh is trying to assure Lamech that he is the father. He requires no assurance that there was a pregnancy! Her response only makes sense if it asserts the plausibility of his involvement in the procreative act. Moreover, the translation "sexual pleasure" is consonant with the following image of her panting during the coital act.

As Fitzmyer notes, this translation of *ʿdynth* as sexual pleasure ought to be compared to the usage of *ʿednâh* in Gen. 18:12. In this text, Sarah hears the promise made regarding future offspring and laughs. She says: "Now than I am withered up (*bĕlōtî*) can I have *ʿednâh,* and my lord also is old." Fitzmyer would render the term *ʿednâh* as sexual pleasure and compare it with the Aramaic cognate *ʿdynth* found in the Genesis Apocryphon. This sense is followed in the *RSV, NAB,* and *JPS* translations.

It is not our point to say that the rabbis knew this particular text in their exegesis of the Eden narrative. Rather, we have rehearsed this material to show the general associations of the root *ʿ-d-n* with the themes of blessing and fertility from the very earliest Northwest Semitic sources down to those of the postbiblical period. Because late biblical texts had associated the end-time with the return of an era of blessing and fertility, it is altogether natural that the rabbis would characterize the first-time as the origin of this blessing and fertility.

This expectation becomes a reality in rabbinic materials. In accordance with this, we find many midrashic texts that not only presume a sexual union of Adam and Eve in the Garden but also emphasize the fertile results. Numerous midrashim declare that Adam and Eve "ascended to bed as two and descended from bed as four (or as some traditions relate, seven)."[30] The sexual encounter in Eden was a particular fruitful one. As is the case in most aggadic expansions of the biblical text, there is an exegetical basis for the tradition. In this case the text is Gen. 4:1–2:

> And the man had sexual relations with ("knew") Eve his wife and she conceived and bore Cain, saying: "I have created man [by means of] the Lord." She continued to give birth to his brother Abel.

This text has several difficulties, but the two that concern us are the phrases "the man had sexual relations with Eve," and "she continued to give birth." The phrase "the man had sexual relations with (literally, "knew") Eve" has some ambiguity because the Hebrew verb can be translated as both a simple narrative past ("knew") and as a pluperfect ("had known"). Those midrashim that presume fruitful sexual relations in the Garden parse the verb as a pluperfect. Rashi also adopts this opinion and tries to establish it on grammatical grounds. He asserts that the emphatic word order is a marker of the pluperfect tense.[31] It is unlikely that the word order necessitates such a translation; one is on safer ground saying that it is simply a possibility.

The phrase "and she continued to give birth" in Gen. 4:2 is also ambiguous. It appears that Gen. 4:2 has telescoped the threefold verbal action of 4:1 (had sex, conceived, gave birth to the simple statement "she gave birth again." But how is one to interpret this abbreviated sequence? Is it simply an ellipsis that presumes the actions of sex and conception, or does it indicate a second birthing experience that follows directly from the first? Modern readers have preferred the former as a simpler reading of the text, but the rabbinic reader—sensitive to the fertile nature of Eden—plays on this narrative ambiguity and describes Eve's first conception as a miraculous one. Not only did she conceive in Eden, but she bore twins (or two brothers and three sisters according to some sources). A late midrashic source even declares that the birth was without pain because of the conception in Eden before the transgression and curse.[32]

The eviction of Adam and Eve from Eden can also be understood in relation to the fertility of Eden. Some rabbinic sources say that Adam goes into mourning upon his expulsion. Thus, as a result of Adam's ritual state, Eve remains barren for the next 130 years (*Genesis Rabbah* 23:4). When the mourning ends, Adam again knows his wife ("rejoices" in *Jubilees* 4:7), and Seth is born. This sequence indicates that the movement from Eden to the outside world was a movement from fertility and sexual joy to barrenness, mourning, and sexual continence.

Let us summarize what we have done. We began by showing the antiquity of the sexual consummation motif before the Fall. The rabbinic position cannot be a reaction to a Christian position. Not only is the rabbinic idea of sexual relations before the fall found in *Jubilees,* but both establish their position on the very same verse. This can hardly be a coincidence. The rabbinic materials preserve an ancient piece of exegesis. But beyond this point *Jubilees* and the rabbis show serious disagreement. For the writer of *Jubilees,* Eden is the prototype of a Temple, a spot of quintessential purity. Thus, the sexual relations of Adam and Eve take place before the entry into the Garden. Rabbinic thought is a bit more complex. On the one hand, Eden represents a concentrated locus of divine blessing—a blessing that actualizes itself in sexual fertility. On the other hand, Eden is a mythic topos for the anticipated joy of the eschaton. Just as marital bliss shall characterize the *Endzeit,* so marital bliss characterized the *Urzeit.*

Notes

1. Among those he cites are the *2 Baruch* (56:6), *The Life of Adam and Eve* (18), and *Jubilees* (4:1). For a variant understanding of *Jubilees,* see the discussion below. *The Life of Adam and Eve* is also problematic for Ginzberg. The text Ginzberg cites (chapter 18) declares that Eve was three months pregnant at some unspecified time after the expulsion. But, if one adds up the time taken by the events that took place after the expulsion in the first seventeen chapters, Adam and Eve are said to have been out of the Garden for only sixty-three days. If the chronology within the book can be taken seriously, then sexual relations had to take place in the Garden. One might also note that after their expulsion, Adam and Eve began to mourn. The ritual state of mourning entails sexual abstinence making it more unlikely that the pregnancy described in chapter 18 could have resulted from a postexpulsion coital act.

2. This was especially true in early Syriac Christianity, which did not have the Apocalypse of John within its Canon.

3. *Genesis Rabbah* 34:14.

4. For the text, see Parisot *Patrologia Syriaca,* 1:817:1–820:18.

5. *Patrologia Syriaca* 1:841:3–9.

6. The term is also the title of the Mishnaic tractate concerning marriage law.

7. The only exception to this would be the mourner who was abstinent for seven days. But the mourner's uncleanness was not caused by the absence of sexual activity alone.

8. This position is argued by Ginzberg (1908–38, 5.134 n. 4 and 1900, 57–58).

9. Indeed, as Heinemann has demonstrated, it can be helpful to begin a tradition-historical investigation of an exegetical theme with the rabbinic materials and then work back through earlier pseudepigraphical works. This is because the Rabbinic materials will often single out the particular textual problem(s) that led to the creation of a supplementary tradition. For a good example of this, see J. Kugel's treatment of the tradition of Joseph's handsome appearance in the work *Joseph and Asenath* (Greer and Kugel 1986, 96–102). The exegetical foundations of the full-blown narrative tradition that is found in this work cannot be appreciated apart from Targumic and Rabbinic sources.

10. This motif is also present in Targum Neophyti and the Fragmentary Targum.

11. The selection is taken from chapter 8. The best edition is that of Schechter (Schechter 1967). This is a reprint of the original 1887 edition. One should also note the translation and commentary of Saldarini (1975).

12. This is taken from *Midrash ha-Gadol*. Also note that Josephus (*Jewish Antiquities* I:34–35) understands this scene in a very similar fashion.

13. Heinemann (1974) has shown time and again how an early cause for a particular aggadic narrative can be forgotten in the subsequent elaboration of the interpretative theme.

14. The text is *Jubilees* 3:2–5a,6. The translation is that of Wintermute (1985).

15. Levenson (1985, 142–45) argues that just as the Temple serves to mark out sacred space and is a spot of rest (*mĕnûḥâh*) so the Sabbath serves to mark out sacred time and serves as a period of rest. The correspondences between the creation of the world the erection of a holy shrine can be seen in these texts, all from the hand of P: Gen 2:1–2 and Exod. 39: 32, 40: 33b–34; Gen. 1:31 and Exod. 39:43; Gen. 2:3 and Exod. 39:43, 40:9. Weinfeld (1981) and Blenkinsopp (1977) have noted these similarities. On postbiblical developments, see the study of A. Green (1980).

16. A similar understanding of the kingdom (*malkûtâʾ* in Aramaic) was present among Syriac writers. As Murray observes (1975, 239, 41), "the early Syriac Fathers remained too close to their Judaeo-Christian roots to move far from the primitive totally eschatological sense of *malkutâʾ*...*[M]alkûtaʾ* is sovereignity in this world under God's governance; he gave it once to Israel and now he has given it to the Romans. It may be a title of supremacy, but it is not the Church."

17. Safrai (1976, 2:205.) has asserted that an even strictor position was advocated by the early *ḥasîdîm*. He claims that they not only "forbade marital relations on the Sabbath, [but] even remained continent from the preceding Wednesday, so that the woman need not be ritually impure on the Sabbath eve by reason of some residue from intercourse." One should note, though, that this assertion is dependent on the assumption that the Babylonian Amoraim have misunderstood an early extra-Mishnaic saying from the tannaitic period (*baraita*). The particular *baraita* is cited in TB *Niddah* 38a and declares that sexual relations were forbidden after Wednesday by the early *ḥasîdîm*. The Amoraic discussion of the *baraita* presumes that the reason is based on the calculation of the gestation period of a woman. If one had sex after Wednesday, the birth might fall on the Sabbath day. L. Finkelstein (1932) argued that the *baraita* reflected an earlier more ascetic branch of Judaism that abstained from sexual relations for three days before the Sabbath so as not to enter that holy day in an unclean state. The figure of three days presumably stems from Exod. 19:10,15. This perspective fell out of favor in the rabbinic period, and so the *halakha* found in this *baraita* was subject to reinterpretation.

18. So BT *Ketubbot* 62b, *B. Qama* 82a, and PT *Ketubbot* 5.6.

19. For example, see *Mishna M. Qatan* 3:6.

20. One should note that in rabbinic legal tradition, sexual relations could begin because they were no longer forbidden. Sexual relations were not required to end the mourning cycle. On the idea that joy constitutes a ritual state that corresponds inversely to that of mourning, see the discussion in the next section below.

21. See the texts from *Jubilees* and *Gilgamesh* cited below. Appropriate biblical texts include: II Sam. 11:27, 12:24 and I Chron. 7:22–23. In BT *M. Qatan* 15b sexual continence is also enjoined on the leper because his state is like that of the mourner.

22. His work includes a table of variants for the fourth and fifth blessings. See pp. 74 and 290.

23. The use of joy in these various languages is developed in considerable detail in my forthcoming book (Anderson 1991).

24. The close association of this eschatological joy with cultic feast has been observed by M. Black (1985, 115–16). The same point has been made about the use of the term "joy" in the kingdom preaching of Jesus [Jeremias 1958, 63, n. 4).

25. This line has been found only in the Old Babylonian recension (Meissner 1902). Note also the Akkadian idiom: *ulṣam epēšu*, literally "to do a joy," idiomatically "to make love." The same root of *ulṣam* (ʿ-*l*-ṣ) is

employed in the Samaritan Targum with this force. Gen. 2:24, "he shall cleave to his wife," is rendered "he shall rejoice with his wife." For other examples see my forthcoming book on joy.

26. The sexual nuance of the term joy is important for interpreting rabbinic discussions of how the mourner was to act on the feast day (BT *M. Qatan* 23b). The ritual requirements of "joy of the feast" took pride of place. This meant that the mourner had to bathe, put on frest clothes and scented oil, eat and drink, and even (according to some) resume sexual relations. These were the discrete behaviors that constituted the ritual state of joy. The Talmud explicitly states: "A mourner does not deport himself as one in mourning during a festival as scripture says: 'You shall rejoice in the feast' (Deut. 16:14)" (BT *M. Qatan* 14b). Because the Sabbath and the feast day were so similar in legal thought, the same type of logic applied to the Sabbath. After the Talmud has cited this proof text from Deuteronomy, the text then describes the exact behaviors that are forbidden to the mourner, one of which is sexual relations. As could be expected, some rabbinic authorities made the logical inference that the commandment to rejoice on the festival took such precedence that even the mourner was to resume sexual relations during this period. This is a remarkable assertion because the punishment for the mourner who would have sexual relations during this period was terribly severe (*M. Qatan* 24a). Some rabbinic authorities even allowed sexual relations for the mourner on the Sabbath, though others disagreed (PT *M. Qatan* 3:5; BT *M. Qatan* 23b–24a). The important point to observe in these discussions is *the legal framework in which these issues are discussed.* These rabbinic texts outline those discrete behaviors that constitute the state of mourning and those that constitute the state of joy and then attempt to reconcile the conflict that arises when the two states might coincide.

27. See Gen. 16:2, 30:3 for a similar usage of *ƀanh.*

28. E.G., Lev. 26:9, 21–22 and Deut. 28:4,18.

29. The form *dynty* would probably be vocalized, *ădîntî.*

30. See, for example, TB *Sanhedrin* 38b and *Genesis Rabbah* 22:2.

31. The expected word order would be verb and then noun. This verse begins with the sequence noun, verb.

32. See Ginzberg 1908–38, 5:134–35, n. 5 in regard to *Midrash Aggada* to Gen. 4:1. This text was unavailable to me.

References

Anderson, Gary
1991 *A Time to Dance, a Time to Mourn: The Expression of Joy and Grief in Israelite Religion.* University Park: Penn State Press.

Albeck, Ch., and J. Theodor
1965 *Bereshit Rabba*. Jerusalem: Wahrmann.

Black, Matthew
1985 *The Book of Enoch*. Leiden: Brill.

Blenkinsopp, Joseph
1977 *Prophecy and Canon: A Contribution to the Study of Jewish Origins*. Notre Dame: University of Notre Dame.

Finkelstein, Louis
1932 *Monatschrift für Geschichte und Wissenschaft des Judentums* 76:529–30.

Fitzmyer, Joseph
1971 *Genesis Apocryphon of Qumran Cave I*. 2nd ed. Rome: Biblical Institute Press.

Ginzberg, Louis
1900 *Die Haggada bei den Kirchenvätern und in der apokryphischen Literatur*. Berlin: Calvary.
1808–38 *Legends of the Jews*. Philadelphia: Jewish Publication Society.

Green, Arthur
1980 "Sabbath as Temple: Some Thoughts on Space and Time in Judaism." In *Go and Study: Essays and Studies in Honor of Alfred Jospe*. Ed. R. Jospe and S. Z. Fishman. Washington, D.C.: B'nai B'rith.

Greenfield, Jonas
1984 "A Touch of Eden." In *Orientalia J. Duchesne-Guillemin emirito oblata*. 219–24. Leiden: Brill.

Greer, Rowan, and James Kugel.
1986 *Early Biblical Interpretation*. Philadelphia: Westminster Press.

Heinemann, Joseph
1974 *Aggadot Ve-Toledotehen*. Jerusalem: Keter.
1977 *Prayer in the Talmud: Forms and Patterns*. New York: De Gruyter.

Huntington, Richard, and Peter Metcalf.
1979 *Celebrations of Death: The Anthropology of Mortuary Ritual*. New York: Cambridge.

Jeramias, Joachim.
1958 *Jesus' Promise to the Nations*. London: SCM.

Klein, Isaac
1972 *The Code of Maimonides, Book 4, The Book of Women*. New Haven: Yale.

Levenson, Jon
1976 *The Theology of the Program of Restoration of Ezekiel 40–48*. HSM. Missoula: Scholars Press.

1985 *Sinai and Zion: An Entry into the Jewish Bible.* San Francisco: Harper and Row.

Meissner, B.
1902 *Ein altbabylonisches Fragment des Gilgamosepos.* MVAG. Berlin: Peiser.

Murray, Robert
1975 *Symbols of Church and Kingdom: A Study in Early Syriac Tradition.* New York: Cambridge.

Parisot, J.
1894 *Patrologia Syriaca.* Paris: Firmin-Didot et Socii.

Rabinowitz, E.
1932 *Midrash HaGadol.* New York: Jewish Theological Seminary.

Safrai, S., and M. Stern
1976 *The Jewish People in the First Century: Historical Geography, Political History, Social, Cultural, and Religious Life and Institutions.* Philadelphia: Fortress.

Saldarini, Anthony
1975 *The Fathers According to Rabbi Natan.* SJLA. Leiden: Brill.

Schechter, Solomon
1967 *Avot de Rabbi Nathan.* New York: Feldheim.

Weinfeld, Moshe
1981 "Sabbath, Temple, and the Enthronement of the Lord." In *Mélanges bibliques et orientaux en l'honneur de M. Henri Cazelles.* Ed. A. Caquot and M. Delcor. 501–12. Neukirchen-Vluyn: Neukirchener.

Wintermute, Orval
1985 "Jubilees." In *Old Testament Pseudepigrapha.* Ed. J. Charlesworth. Garden City: Doubleday.

3

*The Great Fat Massacre: Sex, Death, and the Grotesque Body in the Talmud**

Daniel Boyarin

> Said Rabbi Yohanan, "Rabbi Ishma`el the son of Yose's member was like a wineskin of nine *kav;* Rabbi El`azar the son of Rabbi Shim`on's member was like a wineskin of seven *kav.*" Rav Papa said, "Rabbi Yohanan's member was like a wineskin of three *kav.*" *And there are those who say: like a wineskin of five kav. Rav Papa himself had a member which was like the baskets of Hipparenum.* (Babylonian Talmud, *Baba Metsia,* 84a)[1]

A learned discussion of traditions comparing the size of the penis of our hero with that of others of the Holy Rabbis is not something we expect to find in the Talmud.[2] Enormous phalli, particularly on clerics, inevitably remind of Rabelais,[3] suggesting that our text is part of the grotesque tradition, associated so strongly by Bakhtin with cultural issues centering on procreation (Bakhtin 1984), and indeed, investigation of the text shows that the thematics of the material body, the body of reproduction, is its major emphasis.[4] All that we know of rabbinic Judaism points to reproduction as a cite of central, vital significance in the rabbinic culture, indeed to genealogy as a crucial source of meaning. In Bakhtin's account, the grotesque body is the very triumph of life over death:

> It is the people's growing and ever-victorious body that is "at home" in the cosmos. It is the cosmos' own flesh and blood, possessing the same elemental force but better organized. The body is the last and best word of the cosmos, its leading force. Therefore it has nothing to fear. Death holds no terror for it. The death of the individual is only one moment in the triumphant life of the people

> and of mankind, a moment indispensable for their renewal and improvement. (Bakhtin 1984, 341)

In this chapter I wish to focus on the cultural dynamics of a talmudic text in which the thematics of the grotesque are obsessively present, as in Rabelais. The biography of the holy Rabbi El`azar, the son of Shim`on, in the Babylonian Talmud (Tractate *Baba Metsia* 83b–85a) is surely one of the strangest of "hagiographies" in the literature. With only the slightest gestures at plot-level consistency, the text consists of a series of incidents whose common feature is that they nearly all deal with the body of the subject, and the text is further interrupted by stories about the bodies of other rabbis. On the one hand, the text brilliantly corroborates Bakhtin's reading of the grotesque as powerfully, centrally involved with the reproductive body and thus with reproduction, but on the other hand, this text will show not the body that has nothing to fear but the body in terror and anxiety.

The fabula of the narrative runs as follows:

Rabbi El`azar, the son of Shim`on, is appointed to catch Jewish thieves for the Roman government. Rabbi Yehoshua the Bald meets him and calls him by the insulting epithet, "Vinegar, son of Wine," implying that he is a most unworthy son of a great father. He defends his actions somewhat lamely. When, however, a certain laundryman refers to him by the same designation, he becomes furious and has the man arrested. After calming down, he feels regretful and goes to have the man released but does not succeed. Standing under the crucified laundryman, he begins to cry, whereupon another passing Jew sees him and says that he should not be concerned, for the crucified one and his son had both had intercourse with a married woman on the Day of Atonement, thus committing several capital crimes. The rabbi rejoices and placing his hands on his guts, says "Be joyful, my guts. If you are so accurate when you have no certain information, imagine how accurate you are when you are certain. I am certain that neither rot nor worms will ever prevail over you." In spite of this expression of self-assurance, the text tells us, the rabbi was still not certain, so he actually tests the claim that his guts are impervious during his lifetime, by having several baskets full of fat removed from his stomach with their blood vessels and placed in the sun to see if they rot (which they don't). After some very significant "digressions" that I will be treating at length later on, the story continues by telling us that the rabbi still unsure of himself takes upon himself a penance which resulted in illness such that every morning sixty felt mats soaked with blood and pus were removed from beneath his body. His wife, fearing the other rabbis' reprobation of her husband, prevents him from attending the House of Study, until finally in disgust at his ascetic behavior, she leaves him. He then returns to the rabbinic community, where his first activity is to permit sex for sixty doubtful menstruants, leading to the birth of sixty male children who are named after him. His wife returns to him (although we are never told when, how, or why), and upon his death, he tells her that the other rabbis are still angry with him and will mistreat his corpse, which should be left in the attic, where it does not rot for twenty years or so until finally one day a worm is seen exiting from the ear of the corpse. The rabbi's father communicates from beyond the grave that he would like his son buried beside him, and after some further misadventures, his desire is fulfilled and the corpse is buried. We have then some codas to the story that, as we shall see, powerfully amplify its meaning.

Neither this brief summary of the plot nor my extended reading below can encompass the unencompassable body of this fat text. A complete translation is presented at the end of the discussion.

At first glance, the text seems readable as a sort of social-political satire, an attack on certain rabbis who were grotesquely fat in body and by implication undisciplined and gluttonous and who allowed themselves to be recruited by the Roman authorities to betray their fellow Jews:

> They brought Rabbi El`azar the son of Rabbi Shim`on, and he began to catch thieves [and turn them over to the Romans]. He met Rabbi Yehoshua, the Bald, who said to him, "Vinegar son of Wine: how long will you persist in sending the people of our God to death?!" He said to him, "I am removing thorns from the vineyard." He said to him, "Let the Owner of the vineyard come and remove the thorns." One day a certain laundry man[5] met him, and called him, "Vinegar son of Wine." He said, "Since he is so brazen, one can assume that he is wicked." He said, "Seize him." They seized him. After he had settled down, he went in to release him, but he could not. He applied to him the verse, 'One who guards his mouth and his tongue, guards himself from troubles' (Proverbs 21:23).[6] They hung him. He stood under the hanged man and cried. Someone said to him, "Be not troubled; he and his son both had intercourse with an engaged girl on *Yom Kippur*." In that minute, he placed his hands on his guts, and said, "Be joyful, O my guts, be joyful! If it is thus when you are doubtful, when you are certain even more so. I

> am confident that rot and worms cannot prevail over you." But even so, he was not calmed. They gave him a sleeping potion and took him into a marble room and ripped open his stomach and were taking out baskets of fat and placing it in the July sun and it did not stink. *But no fat stinks. It does if it has red blood vessels in it, and this even though it had red blood vessels in it, did not stink.* He applied to himself the verse, 'even my flesh will remain preserved' (Psalms 16:8–9).

The Rabbi is recruited by the Roman authorities as a sort of collaborator, who turns over Jewish tax evaders to the Roman authorities. This behavior is roundly condemned by the narrative. Rabbi El`azar is called, "Vinegar, son of Wine" [i.e., Wicked One Son of a Saint. see below] and asked, "How long will you persist in sending the people of our God to death?" It is a gross oversimplification of the text, however, to read it in such political terms. Indeed, the text keeps undermining such a reading. On the one hand, the rabbi is referred to as "Vinegar, son of wine," thus seemingly supporting a reading of the text in political terms. But on the other hand, the successful test of his flesh and the strong testimony regarding the sinfulness of the laundryman (who several times over deserved the death penalty) undermine this reading. Moreover, at a later point in the text he is referred to as a saint (precisely when his own child is portrayed as a sinner!) We need more complex cultural models to understand such a self-contradictory text. Bakhtin provides the models. He has discussed similar ambivalences in the European grotesque tradition:

> The soul of the people as a whole cannot coexist with the private, limited, greedy body. There is the same complex and contradictory character in the bodily images related to the banquet; the fat belly, the gaping mouth, the giant phallus, and the popular positive image of the "satisfied man." The fat belly of the demons of fertility and of the heroic popular gluttons (for instance, Gargantua in folklore) are transformed into the paunch of the insatiable simonist abbot. The image, split between these two extremes, leads a complex and contradictory life. (Bakhtin 1984, 292)

It is precisely this complex and contradictory association of the grotesque body, on the one hand with exploitation and on the other hand with such positive images as fertility and fecundity, that will provide an important clue to a richer reading of our text.

The text clearly manifests several of the elements of the grotesque that Bakhtin has identified. As Bakhtin has shown, the grotesque body is the uncontained body. The topoi of exaggerated size, detachable organs, the emphasis on the orifices, and stories of dismemberment are all representations of the body as interacting with the world, not self-enclosed as the classical body:

> All these convexities and orifices have a common characteristic; it is within them that the confines between bodies and between the body and the world are overcome: there is an interchange and an interorientation. This is why the main events in the life of the grotesque body, the acts of the bodily drama, take place in this sphere. Eating, drinking, defecation and other elimination (sweating, blowing of the nose, sneezing), as well as copulation, pregnancy, dismemberment, swallowing up by another body—all these acts are performed on the confines of the body and the outer world, or on the confines of the old and new body. In all of these events the beginning and end of life are closely linked and interwoven. (Bakhtin 1984, 317)

Not surprisingly, the grotesque cultural tradition manifests remarkable ambivalence on this aspect of the body. The opposing principles of corporeal fecundity and corporeal degradation in illness and death are one of the sources of that ambivalence and they are powerfully animated in the talmudic story. Images of decay, dismemberment, and bodily mortification pervade the story.

The rabbi performs a bizarre purity test on himself. In order to demonstrate that his actions with regard to the Jew that he sent to his death were righteous ones, he attempts to prove (to himself) that his body is indeed a classical, impermeable one. He begins by making the claim that since he is so certain that he is righteous, he is equally sure that his body will be impervious to the depredations of worms after his death. That is, he experiences himself as a classical body, the body that is pristine and closed off from the outside world. Ironically enough, the test that the rabbi devises in order to prove his self-image is precisely one that undermines it. He has the integrity of his body violated even in his lifetime in the bizarre operation of removing baskets full of fat from his stomach and having them placed in the sun to see if they will, indeed, be immune from rotting. We have then, a fantastically sardonic moment of the very apotheosis of the grotesque being claimed as a proof for the classic!

As Bakhtin has already pointed out, the image of the body part grown out of all proportion is "actually a picture of dismemberment, of separate areas of the body enlarged to gigantic dimensions" (Bakhtin 1984, 328). The rabbi is clearly grotesquely obese if several baskets full of fat could be removed from his body, and his activity is portrayed as a grotesque violation of the integrity of the body of the Jewish people. The association of the grotesqueness of body and of behavior is underlined by being doubled in another rabbinic figure, Rabbi Ishma`el, the son of Rabbi Yose, who performs similar services for the Roman government and is also marked as an inferior son to a superior father:

> To Rabbi Ishma`el the son of Yose there also occurred a similar situation. Eliahu (the Prophet Elijah) met him and said to him, "how long will you persist in sending the people of our God to death?!" He said to him, "What can I do; it is the king's order?" He said to him, "Your father ran away to Asia-Minor; you run away to Lydia." When Rabbi Ishma`el the son of Yose and Rabbi El`azar the son of Rabbi Shim`on used to meet each other, an ox could walk between them and not touch them.

These rabbis truly are proto-Gargantuas if when they stand together, their stomachs form an arch so big that an ox can walk under it. It is exciting to see how the talmudic text bears out Bakhtin's remarkable insight by combining in one moment the monstrous belly that "hides the normal members of the body" and the actual dismemberment of that monstrous organ. Indeed, the image of what is done to the body of the rabbi is almost comparable to giving birth, to a kind of lunatic Caesarean section. This association makes perfect sense in the logic of the grotesque body because it is precisely in the association of fertility and death that the grotesque draws its power (Bakhtin 1984, 238).

The theme of reproduction begins explicitly to obtrude in the sequel to the anecdote about the two fat rabbis and thus connects the theme of grotesque obesity with the theme of fecundity:

> A certain matron said to them, "Your children are not yours." They said, "theirs are bigger than ours." "If that is the case, even more so!" *There are those who say that thus they said to her: "As the man, so is his virility." And there are those who say that thus did they say to her: "Love compresses the flesh."*

The Roman matron who sees the two obese rabbis cannot believe that they could possibly perform sexually, so she challenges the legitimacy of their children. A highly comic brief linguistic farce ensues. They answer her cryptically, "Theirs are bigger than ours," apparently understanding the matron to have meant that since they have such enormous penises, they could not have intercourse and replying that their wives have even bigger vaginas.[7] The matron, misunderstanding their answer and thinking that they are referring to their wives' abdomens, retorts, "If your wives are even fatter, then all the more so that you could not have intercourse." At this point the fat rabbis finally understand the matron's concern and answer—according to one tradition that the size of a man's genitals is in keeping with the size of the rest of his body, and according to the other, that desire overcomes obesity.

It is at this moment of anxiety about paternity in the text that the account of the gargantuan phalli of the rabbis is mustered. Beginning from this incident and continuing from here, the text produces a phenomenal series of stories that all have anxiety over gender and reproduction as a major motif. The most obvious sign of this thematic concern is the fact that when Rabbi El`azar returns to the House of Study, his first activity is to permit marital sex for sixty women who have had a flux of blood that may or may not be menstrual. According to rabbinic practice, when a woman has a discharge, if it is certainly menstrual blood, then she and her husband are forbidden to have sex until after the period and a purification ritual. However, if it is doubtful as to whether the discharge is menstrual or not, a stain is shown to a rabbi who makes a judgment based on his expertise.[8] In our story, Rabbi El`azar was shown sixty of such stains and judged them all to be nonmenstrual, thus permitting intercourse for these wives. All of the sixty children born of the intercourse permitted by R. El`azar were named after him, signifying him as in some sense their parent. My claim for the significance of this narrative moment in signaling the thematic emphasis of the text is occasioned by its very gratuitousness. We could have had the rabbi performing any feat of halakhic (rabbinic law) ingenuity in order to prove the great loss to Torah of the years that he was away from the House of Study, but precisely the halakhic feat that he performs is one concerned with sexuality and reproduction. The choice of this particular halakhic matter as the example of Rabbi El`azar's great ability is a strong symptom, then, of what our text is "about":[9]

> One day he went to the study-house. They brought before him sixty kinds of blood, and he declared all of them pure. The Rabbis murmured about him, saying is it possible that there is not even one doubtful case among those? He said, "if I am right, let all of the

> children be boys, and if not, let there be one girl among them." All of them were boys. They were all named after Rabbi El`azar. Our Rabbi said, "How much procreation did that wicked woman prevent from Israel!"

The guilt for the prevention of this procreation is displaced from the rabbis themselves who by their undue stringency in applying their laws prevented wives from having intercourse with their husbands and projected onto the wife of Rabbi El`azar whose only guilt was in protecting her husband from maltreatment by those selfsame rabbis. Moreover, the "credit," as it were, for the procreation that took place is taken by the rabbis for themselves in the naming of the children after the rabbi.[10] This reading suggests a source for the tremendous tension that our text manifests around the grotesque, reproductive body. I think that the conflict in the text shows a great deal of anxiety about the role of the rabbinic community in the reproduction and genealogy of Israel and first and foremost about their own genealogies, that is to say, of their own continuation through replication in their offspring.

We find another particularly strong and disturbing connection between the grotesque body of Rabbi El`azar and the female reproductive body in the description of his illness, where the text tells us exactly that "in the evening, they used to fold under him sixty felt mats, and in the morning they would find under him *sixty* vessels full of blood and pus." The text signals by a formal device the gender-related issue at stake here. These sixty vessels of the blood of dying cannot be separated in this text from the exactly sixty issues of feminine blood that were brought before the rabbi in the segment discussed above. Our text of the grotesque body, then, not surprisingly turns very significantly on explicit thematic issues having to do with sexuality, gender, and reproduction. The Bakhtinian concept of the grotesque body and its complex and ambivalent connection with death and birth thus provides a conceptual model for reading what is often taken as a series of individual textual moments as a complex (but not organic) textual system.

The epithet awarded to Rabbi El`azar ben Shim`on, "Vinegar, the son of Wine," can now be read not as a political evaluation but as an expression of the problematic of reproducibility that is the concern of the text.[11] Rabbi Shim`on, the father of our hero, was one of the holiest and most ascetical of all of the rabbis, a man who was famous for his entire devotion to the study of Torah alone, as well as for his implacable opposition to the Romans. His son, as signified by his obesity, as well as by his willingness to serve as errand boy to the Romans, is not "Wine, the son of Wine," as would be hoped for, but "Vinegar, the son of Wine," a decidedly inferior product. Exactly the same applies to Rabbi Ishma`el, the son of Rabbi Yose, again an ignoble son of a noble father. With great [dramatic] irony, it is these two men who are challenged by the Roman matron insisting, "Your children are not yours." Their obesity prevents them, she suggests, from being able to have intercourse with their wives. They answer her, however, in convincing manner that indeed they are the fathers of their children, so as to prevent their children from being mocked. The matron misreads the signification of their bodies, thinking that their grossness and grotesqueness in body signify an interruption of genealogical connection between them and their children. However, we, the readers, know that the genealogical signification which does not obtain is not the physical one between these men and their children, but the spiritual one between these men and their fathers. The fathers were wine; the children are vinegar.

The text, then, seems to bear out the suggestion that its issue is a rabbinic anxiety about their own "continuity through replication." The mistakenness of the matron's taunt that the children of the two fat rabbis are not theirs only underlines through its ironies the truth that they are not truly sons of their fathers. The theme is unmistakably taken up, once more, in the remarkable sequel to our story on the next page of the Talmud:

> Rabbi happened to come to the town of Rabbi El`azar the son of Rabbi Shim`on [after the latter's death]. He asked, "Does that righteous man have a son?" They answered, "He has a son, and any prostitute who is hired for two [coins], would pay eight for him." He came and ordained him and gave him over to Rabbi Shim`on, the son of Issi, the son of Lakonia, the brother of his mother [to teach him Torah].

The son of Rabbi El`azar, he who had once been dubbed "Vinegar, son of Wine," is again presented as an unworthy son to his father. The problematic of continuity through procreation is intensely signified in this brief incident. On the one hand, we have an unbeautiful father, who has a son whose body is so beautiful that whores are willing to pay four times their normal fee in order to sleep with *him*. On the other hand, he is presented again as the highly unrighteous son of a (suddenly saintly) father. Thus, we find the comfort of belief in survival through reproduction is twice challenged in the same figure; he neither looks like his father nor follows in his footsteps. The story, moreover, suggests as well a response to this tragic despair; namely reproduction through education.

This story is immediately doubled by an even more remarkable one:

> Rabbi happened to come to the town of Rabbi Tarfon. He asked, "Does that righteous man have a son?" [for Rabbi Tarfon] had lost his children. They said to him, "He has no son, but he has the son of a daughter, and any prostitute who is hired for four, hires him for eight." He said to him, "If you return [to Torah], I will give you my daughter." He returned.

This is a recapitulation of several of the themes we have seen so far. Rabbi Tarfon has no living sons, and moreover, his [only?] grandson is as far from Torah as could be. Rabbi takes him under his wing through a displaced erotic relationship, a situation that we will be meeting again and interpreting later on. I read here the extraordinary tension that the rabbinic culture seems to feel between the desire on the one hand to pass on the mantle of Torah from father to son and their anxiety that in a profound sense, *people do not reproduce each other, and reproduction is not the answer to death.*

Once again, after Rabbi El`azar's death, his body is put to the test of impermeability. The text produces another very intense image of a grotesque birth out of the flesh of a feminized male (dying) body. This association makes perfect sense in the logic of the grotesque body because it is precisely in the association of fertility and death that the grotesque draws its power (Bakhtin 1984, 238). Moreover, obesity itself is an issue of gender, being associated with the maternal grotesque body[12]:

> When he was dying, he said to his wife, "I know that the Rabbis are furious with me and will not take proper care of me. Let me lie in the attic and do not be afraid of me." Rabbi Shmuel the son of Rabbi Nahman said, "Rabbi Yohanan's mother told me that the wife of Rabbi El`azar the son of Rabbi Shim`on told her that 'not less than eighteen and not more than twenty-two [years] that he was in the attic, every day I went up and looked at his hair, when a hair was pulled out, blood would flow. One day I saw a worm coming out of his ear. I became very upset, and I had a dream in which he said to me that it is nothing, for one day he had heard a rabbinical student being slandered and had not protested as he should have.' "

Again here, we have exactly the same situation of the very zenith of the grotesque in precisely the place where the text is claiming to represent the classical. The theme of the saint's body that does not rot after death is a topos of hagiography.[13] But, the grotesqueness of its handling in this text, and particularly the grotesque denouement with the worm coming out of the Rabbi's ear, suggest not a hagiography, but a satire or parody on hagiographies. Although the text reduces the force of the image by moralizing it, its power "to upset" does not really disappear. If a worm is seen coming out of the ear of a corpse, the suggestion is certain that the cavity is, in fact, full of worms. In order to better understand this moment, we have to remember that until the modern period, the corpse was understood to produce the very worms that devoured it. The corpse is said "to beget" the worms, that is to give birth to them. A more powerful icon, then, of death in life and life in death, of the imbrication of death in the production of life, is hard to imagine.[14] This talmudic grotesque can hardly be said to represent the "last best word of the cosmos."

I have my doubts about Rabelais as well. Certainly the image of an infant so gigantic that he suffocates his mother in being born no more supports these rhapsodic remarks about "triumphant life" than does corpse being consumed by the worms that it has "begotten." Indeed, where Bakhtin talks about "birth-giving death" (1984, 392), I think often we must think of "death-bringing birth."[15] Indeed, I would suggest that it is the very question of reproduction as providing the kind of "triumphant life of the people," the conquering of death which Bakhtin conjures, that is the source of the inner tension of our discourse. For Bakhtin's Rabelais, it is clear that his children will not only repeat the father and render him immortal,[16] but "the father's new flowering in the son does not take place on the same level but on a higher degree of mankind's development. When life is reborn, it does not repeat itself, it is perfected" (Bakhtin 1984, 406 ff.). This utopian desire is, it seems, the exact contrary of the Talmud's fear that the "father's new flowering" will be a bitter one, a Vinegar, son of Wine. Reproduction, then, so far from continuing one's existence into the future, only emphasizes the dissolution that death brings. The reproductive principle was not, it seems, sufficient for this culture to provide a conviction that "death hath no dominion."

Our text, however, rejecting almost entirely the utopian character of reproduction so emphasized by Bakhtin, attempts to provide its own utopian solution, substitution of the phallic mouth for the phallic penis. This substitution, itself, has been brilliantly documented and analyzed by Howard Eilberg-Schwartz (1990, 229–234). Our text shows it to be, however, not the product of discomfort with the body and genealogical reproduction so much as despair at the failure of that ideal. The rabbis are in a strong sense the inheritors of the priestly role in Israel. This transfer of authority is dramatized in the Talmud (*Yoma* 76b), where all of the people who were following the high priest upon his departure from the Holy of Holies on the Day of Atonement turned and followed Shemaia and Avtalyon, semilegendary founding figures of the rabbinic movement, when the latter appeared.[17] Notice that the very activity in which Rabbi El`azar engages, the distinction between menstrual blood and blood that does not cause impurity, is a priestly task *par excellence*. Concerns with procreation and genealogy are very critical in the priestly culture of the Bible, and an impotent priest was even disqualified from serving at the altar and blessing the people.[18] The signifier of biological filiation has a strong anchoring in the values of the culture. As such, the rabbinic mantle should have passed from father to son, as does the crown of priesthood. But it doesn't, at least not in any straightforward way. On the one hand, the rabbis have created a sort of meritocracy to replace the religious aristocracy that the Bible ordains. Filiation is no longer from father to son but from teacher to disciple.[19] But the desire that genetic replicability be homologous with pedagogical replicability persists. For a powerful signifier within the story of this desire and its failure, we need look no further than the following moment:

> As for Torah, what did he mean? When Rabban Shim`on the son of Gamliel and Rabbi Yehoshua the Bald used to sit on benches, Rabbi El`azar the son of Rabbi Shim`on and our Rabbi, used to sit in front of them on the ground and ask and answer. And the rabbis said, "We are drinking their water, and they sit on the ground!?" They built them benches and put them upon them. Rabban Shim`on ben Gamliel said, 'I have one chick among you and you wish to cause him to be lost from me!' " [Apparently, the concern is that by singling him out as talented, the Evil Eye would be attracted to him.] They moved Rabbi down again. Rabbi Yehoshua ben Korha said, "Shall he who has a father live, and he who has none shall die?!" They took Rabbi El`azar down as well. He became upset. He said, "They think we are equals. When they put him up, they put me up; when they put him down, they put me down." Until that day, when Rabbi would say something, Rabbi El`azar the son of Rabbi Shim`on used to say, "There is a tradition which supports

> you." From that day onward, when Rabbi said, "This is my answer," Rabbi El'azar the son of Rabbi Shim'on said, "This is what you will answer; you have surrounded us with vain words, answers that are empty." Rabbi became upset. He came and told his father. He said, "Don't feel bad. He is a lion the son of a lion, and you are a lion the son of a fox.". . . .

Rabban Shim'on ben Gamliel, the patriarch, has power to take care of his son in this world—"Rabban Shim'on ben Gamliel said, 'I have one chick among you and you wish to cause him to be lost from me!' "—, but he cannot guarantee that his son will be superior in learning to the sons of his inferiors in power. On the other hand, the injustice of the power that the father has in this world to promote his inferior son is given a utopian solution in the text when the other Shim'on, who had no power while alive (indeed was considered as if nonexistent then): "Shall he who has a father live, and he who has none shall die?!" can take care of his son from the next world, "Some say that his father appeared to the rabbis in a dream and said, *'I have one chick that is with you, and you do not want to bring it to me.'* " The text thematizes by repeating the exact phrase the conflict that was aroused by the desire that merit and prestige should pass in a homologous way from father to son, only emphasizing the more that they do not in the real world.

The text ends with the comforting conclusion, "Said Rabbi Parnak in the name of Rabbi Yohanan, 'Anyone who is a disciple of the wise and his son is a disciple of the wise and his grandson is a disciple of the wise, the Torah will not cease from his progeny forever.' " According to this apothegm, the very relationship of replication through discipleship is paradoxically precisely what guarantees that one's physical progeny will be a replication of one. The very bravado of this statement, however, reveals more anxiety and the strength of desire for this to be so than any confidence that it is indeed the case.[20]

This problematic orientation toward bodily filiation is figured in our text in another way as well:

> Said Rabbi Yohanan, "I have survived from the beautiful of Jerusalem." One who wishes to see the beauty of Rabbi Yohanan should bring a brand new silver cup and fill it with the red seeds of the pomegranate and place around its rim a garland of red roses, and let him place it at the place where the sun meets the shade, and that vision is the beauty of Rabbi Yohanan. *Is that true?! But haven't we been taught by our master that, "The beauty of Rabbi*

> *Cahana is like the beauty of Rabbi Abbahu. The beauty of Rabbi Abbahu is like the beauty of our father Jacob. The beauty of our father Jacob is like the beauty of Adam," and that of Rabbi Yohanan is not mentioned. Rabbi Yohanan did not have splendor of face.* Rabbi Yohanan used to go and sit at the gate of the ritual bath. He said, "when the daughters of Israel come out from the bath, they will look at me in order that they will have children as beautiful as I am." The Rabbis said to him, "Are you not afraid of the Evil Eye?" He replied, "I am of the seed of Joseph, our father, of whom it is said, 'A fruitful son is Joseph, a fruitful son by the spring' (Gen. 49:22), and Rabbi Abbahu said (of this verse), "Do not read it, 'by the spring' but 'safe from the Eye.'." Rabbi Yosef the son of Rabbi Hanina learned it from here, " 'And they will multiply like fish in the midst of the Land' (Gen. 48:16), just as the fish of the sea, the water covers them and the Eye does not prevail over them, so also the seed of Joseph, the Eye does not prevail over it."

Now, on one level, all we have here is a topos of folk literature that an embryo is affected by appearances which the mother has seen either during pregnancy or at the time of conception.[21] As such, this would not be a particularly remarkable story. However, according to talmudic morality, thinking of another person while having intercourse with one's spouse is accounted as a kind of virtual adultery. The theme of the importance of the sexual partners having no images of another person at the time of intercourse is emphasized over and over in rabbinic literature. It even carries over into halakhic prescriptions for the act of love, e.g., that sexual intercourse should be practiced at an hour when no voices will be heard from the street. Violation of this principle is represented as resulting in children of a sort of mixed genealogy who are not lovely.[22] An exception is made in our case. In fact, I believe that this is a correct reading of the challenge the Rabbis make to Rabbi Yohanan.

> "Are you not afraid of the Evil Eye?" He replied, "I am of the seed of Joseph, our father, of whom it is said, 'A fertile son is Joseph, a fertile son by the spring' (Gen. 49:22), and Rabbi Abbahu said (of this verse), "Do not read it, 'by the spring' but 'out of reach of the Eye'."[23]

Ostensibly, the challenge that the rabbis made to Rabbi Yohanan is something like, are you not afraid that by calling attention to your beauty, you will be attracting the Evil Eye? And the rabbi's reply is made to mean merely, I am of the seed of Joseph who are proof from the Evil Eye. However, I am convinced that there is another meaning lurking within Rabbi Yohanan's words, which the Talmud has either willingly or unwittingly obscured. The whole verse that Rabbi Yohanan quotes is "A fertile son (or young man) is Joseph, a fertile young man by the spring; the daughters walked on the wall." The last word can, however, be taken as a verb meaning "to look." The verse, so read, becomes an exact authorization for Rabbi Yohanan's practice, "a fertile young man is Joseph, he is a fertile young man alongside the ritual bath [=the spring]; the daughters walked to look at him." It is, as if, therefore, what Rabbi Yohanan is proposing is that he would, spiritually, become the father of all of these children, transferring his qualities to them, through the thoughts of their mothers at the moment of intercourse with their physical fathers.[24] If my reconstruction of Rabbi Yohanan's midrash is correct, then, the original challenge must have been "Isn't it immoral for you to be sitting near the ritual bath and introducing yourself into the thoughts of these women as they sleep with their husbands," and Rabbi Yohanan's answer would be: I am exceptional because of my beauty and have a precedent for my actions. Joseph, my ancestor!, also behaved thus. This reading is doubled by Rabbi Yohanan's very claim to be of the seed of Joseph as well, for he certainly could not have meant that literally he was a physical descendant of Joseph, the tribes of Joseph having been long exiled from the Land and lost. He meant, on my reading: I am of the spiritual seed of Joseph; just as he was beautiful of form and spirit and sat by the ritual bath and produced spiritual progeny, so also I. The beauty of Joseph and his ardent sexual purity were, of course, both topoi of the culture and would have been easily recognized in Rabbi Yohanan's claim. Rabbi Yohanan thus embodies the ideology of the classic.[25]

The story of Rabbi Yohanan and Resh Lakish continues the theme of gender, sex, and reproduction. The former is extraordinarily beautiful, nearly androgynous, beardless and so sexually attractive to the masculine Resh Lakish that the latter is willing to perform prodigious athletic feats to get to him. Moreover, compared to the other rabbis, he had the smallest penis as well, in the Hellenistic world a signifier of male beauty.[26] Lest we miss the message, the narrator segues immediately into the story of Resh Lakish's misidentification of Rabbi Yohanan as a woman:

> One day, Rabbi Yohanan was bathing in the Jordan. Resh Lakish saw him and thought he was a woman. He crossed the Jordan after

> him by placing his lance in the Jordan and vaulting to the other side. When Rabbi Yohanan saw Rabbi Shim`on the son of Lakish [= Resh Lakish], he said to him, "Your strength for Torah!" He replied, "Your beauty for women!" He said to him, "If you repent, I will give you my sister who is more beautiful than I am."

As in the *Paideia,* Rabbi Yohanan does manage to produce Resh Lakish as a spiritual copy of him, just as he wished to produce infants who would be physical copies of him. Just as he is effeminate or androgynous, he feminizes Resh Lakish also, and by doing so, reproduces him as a "great man":

> He agreed. He wanted to cross back [vault back on his lance!] to take his clothes but he couldn't. He taught him Mishna and Talmud and made him into a great man.

The feminizing virtue of Torah is strongly represented in this story. As soon as Resh Lakish even agrees to study Torah, he can no longer vault back over the river on his spear! "His strength has been sapped as that of a woman."[27] What we have here is, in fact, an almost exact reversal of the pattern of Greek pederasty, in which an older man, marked as such by his beard,[28] takes an adolescent under his wing and in an erotic relationship educates him and prepares him for full participation in civic life. At the end, the young man is a *hoplites,* a spear-bearer. Here it is the beardless, androgynous one who takes the virile *hoplites* under *his* wing, educates him and makes him a "great man," sapping, however, his physical prowess and disempowering his "spear" in the process. To be sure, within the Jewish moral economy, the homoerotic implications *must* be displaced from a relationship between Resh Lakish and Rabbi Yohanan to his sister, a displacement that the text makes explicit. Rabbi Yohanan's almost androgynous quality is once more underlined in the text further on when in the discussion of why he is not mentioned in a list of beautiful rabbis, it is remarked that the others had splendor of face, but "Rabbi Yohanan did not have splendor of face":

> *Is that true? But haven't we been taught by our master that, "The beauty of Rabbi Cahana is like the beauty of Rabbi Abbahu. The beauty of Rabbi Abbahu is like the beauty of our father Jacob. The beauty of our father Jacob is like the beauty of Adam," and that of Rabbi Yohanan is not mentioned. Rabbi Yohanan did not have splendor of face.*

The Talmud raises an objection to the citation of Rabbi Yohanan as the very embodiment of beauty because there is a tradition that lists beautiful rabbis and does not mention him. The answer is that Rabbi Yohanan, although beautiful, was left out of this list, because he did not possess "splendor of face." This phrase refers to the biblical verse in which we find the injunction to "give splendor to the face of an elder" (Lev. 19:32), which is interpreted in midrash to mean that one must grow a beard. What was lacking, then, in Rabbi Yohanan's beauty was precisely that which defined his beauty for Resh Lakish, his effeminate appearance! The text seems then to contradict itself, asserting that the lack of the beard is a marker of beauty and at the same time that it is a defect in beauty. This text manifests, therefore, an ambivalence or anxiety about the value of virility; on the one hand, the signs of virility are what produce beauty in the male, and at the same time, it is the very lack of those signs that produce the male as beautiful.[29] This ambivalence about the effeminate body of Rabbi Yohanan is thus the double of the ambivalence about the grotesquely masculine bodies of the Fat Rabbis. The ideal male seems to be feminized in this culture, but there would be then an understandable apprehension about the reproducibility of this ideal male.

I would claim that contestation of the significance of physical virility, substituting replication through teaching for replication through reproduction, is an attempt (doomed to failure as it happens) to reduce this anxiety. The production of spiritual children, those who will follow in the moral and religious ways of the parent, is claimed by our text as more important than the production of biological children, not, I hasten to add, because of a hierarchical privileging of "spirit"[30] over body but owing rather to a profound skepticism about replication of the qualities of the parent in the child. Spiritual excellence is claimed as superior to physical prowess. Reversing the Hellenic pattern, the masculine figure joins the "effeminate" one, and while losing his physical virility, becomes nevertheless, or accordingly, a "great man."[31] The narrative seems, therefore, to be challenging the cult of physical virility and male beauty, substituting for it a spiritual reproduction through the oral dissemination of Torah. However, it would be very difficult to claim that our text substitutes for these values anything clear or unambivalent:

> Once they [Rabbi Yohanan and his pupil/child Resh Lakish] were disputing in the Study House: "the sword and the lance and the

> dagger, from whence can they become impure?" Rabbi Yohanan said, "from the time they are forged in the fire." Resh Lakish said, "from the time they are polished in the water." Rabbi Yohanan said, "a brigand is an expert in brigandry." He said to him, "What have you profited me. There they called me Rabbi and here they call me Rabbi!" He became angry, and Resh Lakish became ill. His sister came to him and cried before him. She said, "Look at me!" He did not pay attention to her. "Look at the orphans!" He said to her 'Leave your orphans, I will give life' (Jeremiah 49:11). "For the sake of my widowhood!" He said, 'Place your widows' trust in me' (loc. cit.). Resh Lakish died, and Rabbi Yohanan was greatly mournful over him. The Rabbis said, "What can we do to set his mind at ease? Let us bring Rabbi El`azar the son of Padat whose traditions are brilliant, and put him before him [Rabbi Yohanan]." They brought Rabbi El`azar the son of Padat and put him before him. Every point that he would make, he said, "there is a tradition which supports you." He said, "Do I need this one?! The son of Lakish used to raise twenty-four objections to every point that I made, and I used to supply twenty-four refutations, until the matter became completely clear, and all you can say is that there is a tradition which supports me?! Don't I already know that I say good things?" He used to go and cry out at the gates, "Son of Lakish, where are you?" until he became mad. The Rabbis prayed for him and he died.

Even pedagogical filiation is not left unproblematic by our narrative; the eventual treatment of the student by the teacher and its tragic result are an eloquent exposure of trouble in paradigm. Indeed, the concept of spiritual filiation replacing biological one is given a very bitterly ironic reading, when Rabbi Yohanan replies to his sister that she needn't be concerned about the death of her husband (whom her brother is killing), because God is the "father of orphans." We are left, therefore, with a highly inconclusive evaluation: the text seems neither able to comfortably inhabit nor to reject the importance of biological filiation as a signifier of value. Indeed, the text is not at all sure about the educability (or malleability) of human nature. Both Rabbi Yohanan with his assertion that Resh Lakish is still, as it were, a brigand and the latter's answer that "there they called me Rabbi, and here they call me Rabbi" seem to express great reservation about whether anything at all has changed. So while the raising of spiritual progeny is produced by our text, on my reading, as a solution to a deep-seated problem in the culture, it was itself perhaps no less of a problem for the culture than the problem of procreation that it was supposed to solve. Having downplayed out of a certain despair the consequence of genetic filiation, the culture seems still very uncertain about the reliability of filiation through pedagogy as well.[32] The result is the very anxious and conflicted text we have before us. The problem of the body remains unsolved.

The Tale of Rabbi El`azar the son of Rabbi Shim`on[**] Babylonian Talmud *Baba Metsia 83a–85a*

Rabbi El`azar the son of Rabbi Shim`on found a certain officer of the king who used to catch thieves. He asked him, "how do you prevail over them? Aren't they compared to animals, as it is written 'at night tramp all the animals of the forest' (Psalms 104:20)?" *There are those who say that he said it to him from the following verse: 'He will ambush from a hiding place like a lion in a thicket' (Psalms 10:9).* Said he to him, "perhaps you are taking the innocent and leaving the guilty." He said to him, "how shall I do it?" He said to him, "come I will teach you how to do it. Go in the first four hours of the morning to the wine-bar. If you see someone drinking wine and falling asleep, ask of him what his profession is. If he is a rabbinical student, he has arisen early for study. If he is a day-laborer, he has arisen early to his labor. If he worked at night, [find out] perhaps it is metal smelting [a silent form of work], and if not, then he is a thief and seize him." The rumor reached the king's house, and he said, "Let him who read the proclamation be the one to execute it." They brought Rabbi El`azar the son of Rabbi Shim`on, and he began to catch thieves. He met Rabbi Yehoshua, the Bald, who said to him, "Vinegar son of Wine: how long will you persist in sending the people of our God to death?!" He said to him, "I am removing thorns from the vineyard." He said to him, "Let the Owner of the vineyard come and remove the thorns." One day a certain laundry man met him, and called him, "Vinegar son of Wine." He said, "Since he is so brazen, one can assume that he is wicked." He said, "Seize him." They seized him. After he had settled down, he went in to release him, but he could not. He applied to him the verse, 'One who guards his mouth and his tongue, guards himself from troubles' (Proverbs 21:23). They hung him. He stood under the hanged man and cried. Someone said to him, "Be not troubled; he and his son both had

---

[**]The title, of course, does not exist in the talmudic text. I will provide here brief exegetical notes for difficult passages that are not treated above in the main text.

intercourse with an engaged girl on *Yom Kippur.*" In that minute, he placed his hands on his guts, and said, "Be joyful, O my guts, be joyful! If it is thus when you are doubtful, when you are certain even more so. I am confident that rot and worms cannot prevail over you." But even so, he was not calmed. They gave him a sleeping potion and took him into a marble room and ripped open his stomach and were taking out baskets of fat and placing it in the July sun and it did not stink. *But no fat stinks. It does if it has red blood vessels in it, and this even though it had red blood vessels in it, did not stink.* He applied to himself the verse, 'even my flesh will remain preserved' (Psalms 16:8–9).

To Rabbi Ishma`el the son of Yose there also occurred a similar situation. Eliahu (the Prophet Elijah) met him and said to him, "how long will you persist in sending the people of our God to death?!" He said to him, "What can I do; it is the king's order?" He said to him, "Your father ran away to Asia Minor; you run away to Lydia."

When Rabbi Ishma`el the son of Yose and Rabbi El`azar the son of Rabbi Shim`on used to meet each other, an ox could walk between them and not touch them. A certain matron said to them, "Your children are not yours." They said, "theirs are bigger than ours." "If that is the case, even more so!" *There are those who say that thus they said to her: "As the man, so is his virility." And there are those who say that thus did they say to her: "Love compresses the flesh." And why did they answer her at all? Does it not say, 'Do not answer a fool according to his foolishness'? In order not to produce slander on their children, that they are bastards.*

Said Rabbi Yohanan, "Rabbi Ishma`el the son of Yose's member was like a wineskin of nine *kav;* Rabbi El`azar the son of Rabbi Shim`on's member was like a wineskin of seven *kav.*" Rav Papa said, "Rabbi Yohanan's member was like a wineskin of three *kav.*" *And there are those who say: like a wineskin of five kav. Rav Papa himself had a member which was like the baskets of Hipparenum.*[33]

Said Rabbi Yohanan, "I have survived from the beautiful of Jerusalem." One who wishes to see the beauty of Rabbi Yohanan should bring a brand new silver cup and fill it with the red seeds of the pomegranate and place around its rim a garland of red roses, and let him place it at the place where the sun meets the shade, and that vision is the beauty of Rabbi Yohanan. *Is that true?! But haven't we been taught by our master that, "The beauty of Rabbi Cahana is like the beauty of Rabbi Abbahu. The beauty of Rabbi Abbahu is like the beauty of our father Jacob. The beauty of our father Jacob is like the beauty of Adam," and that of Rabbi Yohanan is not mentioned. Rabbi Yohanan did not have splendor of face.* Rabbi Yohanan used to go and sit at the gate of the ritual bath. He said, "when the daughters of Israel come out from the bath, they will look at me in order that they will have children as beautiful as I am." The Rabbis said to him, "Are you not afraid of the Evil Eye?" He replied, "I am of the seed of Joseph, our father, of whom it is said, 'A fruitful son is Joseph, a fruitful son by the spring' (Gen. 49:22), and Rabbi Abbahu said (of this verse), "Do not read it, 'by the spring' but 'safe from the Eye'." Rabbi Yosef the son of Rabbi Hanina learned it from here, " 'And they will multiply like fish in the midst of the Land' (Gen. 48:16), just as the fish of the sea, the water covers them and the Eye does not prevail over them, so also the seed of Joseph, the Eye does not prevail over it."

One day, Rabbi Yohanan was bathing in the Jordan. Resh Lakish saw him and thought he was a woman. He crossed the Jordan after him by placing his lance in the Jordan and vaulting to the other side. When Rabbi Yohanan saw Rabbin Shim`on the son of Lakish [Resh Lakish], he said to him, "Your strength for Torah!" He replied, "Your beauty for women!" He said to him, "If you repent, I will give you my sister who is more beautiful than I am." He agreed. He wanted to cross back to take his clothes but he couldn't. He taught him Mishna and Talmud and made him into a great man. Once they were disputing in the Study House: "the sword and the lance and the dagger, from whence can they become impure?" Rabbi Yohanan said, "from the time they are forged in the fire." Resh Lakish said, "from the time they are polished in the water." Rabbi Yohanan said, "a brigand is an expert in brigandry." He said to him, "What have you profited me. There they called me Rabbi and here they call me Rabbi!" He became angry, and Resh Lakish became ill. His sister came to him and cried before him. She said, "Look at me!" He did not pay attention to her. "Look at the orphans!" He said to her 'Leave your orphans, I will give life' (Jeremiah 49:11). "For the sake of my widowhood!" He said, 'Place your widows' trust in me' (loc. cit.). Resh Lakish died, and Rabbi Yohanan was greatly mournful over him. The Rabbis said, "What can we do to set his mind at ease? Let us bring Rabbi El`azar the son of Padat whose traditions are brilliant, and put him before him [Rabbi Yohanan]." They brought Rabbi El`azar the son of Padat and put him before him. Every point that he would make, he said, "there is a tradition which supports you." He said, "Do I need this one?! The son of Lakish used to raise twenty-four objections to every point that I made, and I used to supply twenty-four refutations, until the matter became completely clear, and all you can say is that there is a tradition which supports me?! Don't I already know that I say good things?" He used to go and cry out at the gates, "Son of Lakish, where are you?" until he became mad. The Rabbis prayed for him and he died.

And even so, Rabbi El`azar the son of Shim`on did not trust himself, perhaps God forbid, such an incident would befall him again. He accepted painful disease upon himself. In the evening they used to fold under him sixty felt mats, and in the morning they would find under him sixty vessels full of blood and pus. His wife made him sixty kinds of relishes and he ate them. His wife would not let him go to the study-house, in order that the Rabbis would not reject him. In the evening, he said, "My brothers and companions [i.e., his pains], come!" In the morning, he said, "My brothers and companions, depart!" One day his wife heard him saying this. She said, "You bring them upon you. You have decimated the inheritance of my father's house." She rebelled and went to her family home. Sixty sailors came up from the sea and came to him carrying sixty purses and they made him sixty relishes, and he ate them. One day she said to her daughter, "Go see what your father is doing." He said to her, "Ours is greater than yours." He applied to himself the verse, 'From afar she will bring her bread' (Proverbs 31:14).

One day he went to the study-house. They brought before him sixty kinds of blood, and he declared all of them pure. The Rabbis murmured about him, saying is it possible that there is not even one doubtful case among those? He said, "if I am right, let all of the children be boys, and if not, let there be one girl among them." All of them were boys. They were all named after Rabbi El`azar. Our Rabbi said, "How much procreation did that wicked woman prevent from Israel!"

When he was dying, he said to his wife, "I know that the Rabbis are furious with me and will not take proper care of me. Let me lie in the attic and do not be afraid of me." Rabbi Shmuel the son of Rabbi Nahman said, "Rabbi Yohanan's mother told me that the wife of Rabbi El`azar the son of Rabbi Shim`on told her that 'not less than eighteen and not more than twenty-two [years] that he was in the attic, every day I went up and looked at his hair, when a hair was pulled out, blood would flow.[34] One day I saw a worm coming out of his ear. I became very upset, and I had a dream in which he said to me that it is nothing, for one day he had heard a rabbinical student being slandered and had not protested as he should have.' " When a pair would come for judgment, they would stand at the door. One would say his piece and then the other would say his piece. A voice would come out of the attic and say, "I find for the plaintiff and not for the defendant." One day his wife was arguing with her neighbor. She said to her, "May you be like your husband, who is not buried." *Some say that his father appeared to the Rabbis in a dream and said, "I have one chick that is with you, and you do not want to bring it to me."* The Rabbis went to take care of his burial, but the townspeople did not let them, because all of the time that Rabbi El`azar was lying in the attic, no wild animal came to their town. One day, it was the eve of *Yom Kippur,* and the people of the town were worried and they went to the grave of his father. They found a snake which was surrounding the opening of the tomb. They said, "Snake, snake, open your mouth and the son will come in unto his father."[35] The snake opened for them. Our Rabbi sent to her to propose to her. She said, "A vessel which has been used for the holy, shall it be used for the profane?!" *There they say, "In the place where the master hangs his battle-ax, shall the shepherd hang his stick?!"*[36] He sent to her, "Indeed in Torah he was greater than me, but was he greater than me in deeds?" She sent to him, "As for Torah, I know nothing; you have told me, but as for deeds, I know, for he took upon himself suffering."

As for Torah, what did he mean? When Rabban Shim`on the son of Gamliel and Rabbi Yehoshua the Bald used to sit on benches, Rabbi El`azar the son of Rabbi Shim`on and our Rabbi, used to sit in front of them on the ground and ask and answer. And the Rabbis said, "We are drinking their water,[37] and they sit on the ground!?" They built them benches and put them upon them. Rabban Shim`on ben Gamliel said, "I have one chick among you and you wish to cause him to be lost from me!"[38] They moved Rabbi down again. Rabbi Yehoshua ben Korha said, "Shall he who has a father live, and he who has none shall die?!" They took Rabbi El`azar down as well. He became upset. He said, "They think we are equals. When they put him up, they put me up; when they put him down, they put me down." Until that day, when Rabbi would say something, Rabbi El`azar the son of Rabbi Shim`on used to say, "There is a tradition which supports you." From that day onward, when Rabbi said, "This is my answer," Rabbi El`azar the son of Rabbi Shim`on said, "This is what you will answer; you have surrounded us with vain words, answers that are empty." Rabbi became upset. He came and told his father. He said, "Don't feel bad. He is a lion the son of a lion, and you are a lion the son of a fox.". . . .[39]

Rabbi happened to come to the town of Rabbi El`azar the son of Rabbi Shim`on [after the latter's death]. He asked, "Does that righteous man have a son?" They answered, "He has a son, and any prostitute who is hired for two [coins], would pay eight for him." He brought him and ordained him "Rabbi" and gave him over to Rabbi Shim`on, the son of Issi, the son of Lakonia, the brother of his mother [to teach him Torah]. He taught him and spread a mantle over his head. Every day he would say, "I wish to return to my town." He said to him, "They call you 'sage', and place a golden crown on your head, and call you 'Rabbi' and you say, 'I wish to return to my town?!' " He said to him, "Here is my oath that I leave that be." When he became great, he went and studied in the Yeshiva of Rabbi Shemaia. He heard his voice and said, "This one's voice is similar to the voice of Rabbi El`azar the son of Shim`on." They said to him, "He is his son." He applied to him the verse, 'The fruit of the righteous is a tree of life; and he that wins souls is wise' (Proverbs 11:30). 'The fruit of the righteous is a tree of life': this is Rabbi Yose the son of Rabbi El`azar the son of Rabbi Shim`on, and 'he that wins souls is wise': this is Rabbi Shim`on, the son of Issi, the son of Lakonia.

When he died, they brought him to the burial cave of his father. A snake surrounded the cave of his father. They said, "snake, open the door and the son will enter to be with his father." It did not open for them. The people thought that it was because [the father] was greater than the son. A voice came from heaven saying that it was because [the father] suffered in a cave,[40] and the son did not suffer in a cave.

Rabbi happened to come to the town of Rabbi Tarfon. He asked, "Does that righteous man have a son?" [for Rabbi Tarfon] had lost his children. They said to him, "He has no son, but he has the son of a daughter, and any prostitute who is hired for four, hires him for eight." He said to him, "If you return [to Torah], I will give you my daughter." He returned. *There are those who say that he married her and divorced her, and those who say that he did not marry her at all, in order that people would not say that he returned for that.* And Rabbi, why did he go to such lengths? For Rabbi Yehuda said that Rav said *and there are those who say it in the name of Rabbi Hiyya the son of Abba in the name of Rabbi Yohanan and those who say it in the name of Rabbi Shmuel the son of Nahmani in the name of Rabbi Yonathan,* "Anyone who teaches the son of his friend Torah, will be privileged to sit in the Yeshiva on High . . ." Said Rabbi Parnak in the name of Rabbi Yohanan, "Anyone who is a disciple of the wise and his son is a disciple of the wise and his grandson is a disciple of the wise, the Torah will not cease from his progeny forever."

Notes

*A shorter version of this chapter was delivered at the MLA in Chicago in 1990 in the section on nonfictional prose in a session entitled, "The Body and Other Indiscretions." Another version of this study has been published in *The Journal of the History of Sexuality,* 1:4. There I have focused more extensively on comparative and cultural-historical aspects of the text and less on its synchronic meanings. This will eventually be a chapter in a book entitled, *Carnal Israel: Reading Sex in Talmudic Culture* to be published by the University of California Press. I wish to thank Jonathan Boyarin, Steven Fraade, Stephen Greenblatt, Eric Gruen, Elliot Horowitz, Joshua Levinson, Shlomo Naeh, Ilana Pardes, David Resnick, Dov Samet, David Satran, Ellen Spolsky, Shira Wolosky, Eli Yassif, and especially Howard Eilberg-Schwartz for reading earlier versions of this paper and making many helpful comments.

1. This passage, as all of the text here, is translated from the best manuscript of this section of the Talmud, Hamburg 19.

2. It is so unexpected that nearly all commentators quite "interpret" it out of existence. The word "evreh," itself in Aramaic means exactly "member" and can refer, as the English, to other parts of the body. Accordingly some interpreters claim that the innards are being referred to here, while others say it is talking about arms or legs. However, just as in English, the word when unqualified otherwise means *membrum virile*. As we shall see, this interpretation is, moreover, the one strongly suggested by the context. As a hedge, let me say, however that even should my interpretation of this word be less certain than I think it to be, my argument in this paper would not be appreciably weakened.

3. Apparently not so inevitably, since an anonymous reader remarked that he/she found nothing of the grotesque in this text at all!

4. Previous scholarly work on this text has generally focused on determining the so-called "kernel of [historical] truth" that the text is alleged to preserve. Other work has challenged the kernel of truth model. Friedman 1985, Friedman 1989, Meir 1988, and Yassif (1990, 114–9) all challenge the dominant historical interpretations. All of these studies advance our understanding of the redaction of these texts and of their formal literary properties. None attempt to deal with them as culturally significant documents. However, the work that they do is a necessary prelude to the present

analysis, for according to the dominant paradigm in *Science of Judaism* research (the nineteenth-century paradigm still prevalent in Jewish Studies, although receding in the last decade), the stories were not understood as literary documents at all but *mirabile dictu* as more or less accurate historical chronicles. Friedman's studies particularly directly challenge the historical research paradigm.

5. The clever laundryman, who often opposes the rabbis, and sometimes bests them, is a topos of talmudic legend. For a similar confrontation in Greek literature, one could cite the confrontation of Kleon by the "sausage maker" in Aristophanes's *Knights* 877–80, cited in Winkler 1989, 54.

6. Although on the surface the Rabbi is certainly applying the verse to the condemned man, who if he had not been so brazen would not have gotten into trouble, on another (ironic?) level the verse is applicable to Rabbi El'azar himself. He is certainly experiencing a great deal of remorse already at this point and will have considerable troubles later on in the story as a result of his not "guarding his mouth and tongue," by keeping silent and not condemning the laundryman to the Romans. According to one venerable manuscript (the Florence manuscript), the text reads that "he applied to *himself* the verse," thus activating this hermeneutic possibility openly.

7. I owe this interpretation to David Satran and to my student Christine Hayes the brilliant suggestion that the matron meant one thing and the two rabbis another.

8. I will be dealing with the feminist problematic of these practices in another chapter of the present research.

9. I.e., what its cultural business is. Notice that in the parallel text of the Palestinian tradition, nearly the same story is told, but all of the themes having to do with sex and procreation are absent. Thus even a theme like the loss of strength from studying Torah that occurs in the Palestinian text has none of the sexual and gender-related overtones that it has in the Babylonian one. See Mandelbaum 1962, 194ff. That text is accordingly "about" something else.

10. Of course, I am referring here to the narrator or author of our story and not to the rabbis in the diegesis. Compare also *The Fathers According to Rabbi Nathan,* Version A, par. 12, "Moreover, how many thousands there were in Israel named Aaron! For had it not been for Aaron these children would not have come into the world [because he reconciled their quarreling parents]" (Goldin 1955, 64).

11. Once more, the theme already occurs in the Palestinian "sourcetext." My claim is not, therefore, of an absolute conflict between Palestinian and Babylonian ideologies, but of the further development of internal conflict in the relatively Hellenism-free Babylonian branch of the culture.

12. In the classical world, fat men were considered effeminate. See the fascinating discussion of Nicole Loraux (1990, 31–33). Also Paglia 1990, 91 and Traub 1989, 461–4.

13. Recently it was reported in the Israeli press that a group of French Jews, buried in Paris in the mid-nineteenth century were reinterred in a mass grave in Jerusalem because their remains had been disturbed. One was found to have had his corpse preserved intact and was given, therefore, a separate grave since this "miraculous" preservation proved his holiness. A more relevant comparison, perhaps, to a satiric reflection of this topos is of course the story of Father Zosima in *The Brothers Karamazov.* Another possible cultural source for this theme here is a motif of Hellenistic Romances regarding the preservation of a dead lover, which would make it a sort of early "A Rose for Emily." See Hadas 1953, 151.

14. Compare the birth of Pantagruel, as discussed in Bakhtin 1984, 328.

15. These images fit more with Paglia's conception of fecundity as being terrifying, of liquid, female nature gone wild (Paglia 1990). Where I part company with her is at two crucial and related points; one, is her assumption that such images are somehow natural and not cultural in origin and second, her enthusiastic acceptance of the values implied by the imagery of classical male and grotesque female.

16. According to Elisheva Rosen, there is reason to trace Bakhtin's optimistic reading of the grotesque back to Victor Hugo (Rosen 1990, 129).

17. The issue is made even sharper there by the fact that these two rabbis are not only not hereditary priests but they are converts! I am grateful to Joshua Levinson for reminding me of this source.

18. For an excellent discussion of this matter from a comparative anthropology perspective, see Eilberg-Schwartz 1990, 141–176.

19. See Eilberg-Schwartz 1990; 206–216 and 229–234. Of course, the rabbinic interpretation of biblical "father" and "son" as "master" and "disciple" is common. See, for example, *Sifre Deut.* §34 (p. 61), §182 (p. 224), §305 (p. 327), §335 (p. 385). The New Testament polemicizes against the Pharisees for turning their followers against their biological parents. Becoming a "disciple of the sages" often meant accepting a rabbinic father in place of one's biological father. See the story of R. Eliezer b. Hyrcanus in *The Fathers According to Rabbi Nathan,* par. 6, (Goldin 1955, 43), and parallels. However, this meritocracy is also not simple, for on the other hand, the institution of the patriarchate, an institution of both temporal and religious power and prestige, is precisely a hereditary office. The issue of this institution and its hereditary nature is raised in our text in the story of Rabbi El'azar and Rabbi as children, cited immediately below in the text.
But finally, it is rabbi, not Rabbi El'azar, who carries the mantle, not only of political power for his time, but of central cultural prestige for the

Talmudic Judaism of the time of our narrator as well. However, the institution of the patriarchate and its hereditary nature were a source of political and cultural conflict all through the early stages of the rabbinic period. The political dimensions of this cultural conflict are, of course, very significant but beyond the scope of the present chapter. For the passing of rabbinic offices from fathers to sons and the tension of this hereditary principle with that of Torah meritocracy, see Alon 1977, 436–57; Beer 1976, summarized in Beer 1980; and Gafni 1986. I am grateful to Prof. Steven Fraade for these references.

20. It is, indeed, quite ironic that the one figure in our narrative who *does* seem to have transferred his qualities to his son is the laundryman, of whom it is said "that he and his son had intercourse with a betrothed girl on Yom Kippur!" This point strengthens, moreover, my argument against the political historical readings of the text as a critique of collaboration. The laundryman transgressed genealogical rules, marriage rules, and the sacred calendar, a stunningly thorough vindication of Rabbi El`azar against Rabbi Yehoshua ben Korha who used the same epithet that the demonstrably wicked laundryman employed in his attack on Rabbi El`azar. Rabbi El`azar is presented as physically "Oriental," anticlassical, but politically as a Roman "collaborator," and ultimately justified in both respects!

21. "Both the Hippokratics and Soranos recommend preparations prior to intercourse: the prospective mother's sense of sober well-being concentrates her thoughts upon her man and causes her child to look like him, themes that extend far beyond medical circles" (Hanson 1990, 315–6). See also, Huet 1983 and Lloyd 1990, 174.

22. See, e.g., *Babylonian Talmud, Nedarim* 20b.

23. The words for "spring" and "eye" are homonyms in the Hebrew, and the preposition "by" can also mean "above, out of the reach of."

24. It is even possible that this is the original sense of Rabbi Abbahu's midrashic comment as well, for "going up from the Spring" would be a very natural way in Hebrew to refer to returning from the ritual bath.

25. Lest there be any misunderstanding, let me make it explicit that "Rabbi Yohanan" here means the character Rabbi Yohanan in this particular text. Thus, no claim is being made that the historical Rabbi Yohanan was more or less influenced by Greek culture than any other rabbi but only that here he, as the representative *par excellence* of Palestinian rabbinism for the Babylonians, is a signifier of a certain cultural moment and cultural struggle. In other Babylonian stories about him, he himself is represented as grotesque in his person as well.

26. "The Greek aesthetic prefers discreet genitals, small in size." (Lissarrague 1990, 56), and texts cited there. For classical male beauty as being androgynous, see Paglia 1990, 99 ff. In particular, for the small penis as a

standard of male beauty, see Paglia 1990, 114–5. In truth, I must admit, that I am not certain that, given the size of a *kav,* Rabbi Yohanan's penis is actually represented as small, but there can be no doubt that the contrast of nine and seven versus three suggests just that. In any case, we should not misunderstand that the rabbis considered themselves eunuched. Rabbi Yohanan does, after all, have a penis, one of at least normal size.

27. The Talmud in *Sanhedrin* 26b explicitly refers to the Torah as "sapping the strength of a man," and "his strength was sapped as that of a woman" is a common phrase in the talmudic literature.

28. Foucault (1986, 199) remarks on the appearance of the beard as the sign that the relationship between the man and boy must end and that now the young man ought to become the subject and not the object of pedagogy (and pederasty). See also, Frontisi-Ducroux and Lissarrague 1990, 217 and Gleason 1990, 405, n. 63).

29. See Gleason 1990, 400–1 for the sources of one pole of the ambivalence.

30. In fact, one of the main points of this whole research project is to argue against such dualism in rabbinic culture.

31. Jonah Frankel already remarked this reversal of expectations (1981, 73–7). Frankel's reading of the story of Rabbi Yohanan and Resh Lakish is of very great interest, but it entirely removes the story from its literary context as part of a larger narrative text, apparently assuming that it was attached here secondarily and by mere association. However, as Friedman (1985, 79–80, nn. 49, 50) has already shown, there is no doubt but that the present editor carefully wove these two sources into a single narrative text, and it is that text that I am reading here. This does not invalidate Frankel's reading as far as it goes, and indeed it is a necessary supplement to the interpretation I am giving here.

32. I am indebted for this last comment to Dr. David Resnick.

33. Rav Papa is also a legendary fat rabbi, as is known from several other Babylonian talmudic intertexts.

34. For hair that grows after death, see Satran (1989, 119).

35. Snakes protecting saints' tombs is a common feature of rabbinic legend.

36. The sexual imagery of both of these proverbs is quite stark.

37. A common figure for learning Torah from someone.

38. I.e., by distinguishing them as extremely talented children, you are attracting the evil eye to them.

39. There follow here stories about the sufferings that rabbi took upon himself in order to "compete" for holiness with Rabbi El`azar, stories which will be treated in another chapter of the present research.

40. When hiding from the Romans for thirteen years for the crime of studying Torah.

References

Alon, Gedalyahu

1977 *Jews, Judaism and the Classical World: Studies in Jewish History in the Times of the Second Temple and Talmud.* Trans. Israel Abrahams. Jerusalem: Magnes Press.

Bakhtin, Mikhail

1984 *Rabelais and His World.* Trans. Hélène Iswolsky. Bloomington: Indiana University Press.

Beer, Moses

1980 "The Hereditary Principle in Jewish Leadership." *Immanuel* 10 (Spring):57–61.

Beer, Moshe

1976 "The Sons of Moses in Rabbinic Lore." *Bar-Ilan: University Yearbook of Judaic Studies and the Humanities* 13:149–157.

Eilberg-Schwartz, Howard

1990 *The Savage in Judaism: An Anthropology of Israelite Religion and Ancient Judaism.* Bloomington: Indiana University Press.

Foucault, Michel

1986 <Paris: Galliamard, 1984> *The Use of Pleasure.* Trans. Robert Hurley. *The History of Sexuality.* Vol. 2. New York: Random House, Vintage.

Frankel, Yonah

1981 *Readings in the Spiritual World of the Stories of the Aggada.* Tel-Aviv: United Kibbutz Press.

Friedman, Shamma

1985 "Literary Development and Historicity in the Aggadic Narrative of the Babylonian Talmud: A Study Based Upon B.M. 83b–86a." In *Community and Culture: Essays in Jewish Studies in Honor of the 90th Anniversary of Gratz College.* Ed. Nahum W. Waldman, 67–80. Philadelphia: Gratz College.

1989 "Towards the Historical Aggada of the Babylonian Talmud." In *The Saul Lieberman Memorial Volume.* Ed. Shamma Friedman, 4–14. Jerusalem: The Jewish Theological Seminary. preprint.

Frontisi-Ducroux, François, and Françoise Lissarrague
1990 "From Ambiguity to Ambivalence: A Dionysiac Excursion Through the 'Anakreontic' Vases." In *Before Sexuality: The Construction of Erotic Experience in the Ancient Greek World.* Ed. David M. Halperin, John J. Winkler, and Froma Zeitlin. 211–256. Princeton: Princeton University Press.

Gafni, Isaiah M.
1986–87 " 'Scepter and Staff': Concerning New Forms of Leadership in the Period of the Talmud in the Land of Israel and Babylonia." In *Priesthood and Kingdom: The Relations of Religion and State in Judaism and the Gentiles.* Ed. I. Gafni and G. Motzkin, 84–91. Jerusalem: Zalman Shazar Center.

Gleason, Maud
1990 "The Semiotics of Gender." In *Before Sexuality: The Construction of Erotic Experience in the Ancient Greek World.* Ed. David M. Halperin, John J. Winkler, and Froma Zeitlin, 389–415. Princeton: Princeton University Press.

Goldin, Judah, trans.
1955 *The Fathers According to Rabbi Natham.* Yale Judaica Series. New Haven: Yale University Press.

Hadas, Moses, ed. and trans.
1953 *Three Greek Romances.* Garden City, N.Y.: Macmillan.

Hanson, Ann Ellis
1990 "The Medical Writers' Woman." In *Before Sexuality: The Construction of Erotic Experience in the Ancient Greek World.* Ed. David M. Halperin, John J. Winkler, and Froma Zeitlin, 309–338. Princeton: Princeton University Press.

Huet, Marie-Helen
1983 "Living Images: Monstrosity and Representation." *Representations* (4) (Fall):73–87.

Lissarrague, François
1990 "The Sexual Life of Satyrs." In *Before Sexuality: The Construction of Erotic Experience in the Ancient Greek World.* Ed. David M. Halperin, John J. Winkler, and Froma Zeitlin, 53–81. Princeton: Princeton University Press.

Lloyd, G. E. R.
1990 *Science, Folklore and Ideology: Studies in the Life Sciences in Ancient Greece.* Cambridge: Cambridge University Press.

Loraux, Nicole
1990 "Herakles: The Super-male and the Feminine." In *Before Sexuality: The Construction of Erotic Experience in the Ancient Greek World.* Ed.

David M. Halperin, John J. Winkler, and Froma Zeitlin, 21–52. Princeton: Princeton University Press.

Mandelbaum, Bernard, ed.
1962 *Pesikta de Rav Kahana*. New York: The Jewish Theological Seminary of America.

Meir, Ofra
1988 " 'Vinegar, Son of Wine': Between Tradition and Innovation." *Leaves for Literary Research* 4:9–18.

Paglia, Camile
1990 *Sexual Personae: Art and Decadence from Nefertiti to Emily Dickenson*. New Haven: Yale University Press.

Rosen, Elisheva
1990 "Innovation and Its Reception: The Grotesque in Aesthetic Thought." *SubStance* xix(2/3):125–136.

Satran, David
1989 "Fingernails and Hair: Anatomy and Exegesis in Tertullian." *Journal of Theological Studies* 40(1):116–120.

Traub, Valerie
1989 "Prince Hal's Falstaff: Positioning Psychoanalysis and the Female Reproductive Body." *Shakespeare Quarterly* 40 (Winter):456–475.

Winkler, John
1989 *The Constraints of Desire: The Anthropology of Sex and Gender in Ancient Greece*. London: Routledge.

Yassif, Eli
1990 "The Cycle of Tales in Rabbinic Literature." *Jerusalem Studies in Hebrew Literature* 12:103–147.

4

Miẓvot *Built into the Body:* Tkhines *for* Niddah, *Pregnancy, and Childbirth*

Chava Weissler

Introduction

One of the important insights of feminist theory is the alterity, the otherness, of women. Men are the rule, women the exception. Thus, when we ask about the significance of the body in Judaism, we are in the first instance thinking about the significance of the *male* body. The female body, like the female person, is the exception. What, then, does the *female* body signify in Judaism? Perhaps the first additional question should be, to whom? While women as well as men are socialized to see men as the norm, it still may make a difference, in understanding the meaning of the body, whether one is embodied as male or female. This chapter explores the connections between women's bodies and the "women's commandments," especially *niddah,* in two genres of popular religious literature in Yiddish. Ethical literature, written by men, treats women, especially women's reproductive processes, in mythic terms, while devotional literature, which has some female authors, treats women's bodies more concretely.

Recovering women's voices, on this or any other topic, is a difficult process. Traditional Jewish texts are written in Hebrew or Aramaic, by men for a male audience. As a rule, only men mastered Hebrew, the sacred tongue, and the language of scholarly communication. In the late medieval and early modern period, some women in Central and Eastern Europe learned to read Yiddish, the vernacular of Ashkenazic Jewry. But even in popular religious literature in Yiddish, most of the voices are male, albeit often addressed to a female audience. This chapter draws upon an important work from the Yiddish *musar,* or ethical literature, a guide to the observance of the women's commandments, *Ayn shoen froen bukhlein* [A Pretty Little Book for Women], also known as *Sefer mitsvas ha-noshim* [The Book of Women's Commandments], by R. Benjamin Aaron Solnik, first published in 1577.[1] It also makes reference to the *Brantshpigl* [The Burning Mirror], a guide to the upright life addressed to women, by Moses Henoch Altshuler, first published in 1596. Material in these works will be compared to *tkhines,* prayers for private devotion recited by women in Yiddish, published in Western and Central Europe in the seventeenth and eighteenth centuries. While many *tkhines* were written by women, most of the texts to be discussed are anonymous, and I suspect that some of them may have been written by men.[2]

Both the *tkhines* and the ethical works consider the relationship of women's bodies, the biblical story of Eve, and the three "women's commandments," religious acts associated with women since the time of the Mishnah *(ḥallah, niddah,* and *hadlaqah).*[3] And both kinds of texts pay special attention to menstruation as symbolic of the relationship of later women to Eve's punishment. Nonetheless, we shall see a marked difference in attitude toward and significance attributed to women's bodies and bodily processes between the two genres.

Women's Bodies and the Women's *Miẓvot*

There is a well-known rabbinic trope that makes a correspondence between human anatomy and God's commandments. According to this traditional physiology, human beings have 248 limbs and 365 organs, corresponding to the numbers of positive and negative commandments, respectively, and adding up to 613, the traditional number of commandments in the Torah.[4] However, this only describes *male* human beings; women, with a different anatomy, have a different number of limbs. A long *tkhine* to be recited "every day," found at the beginning of *Tkhines* (Amsterdam: 1648), discusses the implication of this difference:

> . . . Strengthen my bones so that I can stand before you and serve your awesome Name with my whole heart, with all my limbs that you have created within me, two hundred and fifty two. You have given and commanded your children Israel to perform two hundred and forty-eight *miẓvot* (commandments), the same number as men have limbs. And you have promised them that if they keep and do these commandments, you will give them the light that is hidden

> for the righteous men and women in the next world.[5] And you have given us women four extra limbs, and you have also given us four *mizvot:* kindling lights to honor the holy Sabbath, and to purify ourselves of our impurity, and to separate *hallah* from the dough of our baking, and that we are obligated to serve our husbands. You have also placed in my body three hundred and sixty five organs—the same number as the negative commandments that you have given to your children Israel . . . (*Tkhines* 1648, no. 1)

Thus, the three women's commandments, which are here bound up with subservience to the husband, are built into women's bodies. Truly, in this case, anatomy is destiny.[6]

The Significance of the Women's *Mizvot*

There is an obvious connection between the three women's commandments and aspects of women's traditional activities: separating *hallah* and kindling Sabbath lights can stand for domesticity, while the observance of menstrual avoidances structures sexuality and reproduction. However, texts going back to the rabbinic period add another level of meaning. They make both the three women's *mizvot* and women's post-Edenic physiology emblematic of and punishment for Eve's sin. In Midrash Tanhuma, beginning of parashat Noah, we read:

> . . . And why were women commanded these three commandments? The Holy One, be blessed, said, Adam was the beginning of my creation, and was commanded concerning the Tree of Knowledge. And it is written with regard to Eve, When the woman saw, etc. [that the tree was good for eating and a delight to the eyes, and that the tree was desirable as a source of wisdom, she took of its fruit and ate.] She also gave some to her husband, and he ate [Gen. 3:6]. Thus she caused his death and shed his blood. And it is written in the Torah, "Whoever sheds the blood of man [Adam], by man shall his blood be shed [Gen. 9:6]." So she sheds her blood, and keeps her period of separation [*niddatah*], in order to atone for the blood of Adam that she shed. Whence comes the *mizvah* of *hallah?* She polluted the *hallah* of the world, as Rabbi Yose b. Dusmeka said: Just as the woman slaps her dough with water and afterwards takes *hallah* [*magbahat hallatah*], so did the Holy One, be blessed, with regard to Adam, as it was written, "And a mist came forth from the ground and watered [the whole surface of the earth]" [Gen. 2:6], and then afterwards, "The Lord God formed

> Adam from the dust of the earth" [Gen. 2:7]. Whence comes the kindling of the lights? She extinguished Adam's light, as it is written, "The light of the Lord is the soul of man [Adam]" [Proverbs 20:27], therefore she must observe the kindling of the light.[7]

Thus, the women's commandments are seen as punishment and atonement for Eve's sin, which is understood, here, as the causing of Adam's death. Menstruation, in this text and others, is seen as part of God's punishment of Eve.[8]

In *Sefer mitsvas ha-noshim,* R. Benjamin Aaron Solnik picks up this midrashic notif and lovingly develops it. He begins by retelling the tale of Eve's sin in the Garden of Eden.

> . . . After Eve ate of the apple, and knew she must die, she wanted her husband to eat of it as well. She said, If I have to die, you have to die with me. And she gave it to him so that he would also have to eat of the apple. Adam, poor thing, at first didn't want to eat of the apple. So she took a tree branch in her hand and beat him until he also ate of the apple. As the verse says, **She gave me of the tree, and I ate** [Gen. 3:12: *Hi natnah li min ha-eẓ va-okhel*]. She gave [it] to me with the tree, and I ate. And because that foolish Adam let his wife beat him, God, blessed be his name, cursed him, for he should not have let a woman beat him, but he should have beaten her . . . for God made the man to rule over the woman . . . (Solnik 1602:3b–4a)[9]

Thus Eve's sin includes insubordination to Adam—even though the biblical text declares that Adam will rule over Eve only *after* they have eaten the fruit, as part of Eve's punishment (Gen. 3:16). But according to the *Sefer mitsvas ha-noshim,* Eve's sin is even worse than that:

> . . . Therefore the woman must also . . . suffer torment and misfortune. And therefore she must have her period every month, and must fast once or twice [a month], so that she will always remember her sin and remain in a constant state of repentance. Just as a murderer continuously does, who must all his days fast once or twice a month, so that he will think about repentance, and regret his sin, so must the woman do as well. Every month she immerses herself in the ritual bath, so that she will remember her sins, and be pious. . . . Therefore, it is fitting for her to recite the prayers for a repentant sinner . . . (Solnik 1602:4a)

Thus, women's very bodies give evidence against them as murderers once a month; the implication also seems to be that because of Eve's sin, all women are "naturally" more sinful than men, and need, therefore, the monthly reminder of their sins that the observance of *niddah* provides. This periodic penitence will ensure the woman's piety, says the author, even after she reaches the age of forty, and, presumably, menopause. "Therefore, dear daughter," this chapter concludes, "God has commanded you these three commandments. If you keep them and do them properly, he will forgive you your sins in this world and the next" (Solnik 1602:4a).

What should give us pause here is the picture of woman as murderer. Solnik seems to like this comparison, and, again, following the midrashic sources, develops it further with reference to the other two commandments as well:

> Women were commanded to kindle the lights, and they are obligated to observe this commandments, because they extinguished the light of the world [no longer just Adam's light], and darkened it . . . And because of her sin, because she ate from the apple, all of us must die. Since she has extinguished the light of our life, she must kindle the lights. (Solnik 1602:4a–4b)

After giving a variety of interpretations for the requirement that the two candles be lit, the author returns to this theme:

> . . . Therefore women must kindle the lights, for they have extinguished our light. And for that reason they must also suffer the pain of menstruation, because they shed our blood. Therefore they have the suffering of menstruation and must immerse themselves. For the immersion is like the repentance of a penitent sinner who was a murderer. And so it is with *ḥallah,* too. For she has spoiled things for us, we who are called **"Israel was holy to the Lord, the first fruits of his harvest"** [Jer. 2:3]; this means in Yiddish: Hallow, Israel, to God, the firstling of his fruit. Therefore she must "take *ḥallah.*" For she is commanded, **"As the first yield of your baking, you shall set aside a loaf [*ḥallah*] as a gift"** [Num. 15:20]; this means in Yiddish, the first part of your dough shall you separate as *ḥallah*. Therefore the woman must keep the three commandments. (Solnik 1602:4b)

What is fascinating here, even beyond the punitive theory the author develops of the women's commandments, is his complete collapse of all women into Eve. For him they are all the same, and the sixteenth-century women he addresses must repent continuously for Eve's "murder" of Adam. Of course, the text of Genesis does indicate that the punishments of both Adam and Eve will apply to future generations, and the midrashic sources also conflate Eve and later women. However, Solnik goes beyond his sources in two ways. First, he repeatedly uses the term "murderer" avoided by the more delicate language of the rabbinic sources. Second, he implicitly describes all women as the murderers of all men, not just of Adam: "They have extinguished *our* light . . . They have shed *our* blood . . ." (emphasis mine). Near the end of the final chapter of the section on *niddah,* which makes up the lion's share of the book, Solnik remarks, ". . . Women, with their apple eating, brought death to the world, and with their piety, which means behaving as set out above, they can bring about the end of death. . . . Thus has the Lord God spoken; may it come to pass speedily and in our days, . . . amen" (Solnik 1602:39b).

The View of the *Tkhines*

While Solnik builds on well-known themes in rabbinic literature, and while these themes are also echoed, if less elaborately, in the *Brantshpigl*'s discussion of the women's commandments,[10] they do not appear in the *tkhines* for the women's commandments. I have yet to discover a *tkhine* that links the three women's *miẓvot* to Eve's sin. The biblical figure more likely to appear in *tkhines* for these *miẓvot* is Hannah (the mother of the biblical prophet Samuel), whose name is an acronym of *ḥallah, niddah,* and *hadlaqah*. According to talmudic exegesis (B. Berakhot 31b), Hannah repeated the phrase "your handmaid" three times in her prayer for a son in order to remind God that she had never transgressed any of the three women's *miẓvot*. As God answered her prayer, Hannah's observance was rewarded with a son, a theme explicitly played out in some *tkhine* texts. Thus, in the *tkhines,* the observance of the women's *miẓvot* is connected with fertility, rather than with penance.

In general, *tkhines* for the women's *miẓvot* stress the rewards for observance and the positive religious significance of the acts. (Some of the specific motifs are also found in the *musar* literature.) The reward most frequently mentioned is pious, scholarly offspring. The light of the Sabbath candles symbolizes the light of Torah and Sabbath peace and joy, while the taking of *ḥallah* is likened to God's creation of humanity, *without* mention of how Eve spoiled that first human loaf (cf. Exodus Rabba 30:13). Both taking *ḥallah* and the kindling of Sabbath lights recall Temple rituals: the *ḥallah* is in memory of the system of priestly tithes, while the kindling of the lights is compared to the action of the High Priest kindling the candelabrum in the sanctuary:

> . . . We must kindle lights for the holy day, to brighten it and to rejoice on it; therewith may we be worthy of the light and the joy of eternal life . . . Lord of the world, I have done all my work in the six days, and will now rest, as you have commanded, and will kindle two lights, according to the requirement of our holy Torah, as interpreted by our sages, to honor you and the holy Sabbath . . . And may the lights be, in your eyes, like the lights that the priest kindled in the Temple. And let our light not be extinguished, and let your light shine upon us. Deliver our souls into the light of paradise together with other righteous men and women . . . (*Seder tkhines* 1650:5b)

Only a small number of *tkhines* for *niddah,* pregnancy, and childbirth raise the topic of Eve's sin. Most *tkhines* for *niddah* are primarily concerned with the themes of purity and impurity, while most *tkhines* for childbirth plead that mother and child may come through the birth alive and unharmed. However, rather than assuming with the *Sefer mitsvas ha-noshim* that all women are complicit in Eve's sin and must suffer for it, those few *tkhines* that mention Eve portray the relationship between Eve's sin and later women's suffering in menstruation and childbirth as problematic. Further, Eve's sin is never described as murder, but rather, disobedience to God.

Three *tkhines* that mention this motif are found in the *Seder tkhines u-vakoshes,* first published around 1750, although at least one of them is considerably earlier. All of these texts raise the question of the relationship between women's present suffering and Eve's sin. It occurs to them to ask the question—even if they also convey the view that God's punishment of women is just. Thus, for example, a *tkhine* to be said during childbirth begins:

> Almighty God, righteous judge, with truth and with justice have you punished as women from the creation of human beings, that we women must bear our children with pain. It is within your power; whomever you punish is punished, and whomever you show mercy is shown mercy, and no one can contradict you. Who would say to you, What are you doing? (*Seder tkhines u-vakoshes* 1762, no. 100)

There *is* question here, even if the *tkhine* asserts that it is improper to ask it. Further, God's "justice," the text implies, is partly a matter of brute power.

A *tkhine* to be said when the woman inspects herself to make certain the flow of blood has ceased, which she must do for seven days before purifying herself by ritual immersion, again articulates and then swallows a question:

> God and my King, you are merciful. Who can tell or know your justice or your judgment? They are as deep as brooks of water and the depths of springs. You punished Eve, our ancient Mother, because she persuaded her husband to trespass against your commandment, and he ate from the tree that was forbidden them. You spoke with anger that in sadness she would give birth. So we women must suffer each time, and have our regular periods, with heavy hearts. Thus, I have had my period with a heavy heart, and with sadness, and I thank your holy Name and your judgment, and I have received it with great love . . . as a punishment . . . (*Seder tkhines u-vakoshes* 1762, no. 91)

This prayer seems chiefly designed to reconcile the women who recited it with both the discomfort of their menstrual cycles and an interpretation of this discomfort as a just punishment. By portraying God's justice as inscrutable, the *tkhine* does recognize, indirectly, that perhaps women's situation might seem unjust, but goes on to squelch this thought by having the reciter thank God for her periodic punishment.

Only one text—significantly, the one that seems to be the oldest, and which gives some indication that it emerged from women's oral tradition—actually dissociates the woman from Eve's sin. This is the prayer for biting off the end of the *etrog* on Hoshana Rabba, a practice thought to ensure an easy childbirth.[11] Although it was later incorporated into *Seder tkhines u-vakoshes* and several other *tkhine* collections, it appears first in the *Tsenerene,* known as the "women's Bible," an enormously popular homiletical work. Since the *Tsenerene* was first published around 1600, this *tkhine* is contemporaneous with the *musar* literature quoted earlier.

The way the *Tsenerene* introduces this prayer makes it sound like a record of women's practice. The context is a discussion of what kind of tree the Tree of Knowledge in the Garden of Eden was:

> Some sages say that it was a citron tree. Therefore, the custom is that women take the *etrog* and bite off the end on Hoshana Rabba [the seventh day of Sukkot], and give money to charity, since charity saves from death (Prov. 6:2), and they pray to God to be protected from the sufferings of bearing the children they are car-

> rying, that they may give birth easily. Had Eve not eaten from the Tree of Knowledge, each woman would give birth as easily as a hen lays an egg, without pain. The woman should pray and should say:
>
> Lord of the world, because Eve ate of the apple, all of us women must suffer such great pangs as to die. Had I been there, I would not have had any enjoyment from [the fruit]. Just so, now I have not wanted to render the *etrog* unfit during the whole seven days when it was used for a *mizvah*. But now, on Hoshana Rabba, the *mizvah* is no longer applicable, but I am [still] not in a hurry to eat it. And just as little enjoyment as I get from the stem of the *etrog* would I have gotten from the apple that you forbade (Jacob ben Isaac of Yanov 1702/3:4b).[12]

The implication, not quite explicitly spelled out, is that since the woman would not have committed Eve's sin, she should not suffer Eve's punishment.[13]

To a greater or lesser degree, all of these *tkhines* distance the woman reciting them from Eve and her sin, at the very least by raising the question of their relationship. Further, while reference to Eve's sin does occur in these texts, it is not presented as the justification for the observance of *niddah* (let alone the other women's *mizvot*). Eve's sin explains why women menstruate and why childbirth is painful. But the observance of *niddah* itself is not described as a continuous penance for Eve's murder of Adam, or even for Eve's disobedience to God's command. Rather, the texts use quite different images, and express quite different views of the meaning and consequences of the observance of *niddah*. The *tkhine* before ritual immersion, for example, uses a vocabulary of purity and cleansing, and articulates the connection of the woman reciting it to other pious Jewish women:

> . . . God, my Lord, may it be your will that my cleanness, and washing, and immersion, be accounted before you like all the purity of all the pious women of Israel who purify themselves and immerse themselves at the proper time . . . (*Tkhines* 1648, no. 14; *Seder tkhines u-vakoshes* 1762, no. 92)

The *tkhine* to be said after immersion is concerned primarily with hopes for pious offspring, whether male or female (*Seder tkhines u-vakoshes* 1762, no. 93).[14] In both these cases, the meaning of the observance of *niddah* for the woman is pictured quite differently from the *Sefer mitsvas ha-noshim*. Further, and this deserves greater attention than I can give it here, the very language describing women's physiological states differs between the two genres. The *tkhines* consistently use a vocabulary of purity or cleanliness, and impurity. Both the *Sefer mitsvas ha-noshim* and the *Brantshpigl,* by contrast, prefer a different terminology. Borrowing from the language of cuisine, they describe the woman as either *kosher* or *treyf.*[15]

Tkhines, Musar, and Women's Alterity

What can we conclude from the differences between the *musar* literature and the *tkhines* on the subject of the women's *mizvot* and women's bodies? Before dealing with the differences, it is important to point out one similarity. Both genres find it necessary to inquire as to the meaning of women's bodies and bodily processes; both genres take men as the norm, and women's bodies as that which needs explaining.

But here the similarities end. For the *musar* works, women are less individualized—they form a kind of cosmic class—and more anomalous. Eve, a disobedient and sinful woman, is fully paradigmatic for all women, whose post-Edenic bodies testify monthly to their sinful natures. Indeed, the *Brantshpigl* makes a direct physiological connection, asserting that the blood of menstruation and childbirth originate in the impure venom that the serpent deposited in Eve (Altshuler 1626, chap. 34, p. 121a).[16] This text also states that men find the sight of menstrual blood revolting and that women should therefore keep bloodstained chemises and sheets hidden from their husbands (Altshuler 1626, chap. 34, p. 120b).

For the *tkhines,* by contrast, the view of women's bodies might appropriately be termed less mythical, more rooted in actual physical realities. The question most urgently addressed by the *tkhines* is that of suffering: the physical discomfort, pain, and danger women experience in menstruation and childbirth. The authors of the *tkhines* want to know why women suffer, not why they bleed, and the blood itself does not inspire them with disgust. Further, since the theology implied in the *tkhine* literature in general asserts that people suffer for their own sins, these texts do find the idea that all women suffer because of Eve's sin problematic.

Can we account for the differences between these two genres by the different genders of the authors? The issue is complex, especially since, if we are to be precise about these anonymous *tkhines*, we need to speak of the gender only of the authorial voice. Yet it does seem that men speaking as men, and women (or men) speaking as women, express different attitudes toward, and have different questions about, women's bodies. Let me be clear here: This is not a matter of individual male malice or prejudice toward women. As other parts of the *Brantshpigl* make abundantly clear, Altshuler rather liked women and keenly appreciated their social importance.[17] Solnik, as a *poseq*, an adjudicator of Jewish law, was quite concerned to extend as much opportunity for religious expression to women as he thought he could justify halakhically.[18] And both men, quite unusually, went to the trouble of writing books for women in Yiddish. Rather, the differences between the two genres are evidence of the multivocality of gender constructions in Ashkenazic culture. And these differences might be phrased as two contrasting questions. The authors of the *tkhines* want to understand how God's justice can require women's suffering. But the authors of the two *musar* works want to know why women are the way they are, whence the archetypal nature of the irreducibly Other springs.

Notes

Acknowledgments. This essay is a revised version of a paper delivered at the Association for Jewish Studies, December 1989. I wish to thank the Annenberg Research Institute for a fellowship (1990–1991) that gave me time to complete the revisions. I am also grateful to Dr. Elizabeth Castelli and Prof. Mordechai A. Friedman (fellow Fellows at Annenberg) for their suggestions for revision and to Dr. Sol Cohen of the Annenberg Research Institute for his gracious bibliographic assistance.

1. The definitive study of this work and others of the same genre is the M.A. thesis by Romer-Segal (1979).

2. For an introduction to the *tkhine* genre, see Weissler 1987 and 1991. For a discussion of additional issues in the construction of gender, comparing Yiddish ethical and devotional literature, see Weissler 1989.

3. Mishnah, Shabbat 2:6. To describe these duties more fully: *Ḥallah*: Anyone, male or female, who mixes up a batch of bread dough of a certain minimum volume, must recite a blessing and separate out a small portion of the dough, which is then, usually, burnt separately in the oven. This is in memory of the system of tithes that were given to the priests and Levites. *Niddah:* A menstruating woman must eschew all physical contact with her husband. After the end of her menstrual period, she must inspect herself

daily for seven days to be certain the flow of blood has completely ceased, and then she must immerse herself in a ritual bath to purify herself before resuming marital relations with her husband. *Hadlaqah:* Shortly before the onset of the Sabbath at sundown on Friday night, the woman of the house (or if she is unavailable, or if there is no woman, the man of the house) kindles at least two lights. (It is forbidden to kindle fire or lights on the Sabbath.) For the woman, this act inaugurates the Sabbath.

4. Targum Jonathan, Genesis 1:27. In the Talmud, the correspondence is given differently: Six hundred thirteen commandments were revealed to Moses at Sinai, 365 being prohibitions equal in number to the solar days, and 248 being mandates corresponding in number to the limbs of the human body (B. Makkot 23b). Another talmudic passage states that the disciples of R. Ishmael, by dissecting the corpse of a prostitute who had been executed, determined that women have 252 limbs (B. Bekhorot 45a).

5. According to B. Hagigah 12a, contemplating future human sin, God hid the primordial light that shone during the seven days of creation, with which one could see from one end of the world to the other, and has laid it up as a reward for the righteous in paradise.

6. One further numerical correspondence suggests that women's and men's bodies must be considered in relation to one another. The number of male and female limbs, 248 and 252, respectively (and it is interesting to note that, in traditional Jewish anatomy at least, women are not *lacking* something, but have *more* anatomical features than men) add up to 500. This figure is used to explain why women light two candles on the eve of the Sabbath. After mentioning other explanations, the *Shloyshe sheorim*, a popular eighteenth-century *tkhine* attributed to the legendary Sore bas Tovim, states:

> **"Ner, ner" adds up numerically to 500.** This means, the numerical equivalent of **candle,** twice, comes out to 500, corresponding to the **organs of man and woman,** the number of organs of the man and of the woman. By the merit of this [commandment], God, blessed be he, will heal the limbs of man and woman. Therefore, one should kindle the lights with great seriousness, and God, blessed be he, will enlighten our children in the Torah . . . (Sore bas Tovim [?] [eighteenth century], section entitled *Dinim fun lekht tsindn*)

7. Tanḥuma, begining of Noah. Tanḥuma is one of the few sources that explicitly state that the women's miẓvot function as an atonement. Yalqut Shim`oni, Genesis 3:31, is dependent on the Tanḥuma. An earlier source is Avot de-Rabbi Nathan, version B, chap. 9 (Schechter 1945, 13), which, however, was not published until the twentieth century. For other texts that connect the three women's miẓvot to Eve's sin, without the idea of atonement, see Bereshit Rabba, 17 (end); B. Shabbat 31b–32a, and Rashi; J. Shabbat 2 *ad. loc.* `al she-einan zehirot . . .

8. B. Erubin 100b; Avot de-Rabbi Nathan, chap. 1.

9. I have been unable to locate a midrashic source for Eve's beating of Adam; this motif does not appear *ad. loc.* in Genesis Rabba, Midrash ha-Gadol, Avot de-Rabbi Nathan, Sefer ha-Yashar, Pirqei Rabbi Eliezer, Yalqut Shim'oni, nor in Gross (1982). It is not cited by Kasher (1929), nor in Ginzberg (1913–1938). Nor is it found in the Yiddish sources Altshuler (1626) and *Odom ve-Khave Lid* ([1658–1705]). Prof. Mordechai A. Friedman suggests that the origin of this interpretation may be in fact that the Aramaic root *yehav* means both 'to give' and 'to beat or strike'; the Yiddish *gebn* also has both meanings.

10. Altshuler 1626, p. 118b (chap. 35) for *niddah*; p. 166a (chap. 36) for *ḥallah*; p. 166a–b, (chap. 37) for *hadlaqah*.

11. The *etrog,* or citron, is used, along with the *lulav,* the palm branch together with myrtle and willow twigs, during the liturgy of the weeklong fall harvest festival of *Sukkot.* For the *etrog* to be fit for ritual use, it must be intact: in particular, the raised blossom-end tip of the fruit, or *pittam,* must not have broken off. There were two, probably interrelated, folk beliefs concerning the *pittam,* of the *etrog.* First, attested in twentieth-century ethnographic and literary materials, is the belief that childless women would conceive if they bit off and swallowed the *pittam;* second, and this is what I find in the *tkhines,* by biting off the *pittam,* pregnant women would ensure a safe and easy childbirth.

12. In addition, the text of the prayer only, but not the introduction, is found in *Seder tkhines u-vakoshes* (1762), no. 89.

13. Interestingly enough, there is another, later *tkhine* for biting off the end of the *etrog* (Sobotki 1718, no. 19), written by a man. While Sobotki mentions that Eve's sin of disobedience, which brought death to the world, is the reason for painful childbirth, he removes all connection between the *etrog* and the story of Eve. Instead, he has the woman petition God for an easy childbirth in part because she has kept the *mizvah* of *blessing* the *lulav* and *etrog.* Also, she says, "May I have my child as easily as I bite off the stem of the etrog." While this text distinguishes the woman who recites it, and has obeyed God's commandment, from the disobedient Eve, it blunts the power of the earlier prayer.

14. This *tkhine* also describes the spirit in which the act of marital intercourse may be consummated in a holy manner. A *tkhine* with rather similar content (although with less explicit discussion of the manner of intercourse) is found in the *Sefer mitsvas ha-noshim,* no. 49. It is the oldest dated *tkhine* extant.

15. The use of the term *treyf* for the menstruating woman requires further investigation. While, in Yiddish, *"treyf"* can mean not only "forbidden

food," but also "forbidden" in a more general sense, it is not usually applied to people, except in an extremely pejorative sense.

16. The origin of this idea may be Tiqqunei Zohar, tiqqun 40, p. 80a. See also B. Shabbat 146a, B. Yebamot 103b, and B. Avodah Zarah 22b; the Talmud sees the impure venom as the source of human lust, and as an explanation of the fact that Adam, Abraham, and Isaac all fathered evil as well as righteous sons. Zohar I 54a and Tiqqunei Zohar, tiqqun 70, 128b, continue the Talmud's concern with evil progeny as the "offspring" of the serpent's impure venom. An early *piyyut* makes a different but related connection between Eve's sin and menstrual blood, stating that the color of menstrual blood is reminiscent of the wine which Eve made Adam drink. (On this reading, the Tree of Knowledge was a grapevine.) (Rabinovitz 1985, 435, cited by Friedman 1990, 2 n.)

17. See, for example, chap. 3, pp. 11a–12a, in which Altshuler explain why he is writing this book in Yiddish for women.

18. See Shulman 1986, a historical study based on Solnik's halakhic works, pp. 22–25, 148, 187.

References

Altshuler, Moses Henoch. 1626. *Sefer Brant Shpigl*. Hanau.

Friedman, Mordechai A. 1990. "Harḥaqat ha-niddah veha-minut eẓel ha-ge'onim, ha-Rambam, u-veno R. Avraham, `al pi kitvei genizat qahir." *Maimonidean Studies*. Ed. Arthur Hyman. Vol. 1. 1–21.

Ginzberg, Louis. 1913–1938. *Legends of the Jews*. Philadelphia: Jewish Publication Society.

Gross, M. D. 1982. *Oẓar ha-aggadah*. Jerusalem: Mosad ha-Rav Kook.

Jacob ben Isaac of Yanov. 1702/3. *Tsenerene*. Amsterdam.

Kasher, Menahem. 1929. *Torah shelemah*. Vol 2. Jerusalem.

Odom ve-Khave Lid. [between 1658 and 1705]. Prague.

Rabinovitz, Z. M., ed. 1985. *Maḥzor piyyutei Rabbi Yannai la-Torah velamo`adim*. Jerusalem and Tel-Aviv.

Romer-Segal, Agnes. 1979. *Sifrei miẓvot ha-nashim be-yidish ba-me`ah ha-tet-zayin*. M.A. thesis. Jerusalem.

Schechter, Solomon. 1945. *Aboth de Rabbi Nathan*. New York: Feldheim.

Seder tkhines. 1650. Amsterdam.

Seder tkhines u-vakoshes. 1762. Fürth.

Shulman, Nisson E. 1986. *Authority and Community: Polish Jewry in the Sixteenth Century.* Hoboken: Ktav.

Sobotki, Matityahu. 1718. *Seder tkhines.*

Solnik, Benjamin Aaron. 1602. *Ayn shoen froen bukhlein (Sefer mitsvas hanoshim).* Basle.

Sore bas Tovim [?] [eighteenth century?] *Shloyshe she`orim.* [n.p.]

Tkhines. 1648. Amsterdam.

Weissler, Chava. 1987. "The Traditional Piety of Ashkenazic Women." In *Jewish Spirituality from the Sixteenth-Century to the Present.* Ed. Arthur Green. New York: Crossroad.

——— 1989. " 'For Women and For Men Who are Like Women': The Construction of Gender in Yiddish Devotional Literature." *Journal of Feminist Studies in Religion,* 5 (2): 3–24.

——— 1991. "Prayers in Yiddish and the Religious World of Ashkenazic Women." In *Jewish Women in Historical Perspective.* Ed. Judith Baskin. Detroit: Wayne State University Press.

5

Purifying the Body in the Name of the Soul: The Problem of the Body in Sixteenth-Century Kabbalah

Lawrence Fine

> Whatever we imagine when we speak of Gnostics renouncing their bodies, or despising the flesh, we should not ignore how intrigued they seemed to have been with their own anatomy, how often they seemed convinced that truths, both pleasant and unpleasant, about their origin and their destiny could be traced within its form and functions.
>
> —Michael A. Williams

It is still commonplace to think of asceticism in the religious traditions of the West as involving uncompromising repudiation and utter loathing of the body. The realities, though, are more complex. Two recent studies on conceptions of the body in Christian tradition speak to this problem in particularly compelling ways. In describing the Desert tradition in early Christianity, for example, Peter Brown makes it clear that "to describe [such] ascetic thought as dualist and as motivated by hatred of the body, is to miss its most novel and its most poignant aspect" (Brown 1988, 235). On the contrary, for the Desert Fathers "life in the desert revealed, if anything, the inextricable interdependence of body and soul" (Brown, 236). For alongside of the vivid exhortations to tame the unruly body, and the array of strategies designed to "trample on the passions," Christian monks could also speak, of "this body, that God has afforded me, as a field to cultivate, where I might work and become rich" (Brown, 236).

Similarly, in her study of the religious significance of food to medieval Christian women, Caroline Walker Bynum challenges conventional wisdom by contending that the extravagant penitential practices of the late Middle Ages should not be understood as world-denying, self-hating responses to the miseries and frustrations of medieval life. To Bynum, female Christian saints and mystics "were not rebelling against or torturing their flesh out of guilt over its capabilities so much as using the possibilities of its full sensual and affective range to soar ever closer to God" (Bynum 1987, 295).

It is precisely this paradox that stands at the heart of much of Western religious asceticism and that, more generally, informs attitudes toward the body.[1] How and why is it that the body—despite the unrelenting anxiety it so often generated for the person in search of spiritual perfection—remained the arena in which so much of that search took place? This paradox is no less striking in the ascetic strategies that evolved in the middle of the sixteenth century among Jewish mystical pietists of the Galilean city of Safed in the land of Israel. Study of this community provides an especially interesting opportunity to ask about the nature of this tension in Judaism. For we have to go back to the second century B.C.E.—to the ascetic enthusiasts who gathered near the shores of the Dead Sea—to find a Jewish community as intrigued by the question of the body as this one.

Breach Within the Body of God in Early Kabbalah

Before turning to the question of the body in the sixteenth century, I want to focus our attention on several critical themes from the earlier medieval tradition of thirteenth-century Spanish Kabbalah.[2] According to the kabbalists, the life of God may be said to comprise two aspects, the first of which is known as *Ein-Sof,* meaning "infinite" or "without end." *Ein-Sof* is that dimension of God that is beyond all human apprehension, the hidden and perfect root of all reality, "which thought cannot attain." This conception, with its radical insistence upon the inability of human beings to know God's essence, strongly reminds us of the "negative theology" of medieval Jewish philosophy. But the kabbalists leave the philosophers far behind when they go on to speak of ten *Sefirot,* divine radiances or lights, *emanations* that flow out of the hidden well-springs of *Ein-Sof.* It is as if the concealed Mystery of all being gives birth to other, more manifest parts of Itself. In contrast to *Ein-Sof,* the *Sefirot* are accessible to the human imagination; they are the "garments," "colors," "faces," "limbs," and "names" of God. The *Sefirot* are outer layers of the hidden dimension of God to which they are intimately bound, ways of naming that which is ultimately beyond naming. They are, say the kabbalists, like the rays of the sun in relationship to the sun itself.[3]

The *Sefirot* may also be understood as the symbols through which countless images from the natural world and human experience are used to convey the multiple dimensions of divine existence. For everything in our experience corresponds to and symbolizes the processes of intradivine life. Among the various symbolic patterns by which the *Sefirot* are imagined, none is more central to kabbalah nor more radical in its implications than the symbolism of divine Body.[4] God's self-disclosure or willed emanation is imagined, among other ways, as the formation and completion of the mystical body of "Primordial Man" *(Adam Qadmon)*. Thus, according to the Zohar (3, 141a–141b, *Idra Rabba)*, a human being below is fashioned in both body and soul in the image of "Primordial Man."

> The [divine] image was perfected that comprises all images, the image that comprises all names . . . when the crowns and the diadems were joined together, then it was the perfection of all, for the image of man is the image of the upper and the lower worlds that are comprised within it.

According to the most common descriptions of this symbolism, the upper triad of *Sefirot (Keter, Hokhmah,* and *Binah)* corresponds to the divine "head," or the several dimensions of God's intellect. *Hesed and Gevurah* represent the right and left arms, *Tiferet* signifies the central part of the body, the divine torso, while *Nezah* and *Hod* symbolize the right and left legs of God's anatomy. The ninth *Sefirah, Yesod,* denotes divine phallus, the vessel through which the procreative vitality of God's life ultimately flows.

The notion of gender is intrinsic to a description of the upper nine *Sefirot*. Besides being portrayed as parts of the divine intellect, the second and third *Sefirot, Hokhmah* and *Binah* are also depicted as masculine and feminine qualities respectively. *Hokhmah* is father *(Abba)* while *Binah* is mother *(Imma),* and by virtue of the former's impregnation of the latter, the seed from which all further reality will derive is sown. *Binah* is represented as a great Sea from which numerous streams flow, and as a cosmic Womb, a powerfully fecund Mother who gives birth to Her chidlren, the lower *Sefirot*. As such, all creation is invested with the qualities of male and female, and is held in balance by them. Thus, the Zohar (3, 290a, *Idra Zuta):*

> This *Hokhmah,* which includes everything, when it emerged from, and was illuminated by *Atika Kadisha (Keter),* was illuminated in

> no other way except as male and female; for this *Hokhmah* extended itself and brought forth *Binah* from itself, and so there existed male and female. *Hokhmah* father, *Binah* mother, *Hokhmah* and *Binah* were equally weighed, male and female, and because of them everything survives as male and female, for were it not so they would not survive.

Taken as a whole, however, the upper nine *Sefirot* are *male* in nature, in relationship to the tenth *Sefirah* who possesses a unique status of Her own. *Shekhinah* (also known as *Malkhut*) is imagined as female, possessing no inherent divine light of Her own but instead filled with the nourishment that She receives from the *Sefirot* above Her, mediated most directly through *Yesod.*[5] The *Shekhinah* goes by an array of names that signify Her female nature: "Daughter," "Lower Mother," "Princess," "Bride," "Queen," "Earth," "Moon," and "Sabbath," to name a few. Whereas the relationship between the upper "parents" *Hokhmah* and *Binah* is continually harmonious, not so with *Shekhinah* and Her male lover *Tiferet.* While their relationship is ideally one of perfect intimacy—signifying the balance and unity of the life of God as a whole—their ties to one another are more typically marked by the tension and struggle that characterize all romantic and erotic relationships. Under certain conditions, the *Shekhinah* is separated, estranged from Her lover, quite literally in exile. Thus, the kabbalists appropriate the older language of midrashic theology and speak of *galut ha-Shekhinah,* the "exile of the *Shekhinah.*" But in kabbalistic terms, such exile now takes on the meaning of disunity or breach *within* the life of God itself.

Human beings play a crucial role in these processes, based on a set of anthropological notions axiomatic to medieval Kabbalah. If God is envisioned in terms of human anatomy, as a *macroanthropos,* the converse is equally true. While everything in nature mirrors some aspect or another of the divine world, the human individual in particular, as the Zohar texts cited above imply, is a microcosmic reflection of the upper realms.[6] To the mystics, the individual signifies the totality of the sefirotic structure and, even more, is imbued with divine life in a substantive way. This is especially true of the soul, the *neshamah,* which is conceived as being consubstantial with God. Just as Gnostics of an earlier age had taught that it was the *pneuma* or soul within a person which constitutes the divine portion, so the kabbalists taught that by virtue of the *neshamah* an intimate and immediate bond exists between human beings and

God. Thus, according to the Safed kabbalist Elijah de Vidas, "souls are flaming threads drawn below from on high, their vitality stemming constantly from their Source" (*Reshit Hokhmah,* Gate of Love, chap. 3).

The divine nature of the soul, and the fact that the individual constitutes a microcosm of the sefirotic world, serve as the basis for the theurgic conviction that every human action reverberates, so to speak, on the level of the *Sefirot.* Theurgy refers to the notion that human activity is capable of exerting influence on realms beyond it. According to this pivotal kabbalistic conception, *it is human sin that violates the unity within the world of divinity,* a rupture conceived primarily, as suggested, as estrangement between male and female, *Tiferet* and *Skekhinah.* The project of all human life is to restore the original balance and harmony of the cosmos through ritual and moral activity accompanied by appropriate contemplation. Every proper deed contributes to the well-being of the life of God while every improper action serves to reinforce the disunity within divine life. Even more, the momentary unification of God brought about by such action enables divine light to flow downward into the material world. That is, earthly gestures animate the life of the *Sefirot* in such a way as to cause vitality from the upper world to descend into the lower. Thus there is a *mutual* and *dynamic* relationship between individuals and the transcendent realm with which they are so intimately connected. As a microcosm, a perfect paradigm of the upper world, and as one link in a cosmic chain of being, a person simultaneously reflects the world of deity and arouses it—only to be aroused and nourished in return.

The cosmic repercussions of religious deeds constitutes one of the most far-reaching and radical conceptions of theosophical Jewish mysticism. God is no longer conceived to be in control of all history in the conventional sense; rather, God's own well-being is determined by what human beings do. With this conception the function of religious practice has been redefined and invigorated with altogether new status.

Having pointed in the direction of some of the fundamental themes pertaining to the connection between God's mystical body/self and the human body/self in earlier Kabbalah, I want to turn our attention to various elaborations and revisions upon these themes in the cultural context of Safed in the sixteenth century. My approach is to explore some of the ways in which meanings and feelings associated with the body are especially apparent in the ritual uses to which the body was put. This was a culture in which ritual and performance (in the broad sense) played an enormous role. It is thus precisely in these cultural expressions that we may best be able to approach not simply the *idea* of the body, but the broader human experience to which our sources attest.[7]

Safed in the Sixteenth Century

The sixteenth century witnessed the striking growth of kabbalistic learning and piety in various parts of the Jewish world. Stimulated especially by the expulsion of Jewry from the Iberian Peninsula in the last decade of the fifteenth century and the migration of Jews to Italy, North Africa, and the Ottoman Empire, Kabbalah became inextricably linked with the messianic enthusiasm that erupted in the wake of these events.[8]

The Galilean city of Safed, which flourished under the relatively benevolent auspices of the Ottoman Empire, became the physical and spiritual center for these developments, as Safed emerged as a mystical community of impressive proportions beginning in about 1530.[9] Moses Cordovero, Solomon Alkabetz, Joseph Karo, Abraham Galante, Israel Najara, Abraham ben Eliezer ha-Levi Berukhim, Elijah de Vidas, Moses Alsheikh, Eleazar Azikri, Hayyim Vital, and Isaac Luria are only some of the vivid personalities who illumined Safed during this period. The spiritual creativity of these individuals left a powerful legacy; virtually all Jewish mystical developments through the seventeenth and eighteenth centuries were influenced in significant ways by the Safed renaissance.

Imitating the Suffering of the *Shekhinah* in the Mystical Experiences of Moses Cordovero and Solomon Alkabetz

The kabbalists of the sixteenth century suffered from a profound sense of exile, something shared, paradoxically, even by mystics living in the land of Israel. The precise degree to which this was a direct result of the recent exiles from Spain and Portugal, or of the accumulated psychological weight of the several centuries of physical dislocation that European Jewry experienced, is difficult to determine. What is, however, undeniable is that Safed Jewry was emotionally preoccupied by an overwhelming sense of *galut* (exile). In my view, this phenomenon is the central ingredient in any effort to come to grips with the perception of the self, and of the body, which these pietists possessed. For these were individuals who were clearly convinced that their sinfulness—conceived in large part as *misuse* of their own bodies—was responsible not only for their own exile but for the breach within the "body" of God as well. Even though earlier kabbalists had spoken, as we have seen, of the exile of the *Shekhinah,* it was the Safed mystics, now especially consumed by a sense of individual and collective responsibility, who took up this theme with even greater enthusiasm. In the process they exhibited a deeply and personally felt identification with the rupture within the body of God, and particularly the misery and torment of the *Shekhinah;* it was precisely this identification that helped shape their self-understanding, including their attitude toward their own physicality.[10]

Among the most explicit and vivid illustrations of the connection between the fate of the *Shekhinah* and their own conception of selfhood is a ritual activity that was practiced by two of the leading Safed kabbalists, Moses Cordovero (1522–1570) and Solomon Alkabetz (c. 1505–1584), known as *gerushin.*[11] *Gerushin* literally means "exiles" or "wanderings." They would "wander" amongst the numerous gravesites in the environs of Safed in self-conscious imitation of the exiled *Shekhinah:*

> A person should exile himself from place to place for the sake of Heaven, and in this way he will become a vessel for the exiled *Shekhinah.* . . . he should humble his heart in exile and bind himself to the Torah and then the *Shekhinah* will accompany him. And he should carry out *gerushin* by exiling himself from his house of rest constantly, after the fashion of Rabbi Shimon [bar Yohai] and his company who exiled themselves in order to study the Torah.[12] And how much better is he who bruises his feet wandering from place to place without horse and cart. Concerning him it is said: 'His hope *(sivro)* is with the Lord his God,' (Ps. 146:5) which they explained from the expression *shever* ('to break'), for he *breaks his body* in the service of the Most High (Cordovero, *Tomer Devorah,* chap. 9).

Elsewhere Cordovero reports that his master Alkabetz "decided upon the innovation that in the summer months especially we should, on occasion, walk barefooted in the mystery of the *Shekhinah" (Sefer ha-Gerushin,* chap. 1). To deliberately "exile" oneself, then, is a symbolic act of humility that enables one to express as well as experience the humiliation to which the *Shekhinah* is Herself subjected. Moreover, it is preferably a form of genuine self-affliction, an opportunity to "break one's body" and to bruise one's feet in the dust, just as the bruised and suffering *Shekhinah* lies in the dust.[13] Yet by such mystical peregrinations Cordovero and Alkabetz were also able to provide *comfort* for the *Shekhinah,* as the heart becomes a dwelling place for Her to rest, a motif that suggests the influence of Sufi piety.[14] Thus, while one subjects the body to shame and humiliation in a powerful act of empathy with the *Shekhinah,* at the same time the body humbled serves as a vessel in which She dwells and finds consolation.

This "incorporation" of the *Shekhinah* within the mystic is taken a step further when we consider that these "exiles" resulted in experiences of sudden, unreflected speech on the part of Cordovero and Alkabetz in which they would utter kabbalistic interpretations of Scripture.[15] This "prophetic" type speech was regarded in kabbalistic terms as deriving from the *Sefirah Malchut,* that is, the *Shekhinah.* As the culminating point of the self-revelatory process within God, She is imagined as the articulate aspect of divinity, symbolized by the "speech" of God, the source of virtually all prophecy and vocal revelation. Thus, the *gerushin* served as a ritualized *technique* by which an adept could transform his body into a vessel for the physical and vocalized manifestation of divine revelation. The body serves then *simultaneously* as an instrument with which to dramatize the bitterness of exile, as well as a medium for revivifying God. While the body—itself in exile—is a natural focus for the exile of the *Shekhinah,* so too is it a perfect vehicle for Her rejuvenation, possessed as it is by a heart in which She is able to dwell.

Mortification of the Flesh and Dreams of Martyrdom in Joseph Karo

In his remarkable confessional diary, Joseph Karo (1488–1575), generally better known for his legal preeminence than for his kabbalistic persona, preserved a record of his unusual mystical experiences.[16] Karo's diary, published under the title *Maggid Mesharim,* reveals to us an individual driven by an intensely felt burden of guilt and anxiety, self-doubt and personal torment. We learn as well that Karo practiced a mystical technique which had the effect of producing automatic speech in a manner similar to that reported by Cordovero and Alkabetz. In Karo's case these experiences followed upon the prolonged repetition of passages of Mishnah. The voice that spoke through his own had a complex identity. Karo regarded it as the personification of the Mishnah itself, identifying it as the *Shekhinah,* and referring to it as his *Maggid,* or angelic mentor.

In these communications, in which the *Maggid* speaks through Karo's own voice and addresses him, the *Shekhinah* is depicted as a tormented and abandoned mother. In impressively guilt-inspiring language, She describes Herself as estranged and anguished because of the failures of others.

> For these many years had My head been fallen with none to comfort Me. I was cast down to the ground to embrace the dunghills. . . . If you could only imagine one millionth of the anguish which I endure no joy would ever enter your hearts and no mirth your mouths, for it is because of you that I am cast to the ground. (Jacobs 1977, 100–1)

Karo's *Maggid* portrays Herself as suffering unimaginable humiliation and as having fallen to the depths of despair. She is a bitter, chastizing mother who admonishes those amongst Her children who have deserted Her. Karo's powerful sense of his own sinfulness and inadequacy led him to believe that the only way to atone for his transgressions, to heal the *Shekhinah,* and to induce Her to communicate with him, was through acts of physical mortification.[17] Thus, Karo's kabbalistic writings are replete with endless exhortations from his *Maggid* to sleep less, eat less, drink less, and generally to minimize the body's enjoyment of physical pleasures to the extent possible. The following is typical:

> Be careful to avoid taking pleasure while eating meat and drinking, or while partaking of any other kind of enjoyment. Act as if a demon were forcing you to eat this food or indulge in the enjoyable activity. You should very much prefer it were it possible to exist without food and drink altogether, or were it possible to fulfill the obligation of procreation without enjoyment. (Fine 1984b, 56)

For Joseph Karo, ascetic behavior was rooted not only in a general desire to repent for supposed sinful behavior but in the simultaneous requirement to focus attention exclusively upon the Mishnah/*Maggid* and her needs. The pursuit of self-gratification is narcissistic diversion from the only true legitimate object of concern.[18] Thus, the *Maggid:*

> . . . hold fast to Me, therefore, and give up bodily pleasures. . . . If you will do this, forsaking bodily pleasures so that your heart and

> mind become a constant nest for the Torah, and if you never cease from thinking on the Torah, then the Holy One, blessed be He, will take delight in you. (Jacobs 1977, 114)

In fact, the very manifestation of the *Maggid* hinges upon Karo's having deprived himself of physical pleasures:

> The eve of the Sabbath, 29th of *Iyyar,* portion *Be-Midbar Sinai.* I ate but little and drank the same and I studied the Mishnah at the beginning of the night. I then slept until daybreak so that when I awoke the sun was shining. I was very upset, saying to myself: "Why did I not arise during the night so that the word should come to me as before?" Nevertheless, I began to rehearse the Mishnah and I studied five chapter. As I was reading the Mishnah the voice of my beloved knocked in my mouth and the lyre sang of itself. It began by saying: "The Lord is with you wherever you go, and the Lord will prosper whatever you have done and will do, but you must cleave to Me and to My Torah and to My Mishnah at all times, not as you have done this night. For although you did sanctify yourself in your food and drink, you slept like a sluggard. . . . For this you deserve that I should leave and forsake you since you give strength to Samael, the serpent and the evil inclination by sleeping until daybreak. But in the merit of the six orders of the Mishnah that you know by heart, and in the merit of the self-tortures and torments you engaged in in years past, and which you still practice, it was agreed in the Heavenly Academy that I should return to converse with you as in former time, and that I should neither leave you nor forsake you. (Jacobs 1977, 111)

Karo's ascetic disposition found its ultimate expression in his zeal to martyr himself "for the sanctification of [God's] Name." His most fervent hope was to have the opportunity to be burnt at the stake! While some kabbalists, such as Isaac Luria, indulged in an imaginative, contemplative exercise of martyrdom, Karo apparently believed that only actual death would satisfy his need for personal atonement and devotion to God. Through repentant acts of self-affliction, Karo hoped to make himself worthy of martyrdom. Yet it was only martyrdom itself that would serve to eradicate altogether the sins for which he felt himself responsible. Thus, martyrdom is conceived as both a privilege granted for virtuous behavior and as an opportunity to complete the process of atonement.

Karo explicitly identified martyrdom through being burnt at the stake with a specific type of animal sacrifice practiced in ancient Israel, namely, the burnt offering. Martyrdom has to be by *fire* because "he who is killed [by the sword] or strangled for the holiness [of God's Name] is like a sin offering or a trespass offering [of which part remains and is eaten by the priests], because his flesh remains in this world . . . but he who is burned for the holiness of God is like a burnt sacrifice which rises wholly upwards" (Werblowsky 1977, 153). Karo thus carried the shame for the body felt by many other Safed kabbalists to an extreme, primarily through his identification of the ultimate service of God with the utter dissolution of the body.

As Karo's biographer, R. J. Z. Werblowsky aptly expressed it: "Karo's fantasies of martyrdom and the penitential discipline of his ascetic life have a common foundation: an oppressive sense of sin and a fervent desire to rid himself of sin as well as of the material body. What mortification can achieve only imperfctly in this life is triumphantly consummated in death by the purifying flame that annihilates both body and sin. A handful of ashes remains on the altar, whilst a spotlessly pure and white soul is received into glory" (Werblowsky 1977, 154).

Thus as with Cordovero and Alkabetz's *gerushin,* in Karo's case the body serves more than one purpose. It is both the locus for intentional acts of deprivation and humiliation as well as the vehicle through which divinity is glorified. Karo must deny his body pleasure in order to atone for his sins and to avoid further ones; but at the same time his body—as the repository of the purified soul—becomes a vessel for the *Shekhinah* when She speaks through it, enabling him to raise Her up from the dust and crown Her with glory. Even more, the body is ultimately a weapon to be used in accomplishing the most perfect and enduring means of worshiping God. Only through an act of dis-embodiment, by surrendering the unblemished body to the altar of sacrifice, can Karo's purified soul serve God fully.

Body and Spirit in the Gnostic Teachings of Isaac Luria

Isaac Luria (1534–1572) is among the several greatest figures in the history of the Jewish mystical tradition and the preeminent personality among the kabbalists of Safed, despite the fact that he lived there for a period of only two years, from 1570 until his death. Luria's charismatic personality produced a significant discipleship in Safed and gave birth to an elaborate tradition of sacred biography. In diverse ways, from the realm of popular piety to abstruse theological speculation, Lurianic Kabbalah exerted tremendous influence upon Judaism in the seventeenth century in virtually all parts of the Jewish world, and well into the eighteenth amongst Eastern European and Near Eastern Jewry.

At the heart of Lurianic teaching is an intricate theogonic and cosmogonic mythology. While the descriptions of divine emanation common amongst the Spanish kabbalists of the thirteenth century were unabashedly anthropomorphic in nature, Lurianic myth carried this tendency to even greater extremes. *The most important symbolic categories of Lurianic myth are drawn from the imagery of human anatomy, biological development, and human sexuality.* While the essential features of Lurianic mythology have been spelled out in many places,[19] and they need not be repeated in all their detail here, I do want to draw our attention to certain themes that are especially germane to notions of the body.

In contrast to earlier Kabbalah, Luria describes the self-disclosure of God as initially entailing an act of *withdrawal (zimzum)* in which God contracts its essence, retreating "from Himself into Himself." That is, He abandons a space within Himself, thereby producing an "empty" region *(tehiru).* This process brings into being the space within which all dimensions of existence will eventually be formed, both on the spiritual and corporeal level. While certain residues of divine light have been left behind in this empty space during the process of withdrawal, a second act takes place in which the divine reenters the *tehiru* with a beam of light termed *Adam Qadmon* (Primordial Man), a symbol that we met earlier in connection with Spanish Kabbalah. Lurianic texts employ two different images to describe the emanative process of *Adam Qadmon*—"circle" and "line." The ten *sefirot* originally took shape in *Adam Qadmon* in the form of concentric circles, after which they reorganized themselves in a line, more precisely, in the shape of a human body.

Even more, *Adam Qadmon* is described as having "ears," a "nose," and "mouth" from which lights were shining. The lights emanating from the "eyes" were different from the others; they were deficient, structured in such a way as to require their containment in "vessels" *(qelim)* of thicker light. Although these vessels were intended to permit the orderly emanation of the lights within them, they proved insufficiently strong for their task and shattered, an event known in Lurianic literature as the "breaking of the vessels" *shevirat ha-qelim).* Most of the lights that had been contained in these vessels returned to their divine source while the remainder fell below into the empty space and attached themselves to the now broken shards of vessels. From these shards, "husks" or "shells" were produced; these "shells" are the evil forces of the "other side" and also form the basis for the material world. The sparks of light that failed to return to their source above remained trapped, as it were, among the "shells." The latter, in turn, are nourished by the sparks that are attached to them and that yearn to extricate themselves from their imprisoned state. Were it not for the sparks that cleave to them, the "shells" would fall away into lifelessness. In a manner, then, that is remarkably similar to certain of the mythic systems of the Gnostics of late antiquity, Lurianic mythology depicts a primordial, intradivine crisis that culminates in the descent of transcendent light into the world of gross materiality, the one inherently opposed to the other.

Tiqqun or "mending" refers to the complex processes by which the ruptured condition of divinity was to be repaired. The primary medium for this repair was the sefirotic light that continued to emanate from *Adam Qadmon* following the "breaking of the vessels." This light was now reorganized under five new structural principles known as *parzufim* (faces). The *sefirah Keter* was reconstituted as *Arikh Anpin* (lit., the Long-Faced One). *Hokhmah* and *Binah* were reformed as *Abba* (Father) and *Imma* (Mother), *Tiferet* as *Zeir Anpin* (the Short-Faced One), and *Shekhinah/Malchut* as *Nuqba de-Zeir* (Female of *Zeir*). The last four *parzufim*, then, correspond to the two pairs of male and female in the older sefirotic schema.

Of particular interest to us is that the processes by which these *parzufim* manifest themselves are described in the language of physiological development: conception, pregnancy, birth, suckling, and maturity. The "parents," *Abba* and *Imma*, engage in coupling known as *zivvug*, resulting in the birth of *Zeir Anpin*. *Yeniqah* (suckling) is the means by which *Zeir* is nourished following its emergence from the womb of *Imma*. By the power of this suckling, *Zeir* grows and matures until He comprises six of the lower *sefirot* (*Hesed, Gevurah, Tiferet, Nezah, Hod, Yesod*). Eventually, *Zeir* and his spouse, *Nuqba de-Zeir*, like *Abba* and *Imma*, stand "face to face" in an intimate relationship of marriage.

According to Lurianic teaching, the soul of the first man, Adam, was constituted of all the various "worlds" and was intended to liberate the divine sparks that remained within the "shells." Insofar as Adam's structure was a perfect microcosm of *Adam Qadmon*, he should have been able to complete the process of "mending" through appropriate contemplative efforts and mystical actions. Having extricated the sparks from the realm of materiality, the cosmos would have achieved a state of perpetual communion with the divine light.

Adam's sin, however, thwarted these goals, throwing the cosmos once again into complete disarray. Adam himself assumed true material form for the first time, interrupting his own communion with the upper spheres and attaching himself to the lower worlds. Many of the soul-sparks of humankind that had been contained within Adam's soul became enmeshed in the world of matter. And the once intimate relationship between *Zeir* and *Nuqba de-Zeir* was transformed into one of "looking back to back." The crisis generated by Adam's failure, then, may be said to have paralleled on an anthropological level what occurred on an ontological plane with the "breaking of the vessels."

In light of Adam's failure, the task of *tiqqun* has fallen to every individual. Each religious action requires precise and rigorous contemplative concentration on the *parzufim* and various combinations of the divine name in order to "raise up the fallen sparks." The focus of concentration is the inner dynamics of reorganization and restructuring that occurs in the course of acts of devotional piety. The primary object of attention is the remarriage of *Zeir* and *Nuqba de-Zeir* and the return of their relationship to one of "face to face." The Lurianic literature contains elaborately detailed guidelines for bringing all this about.

What I have described thus far presents us with a peculiar paradox. The cosmological processes are *spiritual* rather than physical ones. *Adam Qadmon* and the vast combinations of light that constitute its being, the *parzufim,* as well as the souls of humankind, are all spiritual entities. The physical world as we know it, most especially our own material bodies, are unintended byproducts of essentially spiritual processes. More than unintended, the physical realm is fundamentally polluted, and thus set over against the "true" world of the sacred.[20] Yet the central images employed to describe the actions and life processes of these spiritual phenomena are drawn precisely from the most basic *physical* experiences of human life. The divine *organism, Adam Qadmon,* has bodily parts, becomes impregnanted, bears children that it nurses to various stages of maturation and who themselves ultimately engage in love making. Indeed, *sexual intimacy* within the life of God is the paradigmatic expression of divine wholeness.[21] What is evident is that *despite* the disparagement of the physical in favor of the spiritual that underlies Lurianic teaching, Luria held a complex and ambivalent relationship to bodiliness. Michael Williams's (1982) warning that "we should not ignore how intrigued they [i.e., ancient Gnostics] seemed to have been with their own anatomy," applies equally well to Luria's particular brand of gnosticism. Luria was sufficiently fascinated by human anatomy so as to represent the orderly processes of cosmic restitution primarily in terms of physiological development and married sexuality.

Not surprisingly, this paradoxical attitude toward the physical in Luria's account of intradivine life finds its parallel in his account of human life. To begin with, Luria's anthropology points to a harsh repudiation of the human body:

> Man is created from matter and from form, which consists of soul *[nefesh]*, spirit *[ruah]*, and super-soul *[neshamah]*, the divine portion from above, as it is said: "and [God] breathed into his nostrils the breath *[nishmat]* of life" [Gen. 2:7]. And his body is dark matter from the side of the "shell," luring and preventing man from [achieving] perfection of his soul [in order] to cut it off from the Tree of Life. . . . It is known that sin is a blemish, stain, and rust in the soul, and this it is the sickness of the pure soul. When it [is immersed] in filth and stain, it is unable to perceive and achieve the true perfection, which is [attainment of] the mysteries of the Torah. . . . And the transgression becomes a barrier separating the soul from her Creator, preventing her from perceiving and comprehending holy and pure supernal matters, as it is said: "The law of the Lord is perfect, restoring the soul" [Ps. 19:8]. . . . (Vital, *Shaar Ruah ha-Qodesh,* 39)

In classic dualistic style Luria pits soul, whose source is divine, against body, whose source is "dark matter from the side of the shell."[22] It is the material body and its impulse toward sin that stands in the way of the perfection of the soul, "separating the soul from her Creator."[23] Only mortification of the body, acts of penitential asceticism, can heal a soul diseased by misuse of the body:

> When the soul is pure and unblemished, then the supernal holy matters take shape in her, and when she dwells in rust and stain everything becomes bittersweet [i.e., evil appears as good]. [This is] similar to the sick person who, when he is ill, abhors the good things and love things which aggravate his illness. The doctor, in order to restore his health, gives him spices, including gall, by which his nature will return to what it originally was, and his health as before. So, too, the sick soul, to remove the sickness from her, must receive the bitterness of medicine and "return" in [the form of] mortification and fasts, sackcloth, ashes and stripes, ritual immersions, and purifications from filth and the stains of sin.

> [This is] in order to be able to attain and comprehend supernal matters, which are the mysteries of the world. (Vital, *Shaar Ruah ha-Qodesh,* 39)

This medical analogy extends to the role that Luria himself played in relationship to his disciples. As a physician of the soul Luria was able to diagnose the specific spiritual illnesses that his "patient" had and prescribe the necessary remedy. The diagnostic techniques that he practiced included his ability to discern and interpret lights visible in the form of Hebrew letters on the forehead[24] as well as those concealed within an individual's pulse. These techniques themselves suggest the complex relationship between body and soul in Lurianic thinking. The underlying assumption is that the human soul can manifest itself in linguistic signs which appear within or upon the body.

The remedies invariably entailed penitential acts known as *tiqqunei avonot* (amends of sin) whose purpose, in the words of Hayyim Vital's son Schmuel, was to "mend his soul" and "cleanse him from the filth of the disease of his sins" (Vital, *Shaar Ruah ha-Qodesh,* 40–64).[25] The basic act of bodily mortification involved regimens of fasting, with the amount of fasting tied to the nature of the transgression involved. Let us take as an example the prescription for violating the precept to honor one's mother or father. According to Luria, the *parzufim* of *Abba* (Father) and *Imma* (Mother) are associated with the divine name *YaH*. The *gematria* (the numerical equivalent of the Hebrew letters) of this name—when the letters *yud* and *heh* are themselves spelled out as full words—equals twenty-six. This is the number of fasts required to atone for this particular sin, along with a similar number of lashings. Performance of this penance atones for the sin by raising the sinner's consciousness with regard to his act, as well as by "mending" the damage done to the corresponding parts of the divine structure. By concentrating on the precise number of fasts and lashings, their relationship to *YaH* and the *parzufim* of *Abba* and *Imma,* the individual repairs the injury suffered by the divine anthropos.

Other types of self-affliction were also prescribed. The remedy required for one who publicly humiliated another person is unique. He must roll upon thorns called *ortigas,* Spanish for nettles (Vital, *Shaar Ruah ha-Qodesh,* 49). Luria is said to have derived this practice from Proverbs 24:31: "The face thereof was covered with nettles." The word "face" is taken to mean the face of one who has been put shamed in public. Just as the humiliated person is covered with "nettles," the guilty party must suffer affliction with actual thorns.

Luria was especialy concerned with sexual transgressions, which called for particularly elaborate forms of penitence. Thus, a man who was guilty of having had intercourse with his wife while she was a *niddah* (menstruant) was to fast for a total of fifty-nine days, insofar as the three letters that make up the word *NiDaH* equal this number by way of *gematria*. Moreover, he must be lashed and ritually immerse himself in water as a form of purification for each of these days. He is further required to abstain from sexual intercourse during this period, except for the evenings of Sabbaths, festivals, and the New Moon. The penitent must also sleep on the ground (*AFaR,* literally 'dust') during these fifty-nine days. The explanation for this is found in the letters that make up the word *NiDaH, nun, dalet, heh.* The *heh* represents the *Shekhinah* who, as we have seen, is Herself "lying in the dust" as a result of Her exiled condition. She is a roving wanderer *(Nah ve Nad)* in exile, who is in need of restoration. This is symbolized by the letters *nun* and *dalet* *(NaD)* of the word *NiDaH.* The implication is that violation of the law of *niddah* further entrenches the *Shekhinah* in the dust of exile. The penitent must imitate the *Shekhinah* whose suffering he has exacerbated. Luria prescribed still other types of mortification for various transgressions, including rolling naked in the snow and wearing sackcloth and ashes.[26]

The same essential idea is present in all of the *tiqqunei avonot.* A particular transgression has violated the laws that govern the orderly processes within the life of God. Penitential action, along with the appropriate act of mental concentration, can repair the damage. At the same time it serves to cleanse an individual's soul by purging it of the defilement that it incurred through sin. If the body's appetites and misguided motivation lead to transgression and pollution of the soul, acts of self-affliction reverse the consequences of such sin.

While the evidence gathered thus far attests to the *struggle* between body and soul, the problem is more complicated. The purpose in achieving a state of purified soul by means of the *tiqqunei avonot* was to qualify oneself to engage in broader levels of *tiqqun.* Having reached a requisite stage of *personal* sanctification, one was considered to be in a position to achieve more ambitious goals of soul perfection and cosmic mending. In order to realize these goals, the body had an indispensable role to play.

One of the means to accomplish these goals was the performance of all of the *mitsvot* (precepts) enjoined by rabbinic law. The significance of observing the *mitsvot* was grounded, in part, in the need to realize the soul's fullest potential. The structure of the human soul is complex: it possesses 613 "limbs," each one corresponding to one of the 613 *mitsvot* in the Torah as calculated by rabbinic tradition. Moreover, the spiritual physiognomy of every soul has its parallel in the structure of *Adam Kadmon*. By fulfilling each of the *mitsvot* one thus perfects the entirety of one's soul structure and simultaneously contributes to the larger theurgic goals of Lurianic Kabbalah with which we have by now become familiar.[27]

What is clear from all this is that the "limbs" with which Lurianism is truly concerned are those of *Adam Qadmon,* as well as those of an individual's soul that replicate the structure of the supernal anthropos. The "body" that ultimately matters is the *spiritual* "body," human and divine. Nevertheless, the reconstruction of the spiritual realms, the gathering of the holy sparks, hinges on the proper use of the physical body. Insofar as the performance of the *mitsvot* depends in Judaism upon the action of the body, it can hardly be repudiated altogether. And inasmuch as human anatomy on some level replicates the anatomy of God, individuals are endowed with the capacity to do this work.

An excellent example for our purposes is the *mitsvah* of procreation.[28] According to Isaac Luria, a man is required to engage in marital intercourse even while his wife is pregnant or nursing a child, despite the fact that such relations will not result in conception. The reason for this is that such love making has as its purpose the sustaining of the upper worlds and "marital love" within the realm of God. Even the nights and hours during which intercourse is preferred are tied to particular metaphysical consequences. Thus, kabbalists are required to more or less limit sexual intercourse to midnight on Friday nights insofar as the intimacy that takes place amongst the *parzufim* as a result of such love making is the highest possible kind. We even learn about the direction in which a couple should lie during sex in imitation of the direction of the *sefirot*.

This strikes me as a fascinating set of rules for sexual behavior. Aside from the assertion that a wife has the right to demur from conjugal relations during periods when conception cannot take place, even if her husband wishes otherwise, we are told nothing about what it means to make love on the purely *human* level. While it is fair to assume that Luria, following older traditions, would have encouraged sensitivity and gentleness in love making, these are not the articulated concerns. The conscious preoccupation is not with sex as interpersonal relations but with its cosmic or metaphysical implications.[29] Aside from the fact that it can sometimes produce children, sexual relations are important because of the various types of intradivine love that it engenders and its role in the process of cosmic mending. It is as if the purely human character of sexual activity retreats into the background as larger concerns assume center stage.

Nevertheless, despite the radically spiritualized meaning given to sexual relations, the physical act itself was not supplanted. The possibility of abstinence from sex altogether does not seem to have occurred to these kabbalists. Even Joseph Karo, for all his sexual anxieties, doesn't go beyond seeking to avoid *enjoyment* in sex. Sexual continence, *de rigueur* for centuries among Christian monks, was not a legitimate option for these late medieval Jewish men. The success of the spiritual processes with which they were so intensely concerned *depended* on the physical processes intrinsic to rabbinic Judaism. And aside from the question of kabbalistic motivation, the very requirements of Jewish law—and the social character of religious life—imposed unavoidable constraints upon ascetic zeal. While a system such as Luria's was subversive in the sense that it shifted dramatically the *meaning* of religious performance, it never went so far as to express itself in antinomian ways.

Lurianism, then, did not involve utter disparagement of the body as much as it represented an effort to tame it in radical ways, to use the body in the service of precise spiritual goals. Left to its own devices, the body loomed as a potent and terrifying adversary opposing the spirit; but by systematically harnessing and focusing the extraordinary powers of contemplative energy, a person could manipulate the body so as to perfect the true self and help heal the cosmos.

But there is one more crucial and fascinating twist to our problem. While I have argued that the devaluation of the body and the physical realm did not extend to their complete repudiation, Luria does appear to have envisioned a *future* in which things would be altogether different. In the messianic age, when *tiqqun* is accomplished once and for all, existence will revert back to its purely spiritual character. As Hayyim Vital reports *(Shaar Maamare Razal,* 16c) in the name of Isaac Luria:

> The literal meaning of the commandments in Paradise was different and far more spiritual than now, and what pious individuals

> now enact in material performance of the commandments, they will then, in the paradisiacal garment of the soul, so enact as God intended when He created man.

The messianic age will call for a messianic Torah, for "some day people will cast off this material body; they will be transfigured and recover the mystical body that was Adam's before the fall."[30]

For all of its originality and boldness, Kabbalah frequently builds upon dialectical tensions inherent in nonkabbalistic Judaism. Under the auspices of its mythicized metaphysics Kabbalah drives these tensions to a deeper level of intensity and heightens the stakes. This is certainly true when it comes to the question of the body. The paradox of confidence in the body as a vessel through which to seek God, coupled with anxiety about the obstacles it unavoidably imposes, characterizes rabbinic Judaism.[31] As for the kabbalists of the late Middle Ages, this same paradox illuminates and animates the ambivalence with which they looked upon their own bodies.

Notes

1. For an introduction to the problem of asceticism in *early* Judaism, as well as some of the more general methodological issues in the study of religious asceticism, see Fraade (1986).

2. This discussion of kabbalistic themes is limited to theosophical/theurgic mysticism, represented most commonly by the literature of the Zohar. I omit any discussion of the traditions of another Spanish mystic, Abraham Abulafia (1240–1291), whose "prophetic" or "ecstatic" Kabbalah exerted considerable influence upon the history of Jewish mysticism. Abulafia's teachings have a good deal to say about the body, including the need for physical seclusion, fasting, breathing techniques, and bodily movements in the context of mystical contemplation. Concerning Abulafia, see Idel (1988a, 1988b). Nor do I discuss here the ascetic behaviors of the medieval German Pietists, studied in Marcus (1981).

3. For general introductions to early Kabbalah, see Ariel 1988; Fine 1984a; Green 1984; Matt 1983. For a more detailed study of Spanish Kabbalah, see Tishby 1989.

4. For another discussion of the body in kabbalistic literature, see Mopsik (1989).

5. For detailed discussions of the concept of *Shekhinah,* see Tishby 1989, I, 371–422 and Scholem 1991, 140–96.

6. Early medieval kabbalistic sources do not always agree on whether it is both body and soul that constitute the reflected image of the divine or the soul alone. Such ambivalence, and ambiguity, characterize the Zohar itself, although in his Hebrew writings, Moshe de Leon, the author of the bulk of the Zohar, exhibits a view that is clearly Platonic. Thus, for example, in his *Sefer ha-Mishqal* (Basle, 1608, fol. ICd, 2 Cb) de Leon writes: "One has to search and inquire as to who is the 'man', whether it is the body or the Form. To say that of the body that comes from a fetid drop and which is flesh [destined to become] full of worms and maggots, it is said, 'In the image of God created He him', is Heaven forfend, something that will never occur to a wise man." For a discussion of the microcosm motif in kabbalistic and philosophical sources, see Altmann 1969, 1–40 as well as Tishby 1989, II, 677–722.

7. This approach reflects, in part, recent developments in the "anthroplogy of experience" (Turner and Bruner 1986) that puts a premium on ways of understanding stories, rituals, performances as expressions of lived and living experience.

8. See Elior 1986.

9. See Scholem 1941, 244–86; Fine 1984b, 1–24.

10. When I speak of the Safed kabbalists, I have in mind *men*. Much to our misfortune, while our sources have a great deal to say about questions of gender, sexuality, and the feminine within God, they provide us with no information about what women themselves felt and thought. About this subject we are left to speculate. Occasionally, there are morsels of information about women's activities. For example, Abraham Galante reports that "on the eve of the New Moon all the people fast, including men, women, and students," and engage in various types of penitential exercises. See Fine 1984b, 42.

11. This ritual is described in Werblowsky 1977, 51–54.

12. The Zohar, whose teachings purport to be those of Rabbi Shimon bar Yohai, a second-century Palestinian sage, is set against the background of the constant journeys of Shimon and his *havraya,* or circle of disciples. See Tishby 1989, 9–12.

13. Lying, or sitting in the dust, also suggests the act of mourning. In his devotional customs, Cordovero prescribes the following: "Every night one ought to sit on the ground, mourn the destruction of the Temple, and weep on account of one's transgressions which delay the redemption." (See Fine 1984, 36, 51.)

14. Werblowsky (1977, 58) draws attention to this connection. In Cordovero's list of devotional customs, we read the following: "A person should not turn his heart away from meditating upon words of Torah and holiness,

so that his heart will not be empty and void of reflection upon the commandments, and in order that his heart may become a dwelling place for the *Shekhinah."* See Fine (1984b, 34). Idel (1988c, 166–70), in a discussion of what he terms rituals of "drawing-down theurgy," cites several passages in which the body serves as a vessel for the *Shekhinah.*

15. See Werblowsky 1977, 50–55. For other examples of sixteenth-century techniques resulting in experiences of automatic speech, see Fine 1982a; 1982b; 1987.

16. A full-length study of Karo's experiences is found in Werblowsky 1977.

17. Such sentiments are common in the Safed literature. For example, Elijah de Vidas *(Reshit Hokhmah,* Gate of Repentance, chap. 1): "It is appropriate for a person to arouse himself in repentance when he considers that the *Shekhinah* is exiled on his account, as it is written 'And for your transgressions was your mother put away' [Isa. 50:1]. (See Fine, 1984b, 95.)

18. In a somemwhat different way, certain Safed kabbalists insisted on isolation from all material sensation for successful contemplative experience. For example, Hayyim Vital, Isaac Luria's most important disciple, prefaces a description of his own technique of reciting *Mishnah* with these words: "The person must seclude himself in his mind to the farthest limits and divest his body from his soul as if he does not feel that he is clothed in matter at all—as though he is only soul. The more he separates himself from matter the more his inspiration will be increased . . ." (Fine 1982b, 189–90.) On the issue of solitude as an element in mystical contemplation, see Idel 1988b, 103–69.

19. For a detailed study of Lurianic myth see Tishby (1960), in Hebrew. For a briefer account in English, see Scholem (1941).

20. In Luria, this manifests itself not so much in any apparent antagonism toward nature but in the conviction that what really matters are the holy sparks that all things material or physical actively conceal.

21. For a study of these notions in pre-Lurianic Kabbalah, particularly in relationship to the celebration of the Sabbath, see Ginsburg 1989, 101–21 and *passim* as well as Idel 1989.

22. Such a view was also voiced without equivocation by Elijah de Vidas, whose teachings primarily reflect those of his teacher, Cordovero: "The body, which is created from a fetid drop, is a part of this world; its ultimate destiny is destruction . . . This is so because the body derives from the serpent's skin and its evil shell." (See Fine 1984b, 130.)

23. Again, to demonstrate that such views were typical of the Cordoverian tradition as well, let us listen to de Vidas: "No bond can exist between an individual and God unless an individual sanctifies himself, for God is holy and purely spiritual in nature, and you are of a material nature.

How can that which is spiritual bind itself to that which is material unless a person sanctifies himself and practices abstinence from worldly things?" (Fine 1984b, 102–3.)

24. A detailed study of this technique is found in Fine 1986.

25. The *tiqqunei avonot,* along with other matters discussed below, are studied in Fine 1987.

26. Other examples of such mortification practices outside the Lurianic literature abound. See, for example, the report by Abraham Galante about the extreme forms of self-affliction practiced by the community on the eve of the New Moon, and the (probably exaggerated) description of Abraham Berukhim's brutal penitential activities in Fine 1984b, 42: 47–50.

27. The problem of the *mitsvot* in Lurianism is studied in Fine (1988). The belief in metempsychosis, or transmigration of souls *(gilgul),* that Luria taught (along with other Safed kabbalists), is intimately connected to the notion of perfecting the soul. Transmigration was regarded as an opportunity to complete those religious precepts that one had failed to accomplish during one's lifetime. This subject constitutes a major topic in Lurianic teachings. For a survey of the history of *gilgul,* see Scholem 1991, 197–250.

28. See Vital, *Shaar ha-Mitsvot,* 1962, 7–8. Concerning marital sexuality as a mystical rite in pre-Lurianic Kabbalah, see Ginsburg 1989, 289–93 and *passim.*

29. This contrasts strikingly with certain trends in earlier Kabbalah, especially that represented by *Iggeret ha-Qodesh,* an anonymously authored thirteenth-century text. This treatise spells out in great detail the care that a husband should take in the conduct of marital relations in order to be sensitive to his wife's needs. The Hebrew text may be found in Chavel's (1964) collection of Nachmanides' writings, and in English in Cohen 1976.

30. This passage is from *Hesed le-Abraham* by Abraham Azulai (1685, 2:27). The conception of two Torahs, one of a completely spiritual character and one of a material nature, goes back at least as far as the *Raaya Mehemna* and *Tiqqunei Zohar* of the Zoharic corpus. Concerning these motifs, see Scholem 1965, 66–86.

31. This point of view is corroborated by Fraade 1986.

References

Altmann, Alexander
1969 "The Delphic Maxim in Medieval Islam and Judaism." In idem, *Studies in Religious Philosophy and Mysticism.* Ithaca, N.Y.: Cornell University Press.

Ariel, David
1988 *The Mystic Quest: An Introduction to Jewish Mysticism*. New Jersey and London: Jason Aronson.

Brown, Peter
1988 *The Body and Society: Men. Women, and Sexual Renunciation in Early Christianity*. New York: Columbia University Press.

Bynum, Caroline
1987 *Holy Feast and Holy Fast: The Religious Significance of Food to Medieval Women*. Berkeley and Los Angeles: University of California Press.
1991 *Fragmentation and Redemption: Essays on Gender and the Human Body in Medieval Religion*. New York: Zone.

Chavel, Hayyim
1964 *Kitvei Rabbenu Moshe ben Nachman*. Vol. 2. Jerusalem: Mossad Rav Kook.

Cohen, Seymour
1976 *The Holy Letter*. New York: Ktav Publishing.

Cordovero, Moshe
1962 *Sefer ha-Gerushin*. Jerusalem.
1965 *Tomer Devorah*. Tel Aviv.

De Vidas, Elijah
1579 *Reshit Hokhmah*. Venice.

Elior, Rachel
1986 "Messianic Expectations and Spiritualization of Religious Life in the 16th Century." *Revue des etudes juives* 145 (1–2):35–49.

Fine, Lawrence
1982a "Maggidic Revelation in the Teachings of Isaac Luria." In *Mystics, Philosophers and Politicians*. Ed. J. Reinharz and D. Swetschinski. Durham. N.C.: Duke University Press.
1982b "Recitation of Mishnah as a Vehicle for Mystical Inspiration: A Contemplative Technique Taught by Hayyim Vital." *Revue des etude juives* 141 (1–2):183–99.
1984a "Kabbalistic Texts," In *Back to the Sources*. Ed. B. Holtz. New York: Summit.
1984b *Safed Spirituality*. New York: Paulist Press.
1986 "The Art of Metoposcopy: A Study in Isaac Luria's Charismatic Knowledge." Association for Jewish Studies Review 11 (1):79–101.
1987 "The Contemplative Practice of Yihudim in Lurianic Kabbalah." In *Jewish Spirituality* Vol. 2. Ed. A. Green. New York: Crossroad.
1988 "The Study of Torah as a Rite of Theurgical Contemplation in Lurianic Kabbalah." In *Approaches to Judaism in the Medieval Period*. Vol. 3. Ed. D. Blumenthal. Atlanta: Scholars Press.

Fraade, Steven
1986 "Ascetical Aspects of Ancient Judaism." In *Jewish Spirituality* I. Ed. A. Green. New York: Crossroad.

Ginsburg, Elliot
1989 *The Sabbath in the Classical Kabbalah*. Albany: State University of New York Press.

Green, Arthur
1984 "The Zohar: Jewish Mysticism in Medieval Spain." In *An Introduction to the Medieval Mystics of Europe*. Ed. P. Szarmach. Albany: State University of New York Press.

Idel, Moshe
1988a *The Mystical Experience in Abraham Abulafia*. Albany: State University of New York Press.
1988b *Studies in Ecstatic Kabbalah*. Albany: State University of New York Press.
1988c *Kabbalah: New Perspectives*. New Haven: Yale University Press.
1989 "Sexual Metaphors and Praxis in the Kabbalah." In *The Jewish Family*. Ed. David Kraemer. Oxford: Oxford University Press.

Karo, Joseph
1960 *Maggid Mesharim*. Jerusalem: n.p.

Marcus, Ivan
1981 *Piety and Society: The Jewish Pietists of Medieval Germany*. Leiden: E. J. Brill.

Matt, Daniel
1983 *Zohar: The Book of Enlightenment*. New York: Paulist Press.

Mopsik, Charles
1989 "The Body of Engenderment in the Hebrew Bible, the Rabbinic Tradition and the Kabbalah." In *Fragments for a History of the Human Body* Vol. 1. Ed. M. Feher. New York: Zone.

Scholem, Gershom
1941 *Major Trends in Jewish Mysticism*. New York: Schocken.
1965 *On the Kabbalah and its Symbolism*. New York: Schocken.
1991 *On the Mystical Shape of the Godhead*. New York: Schocken.

Tishby, Isaiah
1984 *Torat ha-Ra ve-ha-Qelippah be-Qabbalat ha-Ari*. New Edition. Jerusalem: Magnes Press
1989 *The Wisdom of the Zohar*. Vol. 1–3. Trans. from the Hebrew by D. Goldstein. Oxford: Oxford University Press.

Turner, Victor and Bruner Edward
1986 *The Anthropology of Experience*. Urbana and Chicago: University of Illinois Press.

Vital, Hayyim
1962 *Shaar Maamare Razal*. Tel Aviv.
1962 *Shaar Ruah ha-Qodesh*. Tel Aviv.

Werblowsky, R. J. Zwi
1977 *Joseph Karo: Lawyer and Mystic*. Philadelphia: Jewish Publication Society of America.

Williams, Michael
1989 "Divine Image—Prison of Flesh: Perceptions of the Body in Ancient Gnosticism." *In Fragments for a History of the Human Body* Vol. 1. Ed. M. Feher. New York: Zone.

6

Images of God's Feet: Some Observations on the Divine Body in Judaism

Elliot R. Wolfson

Introduction

The focus of this study is one particular anthropomorphic image that has engaged the religious imagination of Jews in different historical periods. I will treat the development of a cluster of literary motifs that surround the image of God's feet as they emerge from the Bible, the classical writings of the rabbis, and select Jewish mystical texts from Late Antiquity and the Middle Ages. The ensuing examination serves a twofold purpose. First, it provides an excellent window through which to view the role accorded to figural corporealization of God within Judaism. Secondly, an important concern of this investigation will be a reevaluation of our notion of earlier rabbinic sources and their relationship to vestiges of mythical representations of God in the Bible, on the one hand, and ancient mystical and medieval kabbalistic sources, on the other. To anticipate my conclusion: the mythical conception of the divine body, fully represented in the theosophical kabbalistic tradition, is continuous with earlier strands of Israelite religion and rabbinic Judaism that attributed corporeal form to God (Mopsik 1989). In that sense it is inappropriate to view the anthropomorphic mythos of kabbalah as an apologetic concession to "popular religion and of the faith of the common man" due to "gnostic convictions" that, presumably, can be contrasted with a more normative rabbinic approach (Scholem 1987, 211; 1969, 87–117). On the contrary, the mythic transformation must be seen as part of an internal Jewish hermeneutic: just as rabbinic myth (*'aggadah*) is molded from the fragments of myth scattered upon the landscape of Scripture (Heinemann 1974, 19; Boyarin 1990, 93–104), so kabbalistic myth should be seen against the background of the mythical consciousness embedded in the worldview of the rabbis (Idel 1988, 156–157; Fishbane 1991; Liebes 1992). By positing a line of continuity, however, I do not intend to subscribe to the position that the theosophical interpretation articulated by the kabbalists results from a conservative preservation of older esoteric traditions. On the contrary, as the most recent scholarship has suggested (Idel 1981, 1986; Liebes 1988), some of the mythic and theurgic ideas expressed in the kabbalistic literature of the High Middle Ages have resulted from a complex development wherein older traditions are appropriated and expanded in new contexts. The process of mythologization within any religious culture is not a static retrieval of fixed mythologoumena but rather a dynamic recasting and reformulation of *older* traditions in response to the exigencies of the given historical moment. In the case of Judaism, this process is decidedly hermeneutical, resulting from particular strategies of reading, which may at different historical junctures repeat themselves and produce corresponding phenomenological results without any evident connection or direct line of transmission. With such a model in mind we must seek the roots for the mythos and theosophy alike in the hermeneutical patterns of the different Jewish textual communities responding to the shared base text (Scripture) in all its fluidity, obscurity, and complexity.

Biblical Precursors

As with other motifs that have shaped Jewish approaches to theological matters, so too the image of God's feet has its basis in the biblical writings. Within the diverse textual layers of the Bible, one can discern several different images surrounding God's feet. Yet, all of these occurrences can be grouped into two categories: theophany (Exod. 24:9–10; Deut. 33;3; 2 Sam. 22:10; Ps. 18:10) or execution of divine judgment (Isa. 41:2; Hab. 3:5; Lam. 3:34; Nah. 1:3; Ps. 74:3, 77:20; cf. Mic. 1:3). It may be argued that the latter is in effect a subcategory of the former, for the exercise of divine punishment is one particular instance of God's manifestation in the world. From a careful analysis of the relevant material, therefore, it may be concluded that in ancient Israelite culture, God's feet served as a *topos* for divine revelation (Beyerlin 1965, 31).

Despite the many references to the feet of God in ancient Israelite literature, a description of the feet is never given, as we find, for example, in the case of the angelic feet in Ezek. 1:7, a description that had a decisive impact on the recommended posture during prayer in later Jewish sources (Zimmer 1989, 107–108), or in the case of the feet of the Son of God that are explicitly described in Rev. 2:18 in terms reminiscent of the aforementioned verse in Ezekiel as well as the description of the feet of the man seen by Daniel (10:6). The closest one comes to any description related to the feet is in Exod. 24:10, where it is said that the nobles of Israel "saw the God of Israel, and under His feet was the likeness of a pavement of sapphire, like the very sky for purity" (Nicholson 1974; 1975). But here too nothing is said of the feet, only what is beneath them, viz., the likeness of a pavement of sapphire, which, as various ancient and medieval Jewish interpreters and some more recent biblical scholars have noted (Skipwith 1907, 693; Beyerlin 1965, 30–32; Childs 1974, 506–509), may be an elliptical reference to the Ark, frequently designated in Scripture as God's footstool (cf. Ps. 99:5, 132:7; Lam. 2:1; 1 Chron. 28:2; cf. Ezek. 43:7; Isa. 60:13), or the throne that is described in similar terms in Ezek. 1:26 and 10:1 as well as in subsequent apocalyptic literature, e.g., 1 Enoch 18:8. The biblical authors avoid specifying the precise nature of the feet. This evasion seems to me to be quite deliberate. Confirmation of the need to hide God's feet may be found in 2 Sam. 22:10 (Ps. 18:10) where it is said that a thick cloud (*ʿarafel*) is under God's feet (cf. Nah. 1:3). That the cloud functions as a cover hiding the feet is suggested in a later rabbinic interpretation of the verse (*Pirqe Rabbi ʾEliʿezer*, chap. 41, 1970, 95b). Indeed, in several other theophanies recorded in the Bible (generally attributed to P), the thick cloud serves as a cover to conceal God's presence (*kevod YHWH*) depicted as a fiery brightness, splendor, and radiance (cf. Exod. 16:10, 24:16–17, 40:34–35; Lev. 9:23–24; Num. 14:10, 16:19). Mention should also be made of Isa. 6:1, "I behold my Lord seated on a high and lofty throne; and the skirts of His robe filled the Temple." The anticipated reference to God's feet is replaced by the skirts of His robe, which may indeed function as a kind of covering concealing the feet (Beyerlin, 1965, 31, n. 35). In the continuation of that vision, we are told the seraphs each had six wings; with two they covered their face, with two they covered their feet, and with two they would fly. Perhaps the explicitly mentioned covering of the seraphs' feet by wings parallels the implied covering of God's feet by the skirts of His robe. (In the opinion of some scholars the reference to feet here should be interpreted as a euphemism for the genitals [Ben Yehuda, 1960, 7:6421, n. 3]. Such a usage, as will be discussed below, is developed in kabbalistic literature.) The tension between the theophanous tradition, affirming the manifestation of the divine form at a specific moment in Israel's *Heilsgeschichte,* on the one hand, and the effort to curtail the vision by emphasizing that something was not visible, on the other, is implied in Ps. 77:20, "Your way was through the sea, Your path, through the mighty waters; but Your footsteps could not be seen." The tension is highlighted in the midrashic paraphrase of the biblical account in *Pirqe Rabbi ʾEliʿezer* (chap. 42. 1970, 99a): "They saw the Holy One, blessed be He, walking before them, but the heels of His feet were not seen or known." Although God's presence is surely felt at this historical juncture, the feet must nevertheless be hidden: at the point of divine disclosure something remains concealed. This seems to be a consistent pattern in Jewish sources.

Talmudic and Midrashic Sources

I begin my analysis of the images of God's feet in the rabbinic material with a discussion of the particular idiom *ragle Shekhinah,* the feet of the Presence, that appears in three places in the Babylonian Talmud: Hagigah 16a [**A**], Qiddushin 31a [**B**], and Berakhot 43b [**C**]. In the first two cases, the expression occurs in a saying attributed to R. Isaac, a second-century tanna: "whoever commits a transgression in secret it is as if he pushed away the feet of the *Shekhinah,* as it is said, 'The heaven is My throne and the earth is My footstool' (Isa. 66:1)." In the third talmudic source, the expression occurs as part of an anonymous teaching: "The one who walks in a proud manner even for four cubits, it is as if he pushed away the feet of the *Shekhinah,* as it is written, 'His glory fills all the earth' (Isa. 6:3)." A variant of this teaching without reference to the feet of the Presence, appears as well in [**B**] where it is attributed to R. Joshua ben Levi.

An examination of these three sources reveals the following intertextual links: the basic teaching concerning the pushing away of the feet of the *Shekhinah* is that of R. Isaac as found in [**A**]. In the case of [**B**] this teaching is placed in a larger context whence it is evident that the issue is negatively causing pain to the divine. The reference attributed to the anonymous sage in [**C**] is based on the statement of R. Joshua ben Levi in [**B**] which follows the view of R. Isaac. Although in the case of [**B**], R. Joshua's view is not linked to the specific image of pushing away the feet of the *Shekhinah,* as is the case of [C], it is evident that the juxtaposition of his statement to that of R. Isaac is based on the fact that both share the underlying assumption that human action can have an adverse effect on the divine Presence which is immanent in the world. The views of R. Isaac and R. Joshua ben Levi resonate well with other rabbinic pericopae (in some cases also attributed to R. Isaac; cf. *Genesis Rabbah* 19:7) which stress that the righteous cause the *Shekhinah* to dwell on earth while the wicked, conversely, drive the *Shekhinah* away (Marmorstein 1968, 82–83). This point is corroborated in the following passage in *Seder 'Eliyahu Zuṭa'*, 13 (Friedmann 1969, 194): "When [the sinners of Israel] transgress they push away the feet of the *Shekhinah,* as it says, 'His glory fills all the earth' (Isa. 6:3)." In all three talmudic passages, as well as the parallel passage from the midrashic source just cited, the image *ragle Shekhinah* implies God's all-pervasive immanence (Abelson 1912, 112; Goldberg 1969, 365).

The critical question concerns the way one interprets the figural representation of the *Shekhinah,* i.e., is the anthropomorphic expression to be taken literally or metaphorically? Several scholars have argued that the idiom *ragle Shekhinah* functions as a metaphor for God's presence in the world, rather than a literal expression implying that God has a body (Goldberg 1969, 365; Urbach 1979, 40; Scholem 1991, 147). Such an interpretation is rooted, of course, in a larger presumption regarding the rabbinic rejection of the corporealization of God in any literal sense. Urbach's statement that the rabbinic sages acquired from the Bible a "supramythological and supranatural conception of the Deity" (1979, 37) may be considered typical. However, the tenability of such a view as a universal characterization of all rabbinic theology in its formative stages is far from certain, as a variety of scholars have argued (Marmorstein 1968; Smith 1957–58, 474–81; 1970, 325–20; Neusner 1988). Turning to the issue at hand, I would suggest that *ragle Shekhinah,* as the cognate rabbinic expression, *pene ha-Shekhinah,* "face of the Presence," in contrast to the evidently figurative *kanfe ha-Shekhinah,* "wings of the presence" (Goldin 1988, 329–330) should not be construed metaphorically but rather mythically, i.e., it reflects a conception of the divine Presence that is predicated on the figuration of God as body. In this connection, it is of interest to consider the targumic rendering of Song of Songs 5:3, "I had taken off my robe—was I to don it again? I had bathed my feet—was I to soil them again?": "I have already removed my Presence (*shekhinti*) from amongst you, how can I return when you do evil things? And I purified my feet from your impurity, how can I soil them amongst you through your evil deeds?" In this context the divine feet are correlated with the *Shekhinah,* which is linked exegetically to the robe (*kuttonet*) worn by the lover who represents in line with the standard rabbinic exegesis of this book, God. Far from avoiding anthropomorphisms, the Targum here, as has been demonstrated in many instances in the Targumim to the Pentateuch (Klein 1981; 1982), expands the scope of the corporeal representation of God through the allegorical interpretation of the verse.

The notion of divine immanence is expressed positively in terms of the feet of God in another rabbinic statement recorded in *Mekhilta' de-Rabbi Yishma'el* interpreting the words of God to Moses, "I will be standing there before you on the rock at Horeb" (Exod. 17:6): "The Holy One, blessed be He, said to him: In every place where you find the imprint of human feet (*roshem ragle 'adam*) there I am before you" (Horovitz and Rabin 1970, 175; cf. *Tanḥuma'*, Beshallaḥ, 22). The influence of the midrashic text is clearly discernible in the Targum Pseudo-Jonathan on Exod. 17:6 (Ginsburger 1903, 129, n. 2; Schmerler 1933, 105): "I stand before you in the place in which you see the imprint of the foot (*roshem rigla'*)." That the imprint of the human feet refers to the anthropomorphic form of God is supported by the reading of *Mekhilta' de-Rabbi Shim'on bar Yoḥai,* preserved in the thirteenth-century Yemenite collection, *Midrash ha-Gadol* and cited as well in the same century by the Spanish kabbalist, Todros ben Joseph Abulafia (Kushnir-Oron, 1988, 148): "[God] said to [Moses]: In every place that you find the mark of human feet, as it says, 'the semblance of a human form' (Ezek. 1:26), there I will stand before you" (Hoffmann 1921, 181, n. 1; Epstein and Melamed 1955, 118; Margulies 1983, 338). In an effort to validate the anthropomorphic teachings of *Shi'ur Qomah* as an authentic second-century Jewish tradition, Gershom Scholem cited this text, observing that " 'the imprint of the feet of man' in this context refers to the image of the heavenly man mentioned in the Merkabah vision" (Scholem 1965, 129). It may be suggested, however, that the statement in the midrash is actually polemicizing against a view such as the one articulated in the *Shi'ur Qomah* (Cohen 1983, 205, n. 15), for in the case of the midrashic pericope we are not dealing with the gigantic feet of the enthroned anthropos but rather the anthropomorphic form that is immanent in the world (for a different interpretation see Ginzberg, 1968, 6: 20–21, n. 122). In striking contrast to the idea expressed in Ps. 77:20, the passage in *Mekhilta'* affirms the visibility of the divine footprints, the representation of God's presence in this world, precisely the issued raised by the talmudic comments concerning *ragle Shekhinah* cited above. The midrashic idea may be related to a theme found in various magical and religious texts which locate the presence of a being in the impressions that one leaves, especially the footprints (Frazer 1935, 1:207–212). Specifically in terms of Christianity, the midrashic expression *roshem ragle ʾadam* is analogous to the tradition concerning the legendary footprints (*vestigia*) of Jesus implanted on the rock of Ascension, in some cases connected exegetically with Zech. 14:4 (Schapiro 1979, 272–273, 277).

It is evident as well that the rabbis preserved the biblical image of God's feet to denote His manifestation in the context of meting out judgment, often associated especially with Zech. 14:4 (cf. *Mekhiltaʾ de-Rabbi Shimʿon bar Yoḥai,* Epstein and Melamed 1955, 92; *Lamentations Rabbah* 1:50; *ʾEliyahu Rabbati* 30; *ʾAvot de-Rabbi Natan,* A, 34 [Schechter 1887, 102]; *Pesiqtaʾ Rabbati* 31 [Friedmann, 1963, 147a]; *ʾOtiyyot de-Rabbi ʿAqivaʾ* [Wertheimer 1980, 2: 364]; *Exodus Rabbah* 17:4; *Tanḥumaʾ*, ʿEqev, 6 [Buber 1946, 18]; *Aggadat Bereshit,* 54 [Buber 1973, 108]; *Bereshit Rabbati,* to Gen. 2:9 [Albeck 1984, 23]). In such contexts the image of God's feet is not to be treated allegorically. On the contrary, the authors of these midrashic statements assumed some mythical conception of God predicated on the manifestation of the divine Presence in the form of an anthropos. One example will suffice: "R. Yose said: The Presence never descended . . . Did the Presence never descend? It is written, 'The Lord came down upon Mount Sinai' (Exod. 19:20). This was above ten handbreadths. And it is written, 'On that day, He will set His feet on the Mount of Olives' (Zech. 14:4), i.e., above ten handbreadths" (B. Sukkah 5a). God's standing on the Mount of Olives is not a rhetorical trope but rather the mark of the divine presence that will appear in precisely this form. Again, we confront the difference between metaphor and myth.

Still other rabbinic sources can be cited as proof that references to God's feet are not to be taken in an allegorical manner. One of the most important examples is another passage in the *Mekhiltaʾ de-Rabbi Yishmaʾel* (Horovitz and Rabin 1970, 51) in which the midrashist interprets the reference to the "likeness of a pavement of sapphire under God's feet," *kemaʿaseh livnat ha-sappir* (Exod. 24:10) as a sign of God's enslavement when Israel is enslaved below, thus confirming the view put forth in Isa. 63:9 concerning God's suffering when the people of Israel suffer (Idel 1988, 226). This reading is based on an interpretation of the word *livnat* in terms of *levenim*, i.e., bricks, attested in P. Sukkah 4:3 (ed. Venice, 54c), and reflected in the Targum Pseudo-Jonathan on Exod. 24:10 (Ginsburger 1903, 142). That is, just as Israel below is enslaved by the bricks of Egyptian servitude, so too God has to place bricks beneath His feet. The force of this claim is made in a strikingly graphic way in the tradition reported in the name of *Midrash Avkir* by R. Eleazar ha-Darshan in his *Sefer ha-Gemaṭriyot:* "The likeness of a pavement of sapphire—this alludes [to the fact that] just as Israel were treading the mortar with their feet to make bricks, so it was, as it were, above, 'in all their troubles He was troubled' " (cited by Idel 1988, 382, n. 101). In all of these sources the correlation between God's feet and the throne of glory is implicit, a point confirmed in other rabbinic texts as well that decode the biblical image of the feet of God as a metonymy for the throne or footstool (B. Ḥullin 91a; Sanhedrin 38b; Ḥagigah 14a). It must also be noted that the rabbis preserved the biblical practice of referring to the Temple as the footstool or feet of God (cf. B. Makkot 24a).

Another relevant image employed by the rabbis is that of God pounding His feet as an expression not of divine pathos or empathy but anger and vengeance. An illustration of this is found in an aggadic statement found in a number of sources including *Midrash Psalms* 93:5 (Buber 1891, 415), *Pirqe Rabbi 'Eli'ezer,* chap. 5 (1970, 12a), and the *Baraita' de-Ma'aseh Bereshit* (Sed 1965, 60). In this context there is a description of the creation of the waters and their subsequent desire to rise and cover the earth, a common motif in ancient cosmogonic mythologies, remnants of which are found in Scripture (cf. Ps. 74:13; Job 12:15, 38:8; Prov. 8:29). According to the aggadah, God controlled the raging seas by "yelling at them and subduing them under the soles of His feet, and measuring them in the hollow of His hand (cf. Isa. 40:12), so as not to add or diminish, and He made the sand a boundary for the sea." An echo of this conception may be found in a statement attributed to R. Aḥa bar Jacob in B. Berakhot 59a: "He pounds His feet under the throne of glory, as it says, 'The heaven is My throne and the earth is My footstool' (Isa. 66:1)." The statement occurs in the context of various different mythical explanations to account for the physical occurrence of an earthquake (Fishbane 1991). No explanation is offered as to why God would cause the shaking of the earth by pounding His feet, but it may be conjectured that there is a residuum here of a much older myth based on the correlation of human and divine actions. Such a view is expressed explicitly in the following statement in P. Berakhot 9:2 (ed. Venice, 12c): "When Israel do the will of God and bring forth the tithes according to their set regulation, 'the Lord your God always keeps His eye upon it [the land of Israel] from year's beginning to year's end' (Deut. 11:12), and it is not harmed at all. When Israel do not do the will of God and do not bring forth the tithes according to their set regulation, 'He looks at the earth and it trembles' (Ps. 104:32)."

Hekhalot and Shi'ur Qomah Tradition

One of the main aims of the earliest phase of Jewish mysticism represented in the *Hekhalot* literature, which spans a period from the second to the eighth or ninth centuries, is the heavenly ascent culminating in a vision of the enthroned glory (Scholem 1956, 43–50; 1974, 14–21; Gruenwald 1980, 94; 1988, 184; Chernus 1982, 123–146; Elior 1989, 97–120). It is reasonable to expect, therefore, that the anthropomorphic imagery of the divine would be intensified in the redactional units that make up this corpus. Yet, the textual evidence indicates otherwise. In the main units that describe heavenly ascent and visionary experience, the anthropomorphic description is fairly muted. By contrast, the tone of the anthropomorphism reaches an intense and extreme pitch in the cluster of texts known as the *Shi'ur Qomah* whose focus is a detailed description of the divine body.

When we turn specifically to the image of God's feet we note that only sporadic references are made in the *Hekhalot* corpus. In one passage in *Hekhalot Rabbati,* mention is made of the angels beneath God's feet (Schäfer 1981, § 152). In a relatively late text, *3 Enoch,* we find two references to God's feet. In one context Exod. 24:10 is cited as a proof text to support the idea that God has chariots of sapphire (Schäfer 1981, § 37), and in another context there is a description of God placing His foot on the back of the swift cherub at the time that He rides upon it (Schäfer 1981, § 38). By contrast, references to God's feet abound in the *Shi'ur Qomah* texts where specific dimensions are given to them as part of the comprehensive measurement of the divine body (Schäfer 1981, §§ 480, 695, 948; 1984, 130, 132). As a representative example I will cite one critical passage which, in some recensions of the *Shi'ur Qomah* text, appears as Meṭaṭron's initial measurement of the divine body, a point noted already by the Karaite, Salmon ben Yeruḥim (Davidson 1934, 115): "The soles of His feet fill the entire universe, as it is stated,

'Thus said the Lord, the heaven [is My throne] and the earth is My footstool' (Isa. 66;1). The height of His soles is 30,000,000 parasangs" (Schäfer 1981, §§ 480, 695, 948; Cohen 1985, 59, 87, 137). In the continuation of the text, the names of the feet are specified as well as additional measurements, details that vary from one recension to another. What is essential for this analysis is that according to the Jewish esoteric tradition, the biblical image of the earth as the footstool of God (Isa. 66:1; cf. Matt. 5:34–35; Acts 7:49) is not merely a figurative characterization of divine providence but signifies that the divine corpus is large enough to fill the entire universe (cf. Schäfer 1981, 440, 745; 1984, 132). Similarly, in the cosmological treatise, *Baraita᾽ de-Maʿaseh Bereshit,* the throne of glory in the lowest earth is described as the "footstool of the Master of all the earth, as it says, 'The heaven is My throne and the earth is My footstool' (Isa. 66:1) . . . Just as the *Shekhinah* is above so it is below" (Sed 1965, 70–71).

It is noteworthy that the third-century Christian exegete, Origen, relates in his *Homiliae in Genesim* I.13 that precisely such a reading of Isa. 66:1 is assumed by those who interpret the divine image in terms of bodily shape: "those carnal men who have no understanding of the meaning of divinity suppose, if they read anywhere in the Scriptures of God that 'heaven is my throne, and the earth is my footstool' (Isa. 66:1), that God has so large a body that they think he sits in heaven and stretches out his feet to the earth" (Origen 1982, 63–64). It is not stated who these "carnal men" are, but from other comments in Origen's works a likely candidate are Jews who are accused of supposing that God is corporeal based on a literal reading of scriptural anthropomorphisms (De Lange 1976, 44, 126). More specifically, it seems likely that Origen had in mind some Jewish exegetes who were close in spirit to the anthropomorphic speculation evident in the *Shiʿur Qomah* texts (Stroumsa 1983, 271; Cohen 1983, 40, n. 65). The possibility that Origen knew of the *Shiʿur Qomah* was suggested by Scholem (1965, 36–42) on the basis of Origen's characterization of the Song of Songs as one of four biblical texts that the Jews treat as esoteric (Urbach 1971, 252). Scholem's observation is dependent on the presumed relation of *Shiʿur Qomah* to Song of Songs. By contrast, Origen's report regarding those who posit a literal reading of Isa. 66:1 is, in fact, an exact parallel to what one finds in the *Shiʿur Qomah* material. Indeed, this is not simply a stock phrase against Jewish literalism or anthropomorphism but represents a very specific exegesis that appears in the relevant sources. In this connection, mention should also be made of the description of the angel in the book of Elchasai reported by Hippolytus (ca. 170–236), which bears a resemblance to the measurements in the *Shiʿur Qomah* material (Ginzberg 1955, 192; Smith 1963, 151; Cohen 1983, 39, n. 64; Idel 1986, 4), knowledge of which is attested in other excerpts from his writings as well (Alon 1967, 189–190; Baumgarten 1986). The "tracks" of the angel's feet are said to "extend to the length of three and a half schoenoi, which makes fourteen miles, while the breadth is one and a half schoenoi with the height of half a schoenos" (Klijn and Reinink 1973, 115). While the critical verse from Isaiah is not cited here, it is instructive that this second-century text of Jewish-Christian provenance describes the feet of the angel in terms remarkably close to the Jewish esoteric tradition.

In the *Hekhalot* and *Shiʿur Qomah,* references to the feet of God are not to be taken metaphorically but mythically (Cohen 1983, 205, n. 16). Moreover, the rabbinic idiom, *ragle Shekhinah,* which occurs various times in this literature, must also be understood as espousing a patently anthropomorphic conception of God. Thus, in the *Masekhet Hekhalot* it is stated that "under the throne a sapphire stone is fixed beneath the feet of the *Shekhinah,* as it says, 'They saw God and under His feet there was the likeness of a pavement of sapphire' (Exod. 24:10)" (Jellinek 1967, 2:41). In another work, *Seder Rabbah di-Bereshit,* it is stated that the feet of the Presence stand above the heads of the angels who occupy the lower earth. Hab. 3:3 and Isa. 66:1 are cited as proof texts for the notion that just as the Presence is above, so it is below (Schäfer 1981, §§ 745–746; see also § 440). In another passage from this work, one reads of the "four rivers of fire that proceed and come forth from the sweat of the creatures beneath the feet of the glory (*ragle kavod*) [Schäfer 1981, § 784; see § 805] which, no doubt, is a synonym for *ragle Shekhinah.* By way of summary, it can be said that in these ancient Jewish esoteric texts, especially the *Shiʿur Qomah,* special attention is given to God's feet, even though other parts of the divine body are mentioned.

Before turning to medieval Jewish mysticism, let me note that the mythical conception of God's feet in biblical and rabbinic sources influenced certain poetic images, which in turn helped foster subsequent developments in Jewish esoteric literature. Thus, to cite one of many possible examples, I refer to a motif in one of the most prolific *payyeṭanim,* Eleazar Kallir, who apparently lived in Palestine in the sixth century. In the fifth part of Kallir's *ʾereṣ maṭah weraʿashah,* a poetic midrash on Prov. 8:22–29 that begins *ʾalpayim shanah nimttaqti be-ḥikko,* the Torah thus describes herself: "I was dandling on His knee, rejoicing before Him, to praise Him and bless Him" (*Maḥzor* 1599, 240b). This motif is expressed in rabbinic literature as well which, based on the description of Wisdom in Prov. 8:30, described the Torah in its primordial state as rejoicing before God (*Genesis Rabbah* 1:1). A significant variant of this motif occurs in B. Shabbat 89a (cf. Zevaḥim 116a) where the Torah is described as the "hidden delight" (*ḥamudah genuzah*) in which God takes pleasure each day (*mishtaʿasheʿa bah be-khol yom*). To the standard aggadic image Kallir has added the detail that the Torah dandled upon the knee of God, which is itself derived from an expression in Isa. 66:12 describing the people of Israel. In the continuation of the poem, Kallir returns to this image in a section where he narrates the Torah's activity during the creation of the seven heavens: "When He laid the foundation of ʿArafel under His feet, I was dandling on His knees" (*Maḥzor* 1599, 242a). The Torah assumes here, as it does in a variety of rabbinic sources, a female persona vis-à-vis God who is depicted as a male (Wolfson 1989). It is evident, moreover, that the female imaging of Torah on the part of Kallir is not simply metaphorical, but rather mythical. Indeed, as a variety of scholars have noted, in another one of his poems, the *silluq* for *parashat Sheqalim, ʾaz raʾita we-sipparta,* the Torah, called the Princess (*bat melekh*), is described in anthropomorphic measurements reminiscent of the *Shiʿur Qomah* speculation (Wolfson 1989, 278–279). It is thus very unlikely that Kallir intended the female images of Torah to be purely figurative.

A similar description of the primordial Torah is found in the *yoser* for Pentecost, *ʾadon ʾimnani ʾeṣlo shikhnani,* composed by the tenth-century German poet Simeon bar Isaac: "Dandling on His knee, the beginning of His way, I approached His feet, I dwelt in His shadow, my longings were for Him the first of His works (Prov. 8:22) (*Maḥzor* 1599, 235b; Habermann 1938, 42). It is evident that these poets are building upon conventional motifs in rabbinic literature to describe the relationship between the female Torah and the male deity. Significantly, the use of anthropomorphism is augmented in the liturgical poetry, and especially prominent in this regard is the image of God's feet. As will be seen below, in subsequent mystical literature the image of dwelling under the feet assumes a decidedly erotic connotation, as the feet function as a phallic symbol for the masculine aspect of God. It is difficult to conclude definitively if such a meaning is already implied in the poem of Simeon bar Isaac, but it may be suggested that poems such as his did influence later developments.

Image of Divine Foot in Shabbetai Donnolo, Haside Ashkenaz and the Bahir

The motif of God's feet continued to occupy the attention of Jewish poets and mystics through the High Middle Ages. It is especially in the realm of theosophical speculations that this image had its greatest impact. While the most daring applications of anthropomorphic imagery to God appear in the theosophic kabbalah of the twelfth and thirteenth centuries, originating in Provence and Northern Spain, one can chart a development from earlier sources that helped shape the later formulations. In this section I will limit my discussion to the image of God's feet in the writings of Shabbetai ben Abraham Donnolo (913–ca. 982), the main circle of German Pietists led by Judah ben Samuel he-Hasid of Regensburg (ca. 1150–1217) and Eleazar ben Judah of Worms (ca. 1165–ca. 1230), and the *Sefer ha-Bahir,* generally acknowledged to be the earliest kabbalistic document to surface in medieval Europe. While the text of the *Bahir* in the form in which it has been redacted clearly reflects twelfth-century Provence (Scholem 1987, 49–198; Pedaya 1990, 139–164), it has been noted by scholars that contained in the book are older "gnostic" traditions of an Eastern provenance (Scholem 1987, 68–97; Idel 1987, 55–72; 1988, 122–128). Through an examination of the motif of the divine feet, we are afforded an opportunity to cast our glance upon the larger field of inquiry concerning the literary sources for later kabbalistic theosophies as well as the presumed relationship between the Provençal kabbalists and the German Pietists (Scholem 1987, 41–42, 97–123, 180–198, 215–216, 325, n. 261; Dan 1968, 116–129; 1987, 125–140; Idel 1982, 274–277; 1988, 130–132; Farber 1986; Wolfson 1992a).

I begin my analysis with Shabbetai Donnolo. It has been noted by various scholars that the thought of Donnolo had a significant influence on the German Pietists (Epstein 1957, 206–210, 211, 214–216; Scholem 1956, 113, 376, n. 115; Dan 1968, 18, 23, 39, 48, 63, 85, 129, 214; Sharf 1976, 80, 125), as well as on subsequent kabbalists (Neumark 1921, 121, 188–190, 258, n. 4; Vajda 1948, 92–94). In a separate study I have argued that adumbrated in Donnolo's *Sefer Ḥakhmoni,* his commentary on the ancient Jewish esoteric work, *Sefer Yeṣirah,* is a theosophic understanding of the *sefirot* later expanded by kabbalists in the twelfth and thirteenth centuries (Wolfson 1992b). The relevant comment of Donnolo concerning the feet of God occurs in a lengthy passage in the first part of *Sefer Ḥakhmoni* (Castelli 1880, 7–8) on the nature of the divine image (*demut*) and the visible glory (*kavod*). Donnolo compares the theophany recorded in Exod. 24:10 and that of Isa. 6:1–3. Isaiah had a vision of the glory enthroned—as opposed to Moses who saw the back of the glory in a standing position—but even this vision was limited by the fact that what he saw was the outlying part of God's robe, i.e., the glory under God's feet. This is precisely the object of vision for the nobles of Israel who, according to Donnolo, "saw only His glory which is under His feet by means of a sign and symbol (*be-'ot we-siman*)," a formulation based in part on a passage attributed to R. Berechiah in *Exodus Rabbah* 23:15. From the continuation of the passage in *Sefer Ḥakhmoni,* moreover, it is evident that the glory described as under God's feet may be equated with the anthropomorphic appearance that the upper, invisible glory assumes in the prophetic vision (Castelli 1880, 8–9).

The association of the lower glory and the feet, based on Exod. 24:10, is further developed in the esoteric theosophy of the German Pietists. In an anonymous treatise extant in manuscript bearing the title *Sefer ha-Kavod* (the Book of the Glory) and attributed by Joseph Dan (1975, 134–187) to Judah he-Hasid, there is an extended discussion on the images of God's feet that occur in the Bible. The immediate context for this discussion is a discourse on the sin of using that which has been consecrated to God (*ḥerem*) for secular use. The author enumerates eighteen occurrences in the following order: Exod. 24:10; Deut. 33:3; Isa. 66:1, 60:3; Ezek. 43:7; 1 Chron. 28:2; Ps. 99.2, 132:7; Lam. 2:1; Zech. 14:4; 2 Sam. 22:10; Ps.. 18:10; Hab. 3:5; Lam. 3:34; Nah. 1:3; Song 5:15 [read, of course, in light of the allegorical exegesis of the rabbis]; Ps. 74:3, 77:20. At the conclusion of this enumeration, the Pietistic writer observes: "There is nothing that prevents longevity for oneself and others like sinning against that which has been consecrated . . . No one knows about the one who transgresses with respect to what has been consecrated except the Creator, and it is as if one pushes away the feet of the Presence (*ragle Shekhinah*) and, as it were, one burdens the feet of God (*ragle shel Maqom*) . . . Therefore, there are [with respect to God] fourteen [occurrences of] the [expression] rising up (*qumah*) [Ps. 3:8, 7:7, 9:20, 10:12, 12:6 (cf. Isa. 33:10), 17:13, 35:2, 44:27, 74:22, 76:10, 82:8, 132:8, 68:2, and 102:14] corresponding to the fourteen [occurrences] of [the expression] feet (*raglayim*) excluding 'Crushing under His feet' (Lam. 3:34) [in three instances the term *regel* itself is not used], and these correspond to the fourteen [occurrences] of the word *ḥerem* [Josh. 6:17, 18(3x), 7:1 (2x), 11, 12 (2x), 13 (2x), 15, 22:20, to which is added Josh. 6:18 wherein the predicate form, *taḥarimu,* appears]. When one sins with respect to that which has been consecrated one removes the feet of the Presence and prevents the rising up [of God]" (MS Oxford-Bodleian 1566, fol. 106a). Through this complicated web of exegesis, the author has revitalized the biblical mythos of God's feet, expressing it in terms of rabbinic terminology.

It is, however, especially in the writings of Eleazar of Worms, whose knowledge of Donnolo has been well noted in the scholarly literature, that the theosophic import of the image of feet applied to the glory is most fully elaborated. I will cite one representative text from Eleazar's *Commentary on Ezekiel's Chariot* in extenso:

> It is known that the human being is the most glorious of the creatures, and the head of a human is the most glorious of all the limbs, and so it is above. This head is in the image of Jacob . . . who is engraved upon the throne of glory. Concerning him it is said, "[The Lord] has cast down from heaven to earth the majesty of Israel" (Lam. 2:1). "[You are My servant] Israel in whom I glory" (Isa. 49:3). Therefore, it says in Song of Songs, "His left hand was under my head" (Song 2:6), transpose [the letters of *le-ro'shi*, "my head"] and read *yisra'el* [Israel]. Therefore, the diadem of the glory is called Israel . . . for it is made from the praise of Israel and ascends to the throne of glory . . . "And the Lord was standing above him" (Gen. 28:13), as upon the throne above. Thus, "He mounted a cherub" (2 Sam. 22:11) . . . Jacob is called small, and similarly the cherubim have small faces . . . Since the human countenance is that of Jacob engraved on the throne, thus you find the word *'adam* in the last letters [of the expression] "O throne of glory, exalted" (*kisse' kavod marom*) (Jer. 17:12), as well as in the last [letters of] "granting them seats of honor" (*we-khisse' khavod yanḥilem*) (1 Sam 2:8). It is written, "You will see My back" (*we-ra'ita 'et 'aḥorai* (Exod. 33:23) which is numerically equivalent to [the expression] the image of Jacob is engraved on the throne (*demut ya'aqov ḥaquqah ba-kisse'*). And Jacob said, "Am I (*'anokhi*) under God?" (Gen. 30:2), [the word] *'anokhi* is numerically equivalent to *kisse'* (throne) . . . It is written, "And they saw the God of Israel and under His feet etc." (Exod. 24:10), it should be read as Israel under His feet. (MS Mussayef 145, fol. 35b; corrected in part by MS Paris, Bibliothéque Nationale 850, fols. 56b-57a)

In accord with his usual exegetical manner, Eleazar connects seemingly disparate issues through word associations and numerological equivalences. The first and most surprising connection is that between the back of God and the image of Jacob engraved on the throne, a motif that is found in early aggadic sources (*Genesis*

Rabbah 68:12, 82:2; B. Ḥullin 91b) and in the Targum Yerushalmi and Targum Pseudo-Jonathan to Gen. 28:12. Whatever the original idea behind this image (Ginzberg 1968, 5:290, n. 134; Smith 1970, 284–286; Altmann 1981, 13; Halperin 1988, 121), it became one of the most popular motifs in Jewish liturgical poetry and mystical literature in Late Antiquity and the Middle Ages. In the case of Eleazar, as I have shown in great detail in a separate study, the image of Jacob is treated hypostatically as the lower glory (Wolfson 1992a). In the passage cited above, Eleazar draws specifically upon a comment attributed to R. Joshua ben Naḥman in *Lamentations Rabbah* 2:2, interpreting the verse, "He cast down from heaven to earth the majesty of Israel" (Lam. 2:1). In that context the image of Jacob engraved on the throne is named *Tif'eret Yisra'el* (the majesty of Israel) on the basis of the verse in Lamentations and is compared parabolically to a king's crown. In Eleazar's text the image of Jacob is also referred to as the crown (*'aṭeret ha-kavod,* diadem of the glory), but for him the literary motif has been transformed into a theosophic symbol. Eleazar's description of the crown reflects as well the ancient merkavah tradition (Farber 1986, 231–234) according to which the crown, named Israel or having the name of Israel engraved upon it, is made from the prayers of Israel and is placed upon the head of the glory by an angel—according to some sources Sandalphon (Lieberman 1970, 13–14) and according to others Meṭaṭron (Cohen 1985, 36, n. 38, 128, 149). The identification of the crown as the image of Jacob is clearly based on the fact that Jacob is interchangeable with Israel (i.e., the crown, which is named Israel, is Jacob's image). In another important Pietistic text, extant in MS JTSA 1786, fol. 43a, the crown, identified with prayer, is called Sariel (the letters of *Yisra'el*), which is, in turn, identified with the throne (Idel 1988, 193). It is noteworthy that the crown is described as the throne in a way that parallels the description of Jacob's image as a throne. In still other contexts Eleazar identifies the image of Jacob with the letter *shin* said to be on the head phylacteries worn by God or with the phylacteries themselves (Wolfson 1992a). The association of the crown and the head phylacteries is another ancient motif in Jewish esotericism (Bar-Ilan 1987). It is understandable, then, why Eleazar would substitute the phylacteries for the crown, both of which are identified as the image of Jacob on the throne.

From the passage cited above it also appears that the image of Jacob is the cherub referred to in the expression *'appe zuṭrei,* the "small face." This identification is based on the fact that both items are connected terminologically with the issue of smallness, *qaṭnut*. In B. Ḥullin 60b, Jacob, together with Samuel and David, is called "the little one." It is possible that the designation *ya'aqov ha-qaṭan* is based on Amos 7:2, "How will Jacob survive? He is so small," *mi yaqum ya'aqov ki qaṭon hu'*, which, in turn, is probably based on the statement attributed to Jacob in Genesis 32:10, "I am unworthy of all the kindness," *qaṭonti mi-kol ha-ḥasadim*. On the other hand, in B. Ḥagigah 13b the face of the cherub (*pene ha-keruv*) is contrasted with the human face (*pene 'adam*) mentioned in Ezek. 10:14 insofar as the former is characterized as the "small face" (*'appe zuṭre*) and the latter as the "great face" (*'appe ravreve*). Eleazar combines these two motifs and forges an identification of Jacob's image with the cherub. This is alluded to as well in the verse, 'He rode upon a cherub,' i.e., God rode upon the image of Jacob. From the other scriptural verses cited by Eleazar, it also emerges that Jacob's image, which is the cherub, is the throne upon which the glory sits. The point is derived exegetically from several verses, including the utterance of Jacob in Gen. 30:2, *ha-taḥat 'elohim 'anokhi,* that Eleazar reads as "I am under God." i.e., Jacob is the throne to God. This interpretation is supported by the fact that the word *'anokhi* is numerically equivalent to *kisse'*, throne. At the end of the passage, Eleazar informs the reader that Jacob's image is to be identified with the God of Israel seen by the nobles of Israel, for the name Israel designates the lower power in the divine realm, symbolized in Scripture by the expression "and under His feet."

In another Pietistic work, the commentary on the forty-two-letter name of God attributed to Hai Gaon and included in Eleazar's *Sefer ha-Ḥokhmah,* the Presence (*Shekhinah*) of God is described in a number of terms that scholars have considered to be proto-kabbalistic in tone (Dan 1968, 119–127; Farber 1986, 231–244; Scholem 1987, 98, 184–185; Idel 1988, 195). These include diadem (*'aṭarah*), prayer (*tefillah* or *ṣelota'*), the heavenly voice (*bat qol*), the tenth kingship (*malkhut 'asirit*), the secret of all secrets (*sod kol ha-sodot*), the king's daughter (*bat melekh*), and the bride (*kalah*) who sits to the left of God, the groom (MS Oxford-Bodleian 1812, fols. 60b–61a). In a second passage the Presence of the Creator (*shekhinat ha-bore'*) is called daughter (*bat*) as well as the tenth *sefirah,* and kingship (*malkhut*) for the crown of royalty (*keter malkhut*) is on His head (Scholem 1987, 185–186). In yet a third passage the tenth kingship is identified as the supernal crown (*keter 'elyon*), the image of God (*temunat YHWH*), and the shoe (*pazmeqe*) of God (MS Oxford-Bodleian 1812, fol. 63a). I suggest that the image of the shoe should be understood in terms of the other notion mentioned above concerning the glory of Jacob under God's feet, i.e., the *Shekhinah* supports that which is above her in the same way that a shoe supports the foot. It is possible that the symbolic identification of the shoe and the *Shekhinah* underlies the well-known folk legend concerning Enoch the cobbler, which the fourteenth-century kabbalist Isaac ben Samuel of Acre attributes to a German source, R. Judah ha-Darshan ha-Ashkenazi (Scholem 1956, 365, n. 101; 1969, 132). If one assumes that the shoe stands symbolically for the Presence, then Enoch's stitching may have an implicit theurgical implication. This is precisely the meaning accorded the legend in later kabbalistic and Hasidic sources (Wolfson, 1992c), but it may already be implied in the original version.

A striking similarity to the Pietistic conception outlined above is found in *Sefer ha-Bahir*. The possible connection between the *Bahir* and the German Pietists has been duly noted in scholarly literature (Scholem 1987, 97–123, 180–198; Farber 1986), and here I would like to add another intriguing example to this discussion. In one passage the last two of the ten divine *logoi (ma'amarot)* are described as follows:

> What is the ninth? I said to him: The ninth and tenth are together, one corresponding to the other. The one is higher than the other by [a measure of] 500 years. They are like two ophanim, one holding on to the north side and the other to the west, and they go to the lowest earth. What is at the lowest? The last of the seven lands below. And the end of the Presence (*sof shekhinato*) of the Holy One, blessed be He, is under His feet, as it says, "The heaven is My throne and the earth is My footstool" (Isa. 66:1). (*Sefer ha-Bahir,* ed. Margaliot, 1978a, § 169)

The tenth of the divine emanations is thus referred to as the "end of the Presence" (*sof ha-Shekhinah*) that is said to be under God's feet. (Elsewhere in the *Bahir* §§ 82, 168, 172, the feet or legs of God are mentioned as part of the enumeration of the limbs that constitute the holy forms [Idel 1988, 126] of the divine image; Scholem 1991, 44–45.) This emanation, united with the ninth like two ophanim, is also identified as the lowest earth, a term derived, as Scholem already pointed out (1923, 122, n. 3), from a passage in the *Baraita' de-Ma'aseh Bereshit* that I mentioned above in another context. (It is of interest to note that the end of that text is interpreted in *Sefer ha-Bahir* § 171.) In the *Bahir* this cosmological term is theosophically transformed, for the lowest earth now connotes the last of the divine emanations, the *Shekhinah*. Hence, in another passage the "earth" is identified as the "throne of the Holy One, blessed be He, which is a precious stone, and it is the sea of wisdom" (§ 96). In the continuation of that passage, the interpretation of Exod. 24:10 attributed to R. Meir in B. Menaḥot 43b is cited. According to R. Meir, the "likeness of the pavement of sapphire" under the feet of God refers to the throne of glory described in Ezek. 1:26 "in appearance like sapphire." In terms of the kabbalistic symbolism in the *Bahir*, the sapphire stone under the feet of God alludes to the throne that is the *Shekhinah*. It will be readily acknowledged that the bahiric conception is parallel to the German Pietistic idea of the lower glory that is said to be under the feet of God, an image which is depicted as well in the symbolic identification of the *Shekhinah*, also called the tenth *sefirah*, as the shoe, presumably worn by the divine foot.

It is noteworthy that just as Eleazar characterizes the lower glory as the crown, phylacteries and throne, so in the *Bahir* one finds a convergence of these three symbols. Thus, for example, the title "precious stone" is applied to the ascending crown in § 91 (cf. § 72 and § 33 where the crown is characterized in terms of Lam. 2:1 just as we found in the case of Eleazar) and to the throne in § 169. Lest one protest that this is a mere coincidence, mention should be made of two other passages that specifically deal with the interchange of all three symbols. In § 37 the following parable is given: "A king had a throne. Sometimes he took it and placed it on his arm and sometimes on his head. They asked him: Why? Because it is beautiful and he could not bear sitting on it." The reference to the arm and head brings to mind the traditional phylacteries. Indeed, in a second passage a similar parable occurs and is interpreted in precisely this way: "You say [that the sixth of the ten *logoi*] is His throne? It has been said that it is the crown of the Holy One, blessed be He . . . This may be compared to a king who had a beautiful and fragrant object which he loved alot. Sometimes he placed it on his head, and that is the head phylacteries, sometimes he took it on his arm in the knot of the phylacteries of the arm, and sometimes he lent it to his son to sit upon. Sometimes it is called his throne, for he carries it on his arm like an amulet, which is like a throne" (§ 152). The convergence of these different symbols in the case of both Eleazar of Worms and the *Bahir* is striking, and seems to point to common and probably older sources (Farber 1986, 247).

The full force of this symbolism may be gathered from a later source, *Ra'aya Mehemna'* (Faithful Shepherd), the anonymous fourteenth-century kabbalistic exposition of the biblical commandments included in the standard editions of the *Zohar.* In one passage the *Shekhinah* is described as the point that is "sometimes a diadem, sometimes a throne to sit upon, and sometimes a footstool" (*Zohar* 3:248b). Similar terminology is used in a passage in *Tiqqune Zohar,* written by the same author: "From the aspect of the vowels *Shekhinah* is the daughter of the king, His footstool, and from the aspect of the accents she is called 'a capable wife, a crown for her husband' (Prov. 12:4)" (*Zohar Ḥadash,* ed. Margaliot, 1978c, 101a–b). It yet another passage the dual symbolism of the *Shekhinah* is expressed in terms of two different vowels that are, respectively, above and below the corresponding letter: "As a *ḥolem* she is a crown on his head, and as a *ḥiriq* a throne beneath him . . . When she is above [she is] a crown on his head, and she is the daughter [alternative reading: she goes down] beneath his feet" (*Tiqqune Zohar,* 10, ed. Margaliot, 1978b, 25a). In this context, then, the image of the throne is connected with the posture of being beneath the feet of God, applied, according to one reading, to the daughter. Although the symbolism here in comparison to the *Bahir* or Eleazar of Worms is considerably more complex, one can still recognize the influence of the earlier sources.

Images of God's Feet in Zoharic Literature

With the further literary development of kabbalistic theosophy in the twelfth and thirteenth centuries, the boldness of the anthropomorphic expression was considerably augmented. One of the distinctive features of anthropomorphic speculation on the part of kabbalists, already apparent in the *Bahir,* as we have seen, is the attribution of gender to the divine. Indeed, some of the most recondite teachings of the kabbalists relate specifically to the androgynous nature of God. Divine processes are portrayed in vividly sexual terms, a tendency that reaches its climax in the theosophy of Isaac Luria (1534–1572), organized and disseminated by his disciples. It is my intention in this section to focus on the instrumental role played specifically by the image of God's feet in the anthropomorphic speculations of the zoharic corpus, occasionally drawing upon the writings of other thirteenth-century Spanish kabbalists who were presumably part of the circle responsible for the literary production of the *Zohar* in Castile (Liebes 1989), as well as some later echoes of these ideas in the Lurianic kabbalah of the sixteenth century.

In one of its symbolic usages, the feet of God in the *Zohar* represent the attribute of divine judgment or angelic beings in a lower realm of being which emanate from that attribute. Thus, for example, in one text the expression, *ʾoraḥ raglav,* "the way of his feet," in Isa. 41:3 (rendered in accord with the reading of the *Zohar*) is interpreted as follows: "What are 'His feet?' These are the angels which are beneath the Holy One, blessed be He, as it says, 'On that day, He will set His feet etc.' (Zech. 14:4)" (*Zohar* 1:86a; cf. *Tiqqune Zohar* 18, ed. Margaliot, 1978b, 32b, 70, 113a; Idel 1986, 44–45, 56). The theme of the zoharic section from which the above passage is extracted is the administration of divine judgment in the upper and lower worlds, and it is evident that this is precisely the function of the angels designated as God's feet. In a second passage in the *Zohar,* a similar interpretation of the divine feet is offered, but in more strikingly mythic terms. In that context, it is stated that within each person are comprised the ten holy emanations (*sefirot*) and the ten demonic powers; the former are said to be represented by the fingers of the hands and the latter by the toes. Having established that correspondence, the zoharic authorship poses an obvious exegetical question: "If so, what is the meaning of 'On that day, He will set His feet' (Zech. 14:4)'? His feet [refers to the feet] of the [divine] body [which] are the masters of judgment (*maʾrehon de-dinin*) who mete out punishments, and they are called masters of the feet (*baʿale raglayim*). Some of them are strong, and the masters of judgment below are united to the lower [i.e., unholy] crowns" (*Zohar* 3:143a, *ʾIdraʾ Rabbaʾ*).

Although the zoharic imagination has obviously carried us far from the biblical text, it is important to stress the line of continuity. As I indicated above, the image of the feet of God frequently appears in biblical contexts that involve the execution of divine judgment. Such an idea, reiterated in the rabbinic corpus as well, presumably fostered in the mythic consciousness of the medieval Spanish kabbalist the idea of a group of angels whose purpose it is to administer divine judgment and avenge wrongdoings. By identifying the feet of God with angels, the *Zohar* turns the exegetical wheel in compliance with an earlier turn in Jewish sources. Indeed, on another occasion the *Zohar* interprets God's feet mentioned in Isa. 41:2 as a reference to the attribute of judgment (*din*) or strength (*gevurah*), the fifth of the ten gradations (*sefirot*) in the divine pleroma (*Zohar* 2:139b). Through its theosophic prism the *Zohar* reflects the biblical locution and thereby recovers an ancient symbol of Israelite myth.

In addition to this symbolism, one finds that in the *Zohar* the term *regel* can either apply to the masculine aspect of God (in most cases the ninth emanation, *Yesod,* which corresponds to the divine phallus) or to the feminine (the tenth emanation, *Shekhinah*). The bipolar nature of the symbol *regel* is not unique as there are several such symbols in the *Zohar* that can represent the masculine and/or the feminine. With respect to the masculine signification of *regel,* it should be noted that the zoharic symbolism is rooted in a much older tradition whereby the foot functions as a euphemism for the phallus. This usage is found in various cultures (Schultze-Galléra 1909) and is attested in the classical sources of Judaism, including the Bible (Exod. 4:25; Judges 3:24; 1 Sam. 24:3; Ruth 3:7–8; see also Gen. 49:10 and Rashi's commentary on 2 Sam. 19:25 based on B. Yevamot 103a) and rabbinic literature (M. Shabbat 9:5; Bava Batra 2:1; Niddah 9:6–7; B. Berakhot 23a; Sanhedrin 108b; Yevamot 103a). I note, parenthetically, that biblical usage attests as well that feet can function as a euphemism for the female genitals, as in the case of Deut. 28:57. (A modern reverberation of this symbolism may be found in the psychoanalytic category of the foot-fetishist; Freud, 1966, 348–349.) Still, the dominant symbolic connotation of feet in the Jewish texts is phallic in nature, and it is precisely this symbolism that is most prominent in the kabbalistic literature. The impact of the phallic interpretation of foot in subsequent kabbalistic and Hasidic literature cannot be overemphasized. Numerous examples could be provided from these sources, especially Hasidic (Wolfson, 1992c), but here I will mention only one startling illustration from the *Kanfe Yonah* of Moses Yonah, one of the disciples of Luria. In the context of discussing the theosophical ramifications of homosexuality (*mishkav zekhur*), Moses Yonah asserts that the term *regel* is numerically equivalent to *zekhur* (i.e., both words equal 233), which is associated with *Yesod,* the *membrum virile* in the divine anthropos and hence the masculine (*zakhar*) potency *par excellence* (MS Sasson 993, 208). Without entering into the details of Moses Yonah's exposition, let me simply note that he recommends that the means of atonement for sexual relations with another male consists of fasting 233 consecutive days, corresponding to the word *regel* (ibid., 210; cf. Azikri 1966, 200; Sha'ar ha-Kelalim, ch 11).

The masculine signification of the feet is evident in the following zoharic interpretation of "Righteousness calling him to his feet" (Isa. 41:2):

> Righteousness constantly calls to the speculum that shines, and it never rests. Righteousness constantly stands by His feet, she is not

removed from there, she calls and does not rest, as it is written, "O God, do not be silent; do not hold aloof; do not be quiet, O God!" (Ps. 83:2) (*Zohar* 2:140a).

The feet of God thus represent the masculine potency, identified further as the speculum that shines, which is united with the feminine *Shekhinah,* whose desire to receive the influx from the masculine is here depicted by the image of Righteousness calling out to the feet in a continuous manner. That the feet function as a euphemism for the phallus is attested as well from the zoharic interpretation of David's command to Uriah, the husband of Bathsheba, "Go down to your house and bathe your feet" (2 Sam. 11:8): "He ordered him to have intercourse with his wife" (*Zohar* 1:8b). The symbolic use of the foot to characterize the erotic relationship between male and female potencies of God is rendered explicitly in another zoharic text: "See what is written, '[Jacob] drew his feet into the bed' (Gen. 49:33), the sun entered into the moon" (*Zohar* 1:248b). In typical fashion the *Zohar* illuminates one set of symbols by means of another, indicating hermeneutically that the world of divine reality can be portrayed only through the maze of symbolic representation. In this case the kabbalistic interpretation of the verse follows several other more literal and homiletical approaches. Read kabbalistically, Jacob refers to *Tif'eret,* the sixth emanation, and the bed to *Shekhinah,* the tenth. Hence, the symbolic meaning of Jacob's placing his feet on the bed is the unification of the masculine and feminine potencies, and the feet correspond to the conduit uniting male and female, i.e., the phallus, which is *Yesod,* the ninth emanation. This process is alluded to as well in the remark, "the sun entered the moon," for the sun represents the male (*Tif'eret*) and the moon the female (*Shekhinah*). Jacob's placing his feet on the bed, therefore, is a symbolic depiction of the unification of masculine and feminine potencies in the divine world. According to another interpretation offered by the *Zohar,* this verse indicates that at the moment of his death, the earthly Jacob actually (and not merely symbolically) united with the *Shekhinah,* thereby causing the arousal above resulting in the unification of the male and female aspects of the divine: "Come and see: Jacob entered into the moon [i.e., the *Shekhinah*] and produced in her fruits [i.e., souls] for the world. There is no generation in the world that does not have the fruit of Jacob in it, for he initiated the arousal above, as it is written, 'he drew his feet into the bed' (Gen. 49:33), for it is certainly the bed of Jacob" (*Zohar* 1:249a). Elsewhere the *Zohar* relates that the unification of Jacob with *Shekhinah* may be likened to a kind of death: "When did [Jacob] die? At the time of which it is written, 'he drew his feet into the bed.' 'The bed'—as it is written, 'This is Solomon's bed' (Song 3:7), for regarding this bed it is written, 'Her feet go down to death' (Prov. 5:5). Therefore, it is written, 'he drew his feet into the bed,' followed by 'he was gathered to his people' " (*Zohar* 2:48b). Jacob's entering into the feminine Presence, symbolized by the language of drawing his feet on the bed, eventuates in an ecstatic death, as the *Shekhinah* is frequently characterized in the *Zohar* as the locus of death. Indeed, in yet another passage the *Zohar* mandates that the ecstatic death realized through unification with the feminine Presence must be reenacted by every male Jew at a particular moment in the morning prayers; "After a person has completed the *ʿAmidah* prayer [i.e., the eighteen benedictions recited in a standing posture] he must appear as if he departed from the world, for he has separated from the Tree of Life [*Tifʾeret*] and gathered his feet upon that Tree of Death [*Shekhinah*] . . . as it is written, 'he drew his feet into the bed' " (*Zohar* 3:120b).

In another context the *Zohar* utilizes this symbolism to explicate Ruth 4:7, "Now this was formerly done in Israel in cases of redemption or exchange: to validate any transaction, one man would take off his sandal and hand it to the other. Such was the practice in Israel."

> Come and see [what is written] "And [God] said [to Moses]: Do not come closer. Remove your sandals from your feet" (Exod. 3:5). Why is a sandal mentioned here? Rather this indicates that [God] commanded him concerning his wife, to separate from her, and to unite with another wife, the holy light above, which is the *Shekhinah* [Scholem 1991, 183, 298, n. 77]. He establishes that sandal in another place, he removes it from this world and establishes it in another world. Accordingly, [it has been taught] whatever a deceased person gives someone in a dream is [a] good [sign], but if he takes an item from the house it is [a] bad [sign], for example, one's sandal (cf. B. Berakhot 57b). Why? Because he removes his feet, which are the foundation of a person, from this world and gathers them in the other world, the place wherein death dwells, as it is written, "How lovely are your feet in sandals, O daughter of nobles" (Song of Songs 7:2). (*Zohar* 3:180a)

From this passage it is clear that the sandal symbolizes the feminine and the foot the masculine, or, more specifically, the phallus. The symbols have a twofold connotation: they refer to mundane realities and their correlates in the divine realm, the sandal symbolizing the *Shekhinah* and the foot *Yesod*. Interestingly, in an earlier stratum of *Zohar,* the *Midrash ha-Ne'elam* on Ruth, the shoe symbolizes the male genitals: " 'So when the redeemer said to Boaz, 'Acquire for yourself,' he drew off his sandal' (Ruth 4:8) . . . [This alludes to] the arousal of the phallus, and it is a euphemism. When the Righteous (*ṣaddiq*) is aroused by the right [side], immediately 'he drew off his sandal.' This is the arousal in relation to the lower world" (*Zohar Ḥadash,* ed. Margaliot 1978c, 88b–c). In this context, then, the drawing off of the sandal functions as a euphemism for the erection of the phallus. Theosophically, the passage alludes to the relationship of *Yesod,* symbolized by Boaz or the Righteous, and *Shekhinah,* the lower world (Mopsik 1987, 181). In the kabbalistic explanation of the biblical injunction of *ḥaliṣah,* the removal of the sandal of the brother-in-law who refuses to fulfill the law of levirate marriage (see Deut. 25:9), contained in the *Piqqudin* section of *Zohar* (3:308b), with a parallel in the *Sefer ha-Rimmon* (Wolfson 1988, 253) and *Sefer ha-Mishqal* (Wijnhoven 1964, 145–146) of Moses de León (1240–ca. 1305), the same symbolism is employed. That is, the removal of the sandal by the woman of the deceased man substitutes for her having intercourse with her brother-in-law, for the sandal symbolizes the place of the "perfection of the human feet" (*tiqquna' de-raglin de-var nash*), i.e., the *sefirah* of *Yesod,* which is the source of the life-force that sustains the *Shekhinah* and all worlds below her. By taking the sandal, the wife, in effect, is imparting eternal life upon her deceased husband so that his name will not be erased. What is essential to reiterate is that the masculine aspect of the divine is here characterized as the sandal. By contrast, it is clear that in the latter stratum of the *Zohar,* the sandal is a symbol of the feminine. When applied to the divine realm, the sandal refers to the *Shekhinah,* a point made by the *Zohar* specifically in connection with the sandal of *ḥaliṣah.* The latter symbolism is reminiscent of what we detected in the pseudo-Hai passage contained in Eleazar of Worms' *Sefer ha-Ḥokhmah,* wherein the *Shekhinah* was designated as the shoe (*pazmeqe*) of God. Utilizing this symbolism, the *Zohar* explains God's command to Moses to remove his sandal, i.e., to separate from his wife, so that he can unite with the other sandal that is the *Shekhinah,* the feminine Presence (cf. *Zohar* 3: 148a; *Zohar Ḥadash,* ed. Margaliot, 1978c, 72d; *Tiqqune Zohar* 21, ed. Margaliot, 1978b, 60b). Building upon a motif found in earlier aggadic sources (Liebes 1976, 182–184), the *Zohar* expresses Moses' refraining from conjugal relations with his wife after he was united with the Presence in terms of the symbolism of the feet and the sandal.

From the examples I have adduced, it can be concluded that the foot functions in the zoharic literature as a euphemism for the phallus, human and divine. As I mentioned at the outset, however, the foot can also serve in the *Zohar* as a symbol for the feminine. Precisely such a symbolic correlation underlies the zoharic interpretation of the verse, "He guards the feet of His faithful" (1 Sam 2:9): "[The word] faithful (*ḥasidav*) is written in the singular (i.e., according to the Masoretic spelling, the word can be read as *ḥasido*), and this refers to Abraham, for the Holy One, blessed be He, constantly watches him . . . And the [word] feet (*ragle*) refers to his wife, for the Holy One, blessed be He, send His Presence with her and watches her constantly" (*Zohar* 1:112b). As might be expected the image of the feet, the lowest part of the body, was applied as well to the feminine in the divine realm, the last of the emanations. To be sure, the *Shekhinah* is also depicted by other anatomical parts and, on occasion, as a distinct feminine form that is a counterpart to the masculine. The logic of the mythic representation of the *Shekhinah* in terms of foot imagery is well captured by Moses Cordovero (1522–1570) in the lexical chapter of his opus, *Pardes Rimmonim,* s.v., *raglayim:* "All [such images] refer to *Malkhut* [i.e., *Shekhinah*], and she is called feet in the mystery of the lower aspect which is clothed in the [demonic] shell, according to the mystical import of 'I had bathed my feet—was I to soil them again?' (Song of Songs 5:3), and she disseminates the sparks clothed in the shells" (1962, pt. 2, 39b). In the zoharic corpus this aspect of *Shekhinah* is related especially to Prov. 5:5, "Her feet go down to death" (*Zohar* 1:35b, 161b, 190a, 221b; 2:48b; 3:107b, 251b). We have already encountered the use of this verse in one of the texts cited above to indicate that the divine Presence delves into the depths of the demonic symbolized by death. The characterization of the *Shekhinah* as descending to death is a perfect example of a tendency on the part of the *Zohar* to depict the last of the divine emanations in terms also used to represent the demonic other side (Tishby 1971, 1:223–226). The issue of death is particularly relevant, for in some contexts, the *Shekhinah* is identified as the cause of death (Tishby 1971, 1:222–223) whereas in other cases death is attributed to the demonic realm, and especially the feminine counterpart of the *Shekhinah,* the serpent or Lilith (Tishby 1971, 1:299–300). In any event, the verse from Proverbs provided the *Zohar* and subsequent kabbalists with yet another important foot image to apply to the *Shekhinah,* especially to characterize her state of exile amongst the demonic shells. In the kabbalah of the sixteenth century, this image took on added significance as the disciples of Luria explained the ritual of washing one's feet in hot water on Friday afternoon (and days before festivals) as a theurgical purification of the feet of the Presence from the impurity of the shells. Thus, e.g., in the *Sha'ar ha-Kavvanot* of Ḥayyim Vital (1542–1620), the matter is put as follows:

> Another [mystical] intention that one must have with respect to the washing of the face, hands, and feet in hot water on Friday. The reason is that during the week the *Shekhinah* [is in the status of] "Her feet go down to death," and now [before the Sabbath] she washes her feet from that filth which cleaves to that place. And her feet rise [to holiness] . . . according to the mystery of "I had bathed my feet—was I to soil them again?" (Song of Songs 5:3) by bringing her down again to the place of the shells. (1963, 63a)

The washing of the feet is thus a purificatory rite to purge the *Shekhinah* of the forces of impurity attached to her feet. It is also clear, however, that Vital, following a passage in the *Zohar* 1:8b cited above, viewed washing the feet as a euphemism for coitus, especially as applied to the divine realm. "Do not wonder," he writes in one place in *Sha'ar Ma'amere RaZa"L,* "that *Yesod* [i.e., the divine phallus] is also called foot, the reason being that sexual union is called washing the feet, as King David, peace be upon him, said to Uriah, 'Go down to your house and bathe your feet' (2 Sam. 11:8), his intention being that he should have intercourse with her. This too is the mystery of 'I had bathed my feet—was I to soil them again?' (Song of Songs 5:3)" (1898, 8c–d). By washing one's feet, then, one cleanses the *Shekhinah* and prepares her for union with the male aspect of the divine, a union that is alluded to by the feet. The implicit sexual function of this rite is underscored in a parallel version contained in the *Peri 'Eṣ Ḥayyim,* edited by Meir Poppers (d. 1662), where one finds an additional detail with respect to drying oneself after the washing: "When the person dries his hands and feet after the bathing and purification he should intend the name Sandalphon because he has become a sandal for the feet of the *Shekhinah* on Friday when she adorns herself for the union of Sabbath evening, and the *Shekhinah* at that time has washed her feet" (1980, 385). The full theurgical significance of this last comment can only be appreciated if one bears in mind the mystical intention imparted by kabbalists to the act of putting on shoes each morning. I will present here one example from the *Kanfe Yonah* of Menaḥem Azariah da Fano (1548–1620). According to Fano, following earlier sources (see, e.g., Karo 1990, 85, 106; Vital 1980, 609), the right shoe (male) corresponds to Meṭaṭron and the left (female) to Sandalphon (cf. *Zohar Ḥadash*, ed. Margaliot, 1978c, 38d; *Zohar* 3:281a [*Ra'aya Mehemna'*]). By putting on one's shoes, beginning with the right, one symbolically binds these angels to the feet of the *Shekhinah* so that the demonic shells will not be attached to her (1786, pt. 3, § 67, 16c). In effect, then, the tying of the shoes has the same theurgical impact as the ceremony of the feet washing.

I would like to conclude with a discussion of one more aspect of the image of God's foot in the *Zohar* and related kabbalistic literature. Given the bipolarity of the symbol of the foot, referring to both the masculine and feminine potencies of God, this imagery assumed a rather significant erotic connotation that kabbalists themselves tended to treat as highly esoteric. The *Zohar* employs this imagery in a text that had a profound influence on the eschatological and messianic speculation of Lurianic kabbalah, Sabbatianism, and Hasidism. The relevant passage is part of an extended reflection on the history of the Jewish people from biblical times, presented in terms of the theosophic processes in the sefirotic pleroma and the corresponding esoteric knowledge appropriate to each epoch. I begin my citation with the destruction of the Second Temple and the consequent exile:

> Afterwards their sins caused the foreskin [i.e., the demonic power or Rome] to rule, and [they] were banished from the Second Temple to the outside, and they descended from there to the roundings of the thighs below, until they dwelt below in the feet. When they settled in the feet, then [it is written] "On that day, He will set His feet" (Zech. 14:4). And the world in every matter will be governed by the upper mystery as is appropriate. Even though they were banished [from the Temple] they have not deserted it, and they always hold on to it. He who knows and measures with the measurement of the measuring line (*be-shi'ura' de-qav ha-middah;* cf. Jer. 31:39), the length of the extension from the thighs to the feet, he can know the length of the duration of the exile. This is a secret amongst the reapers of the field [i.e., kabbalists], and all is a supernal mystery . . . When the exile is terminated, in the extension of the feet, then "On that day, He will set His feet," and the spirit of impurity, the foreskin, will be removed from the world, and Israel will be restored to rule alone as is fitting. (*Zohar* 2:258a)

In the continuation of the passage the *Zohar* goes on to describe the process of restoration that is depicted as an overflow of prophetic influx caused by a union of *Yesod* (Joseph the Righteous) and the *Shekhinah* (the hidden and concealed palace). The overflow proceeds from the thighs, i.e., *Neṣaḥ* (Eternity) and *Hod* (Majesty), the seventh and eight emanations, until "the feet reach the feet." This last expression, *ʿad de-maṭu raglin be-raglin,* was interpreted in the Lurianic, Sabbatian, and Hasidic traditions, as the stage right before the coming of the Messiah when the demonic shells lodged in the heels of the cosmic Adam, or, alternatively, the satanic Adam, will be redeemed, and hence was connected with the rabbinic motif of the footheels of the messiah, *ʿiqvot meshiḥaʾ* (Wolfson 1992c). It seems to me, however, that in the context of the *Zohar,* the expression "when the feet reach the feet" signifies the union of the divine phallus (*Yesod*) and the feminine Presence (*Shekhinah*), or, as Cordovero puts it in his commentary on this passage, "the male becomes one with the female, the feet together with the feet" (Azulai 1973, 267a). The time of redemption is thus characterized as the moment when the feet reach the feet, i.e., when male and female embrace, a theme that is central to the messianic speculation of the *Zohar* (Liebes 1982, 157–170, 175–207). When the divine feet are united, the Jews will be released from their state of entrapment in the feet of the demonic power. This is the esoteric knowledge attained by one who calculates by means of the measuring line (*Zohar* 2:233a; *Zohar Ḥadash,* ed. Margaliot, 1978c, 56d–58d; Liebes 1976, 146, 163; Wolfson 1990, 231–232, n. 132) the duration of the exile by measuring from the thighs to the feet.

The erotic implications of the zoharic expression "when the feet reach the feet" can be gathered from a text written by Joseph Hamadan, a kabbalist who was apparently active in the last decades of the thirteenth century and who may have been part of the zoharic circle (Liebes, 1989, 25–34). In one of his works, *Sefer Tashaq,* he writes:

> The holy feet of the Matrona embrace the pillar upon which the world stands [i.e., *Yesod*], as it is written, "Righteousness is the foundation of the world" (Prov. 10:25) . . . Moreover, we have learnt the secret regarding the holy feet of Matrona and the holy feet of the Holy One, blessed be He: there are four feet corresponding to the four holy beasts in the holy chariot, in the image of a human, lion, eagle, and ox . . . The holy feet [of the Matrona] stand with the feet of the Holy One, blessed be He, and they form a circle. The top of the right foot of the Holy One, blessed be, embraces the top of the left foot of Matrona, and the top of the left foot of the Holy One,

> blessed be He, embraces the right foot of Matrona, and their heels are joined, one foot to the other, and in the space between them sit the souls of the pious and the angels. (Zwelling 1975, 328–329, 335)

The sexual play of the male and female is here clearly expressed in terms of the feet. Hamadan, unlike the *Zohar,* does not place this in an eschatological context, which is consistent with the lack of a messianic element in his writings (Liebes 1982, 102). Nevertheless, it is obvious that his imagery is helpful in decoding the reference in the *Zohar* to the feet reaching the feet. It is instructive that the author of the *Zohar* contextualized the eroticism of the divine feet in a messianic setting. The zoharic tradition had an enduring impact on subsequent kabbalists, as may be seen, for example, in the following statement of Moses Ḥayyim Luzzatto (1707–1746), reflecting on the messianic era: "In that time it will be said with respect to Israel, 'Then (*'az*) the lame shall leap like a deer' (Isa. 35:6), for they will have only one foot, and through Your unity, which is [alluded to in the word] *'az* [the *'alef* refers to the upper three *sefirot,* and the letter *zayin* to the lower seven], [the name] YAHDWNHY [a combination of YHWH and Adonai, which correspond respectively to the masculine and feminine potencies of the divine], which will be revealed to them, the two feet will be joined as one. Then Israel will go safely (cf. Prov. 3:25), as it is written, 'On that day, He will set His feet on the Mount of Olives' (Zech. 14:4)" [1979, 259]. Elsewhere Luzzatto characterizes the two messianic figures, Messiah son of Joseph and Messiah son of David, as the two feet presently in exile but that will in the future redeem the Jewish people (1990, 17). Insofar as the two messiahs correspond respectively to *Yesod* and *Shekhinah,* the masculine and feminine gradations, it is fair to assume that implicit here is the erotic connotation of the feet articulated by Luzzatto in the other context. Given Luzzatto's intense messianic striving based heavily on the *Zohar* (Tishby 1982, 186–203; Liebes 1982, 111–113; Carlebach 1990, 199–203), one should not be surprised at this appropriation and application of the zoharic symbol of the feet to characterize the union of masculine and feminine potencies in the time of redemption.

Conclusion

To sum up, I have traced in this study some of the relevant images connected with the feet of God in Jewish sources from the biblical to the medieval period. It is evident that despite the fact that the divine feet are never fully described in the history of Judaism, this image played a decisive role shaping the theological imagery of Jewish writers through the centuries. The biblical conception of the feet as an instrument of divine judgment was preserved in later rabbinic and mystical literature. In addition, the appearance of this image in theophanic contexts, especially Exod. 24:10, provided an impetus for the development of anthropomorphic speculation on the feet in the esoteric traditions cultivated by Jews from Late Antiquity through the High Middle Ages. While other bodily limbs are attributed to God in the relevant literature, the feet had a special significance in the mythic imagination of mystic visionaries, midrashists, and liturgical poets. Additionally, as I have suggested, speculation on the feet of God played a crucial role in some of the medieval theosophical texts that helped foster both German Pietism and Provençal-Spanish kabbalah. What is perhaps the profoundest set of symbols connected with the feet appears in the *Zohar* where, as we have seen in detail, the feet correspond to the male and female potencies of the divine anthropos. This symbolic correspondence allowed the *Zohar,* and subsequent kabbalists, to depict the *hieros gamos* of the sefirotic world in terms of images of the foot. As one final illustration of this process I conclude with a statement of Ḥayyim Vital, contained in the collection *Shaʿar Maʾamere RaZa"L:* "just as there are feet in the male, which are [the *sefirot*] *Neṣaḥ, Ḥod,* and *Yesod* . . . there are feet in the female . . . for the female is called the feet of her husband, for she sits at the feet, as it says, 'she uncovered his feet' (Ruth 3:7)" [1898, 9b]. The complicated mythology woven by the medieval kabbalist is, at least in part, based on the euphemistic use of feet for the genitals attested in the classical texts of Judaism. In that respect the kabbalistic mythos is not so much a gnostic transformation as it is the hermeneutical recovery of an ancient symbolism.

References

Abelson, Joshua
1969 *The Immanence of God in Rabbinical Literature*. New York: Hermon Press.

Albeck, Chanoch
1984 *Midrash Bereshit Rabbati*. Jerusalem: Mekize Nirdamim.

Alon, Gedalyahu
1967 *History of the Jews in Eretz-Israel*. Vol. 1. Jerusalem: Magnes Press.

Altmann, Alexander
1981 *Essays in Jewish Intellectual History*. Hanover, N. H.: University Press of New England.

Azikri, Eleazar
1966 *Sefer Haredim*. Jerusalem: Defus Ha-'Ivri.

Azulai, Abraham
1973 *'Or ha-Ḥammah* 3 vols. Bene-Beraq: n.p.

Bar-Ilan, Meir
1987 "The Idea of Crowning God in Hekhalot Mysticism and the Karaitic Polemic." *Jerusalem Studies in Jewish Thought* 6 (1–2): 221–234. In Hebrew.

Baumgarten, Joseph M.
1986 "The Book of Elkesai and Merkabah Mysticism" *Journal for the Study of Judaism* 17:212–223.

Ben Yehuda, Eliezer
1960 *A Complete Dictionary of Ancient and Modern Hebrew*. New York: Thomas Yoseloff.

Beyerlin, Walter
1966 *Origins and History of the Oldest Sinaitic Traditions*. Oxford: Basil Blackwell.

Boyarin, Daniel
1990 *Intertexuality and the Reading of Midrash*. Bloomington: Indiana University Press.

Buber, Salomon
1891 *Midrash Tehillim*. Vilna: Romm.
1946 *Midrash Tanḥuma'*. New York: Sefer.
1973 *Aggadat Bereshit*. Jerusalem: n.p.

Castelli, David
1880 *Il Commento di Sabbatai Donnolo sul Libro Della Creazione*. Firenze.

Carlebach, Elisheva
1990 *The Pursuit of Heresy: Rabbi Moses Hagiz and the Sabbatian Controversies*. New York: Columbia University Press.

Chernus, Ira
1982 "Visions of God in Merkabah Literature," *Journal for the Study of Judaism* 13:123–46.

Childs, Brevard
1974 *The Book of Exodus: A Critical, Theological Commentary.* Philadelphia: Westminster Press.

Cohen, Martin S.
1983 *The Shi'ur Qomah: Liturgy and Theurgy in Pre-Kabbalistic Jewish Mysticism.* Lanham, Md.: University Press of America.
1985 *The Shi'ur Qomah: Texts and Recensions.* Tübingen: J. C. B. Mohr.

Cordovero, Moses
1962 *Pardes Rimmonim.* Jerusalem: n.p.

da Fano, Menahem Azariah
1786 *Kanfe Yonah.* Koretz: n.p.

Dan, Joseph
1968 *The Esoteric Theology of Ashkenazi Hasidism.* Jerusalem: Bialik Institute. In Hebrew.
1975 *Studies in Ashkenazi-Hasidic Literature.* Ramat-Gan: Massada. In Hebrew.
1987 "A Re-evaluation of the 'Ashkenazi Kabbalah'." *Jerusalem Studies in Jewish Thought* 6 (3–4):125–140. In Hebrew.

Davidson, Israel
1934 *The Book of the Wars of the Lord.* New York: The Jewish Theological Seminary of America.

de Lange, Nicholas
1976 *Origen and the Jews.* Cambridge: Cambridge University Press.

Elior, Rachel
1989 "The Concept of God in Hekhalot Literature" In *Binah: Studies in Jewish History, Thought, and Culture.* Ed. Joseph Dan, 2:97–120. New York: Praeger.

Epstein, Abraham
1957 *Mi-Qadmoniyot ha-Yehudim: Kitve R. Avraham Epstein.* 2 vols. Ed. A. M. Habermann, Jerusalem: Mosad Harav Kook.

Epstein, J. N. and E. Z. Melamed
1955 *Mekhilta d'Rabbi Sim 'on b. Jochai.* Jerusalem: Mekize Nirdamim.

Farber, Asi
1986 "The Concept of the Merkabah in Thirteenth-Century Jewish Esotericism—Sod ha-'Egoz and Its Development." Ph. D. diss., Hebrew University, Jerusalem. In Hebrew.

Fishbane, Michael
1991 " 'The Holy One Sits and Roars': Mythopoesis and the Midrashic Imagination." *Journal of Jewish Thought and Philosophy, 1*:1–21.

Frazer, James George
1935 *The Golden Bough*. 12 vols. New York: Macmillan.

Freud, Sigmund
1966 *The Complete Introductory Lectures on Psychoanalysis*. Trans. and ed. James Strachey. New York: W. W. Norton & Company Inc.

Friedmann, Meir
1963 *Pesikta Rabbati*. Tel-Aviv: Offset.
1969 *Seder Eliahu Rabba and Seder Eliahi Zuta* (Tanna d'be Eliahu). Jerusalem: Wahrmann Books.

Ginsburger, Moses
1903 *Pseudo-Jonathan (Thargum Jonathan ben Usiel zum Pentateuch)*. Berlin: S. Calvary.

Ginzberg, Louis
1955 *On Jewish Law and Lore*. Philadelphia: The Jewish Publication Society of America.
1968 *The Legends of the Jews*. 7 vols. Philadelphia: The Jewish Publication Society of America.

Goldberg, Arnold
1969 *Untersuchungen über die Vorstellung von der Schekhinah in der Frühen Rabbinischen Literatur, Talmud und Midrasch*. Berlin: Walter de Gruyter.

Goldin, Judah
1988 *Studies in Midrash and Related Literature*. E. Barry L. Eichler and Jeffrey H. Tigay. Philadelphia: The Jewish Publication Society.

Gruenwald, Ithamar
1980 *Apocalyptic and Merkavah Mysticism*. Leiden: E. J. Brill.
1988 *From Apocalypticism to Gnosticism*. Frankfurt am Main: Peter Lang.

Habermann, Abraham Meir
1938 *Liturgical Poems of R. Shimʿon bar Yiṣḥâq*. Berlin: Schocken.

Halperin, David J.
1988 *The Faces of the Chariot*. Tübingen: J. C. B. Mohr.

Heinemann, Isaak
1974 *Darkhe ha-ʾAggadah*. Jerusalem: Magnes Press.

Hoffmann, David
1921 *Midrasch ha-Gadol zum Buche Exodus*. Berlin: Mekize Nirdamim.

Horovitz, H. S. and Rabin, I. A.
1970 *Mechilta d'Rabbi Ismael*. Jerusalem: Wahrmann Books.

Idel, Moshe
1981 "The Concept of torah in Hekhalot Literature and Its Metamorphoses in the Kabbalah." *Jerusalem Studies in Jewish Thought* [Heb.] 1:23–84.
1982 "The Sefirot above the Sefirot." *Tarbiz* 51:239–280. In Hebrew.
1986 "The World of Angels in Human Form." *Studies in Jewish Mysticism, Philosophy, and Ethical Literature Presented to Isaiah Tishby on his Seventy-fifth Birthday*. 1–66. Jerusalem: Magness Press. In Hebrew.
1987 "The Problem of the Sources of the *Bahir*." *Jerusalem Studies in Jewish Thought* 6 (3–4):55–72. In Hebrew.
1988 *Kabbalah: New Perspectives*. New Haven: Yale University Press.

Jellinek, Adolph
1967 *Bet ha-Midrasch*. 3rd ed. 6 vols. Jerusalem: Wahrmann Books.

Klien, Michael L.
1981 "The Translations of Anthropomorphisms and Anthropopathisms in the Targumim," *Congress Volume: Vienna 1980. Supplements to Vetus Testamentum* 32:162–177.
1982 *Anthropomorphisms and Anthropopathisms in the Targumim of the Pentateuch*. Jerusalem: Makor Publishing Ltd. In Hebrew.

Klijn A., and G. J. Reinink
1973 *Patristic Evidence for Jewish-Christian Sects*. Leiden: E. J. Brill.

Karo, Yosef
1990 *Maggid Mesharim*. Petah Tiqvah: n.p.

Kushnir-Oron, Michal
1989 *Shaʿar ha-Razim*. Jerusalem: Bialik Institute.

Lieberman, Saul
1970 *Shkiin*. 2d ed. Jerusalem: Wahrmann Books.

Liebes, Yehuda
1976 *Sections of the Zohar Lexicon*. Ph.D. diss., Hebrew University, Jerusalem. In Hebrew.
1982 "The Messiah of the Zohar." in *The Messianic Idea in Jewish Thought: A Study Conference in Honour of the Eightieth Birthday of Gershom Scholem*, 87–236. Jerusalem: The Israel Academy of Sciences and Humanities. In Hebrew.
1988 "The Kabbalistic Myth of Orpheus." *Jerusalem Studies in Jewish Thought* [Heb.] 7:425–60. In Hebrew.
1989 "How the Zohar was Written." *Jerusalem Studies in Jewish Thought* 8:1–72. In Hebrew.
1992 "De Natura Dei: ʿAl ha-Mitos ha-Yehudi we-Gilgulo." In *Efraim Gottlieb Memorial Volume*. Jerusalem: Bialik Institute.

Luzzato, Moses Hayyim
1979 *TQTW [515] Tefillot*. Bene Beraq: S. Ulman.
1990 *Ma'amar ha-Ge'ullah* Jerusalem: Ma'or Yisra'el.

Mahzor Ashkenazi Rite.
1599 Venice.

Margaliot, Reuven
1978a *Sefer ha-Bahir*. Jerusalem: Mosad Harav Kook.
1978b *Tiqqune Zohar*. Jerusalem: Mosad Harav Kook.
1978c *Zohar Ḥadash*. Jerusalem: Mosad Harav Kook.

Margulies, Mordecai
1983 *Midrash Haggadol on Exodus*. 4th ed. Jerusalem: Mosad Harav Kook.

Marmorstein, Arthur
1968 *The Old Rabbinic Idea of God*. Pt. 2: Essays in Anthropomorphism. New York: Ktav.

Mopsik, Charles
1987 *Le Zohar: Le Livre de Ruth*. Lagrasse: Editions Verdier.
1989 "The Body of Engenderment in the Hebrew Bible, the Rabbinic Tradition and the Kabbalah." In *Zone: Fragments for a History of the Human Body*. Pt. 1, 48–73. Ed. Michel Feher, Ramona Naddaff, and Nadia Tazi. New York: Urzone Inc.

Neumark, David
1921 *Toledot ha-Pilosofia be-Yisra'*el. 2 vols. New York: The Stybel Publishing House.

Neusner, Jacob
1988 *The Incarnation of God: The Character of Divinity in Formative Judaism*. Philadelphia: Fortress Press.

Nicholson. E. W.
1974 "The Interpretation of Exodus XXIV 9–11." *Vetus Testamentum* 24:77–97.
1975 "The Antiquity of the Tradition in Exodus XXIV 9–11." *Vetus Testamentum* 25:69–79.

Origen
1982 *Homilies on Genesis and Exodus*. Trans. Ronald E. Heine. Washington, D.C.: Catholic University of America Press.

Pedaya, Haviva
1990 "The Provençal Stratum in the Redaction of *Sefer ha-Bahir*." *Jerusalem Studies in Jewish Thought* 9:139–164. In Hebrew.

Pirqe Rabbi 'Eli'ezer
1970 With notes by David Luria. Jerusalem: n.p.

Schäfer, Peter
1981 *Synopse zur Hekhalot-Literatur.* Tübingen: J. C. B. Mohr.
1984 *Geniza-Fragmente zur Hekhalot-Literatur.* Tübingen: J. C. B. Mohr.

Schapiro, Meyer
1979 *Late Antique, Early Christian and Medieval Art: Selected Papers.* New York: George Braziller, Inc.

Schechter, Solomon
1887 *ʾAvot de-Rabbi Natan.* Vienna.

Schmerler, B
1933 *ʾAhavat Yehonatan.* Bilgoraj: N. Kronenberg.

Scholem, Gershom
1923 *Das Buch Bahir.* Leipzig: W. Durgulin.
1956 *Major Trends in Jewish Mysticism.* New York: Schocken Books.
1965 *Jewish Gnosticism, Merkabah Mysticism, and Talmudic Tradition.* New York: The Jewish Theological Seminary of America.
1969 *On the Kabbalah and Its Symbolism.* Trans. Ralph Manheim. New York: Schocken Books.
1974 *Kabbalah.* Jerusalem: Keter.
1987 *Origins of the Kabblah.* Ed. R. J. Zwi Werblowsky. Trans. Allan Arkush. Princeton: Princeton University Press.
1991 *On the Mystical Shape of the Godhead.* Ed. Jonathan Chipman. Trans. Joachim Neugroschel. New York: Schocken Books.

Schultze-Galléra, Siegman
1909 *Fuss- und Schusymbolik und- Erotik.* Leipzig.

Sed, Niolas
1965 "Une cosmologie juive du haut Moyen Age: La Berayta di Maʿaseh Bereshit." *Revue des études juives* 124:23–123.

Sharf, Andrew
1976 *The Universe of Shabbetai Donnolo.* New York: Ktav.

Skipwith, Grey Hubert
1907 "The Lord of Heaven." *The Jewish Quarterly Review, o.s.* 19:688–703.

Smith, Jonathan Z.
1970 "The Prayer of Joseph." In *Religions in Antiquity: Essays in Memory of Erwin Ramsdell Goodenough.* Ed. J. Neusner, 254–294. Leiden: E. J. Brill.

Smith, Morton
1957–58 "The Image of God." *Bulletin of the John Rylands Library* 40: 474–81.
1963 "Observations on *Hekhalot Rabbati.*" In *Biblical and Other Studies,* 142–60. Ed. A. Altmann. Cambridge: Harvard University Press.

1970 "On the Shape of God and the Humanity of Gentiles." In *Religions in Antiquity: Essays in Memory of Erwin Ramsdell Goodenough*. Ed. J. Neusner, 315–20. Leiden: E. J. Brill.

Stroumsa, Gedaliahu

1983 "Form(s) of God: Some Notes on Meṭaṭron and Christ." *Harvard Theological Review* 76:269–288.

Tishby, Isaiah

1971 *Mishnat ha-Zohar.* Jerusalem: Bialik Institute.

1982 *Paths of Faith and Heresy.* Jerusalem: Magnes. In Hebrew.

Urbach, Ephraim E.

1979 *The Sages Their Concepts and Beliefs.* 2 vols. Trans. Israel Abrahams. Jerusalem: Magnes Press.

Vajda, Georges

1948 "Quelques traces de Sabbatai Donnolo dans les commentaires medievaux du Sefer Yeçira." *Revue des études juives* 108:92–94.

Vital, Hayyim

1898 *Sha'ar Ma'amere RaZa*"L. Jerusalem: n.p.

1963 *Sha'ar ha-Kavvanot.* Jerusalem: Meqor Hayyim.

1980 *Peri 'Eṣ Ḥayyim.* Jerusalem: 'Or ha-Bahir.

Wertheimer, Shlomo A.

1980 *Battei Midrashot.* 2 vols. Jerusalem: Ktab Wa-Sepher.

Wijnhoven, Jochanan H. A.

1964 *Sefer ha-Mishkal.: Text and Study.* Brandeis University, Ph.D.

Wolfson, Elliot R.

1988 *The Book of the Pomegranate: Moses de León's Sefer ha-Rimmon.* Atlanta: Scholars Press.

1989 "Female Imaging of the Torah: From Literary Metaphor to Religious Symbol." In *From Ancient Israel to Modern Judaism Intellect in Quest of Understanding: Essays in Honor of Marvin Fox.* Ed. Jacob Neusner, Ernst Frerichs, and Nahum Sarna, 2:271–307. Atlanta: Scholars Press.

1990 "Letter Symbolism and Merkavah Imagery in the *Zohar*." In *'Alei Shefer: Studies in the Literature of Jewish Thought Presented to Rabbi Dr. Alexandre Safran.* Ed. Moshe Hallamish. Bar-Ilan: Bar-Ilan University Press.

1992a "The Image of Jacob Engraved Upon the Throne: Further Speculation on the Esoteric Doctrine of the German Pietists," *Ephraim Gottlieb Memorial Volume.* Jerusalem: Bialik Institute. In Hebrew.

1992b "The Theosophy of Shabbetai Donnolo, With Special Emphasis on the Doctrine of *Sefirot* in *Sefer Ḥakhmoni." Frank Talmage Memorial Volume.* Ed. Barry Walfish.

1992c "Walking as a Sacred Duty: Theological Transformation of Social Reality in Early Hasidism." *Polin.*

Zimmer, Eric
1989 "Poses and Postures during Prayer." *Sidra* 5, 89–130. In Hebrew.

Zwelling, Jeremy
1975 "Joseph of Hamadan's Sefer Tashak: Critical Text edited with Introduction." Ph.D. diss., Brandeis University.

7

God's Body: Theological and Ritual Roles of *Shi'ur Komah*

Naomi Janowitz

> "Rabbi Ishamel says: What is the measure of the body of the Holy One? . . . The height of his soles is 30,000,000 parasangs; its name is Parmeseh."
>
> *Shi'ur Komah* (Sefer Haqqomah 51, 54)[1]

> From what quarter was this monstrosity smuggled in?
>
> Heinrich Graetz[2]

Let us follow for a moment Xenophanes' musing that if cows had a religion, they would imagine their gods to be cows.[3] The theological debates among the rival cow theologies might include the Angus cows expressing shock at Hereford documents that describe young cows "waiting at night for visions of their god in the shape of a young bull," and at rituals that include the drinking of milk. Meanwhile Hereford warn, "Do not, like an Angus, suppose concerning an incorporeal being that distinctions of male or female hold good. You may hold such language about them, just as you would even about your own body, for your soul is nominally called feminine, yet in reality it is neither male nor female."[4] Meanwhile the Jersey reject both the Angus and the Hereford claiming that "our God is closer to Aristotle's Unmoved Mover than to the bovine deities of the Angus Testament and the Hereford."[5]

Next the cow scholars enter. Those from the Wissenschaft des Kuhetums report that after careful historical research they have decided that the Angus never had bovinomorphic conceptions of their deity, except due to outside influence. The Revisionists claim after their careful research that the Angus theology was always bovinomorphic, except when led astray by outside influence. Finally the deconstructionist cow scholars state that after careful research, they have decided that cows do not exist, but that in certain circumstances of privileged discourse, those with hegemonic power are permitted to eroticize their gaze and state "udder."

As this allegory demonstrates, charging ones opponents with being "anthropomorphic" has been used as a means of both inter- and intrareligious attack; like the words "decadent," or even better "obscene," someone is saying that someone else has "bad taste" in their God-language. The notion of anthropomophism is very vague; Judaism, Christianity, and Islam have all used human (mostly male) analogies to describe their deities. Over time customs, or aesthetics, change as to which type of analogies are acceptable and which are simply out of fashion. In the world of attack and counterattack between Jews and Christians, positions had to be caricatured to distinguish between extremely similar beliefs, and charges of poor choice of God language were one means used. For example, the "Hereford" quote from Justin Martyr distorts the fact that Christians made use of similar male/female distinctions when it suited them.

Modern debates about anthropomorphism mainly repeat the Late Antique polemics or attempt to construct a new anthropomorphism-free history based on modern aesthetics. Texts in the Jewish tradition that discuss the deity in bodily terms have elicited concern, amusement, and scorn from Jews, ancient and modern. Descriptions of the deity's body appear to threaten the purity of Judaism, its monotheistic stance, perhaps its anti-idolatry stance. The insistence by some to exaggerate anti-anthropomorphic sentiments in Jewish texts in the face of overt evidence to the contrary is best illustrated by Joseph Dan's statement that *Shi'ur Komah,* a text which enumerates God's limbs, is "anti-anthropomorphic."[6] A more subtle version of this emphasis is found in the standard description of Targumic translations as motivated by the desire to eliminate biblical anthropomorphisms.[7] Chipping away consistently at this stance, Michael Klein points out that avoidance of human attributes is not found consistently among the translators, and more importantly, it is possible to find other motives for word choices.[8] Klein has demonstrated the extent to which the finding of anti-anthropomorphic stances is simply a continuation of one position internal to a Jewish debate about God (1972, 1979). The less anthropomorphism is an affront to scholars, the less likely they are to find anti-anthropomorphic attitudes in Jewish texts.

Daniel Boyarin helps to redress the balance by taking up the stance of those rabbis who argued for the bodily epiphanies of the deity (1990). They strove to repeat these epiphanies by means of martyrdom and midrash. By offering himself up to death, as seen in the stories about Akiba, a rabbi could summon God's presence. In a perhaps less final and dramatic manner, the divine presence could also be summoned in the process of studying and interpreting Torah.[9] Boyarin concludes

> In order to recover the erotic visual communion that obtained between God and Israel at Mount Sinai, Ben-Azzai engages not in a mystical practice but in a hermeneutic one, the practice of midrash. (1990, 550)

Taking a slightly different approach, Gedaliahu Stroumsa argues that the rabbis (and the authors of *Shi'ur Komah*) turned to "mystical anthropomorphism" in an attempt to find a middle ground between the dualist gnostics who say "no man hath seen God" and a literalistic view, which he calls "simple anthropomorphism."

> It seems, indeed, that mystical anthropomorphism may have been an alternative solution to the above-mentioned antinomy between 'simple' anthropomorphism and dualism for a religious thought which did not, as did Alexandrian Christianity, encounter Platonism.[10]

While these contributions are more nuanced than previous scholarship, there is still a tendency to match specific attitudes toward the body with specific groups that oversimplifies the material[11] and to rely on polemical statements as if they were straightforward descriptions.[12] Modern scholars have recapitulated the positions from the ancient debates, the majority siding with an "allegorical" reading of biblical descriptions of God, but with a few siding with the "literal" reading. Such strategies necessitate distortion of the other side, just as they did in the ancient world. On the one hand, single-minded alignment with allegorical readings becomes defensive when employed to attack any texts that do describe God's body. When Jews at times felt uncomfortable about the implications of thinking about God's body, the biblical images were not completely abandoned, but reinterpreted. On the other hand, the pro-body side must equate Judaism with a "literal" reading of the

Scriptures, the same ill-suited and pejorative label used to attack the Jews in Late Antiquity.

These issues are raised in a dramatic manner by *Shi'ur Komah,* a text that presents a limb-by-limb description of the Deity, beginning with the feet and ending with the head. It includes the astronomical sizes for each limb ("the height of his neck is 130,000,000 parasangs"), the name of each limb, and promises of considerable rewards ("if you recite this you will gain eternal life"). Gershom Scholem, a champion of oft-maligned texts, summarized it as ". . . an anthropomorphic description of the divinity, appearing as the primal man, but also as the lover of the Song of Songs together with the mystical names of his limbs."[13]

Two issues will be raised about this bewildering and fantastic text: 1) the theological contributions of this type of bodily description of God and 2) the ritual functions of the text.

Thinking about Cosmic Bodies

Instead of designating an *Urschrift,* the phrase "shi'ur komah" refers to a category of knowledge represented in a cluster of similar text titles and phrases including The Book of the Dimensions (*Sefer Ha-Komah*), the Book of the Measurement (*Sefer Ha-Shi'ur*), and even "l'etendue de mon corps" (Second Enoch, Valliant 39). Idel argues that the term is used generally for a secret dimension of Torah, mentioning another variant in the *Alphabet of R. Akiba*, "the measurement of the dimensions of the names of God."[14] These phrases refer to the same type of information (size of limbs, names of limbs) but do not point to an original wording. The pragmatic implications of these texts are expressible in manifold specific wordings.

As if to make this very point, all five versions of *Shi'ur Komah* used in Martin Cohen's recent edition explicitly identify the material in the text, often by using the device of question and answer (e.g., "I asked, teach me the measurement of our Creator . . . he said to me the shi'ur komah").[15] These statements establish the text as having whatever is necessary to qualify as "Shi'ur Komah."

Biblical stories contained tales of the Deity that included numerous limb and body references.[16] By the time of the Late Antique biblical interpretations and controversies that concern us, there was widespread disagreement as to how these older stories should be understood. This entire debate was shaped by Late Antique cosmological conceptions and then-contemporary theological issues.

Nilsson's classic statement about the shift from the earliest Greek religion to its Greco-Roman manifestations is still the best concise description of the cosmological shift. He wrote:

> The old cosmology was shattered and the universe expanded dizzily. Earth occupied the center, surrounded by the atmosphere, and around it turned the seven spheres of the heavenly bodies, that of the moon being the lowest, while the eighth and highest was the sphere of the fixed stars in which the Zodiac with its twelve signs, the path on which the heavenly bodies travelled, occupied the most important place . . . Under the influence of Platonic thought this distinction (Between sublunary and superlunary) was deepened, so that the mutable, perishable sublunary world became the inferior, even the abode of evil, while the imperishable and eternal superlunary region was the higher and divine. Since the earth was peopled by human beings, the superlunary region by gods, there appeared a gap which must be filled if the air was not to be left uninhabited. The answer was given in accordance with ancient popular belief; the air was the abode of souls and daimones, the mediators and intermediate beings between gods and men, who are active in that space.[17]

The far-off God of Late Antiquity was less likely than his biblical forerunner to manifest himself directly on earth. While the Deity no longer walked in the garden, in special circumstances some form of manifestation on earth was not only possible but demanded. How did he manifest and reveal himself on earth? On this general issue, what Nilsson writes about Greco-Roman religions is true of Judaism as well. "Epiphanies of the gods were no longer their personal appearances but manifestations of their power (1963, 107)." If someone claimed to see this god, had he truly seen the deity or just his "power"?[18] Supernatural manifestations could also be proof of the presence of angels, daimons, or spirits. Thus we are left with two issues, both of which influence *Shi'ur Komah,* first, the need to reinterpret the biblical epiphanies and second, the complexity of distinguishing between supernatural manifestations.

Against the background of this web of supernatural forces, there is no single stance, nor even two or three stances, in rabbinic literature about the possibility of humans seeing their deity. According to the heikhalot (palace) texts associated with *Shi'ur Komah,* a special cadre of individuals was able to traverse the heavens and ascend to see the deity. These trips were full of dangers and the descriptions replete with warnings. While some scholars read these prohibitions straightforwardly as proof that no one can see God,[19] Ira Chernus's more considered reading of the threats about potential bodily destruction concludes, "Since the dangers are the price one must pay for the ultimate vision of God, their existence in fact confirms that such a vision is possible."[20] *Shi'ur Komah* reflects inner tensions on this subject, heightened perhaps by the long history of redaction during which aesthetics shifted. With characteristic straightforwardness, *Shi'ur Komah* states, "I saw the King of the universe sitting upon an exalted and lofty throne."[21] The "I" of the text can still use standard tropes of God's hidden nature to describe the vision.[22] An entire vision can be reinterpreted simply by changing the identity of the power to a lower level of divinity.[23]

In *Shi'ur Komah,* the exegetical question is how to interpret the Scriptural traditions that God made himself manifest in bodily form in the expanded cosmology of Late Antiquity when there are seven heavens and not one. Read through "modern" eyes, the older throne vision could be understood as a type of throne unknown on earth, a cosmic throne, and the body that sat on it a type of body unknown on earth, a cosmic body. This is not a literal reading of Scriptures; the new divine body has little in common with the Scriptural body other than that it is a projection of humans (and in this case, men). God's giant body is described in a manner that would have shocked the biblical authors. Indeed, the very definition of a body has changed—we do not find limb by limb body descriptions in the biblical texts.

Greco-Roman religious texts are replete with descriptions of huge deities, many sounding like "incredible hulks" bursting out of their previous, much smaller clothing. Martin Nilsson cites an Orphic Hymn that describes the giant Zeus of Late Antiquity, sitting on his giant throne.

> The eyes of all mortals have but mortal pupils,
> Too weak to behold Zeus, who governs all.
> For he is enthroned in the brazen heaven
> On a throne of gold, but his feet are set upon the earth.
> And his right hand he has stretched out to the limits of Ocean,
> From all quarters.[24]

Shi'ur Komah's giant figure is by no means unique;[25] similar figures include a huge angel who reaches from heaven to earth and who on occasion is called upon to take prayers up to heaven (*B. Hag 13b*), a gigantic primal Adam who was shrunk to human size,[26] and even to a divine figure.[27]

What purpose is filled by describing God's body this way? Psychological readings of such figures are tempting, although it is open to debate whether a gigantic body is reassuring or terrifying.[28] In these bodily descriptions, God's body has been "cosmicized." Knowing about the body is now a form of cosmological knowledge, which, again, was not true in the Scriptures. In *Shi'ur Komah,* to ask "teach me the dimensions of the (divine) body" is to hope to understand the most hidden structure of both the deity and the cosmos.[29] In fact, this version of cosmological speculation shrinks previous generations of speculation (earth and one heaven) into a tiny piece or section of the new cosmology. The verse from Deut. 33:27 "and beneath his arm, the universe" is cited to prove that the universe is a mere appendage to this deity.

> The entire universe is hung on it [God's arm] like an amulet on the arm of a hero as it is stated [in Scripture]: And beneath [his] arm—the universe.[30]

In one devastating move, earlier cosmological traditions have been shrunk down to pocket-size. A tour of the body replaces the now minor-size tours of heaven and hell. God's limbs are his structure, his essence; to know this is to know how the cosmos fits together, to know the secrets of its existence. Cosmological information is qualitatively different because of its status as esoteric knowledge, a quality scholars try to capture, with only partial success, by calling it "gnosis." The efficacy of the text, the list of promises that accompany it, is in part due to this type of knowledge.

The numerical dimension of *Shi'ur Komah* constructs a "science" of cosmology. The exaggerated exactness of the numbers, preserved even in the fantastic sizes, concretizes the details of cosmology so that they are both cosmic and accessible, divine and yet knowable and usable. The numbers give an air of fixity and precision equivalent to the placement of hells and rivers in other types of cosmological speculation.

Filling up the cosmos with God's limbs and names is not that different from filling it up with other metaphorical manifestations common in Judaism and Christianity, such as qualities. Thinking by means of limbs is one mode of conceptualizing how the deity is both manifest and transcendent. This mode redefines what it is to have a body. A body can be made of the mysterious element "tarshish,"[31] be equal in size to the cosmos, and consist of a totality of powerful individual parts (limbs/names).

Ironically, as cosmologies shift, it is the texts that are most traditional, which, like *Shi'ur Komah,* attempt to exegete Scriptural descriptions of God, that appear most out of whack. God's arm, referred to throughout the Hebrew Bible, when transposed to the much larger cosmology, appears doubly ludicrous, once for its size and once due to the altered aesthetic of those who dictate that God is "beyond limbs."

Transforming Bodies: *Shi'ur Komah*'s Ritual Role

Shi'ur Komah promises the reader a stunning hodgepodge of rewards. In one version R. Ishmael states:

> He who recites this secret shall have a glowing face and an attractive body and his fear shall be cast upon his fellow men and his good name shall go (i.e. be known) among all Israel; and his dreams shall be peaceful and his Torah shall be stored up in his hand (such that) he never forgets words of the Torah for all his days. It is good for him in this world and peaceful for him in the world to come. The evil inclination shall hold no sway over him and he shall be saved from the spirits, daimons, danagers and robbers, from all wild animals, from snakes, scorpions and imps. (*Siddur Rabbah* 139–144; Cohen 1984, 53)

This is followed by yet another guarantee that "once we learned the dimensions of our Creator, it was good for us in this world and it would be good for us in the next world" (182–184).[32] A series of eight blessings is appended, which request the specific benefits listed in the previous guarantees.[33] This very self-conscious equation of knowledge of "the measurement" with securing a place in the world to come functions as an interpretive frame for the entire text. The text explicitly claims that the person who learns the text can be transformed by it. The identity of the reciter of the text, is radically altered.

The performative or transformational dimension of the text has several facets. Each of God's limbs has a name. Divine names are the essence of the rabbinic ritual language system; names of God contain the creative force by which God effects all divine transformations including the creation of the world.[34]

In *Shi'ur Komah,* the names of the limbs embody the performative force of each particular bit of the deity. God is conceived of as a collection of powerful forces (limbs), each force being captured in the name of a limb. God's power is concretized and delineated and defined in each act of naming. Every single name embodies its particular limb, this time at the level of language. Thus the reciting of the list of names is a series of minitransformational moments.[35]

The list of limbs highlights the similarities between the reciter and the deity. Both have the same basic body parts: soles of the feet, ankles, knees, thighs, shoulders, neck, face complete with mouth, eyes, tongue, and even a beard. This body is, in fact, a body as *Heikhalot Zutratey* 40b says "He is like us, as it were, but greater than everything." The similarities between the deity and the reciter cannot be avoided, but instead are reinforced. The difference between God and men is that each of God's limbs is much larger and is "named." Knowledge of the exact size of each limb and its name can overcome this difference. As each item is learned and invoked, what it is to have a human body is transformed. The body of the reciter has been identified limb by limb with an analogous but supernatural body. This body is not a confining, earthbound body.

A multitude of Late Antique texts describe similar transformations from human to superhuman using diverse strategies to minimize the identity of the human as an earthbound being and to develop identifications with supernatural beings. A. D. Nock cites a process of self-identification between officiant and deity found in the Greek Magical Papyri, where the officiant states, "Your name is mine and my name is yours, for I am your image."[36] The similarity of images invokes a similarity of identity, conceived in terms of similar names.

Third Enoch describes another mode of transformation reminiscent of our text. Enoch-Metatron narrates that he was taken up from earth by the deity. "After all these things the Holy One, blessed be He, put His hand upon me and blessed me with 5360 blessings and I was raised and enlarged to the size of the length and width of the world" (9:1–2; Odeburg, ed.). He receives a throne and a new name, "The Lesser YH," both of which attest to his "divinization." Enoch in earlier texts such as *First Enoch* was simply given a tour of the cosmos, including the heavens and the hells full of angels being punished. Here the cosmological themes are included but redone exactly as described above. His tour is more extensive and the knowledge imparted on the tour is part of the transformational process. The earlier version of Enoch's trip says little about his body. Now the process of taking his place among the supernatural powers involves not getting rid of the body but using the transformation of the body as a symbol of the other, more important transformation from human status.

This text tells us more about humans than about gods. Humans have the same components as deities; they lack only the cosmicness of the deity. This text thinks about limbs in order to transcend them. The reciter is not more fleshly, more "in the body" at the end of this text. *Shi'ur Komah* seeks transformation by means of the clever device of reinterpreting the very notion of body. The human body as we know it is not the sum total of bodily existence in the cosmos.[37]

Martin Cohen classifies *Shi'ur Komah* as an example of Jewish theurgy.[38] Popularized by E. R. Dodds's classic article, theurgy is a term apparently first coined by the Julian father-and-son team at the time of Marcus Aurelius.[39] It contrasts the "theologos," one who is a words-about-gods expert, with the "theourgos," who is a divine-action specialist. Theurgic rituals have a compulsive or magical quality about them, at least to the outside observer, and activate or influence divine forces; they bring results.

The use of the term "theurgy" for Jewish rituals is undergoing a major renaissance; it is currently used to replace the controversial term "magic,"[40] For example, the famous story about Honi the Circle-drawer, who drew a circle and stood inside it until the deity sent rain, was labeled "magic" in a 1955 article by Judah Goldin and then taken out of that category by him in a 1963 revision. The story is currently referred to as an example of theurgy.[41] The merit of the current discussions about theurgy are that they have focused closer attention on the dynamics of ritual and permit more detailed and less pejorative analysis than the sweeping term "magic."[42]

Applying the term "theurgy" to Jewish text implicates the problems that accompany its use with other Greco-Roman texts, as a review of Dodds's strategy demonstrates. Dodds, among others, hesitated to call the ritual acts of philosophers "magic," though these actions smacked of an efficacy that usually relegated such acts to that category.[43] Fixing upon the term "theurgy" permitted him to carve out a third category between magic and religion; theurgy is goal-directed behavior done to achieve distinct ritual ends, but it is not, in scholarly eyes, crude magic.[44] Dodds writes, "Whereas vulgar magic used names and formulae of religious origin to profane ends, theurgy used the procedures of vulgar magic primarily to a religious end (1951, 291)." When Dodds first introduced the term he included two narrowly defined types: 1) use of symbola or synthemata and 2) employment of an entranced "medium." Due to its precarious position between religion and "magic," the definition of theurgy has an inherent tendency to broaden dramatically. As scholars find more and more religious behaviors that look magical, but have religious aims, the term "theurgy" expands. "Theurgy" consumes all modes of religious ritual behavior, until, as a recent article states, it has the aim "to embrace God and be embraced by God."[45] What since Plato does this not include?

Another problem with the application of this very specific and yet very general use of the term theurgy to Jewish texts is highlighted by Moshe Idel's classification of types of Jewish theurgy. Idel defines theurgy as "operations intended to influence the Divinity, mostly in its own inner state of dynamics, but sometimes also in its relationship to men (1988, 157)." This definition will automatically exclude *Shi'ur Komah* because the focus is not on affecting the deity but the reciter. It is no surprise then that Idel argues that Midrashic-talmudic "augmentation"[46] differs from *Shi'ur Komah* and the other hekhalot texts as follows:

> The former [heikhalot texts] envisions an enormous, static Divinity, the knowledge and repetition of whose precise dimensions constitute a salvific gnosis—hence the implicit static feature of this theology: were the sizes to change, the importance of this knowledge would diminish. The latter literature [midrashic-talmudic] is primarily interested in a dynamic concept that stresses the changes occurring in the divine Dynamis. (1988, 158)

These two approaches conceive of distinct roles for humans: "whereas the *Shi'ur Komah* gnosis is imposed on the mystic as a revelation from above, the talmudic-midrashic tradition is primarily interested in an active attitude of man, who is portrayed as the clue to the amount of divine energy" (1988, 158).

Our analysis undercuts this distinction between static and dynamic conceptions of the deity; the deity appears to be static in *Shi'ur Komah* because the text is concerned with human transformations. The distinction emerges from his basic definition of theurgy that highlights issues of the deity's influencibility (hence static vs dynamic).

We must step back then and ask, what qualities are scholars trying to capture in using the term theurgy? The idea implied by "theurgy" is the revelation of divine power on earth. Whenever this is done, something dynamic has happened. People who were able to coordinate this process seem to become "magicians" because they become indistinguishable from the revelation of divine power they unleash. *Shi'ur Komah* results in a man with cosmic power, a holy man. Peter Brown's writings about the holy man seem particularly relevant here. He states that "in the popular imagination, the emergence of the holy man at the expense of the temple marks the end of the classical world" (1971, 102). Unlike texts that attempt to manipulate a minor supernatural power by invoking its name and giving it an order[47] or that attempt to "augment" a high power to bring about some result, *Shi'ur Komah* aims at different category of cosmic interaction. The transformation of the ritualist appears to be permanent as opposed to those transformations that attempt to gain momentary power. There would then be no need to call on an angel to complete a task. The ritual is effected without the manipulation of objects, again distinguishing it from other transformative rituals.

For humans to think about gaining divine powers, they rely on some projected analogy, making the gods in their image in some way, shape, or form. The details of these analogies (my mind is like God's, my spirit is like God's, my limbs are like God's) are as unlimited as the human imagination.

Notes

1. Translations of *Shi'ur Komah* [The Measurement of the (Divine) Dimension] are cited according to Cohen's edition (1985), including the specific text and line number. Some of the translations have been adapted slightly. Scholem believed it was among "the older possessions of Jewish Gnosticism" (1954, 66) and argued that the original version of the text was the one found in *Merkabah Rabbah* (1965, 27). Cohen has subsequently argued that the original text, which was composed in the early Gaonic period in Babylonia, is best represented by manuscript British Museum 10675, which he dated to the tenth or eleventh century (1985, 5). This text was the result of "an actual experience of mystic communion with God" (1983, 69). Schaefer examined the manuscript and believes that it is probably from a much later date and generally rejects the search for an original text (1988, 75–83).

2. *Mystische Literatur,* p. 142, cited by Cohen 1983, 15–16.

3. DK 15 and 16.

4. Paraphrased from Justin Martyr *Dialogue* chap. 112.

5. This quote is paraphrased from a recent book on Islam by Ruthven (1984, 40).

6. He writes, "Paradoxically enough we have here an attempt at anti-anthropomorphic writings, at least when compared to the simple understanding of the Song of Songs as a divine auto-portrait . . . It is possible that this work includes a polemical refutation of earlier views of Jewish mystics whose concept of God was simpler and more anthropomorphic." (1979, 15)

7. Of the many scholars who have written about anti-anthropomorphic tendencies in the Targums, David Halperin is particularly articulate on the topic and some of its problems. He writes, "When the Targum's translators relentlessly throttle back anything that might imply God has a human-like body, I suspect that they are repressing what they know to be powerful tendencies in themselves and in their hearers. Unchecked, these tendencies might burst forth into what most monotheists would regard as lunacy. And burst forth they do, in *Shi'ur Komah* and the rest of the Hekhalot. Put another way, the anthropomorphism of the Hekhalot represents the synagogue tradition's urge to make God as concrete and tangible to his worshippers as possible. The anti-anthropomorphism of the Targum's represents the tradition's effort to police its own impulses" (1988, 407). This position leads to finding contradictions between the usage of similar phrases in Targumic texts and in *Shi'ur Komah*. "The Aramaic translator of Ezekiel 1:27 had recoiled from its anthropomorphic reference to God's loin, and had therefore shrouded these parts in an impenetrable fog of euphemisms. Now comes a writer who is so under the spell of the Targum to this passage that he cannot resist imitating its language—and he uses the Targum's phraseology in the course of a limb-by-limb description of God's utterly human-like body! If the Targum so influenced him, why did its lesson, that one may not describe God in human terms, have so little impact on him?" (1988, 406).

8. For example, Klein argues concerning the substitution of "before" for the particle denoting direct object that, contra those who interpret its use as a means of avoiding anthropomorphism, "It occurs as an expression of deference to respectable person or institution. It also occurs as a natural result of the idiomatic variance between biblical Hebrew and Targumic Aramaic, or simply as the translation of a biblical phrase that was understood figuratively" (1979, xxvi). Similarly, the elaborate inclusion of Memra, the Aramaic word for "word," as the source of the deity's speech instead of the Deity—about which a great deal of ink has been spilt—incorporates an ideology of God's mode of speaking and is not an attempt to avoid a too-human portrayal of God as speaking. See Janowitz (1992).

9. For example, the rabbis frequently incorporate deixis such as "*this* is my God," which indicates that Rabbi Akiba can literally point to the Deity.

10. 1983, 353.

11. For example, the statement "No man has seen God" reflects not only gnostic sentiments but rabbinic and Christian ones also.

12. Stroumsa cites Origen's statement that Jews reject exegesis as if this were a factual description (1983, 351). According to Boyarin, it was only Hellenistic influence that caused Jews to refrain from the use of bodily images. In rebuttal, Michael Klein writes, "What is also clear is that the anti-anthropomorphic tendencies reflect an internal development within Judaism and are not the result of Hellenistic influence, which they antedate." (1972, vi) Marmorstein's discussion is illuminating on this point, though it must be read with some caution (1968; reprint of 1937).

13. 1987, 20.

14. 1981, 38.

15. R. Ishmael said to him, "How much is the measurement of the body of the Holy One which is hidden from all men?" (*Sefer Raziel* 98–99); "This is the size of the (divine) body as stated in the Book of the Dimensions." (*Sefer Hashi'ur* 1); R. Ishmael says, "What is the measure of the body of the Holy One." (*Sefer Ha-qomah 5*); "And I said to him: Teach me the dimensions of the Holy One." (*Siddur Rabbah* 55–6); "I said to the Prince of the Torah, Rabbi, teach me the measurement of our creator and he said to me the shi'ur komah" (*Merkabah Rabbah* 4–5).

16. See for example Dan. 7:9–10, I Kings 22:19, Isa. 6:1ff, Ezek. 3:22–24, 8:1ff, 10.

17. 1948, 99–100.

18. Note, for example, the frequent use of the term *kavod* (glory) by the rabbis to refer to an epiphany.

19. Scholars do this by emphasizing anti-vision stances attributed to one rabbi or found in one text.

20. 1982, 129. Given the hazards of heavenly travel portrayed in the texts, this seems a judicio statement.

21. *Merkabah Rabbah* 1–2.

22. "R. Ishmael said to him (the Angel of the Presence), How much is the measurement of the body of the Holy One, blessed be He, which is hidden from all men?" (*Sefer Raziel* 98–99).

23. When one sees a flaming figure like a man, is that the deity or just an angel? The texts seen confused or ambivalent at times. For example, Scholem notes that in *Maaseh Merkabah* paragraph 22, a figure with an angelic name and a figure with a divine name "are identical." (1965, 109)

24. Nilsson 1963, 105–6, citing *Orphicorum fragmenta*. Ed. Kern, no. 245 with F. R. Walton's translation.

25. Lieberman first drew attention to the Talmudic citation of *Shi'ur Komah* in the baraita in B. Ber 44a, which states "[The nose is optimally as long] as the little finger." (1965: 120)

26. For numerous citation on this topic see Ginzberg, *Legends of the Jews,* V:79.

27. *Sefer Heikhalot* 5.3 states, "The primal Adam looked upon the image of the shape of the splendor of the Presence, since its splendor would go from one end of the universe to the other."

28. Halperin describes the role of fantasies about a giant angel figure. "Their message, the supreme dignity and importance of the synagogue sounds very much like compensation for a reality in which the worshippers felt themselves neither dignified nor important (1988, 139, but compare p. 140)."

29. Smith writes, "One way of stating this shift is to note that the cosmos has become anthropologized. The old, imperial cosmological language that was the major mode of religious expression of the archaic temple and court cultus has been transformed . . . Rather than a sacred place, the new center and chief means of access to divinity will be a divine man, a magician, who will function, by and large, as an entrepreneur without fixed office and will be, by and large, related to 'protean deities' of relatively unfixed forms whose major characteristic is their sudden and dramatic autophanies. Rather than celebration, purification and pilgrimage, the new rituals will be those of conversion, of initiation into the secret society or identification with the divine man." (1978, 187)

30. *Merkavah Rabbah* 146–147; Cohen 1985, 69.

31. The term *tarshish* (Song of Songs 5:14) refers to some type of precious stone, possibly topaz, beryl, or marble.

32. Scholem cites *Merkavah Shelemah,* "Whoever knows the measurements of our Creator and the glory of the Holy One, praise be to him, which are hidden from the creatures, is certain of his share of the world to come (38b). Cf. b. Niddah 73a, "Whoever repeats halacha every day may rest assured that he will be a son of the world to come."

33. In *Siddur Rabbah* Akiba promises that anyone who knows the measurements of the Creator "may be secure that he has (a portion in) the world to come, and that it will be well for him in the future, and he must (recite it) in holiness and in purity on Mondays and on Thursdays and on all fast days."

34. See Janowitz 1989.

35. This same obsession with the creative power of names flourishes in even denser forms, in the letter-investigations of *Sefer Yetsira* and the "divine nonsense" of *Maaseh Merkavah.*

36. 1972, 192.

37. Contrast, for example, the idea found in *The Hypostasis of the Archons* that Adam was created based on a distorted water reflection of what divinities look like.

38. 1983, 137.

39. In addition to Dodds 1951, see Janowitz forthcoming.

40. See for example Cohen 1983, Lightstone 1984, 23, 25, 28, and Schaefer 1988, 291.

41. See for example Lightstone 1984, 25–28.

42. Contrast Schaefer's use of the term magic. He differentiates between two themes in the Hekhalot texts, the theme of heavenly journey and something he calls "adjuration," which includes revelations by a angel figure, requests for help of any sort, and liturgical compositions. The heavenly journeys are "magical" because they are associated with the "magical" adjurations; often the end of a journey results in a request for some sort of help. "In both cases [heavenly journey and adjuration] the means of achieving this is magic. The worldview which informs these texts is this one which is deeply magical. The authors of the Hekhalot literature believed in the power of magic and attempted to integrate magic into Judaism" (1988, 290).

Since these texts are by definition "magic" and the rabbis reject "magic," these texts must be rejected by the rabbis. There is no way out of this circle. Schaefer states, "The Merkabah mystic to whom the Hekhalot literature is addressed does not expect to ascend to heaven in ecstasy and makes no claim to have done so. Rather, by means of magical and theurgic practices he repeats the heavenly journey of his heroes, Moses, Ishmael and Aqiva" (1988, 294).

Except for the juxtaposition of the word "ecstasy" with "magical and theurgic," the difference between "ascending to heaven" and "repeating the heavenly journey of his heroes" is not explained.

43. Dodds wrote his article to defend Plotinus against the charge of being a theurgist, let alone a magician. He admits that Plotinus believed in the power of magic, but states, "Could any man of the third century deny it?" (1951, 285).

44. When the term theurgy is used to describe Jewish texts, it permits scholars to adopt a similar strategy; the Jews who used these texts are free from charges of being magicians and engaging in magical practices. Idel stresses that "in contrast to the magician, the ancient and medieval Jewish theurgist focused his activity on accepted religious values" (1988, 157). Since in the vast majority of uses, the pejorative "magic" is not a word of self-description, the "Jewish magician" against whom the Jewish theurgian is articulated is an extremely elusive character. We do not have a single text that called itself "Jewish magic." The *Book of Secrets* does not include the term, though Michael Morgan adds the word "magic" several places in his translation just as Cohen adds the word "magic" several places in *Shi'ur Komah*.

45. Luck 1989, 200.

46. Idel subdivides theurgy into two types, augmentation and drawing-down theurgy, and characterizes a third type of related activity as "universe-maintaining." The first type, augmentation, exhibits "a direct dependence of the power of the divine Dynamis upon human activity; the way to increase it is to fulfill the divine will, which is presumably tantamount to performing the commandments" (1988, 158).

Human activity has the potential of either adding to the Godhead or diminishing it. For example, in *Pesikta de-Rav Kahana,* R. Yehuda bar Simon in the name of R. Levi ben Parta interprets the phrase "Through God we shall act with power" (Ps. 60:14) as "in God we shall make power." The same authorities similarly rail against adultery in *Leviticus Rabbah,* "You have weakened the Rock that formed thee—you have diminished the power of the Creator." The most dramatic example he mentions is the Talmudic story of Rabbi Ishmael, described as the High Priest, blessing Akatriel YH Zevaot God: "Let your mercy conquer your anger, and your mercy overflow onto your attributes, and may you behave regarding your sons according to the attribute of mercy (*b. Ber.* 7a)."

In the second type of theurgy, drawing-down, human activity causes the divine presence to either descend from heaven or to retreat there. "This manifest correlation between human acts and the divine presence must be understood as the result of a theurgical conception of the commandments, whose performance is seen as having substantial bearing on the Divinity; the commandments not only draw it downward but also facilitate its indwelling" (1988, 167).

To find evidence of this as a ritual practice, and not just a theme of retreat and ascent as in the *Book of Enoch,* Idel turns to the Prince of the Torah adjurations. These adjurations cause an angel to appear for the purpose of receiving a revelation. As is often true of these texts, there are hints that the presence which descends is a divine "presence."

Idel's third type of activity, "universe-maintaining," includes any references to the importance of human action in maintaining the world. The Jews' acceptance of the Torah preserved the world, as do the sacrifices (170–172).

47. See, for example, *The Book of Secrets.*

References

Boyarin, Daniel

1990 "The Eye in the Torah: Ocular Desire in Midrashic Hermeneutic." *Critical Inquiry* 16.3:532–550.

1989 "Language Inscribed by History on the Bodies of Living Beings: Midrash and Martyrdom." *Representations* Winter, no. 25:139–151.

Brown, Peter
1971 *The World of Late Antiquity.* London: Thames and Hudson.

Chernus, Ira
1982 "Visions of God in Merkabah Mysticism." *Journal for the Study of Judaism* 13.1–2:123–146.

Cohen, Martin
1983 *The Shi'ur Komah: Liturgy and Theurgy in Pre-Kabbalistic Jewish Mysticism.* Lanham, MD: University Press of America.
1985 *The Shi'ur Komah: Texts and Recensions.* Tubingen: Mohr.

Dan, Joseph
1979 "The Concept of Knowledge in the *Shi'ur Komah.*" In *Studies in Jewish Religious and Intellectual History presented to Alexander Altmann on the Occasion of His Seventieth Birthday.* Eds. Stein and Lowe. University of Alabama.
1984 *Three Types of Ancient Jewish Mysticism.* Cincinnati: University of Cincinnati.

Dodds, E. R.
1951 "Theurgy and its Relationship to Neoplatonism." *The Greeks and the Irrational.* Berkeley: University of California Press 283–299.

Ginzberg, Louis
1937 *The Legends of the Jews.* Philadelphia: The Jewish Publication Society.

Goldin, Judah
1955 "The Magic of Magic and Superstition." In *Aspects of Propaganda.* Ed. E. Schussler-Fiorenza. Notre Dame: University of Notre Dame Press, 115–147.
1963 "On Honi the Circle-Maker: A Demanding Prayer." *Harvard Theological Review* 56 233–274.

Halperin, David
1988 *The Faces of the Chariot.* Tubingen: Mohr.

Idel, Moshe
1981 "The Concept of Torah in Hekhalot Literature and its Metamorphoses in Kabbalah." *Jerusalem Studies in Jewish Thought* 1:23–84 (Hebrew).
1988 *Kabbalah: New Perspectives.* New Haven: Yale University Press.

Janowitz, Naomi
1989 *The Poetics of Ascent: Theories of Language in A Rabbinic Ascent Text,* Albany, NY: State University of New York Press.
1991 "Re-creating Genesis: The Metapragmatics of Divine Speech." *Reflexive Language: Reported Speech and Metapragmatics* Ed. John Lucy. Cambridge: Cambridge University Press.
forthcoming *The Artifice of Theurgy.*

Klein, Michael
1972 *The Translation of Anthropomorphisms and Anthropopathisms in the Targumim.* Israel.
1979 "The Preposition KEDEM (before): A Pseudo-anti-anthropomorphism in the Targumim." *Journal of Theological Studies* n.s. 30.2:502–507.

Lieberman, Saul
1965 "Mishnat Shir Hashirim." In *Jewish Gnosticism Merkabah Mysticism and Talmudic Tradition* Ed. G. Scholem. 2nd ed., 118–126. New York: Jewish Theological Seminary.

Lightstone, Jack
1984 *The Commerce of the Sacred: Mediation of the Divine among Jews in the Graeco-Roman Diaspora.* Chico, California: Scholars Press.

Luck, Georg
1989 "Theurgy and Forms of Worship in Neoplatonism." In *Religion, Science, and Magic: In Concert and In Conflict,* 185–225. Oxford: Oxford University Press.

Marmorstein, A.
1968 *The Old Rabbinic Doctrine of God II. Essays in Anthropomorphism.* Reprint of 1937. New York: Ktav.

Nilsson, Martin
1948 *Greek Piety.* Oxford: Clarendon Press.
1963 "The High God and the Mediator." *Harvard Theological Review* 56.2:101–120.

Nock, A. D.
1972 "Paul and the Magus." In *Essays on Religion and the Ancient World,* 1:374–386. Oxford: Clarendon Press.

Ruthven, Malise
1984 *Islam in the World.* New York: Oxford University.

Schaefer, P.
1988 *Hekhalot-Studien* Tubingen: Mohr.

Scholem, Gershom
1954 *Major Trends in Jewish Mysticism* (reprint) New York: Schocken.
1965 *Jewish Gnosticism, Merkabah Mysticism and Talmudic Tradition.* 2nd ed. New York: Jewish Theological Seminary.
1987 *Origins of the Kabbalah* New York: Jewish Theological Seminary.

Smith, Jonathan Z.
1978 *Map is not Territory.* Leiden: Brill.

Stroumsa, Gedaliahu
1983 "The Incorporeality of God." *Religion* 13:345–358.

8

The Body Never Lies: The Body in Medieval Jewish Folk Narratives

Eli Yasif

The importance of the human body in folk creativity is not a coincidence. The body as the most concrete dimension of human life is essential to the very nature of folklore. Indeed, the most common and basic character of all folkloric creations—different from all other forms of artistic and cultural creativity, whether verbal, visual, or cognitive—is the prominence of their directness and concreteness. This special character of folkloric creativity has often been attacked as simplistic, trivial, and primitive. Such hostile attitudes emerge from the very fact that folklore rarely uses philosophical or descriptive means, concentrating on the tangible level of creativity, on narrative plot, and the transformation of feelings, anxieties, and tensions into concrete expressive modes.[1]

The explanation for this phenomenon is not, as folklorists have known for a long time, the shallowness of folk thinking, or the inability of the folk artist to create a complicated and subtle work. Rather, this character of folklore springs from the medium of communication and the audience for whom the folkloric work is intended. The medium is mainly oral and so the artistic shaping of the work, as well as its messages, have to be clear, easy to understand and remember (Utley 1965; on orality versus literacy in folklore see Gaster 1971, 1005–38; Wesselski 1925; Yassif 1987). In other words, it has to be concrete. In most cases, the folkloric work is intended for the most inclusive spectrum of society—the learned and the simple, the mature and the child (Ben-Amos 1971; Dundes 1980; Fischer 1963; Oppenheimer 1977). The concrete is the only means of communication that such a wide range of people can share: the simple will understand it literally while the learned may comprehend it as symbolic. In this way it can always transmit a message to everyone.

It is not just the centrality of the body in Jewish folklore that makes the study of Jewish folklore critical for the larger project of understanding how Jews come to terms with their bodies. In addition, folklore enables us to see how Jews who were not part of the intellectual elite thought about their bodies. The bias among those who study Jews and Judaism has been to concentrate on the writings of the learned: writers, historians, theologians, and religious virtuosi. But the views of these elite reflect only a very thin elitist crust of society. While this focus is somewhat understandable given the paucity of evidence that survives from the past, we must not forget, as sometimes seems to happen, that the views of thinkers such as Philo or Maimonides on issues such as the human body do not represent the attitudes of all Jews in the time. While thinkers such as Philo and Maimonides undoubtedly hope their ideas would become accepted by a wide range of Jews, it is doubtful this happened. For example, Maimonides' opposition to astrology and popular messianism of his own time is well known. But we know from his own writings and from much other evidence that such beliefs were very popular nonetheless (Hartman 1978–79, 1989; Marx 1926). It is significant in particular for this study that many teachers of virtue (musar)—such as Rabbi Bahye, Moshe de Leon, Maimonides, and others, strongly denounced the occupation with narrative and literary fiction as a waste of time (Dan 1974, 6–12; Leviant 1969, 55–58; Malachi 1982; Yassif 1988–89). But obviously these attitudes in no way put a stop to the creation, transmission, and copying of narratives in medieval Jewish culture.

What I am suggesting, then, is that there is a danger that the study of different Jewish attitudes to the body will reflect exclusively the attitudes of an elite layer of the learned and ignore the "mute cultur" of the Jewish Middle Ages, the culture of those who did not write *on* the body but lived it. It would of course be a mistake to claim that the religious and moral leadership were not influenced by folk customs and beliefs or that their ideas did not penetrate into folk culture.[2] Nonetheless, the observation of the division between the precepts of the elite and the culture of the folk is essential both methodologically and factually (Davis 1974; Gurevich 1988; Isambert 1977; Le-Goff 1980; Manselli 1975; Muchembled 1985).

Attitudes toward the body embedded in folktales, beliefs, customs, or rituals reflect more than the opinions or ideas of one person only. These folk creations are formed in the melting pot of society. They are created and re-created by many individuals, generation after generation, and so become an asset of society. This is exactly the meaning of folk culture: not that it is the culture of "simple people" but that it passes through the barriers of society and thus belongs to the common denominator of the many individuals included in it (Ben-Amos 1971; Dundes 1975, XIII—XXII; Jakobson and Bogatyrev 1929).

I approach the question of the human body in medieval Jewish folklore through a discussion of one of the most popular narrative works of the period: *The Alpha-Beth of Ben Sira* (ninth–tenth centuries). In this work, there appear for the first time some of the most popular themes of Jewish folklore: an account of Jeremiah who is forced to spill his semen into the waters of a public bath by the wicked sons of Ephraim, and Jeremiah's daughter who, having been miraculously impregnated from the semen, gives birth to the *wunderkind* Ben-Sira. There is the tale of Queen of Sheba, whose legs Solomon wants to reveal in order to determine if she is a woman or a demoness. When he discovers that she has very hairy legs, he invests in a depilatory cream, removes her hair, and makes her a woman. He then lies with her, and she subsequently gives birth to Nebuchadnezzar, the greatest of the Eastern kings. Also for the first time appears the story of Lilith, Adam's first wife, who refused to lie under him during the sexual act and instead insisted on being on top. In the quarrel between them, she leaves him and becomes the chief demoness (Dan 1966; Lachs 1973; Yassif 1985).

Given the open and frank attitude toward the body in these stories, it is not surprising that already in the eleventh century there was strong opposition to copying, reading, or even mentioning the *Alpha-beta*. Some religious authorities went so far as to claim that it would be considered a *mitzvah* (a blessed act) to burn this book on a Yom Kippur that falls on a Sabbath (Yassif 1980, 104–09). Rabbinical authorities considered the bluntness of this work on matters such as masturbation, intimate parts of the body, and positions during sexual intercourse to be immoral and dangerous. However, it is important to remember that the *Alpha-Beth of Ben Sira* was among the most copied of popular texts of medieval Jewish society. Over 150 copies of manuscripts from the eleventh to the seventeenth centuries are still extant (Yassif 1985, 183–90). In other words, large numbers of Jews rejected the conservative attitude of the learned and moralists on such matters and continued relating, copying, and reading the narrative traditions of the *Alpha-Beth of Ben Sira*.

Some of the narratives come into the *The Alpha-Beth of Ben Sira* via Iranian and Arabic traditions. The narrative about the impregnation in the bath is an old Iranian myth about Zoroaster the prophet, who spilled his semen in a sacred pond from which the divine virgin was impregnated and gave birth to the messiah (Lévi 1891; Yassif 1985, 30–39, 197–201). The tale of the Queen of Sheba was originally an Arabic novella on Solomon and Sheba that was very widespread in the writings of early Moslem writers (Chastel 1939; Prichard 1974; Yassif 1985, 50–59, 217–18). I emphasize these facts in order to make the point that, although these narratives were partly borrowed from international folklore, they nonetheless reflect Jewish attitudes toward the body. In the study of folklore it is not the origin that is the essential factor but its adoption by and incorporation into a given culture. Once these traditions entered Jewish folklore they were told and retold orally, were copied again and again in different versions; in other words, they were transformed so that they became a part of Jewish culture and so reflected its attitudes.

Consider the folk traditions about the immortals. The stories tell of thirteen men and one bird who did not die but entered bodily into heaven. Whereas in normative religious sources, true immortality is normally thought of as being of the spirit, these thirteen exemplary figures receive from God a concrete, physical reward. Of special interest is the story about the nonhuman figure, the *Hol* or *Milham,* the immortal bird.

This bird was the only creature that did not accept Eve's offer to eat of the forbidden fruit and thus received the gift of immortality (Pagis 1962; Yassif 1985, 92–97). This is, of course, the famous myth about the Phoenix, the eternal bird that once in a thousand years is burned with its nest and from the flames emerges as a new Phoenix to live for another thousand years (Suhr 1976; Thompson 1955–58, motif A37). We see here one of the main differences between the international and Jewish versions of this myth. In the former, the body is destroyed and resurrected in a continuous periodicity: the concept of eternity is periodical. Not so in the Jewish myth in which eternity is the survival of the body and spirit together. And it is here on this issue of the body that the folklore tradition breaks with elitist Jewish sources. A mode of existence that is not physical or that is only spiritual cannot be comprehended. The spirituality of eternity is a concept that was created and developed by scholars and theologians but was never accepted by many people who considered existence in this world and after as consisting of a body and spirit that were inextricably entangled.

When we examine the folk traditions of Jewish society in the Middle Ages, we see that they had a complicated system of attitudes toward the body. I will try to describe this complexity of attitudes and approaches in four categories. These categories are synonymous with four levels of narrative analysis: plot, content, conceptual structure, and function. They were not imposed upon the texts but emerged from a detailed analysis of the place of the body in hundreds of medieval folk narratives in manuscripts and early prints. The examples I will present are only a selection from a multitude of texts which can be shown for each one of these categories.

The narrative category: The body as the essence of the narrative conflict

In many of the folk traditions, an overt bodily act is the starting point of the narrative development—the initial conflict from which the plot emerges. The tale type about the bridegroom contest starts with a poor young scholar who loves his rich niece and wants to marry her but whose mother wants her to marry her rich but ignorant nephew. The head of the yeshiva, where the young man studies, instructs him to kiss the girl, to hug her, and then to lie beside her in bed. The couple is discovered by her parents, and so the boy has to run away from his hometown, to be condemned to wandering and danger—the main part of the narrative (Aarne-Thompson 1965: tale type 653; Bin-Gorion 1990: 389–390; Lévi 1896–7: 67–76; Thompson 1977: 81–82; Yassif 1984: 420). In another tale type, King Solomon knows from the start that his daughter will marry a poor man, so he hides her in a tower on a solitary island. This stratagem is unsuccesful. After an eagle has landed the destined husband on top of the tower, they lie together and thus commit "marriage effected by sexual intercourse" (Sadan 1973; Shamir 1991; Shenhar 1984; Urbach 1973). In another very popular tale type, "the weasel and the well" legend, a young man hears cries for help from a deep well. In return for rescuing the girl who has fallen into it, he makes her promise that she will lie with him after he pulls her out of the well (Bin-Gorion 1990: 170–172; Sadan 1957). Here, too, the exceptional bodily act that is committed outside the normative frame permitted by society is the main driving force behind the ensuing narrative. It is important to point out that, in all three narratives, what began as an anti-normative act, is transformed in the end—after the marriage—into a legitimate deed. In any case, it is clear from these traditions, and many others as well, that the sexual tension, the physical, bodily proximity that is often uncontrollable by the legal and normative regulations of society, is translated here into narrative language and becomes the impetus of a complicated narrative.

The thematic category: The body as sin and punishment

The typical frame of the religious folktale and exemplum is the double structure: sin and its punishment, religious precept and its reward. With the help of such a narrative structure, society attempts to propagate and deepen its system of laws and norms of behavior, to threaten by punishment, to seduce through rewards (Aarne-Thompson 1965: 254–284 [religious tale types]; Bremond-Le-Goff-Schmitt 1982). However, the folk traditions do not do this by means of philosophy or rhetoric but with the concrete tools of the narrative plot. The listeners can actually see how these prohibitions and precepts act in real life, in concepts understood and known to them from everyday reality. Thus, most of the sins in the religious exempla are bodily sins and punishments are of the body.

One of the best known traditions in Jewish society of the Middle Ages is the legend about Rabbi Akiba and the wandering dead. In a dark forest, Rabbi Akiba meets a Jew who was punished after his death by eternal wandering and hard labor. The Jew tells the rabbi that these severe punishments would be eased if his son learned to recite the kaddish for him. Rabbi Akiba accordingly finds the dead man's home and teaches the prayer to his son. The dead man appears in a dream and tells the rabbi that he has been saved. The different versions of the story enumerate different sins: avarice, usury, but mainly sexual sins: he had intercourse with a betrothed woman, he was the father of bastards, he committed homosexual acts, and so on. The punishment is always physical: eternal wandering; carrying heavy loads; or gathering wood all day and burning himself every night with it (Lerner 1988).

In another popular story, Rabbi Meir, a young talmudic scholar, is a guest in a house of a certain cook. When the cook has to leave home, his young wife gives Rabbi Meir wine and, on his falling asleep, lies with him. In the morning when the scholar is amazed that she approaches him with too much intimacy, she proves to him by hidden signs on his body that they had been together at night. He turns to his rabbi and asks for atonement. The rabbi orders him to be tied to a tree in the forest and be left for three days, whether he lives or dies. A lion approaches him every day, and on the last one hits the young scholar with its paw, and this causes the man to limp to the end of his life (Bin-Gorion 1990: 145–148).

This category of the function of the body appears in dozens of other stories as well. The theme that most typically underlies the religious folktale is the 'measure-for-measure'—a devise which forms a balance and emphasizes the correspondence between sin and punishment. This balance is the strongest proof provided to society that the calamity which hits the hero is the outcome of a specific sin—the final proof of the control of God over this world (Scholem 1989: 176–183; Urbach 1969: 386–387). This is why, in all the stories belonging to this category, punishments of the body were chosen for bodily sin.[3] We should emphasize here that the punishment in these stories was not the sending of the sinner to hell or depriving him of heaven, but the imposition of concrete bodily suffering: hard labor, burning of the body, disablement. The punishments are ostensible and concrete, because only in this way could they fulfill their function.

A second observation we should make here is that the heroes of these stories never took *upon themselves* the task of their own punishments. They were punished by the rabbi, or by God. This observation is further proof of what we already know about the Jewish rejection of ascetism and of deliberate injury committed to one's own body, either as punishment or as purification (Guttmann 1964; Fraade 1988; Urbach 1988: 437–458).

The structural category: The opposition of body and spirit

It is a well-known fact that the contrast between spirit and body in Judaism does not have the central place it occupies in Hellenistic or Christian cultures. Jewish rituals and beliefs are directed toward the creation of unity between them, and they are considered as a single entity created "in the image of God" (Altman 1968; Marmorstein 1950: 145–161). This is what makes it much more interesting to investigate the relationships between body and spirit in the realm of Jewish folk culture.

The biographical legends about Rashi cannot be a reliable source for his real life's story. Rather than adding any new knowledge about him, these legends, which circulated many years after his death are designed, in fact, to reflect attitudes and beliefs of the Jewish society of the times in which they were created (Berger 1958; Yassif [1992]). One of the most popular of these is the birth legend of Rashi. As a true folktale, it appears in many versions. In one of them, Rashi's father is depicted as a rich merchant of precious stones. When a very special diamond is stolen from the cross in the central church in the capital, messengers find a stone as precious as the original in his possession. In order not to assist the Christians in their ritual, he throws the diamond into the water and so willingly loses his most precious material possession. However, a heavenly voice tells him that a son will be born to him who will enlighten the eyes of all Israel with his wisdom (Bin-Gorion 1990: 302–303; Ginzberg 1960: 239–240; Ibn-Yahya 1866: "Rashi"). At the outset, it is possible to interpret this story as the relinquishing of physical possessions for spiritual values—that is, the Jewish prohibition of dealing in Christian ritual artifacts. However, it has to be emphasized that Rashi's father receives a very physical reward—a celebrated and famous son. Thus, even in a story where the contrast of body and spirit is prominent, the victory of spirit is not complete but has to be balanced by the physical, corporal, element.

Another, later version of the same story, reinforces this conclusion. In this version, Rashi's father is a very poor man and serves as the beadle of the local synagogue. Every day he gets on his knees and wipes the floor in front of the ark with his beard, saying that others honor the Torah with their money but he does so with his body. As a reward, Elijah appears before him and tells him that a wonderful son is going to be born to him—one who will open the Torah for all Israel (Razahbi 1940). As in the first version, the contrast of body and spirit is emphasized here as well: Rashi's father bends his *body* before the *spirit*—the Torah. However, this story has another interesting version; there is evidence that Rashi and his colleagues, while students at the yeshiva in Worms, used to relate anecdotes about their celebrated and eccentric teacher, Rabbi Yaakov ben Yakar. This type of folklore is widespread on every campus, and in folkloric scholarship is called "academia folklore" (Toelken 1986). One of the stories told about Rabbi Yaakov is that he used to appear barefooted in public and also wiped the floor in front of the holy ark with his beard (Grossman 1988: 233–249; Sepher Hassidim 1924: 245). We can assume that something very common in folklore happened here: the transmission of a folk tradition from one figure to another, from the unknown person to the famous one. As Rashi himself used to tell this anecdote, among others, about his beloved teacher, the next generation, to whom Rabbi Yaakov ben-Yakar meant nothing, transposed the tale to Rashi himself. However, what is interesting for us here is the fact that, in the anecdote, Rabbi Yaakov does not receive any reward at all. His reward is the deed itself. As this "learned" anecdote was accepted as a folk tradition and crystalized in successive generations by Jewish society, it clearly underwent many changes. The important one for us here is that in the folk legend, Rashi's father, unlike Rabbi Yaakov, receives a concrete reward; Rashi's father humiliates himself before the Torah, but his son will raise his social status a hundred times more.

We have now learned that, although medieval folk traditions present the contrast between body and spirit, the superiority of spirit over body is never total. The true reward, according to popular culture, should have physical implications. In the opening conflict of the narrative, the stories emphasize the clash between spirit and body in the hero's conscience. And though his preference is for the spirit, the final phase of these narratives prove that, in the eyes of society, victory of spirit can never be complete without the framework, the concrete basis, of the body.

The function category: The body as protest

In the eleventh-century family chronicle *The Scroll of Ahimaaz,* the founder of the family, Rabbi Shefatia, is the hero of a whole cycle of legends. He is the leader of the Jewish community, head of the yeshiva, a poet, and a mystic. The legends relate his great deeds as political leader, as magician who rescues his community, and his leadership in Torah. One story in this cycle, however, stands out: the tale of the marriage of his daughter, Kassia. There are many who desire to marry Kassia, but her mother refuses them all because she wants someone like her father: great in riches, in Torah, and possessing social status. One night, at midnight, when Rabbi Shefatia rises, as usual, to pray and study, his daughter also rises to help him wash his hands. She is wearing only a light nightgown. Rabbi Shefatia suddenly sees that "her pomegranates have budded and her time of love has come." Immediately after completing his prayers, he wakes his wife, shouting, "Why have you prevented our daughter from marrying when her time has come?" The next day, he gives her to his brother's son (Klar 1974: 26–27; Salzman 1924).

In this story, the contrast between body and spirit is ostensible as well: the father rises to busy himself with Torah and clashes with a bodily, erotic phenomenon. However, it is not merely a contrast between body and spirit that is presented here but between the spiritual existence of the father and the physical, sensuous life of his daughter. The rabbi-leader who is occupied all his days in community affairs and the study of Torah is blind to the human drama developing in his own house. In this story the body does not stand merely as a contrast to the spirit but as an element of protest against it. The body here functions as a means by which the blindness of the great leader is presented, and with it, the blindness of the world of Torah to the bodily needs of the members of the Jewish community.

And a further example: among the most important folk traditions of the Middle Ages are the Dybbuk (possession) stories, both in Jewish and Christian traditions (Crapanzano and Garrison 1977; Erickson 1977; Nigal 1983; Oesterreich 1930; Zaretsky and Shambaugh 1979). Let me refer to only one example—that of Rabbi Hayyim Vital, Luria's disciple in Safed of the sixteenth century. A dead man's spirit, which has penetrated a woman's body, tells the exorcist, Rabbi Hayyim Vital, about the sins it has committed; and they are mainly sexual. However, it is the sins of the woman possessed that are interesting:

> Who gave you permission, asked the rabbi, to enter this woman's body? And the spirit replied: I stayed in her house one night, and in the morning I watched her rise up and wishing to strike a light from the flint and steel. But the sparks would not catch on the tinder. Then she grew angry and flung the flint and steel to the ground and in her rage said: Devil take it! and because she mentioned the devil I had permission to enter into her . . . Now was it because of this sin, asked the rabbi, that they permitted you to enter her body? To which the spirit answered: this woman is a hypocrite and does not believe in the exodus from Egypt at all. On Passover Eve when all Israel rejoices and utters praises and tells of the exodus from Egypt, she regards it as nonsense and a mockery and a joke, and thinks to herself that this miracle will never happen. The Rabbi at once asked the woman: Do you fully believe that the Holy and Blessed One created heaven and earth . . . etc . . . Yes she said, I believe it all (Bin-Gorion 1990: 325; Nigal 1983: 67–70).

The woman had transgressed and was skeptical about basic beliefs of Judaism, and so was punished. Only the full acceptance of Jewish values enabled her release from the spirit. Possession is a typical psychosomatic symptom. It causes alterations in the physiological state that emerge from psychotic conditions. It should be clear that the possessed are using their *bodies* in order to express extreme spiritual attitudes. What the possessed woman actually said, through the spirit, is that she entered into an antisocial and religious position which made her deny the basic beliefs of her own society. This *psychotic* development was transformed to a *somatic* reaction—alterations in the regular functions of the body (Bilu 1979, 1983; Bourguignon 1976; Lewis 1966; Prince 1968).

In this tale the dybbuk is the development of a state in which the woman can have control over her life and destiny. In medieval traditional society, where she is almost totally under the domination of father or husband, she has almost no control over her own life. The entrance into this hysterical state enables her to have *some* control over her decisions and deeds.[3] Anski's famous play, "Between the Two Worlds," (or "The Dybbuk"), based on East European folklore, attests to the same phenomenon. The spirit of the young man whom the girl could not marry possessed her. As the young woman could not control her life and choose the man she loved in the real world, the entrance into an hysterical state enabled her to achieve her will outside the framework of society and reality (Ansky 1974).

The last example of the fourth category, the body as protest, is chosen from another genre of medieval narrative: the heroic jest. This is a tale about Joab, David's army leader, who had tried for six months to conquer a walled city. In the narrative he ordered his soldiers to shoot him into the city over the high walls, where he intends to fight the enemy from the inside until blood flows under the city's gates, when his army will join him. When he falls into the courtyard of a poor family, his mighty sword breaks into pieces and he faints. The pregnant woman living there helps him and feeds him. He then goes out and asks a blacksmith to produce another sword for him. This he tests on the blacksmith, cutting his body in two. He then kills hundreds of people in the streets, until his hand sticks to the sword. He returns to the house where he has been sheltered, where the pregnant woman realizes that he is the murderer. So he stabs her in the belly, inserts his hand into it, and the hot blood frees his hand from the sword. He continues to fight until the blood flows under the gates. He then climbs the tower and calls to his army from there (Ginzberg 1913: vol. 4, 98–101; Yassif 1979).

An analysis of this cruel and strange story proves that it is built out of a series of conditions (or quests) in the first part of the story and their fulfilment in the second part: the test of Joab's army, which is fulfilled in the end; the blood that had to flow under the gates; the separation of Joab from his army when he is shot over the walls; and the renewal of his contact with the army in the same way. The narrative pattern that was posed in the first part of the story was fulfilled in the second part. The only two episodes that do not fit into this pattern of condition-and-fulfilment are those of the blacksmith and the pregnant woman. These are the only episodes in which the hero meets the human face of the enemy, not its war machine. In both, he is contrasted with simple, common people, not warriors or nobility, and in both, these are the only people who help him to fulfill his mission. In both episodes, their reward is cruel murder in cold blood by penetrating aggressively *into their bodies*. A close reading of the story has to take into account that the identification of the listeners (or readers) of the story cannot be with the cruel warrior, Joab. He represents here the figure of the medieval knight, who brutally uses simple folk for his goals. The identification is with the poor woman and blacksmith who are trampled by the aggressive system of the knightly order. To these same simple folk who were run down by the warriors (the crusaders, for example), the Jews also belonged.

It is possible to say that, in this example as well, the body is used as a means of expressing the protest, the outcry exemplified in the story. Through the manipulation of a biblical hero, the protest of a whole class, of a whole people, is revealed here.

The four categories we have examined represent four functions that the body fulfills in Jewish folklore of the Middle Ages. In all four, the body stands in conflict with other elements acting in the story: with social norms or religious precepts, with personal or national injustices, or with the spiritual concept of life. Students of folk narrative acknowledged a long time ago that the basis of the narrative plot is the conflict between individuals, moral values, classes, or nations (Dundes 1976; Lévi-Strauss 1963; Olrik 1965). The attempt to reveal this initial conflict proves to be the best means to get to the deep meaning of the story or its social function. This is what I have tried to do through these categories: to expose the conflicts that serve as the basic structure of narratives concerned with the body.

The picture revealed by these series of conflicts and opposing elements is that the body is used by the society which created and transmitted the stories as a means of exposing attitudes toward the main categories of life: the surrounding gentile world, the boundaries of Judaism, the social structure, and especially the concept of *spirituality* that dominated Jewish history. All these tales present an attitude toward the body that is different from the Jewish learned elite and from Christian culture. We do not find in Jewish medieval folklore any stories about miracles happening to the body: physiological alterations such as metamorphoses, decomposition of the body into its parts, with every part performing miracles; special odors or liquids of the dead body; the stigmata; or other motifs such as those that inundate the Christian folklore of the Middle Ages.

On the other hand, we can discern a certain suspicion toward the concept of spirituality in Judaism. Folk traditions were never satisfied with the spiritual categories. The attitude toward the body was never expressed directly. It was not the *theme* of the stories or their main subject. It was expressed indirectly, as serving secondary, narrative goals. The stories can be considered therefore as unintended evidence of the attitude toward the body that is much more reliable than any direct, intended expression about it. These traditions enable us to get to the real meaning of the body in the Jewish society of the times, not to what some moralists would like it to be. Jewish society of the Middle Ages—in the largest meaning of this term—considered the body as a vehicle to express reactions to the conflicts and tensions of its life. This is the element that endows meaning to the everyday conflicts of reality. The body is not an entity superfluous to the spiritual life of Jewish society, as some of the medieval thinkers would have liked us to believe; it is a central means *through* which the individual and the social truths of Jewish life are exposed. It might be said by a pun on a Hebrew proverb about the integrity of the spirit that in the eyes of the folk, for all that, *the body will never lie*—the spirit might do so, in many cases.

Notes

*A shorter version of this paper was read in a conference on "People of the Body/People of the Book," held at Stanford and Berkeley, April 1991.

1. The concrete character of folklore was accepted as a premise since the beginning of the study of folklore in the nineteenth century, although it was obscured by the other major debates that dominated the field, as the savage, the search for origins, nationalism, et. al. See for example Cocchiara 1981. Discussion of this element from different points of view see: Dundes 1965:1–3; Jakobson and Bogatyrev 1929; Lüthi 1982: 11–23, 1984: 1–75; Propp 1984: 16–38; Utley 1965.

2. On the clash between the legal, rabbinic institutions and folk religion and culture in Judaism see for example: Horowitz 1989; Lauterbach 1925; Lauterbach 1935.

3. A similar interpretation has been suggested to another feminine behavior in the Middle Ages, that of fasting-to-death. See: Bell 1985; Bynum 1987.

References

Aarne A. and S. Thompson
1961 *The Types of the Folktale. A Classification and Bibliography.* Helsinki: Academia Scientiarum Fennica.

Altman, A.
1968 "Homo Imago Dei in Jewish and Christian Theology." *The Journal of Religion* 48:235–259.

Anski, S.
1974 *The Dybbuk (Between Two Worlds).* Trans. from the Yiddish by S. Morris Engel. Los Angeles: Nash Pub.

Bell, R. M.
1985 *Holy Anorexia.* Chicago: University of Chicago Press.

Ben-Amos, D.
1971 "Toward a Definition of Folklore in Context." *Journal of American Folklore* 84:3–15.

Berger, I.
1958 "Rashi in the Folk-Legend." In *Rashi—His Work and Personality.* Ed. S. Federbush, 147–179. Jerusalem: Mossad Harav Kook (Hebrew).

Bilu, Y.
1979 "Demonic Explanations of Illness Among Moroccan Jews." *Culture, Medicine and Psychiatry* 3:363–380.
1983 "The Dybbuk in Judaism: Mental disorder as cultural resource." *Jerusalem Studies in Jewish Thought* 2:529–563 (Hebrew).

Bin-Gorion, M. J.
1990 *Mimekor Yisrael, Classical Jewish Folktales.* Abridged and Annotated Edition. Trans. from the Hebrew by I. M. Lask. Prepared with Introduction and Headnotes by Dan Ben-Amos. Bloomington and Indianapolis: Indiana University Press.

Bourguignon, E. (ed.)
1973 *Religion, Altered States of Consciousness and Social Change.* Columbus: Ohio State University.

Bremond, C., J. Le-Goff and J. C. Schmitt.
1982 L'Exemplum. Typologie des sources du Moyen Age Occidental, No. 40. Turnhout: Brepols.

Bynum, C. W.
1987 *Holy Feast and Holy Fast.* Berkeley: University of California Press.

Chastel, A.
1939–40 "La légende de la Reine de Saba." *Revue de l'Histoire de Religions.* 119:204–225, 120:27–44, 160–174.

Cocchiara, G.
1981 *The History of Folklore in Europe*. Trans. from the Italian by John N. McDaniel. Philadelphia: Institute for the Study of Human Issues.

Crapanzano, V. and V. Garrison., eds.
1977 *Case Studies in Spirit Possession*. New York: J. Wiley.

Dan, Y.
1966 "The Riddle of the Alpha Beth of Ben-Sira." *Molad* 23:490–496 (Hebrew).
1974 *The Hebrew Story in the Middle-Ages*. Jerusalem: Keter (Hebrew).

Davis, N. Z.
1974 "Some Tasks and Themes in the Study of Popular Religion." In *The Pursuit of Holiness in Late Medieval and Renaissance Religion*. Ed. C. Trinkaus 307–338. Leiden: Brill.

Dundes, A.
1965 *The Study of Folklore*. Englewood Cliffs: Prentice Hall.
1975 *Urban Folklore from the Paperwork Empire*. Austin: American Folklore Society.
1976 "Structuralism and Folklore." *Studia Fenica* 20:75–93.
1980 "Who are the 'Folk'?" In *Alan Dundes, Interpreting Folklore*, 1–19. Bloomington and Indianapolis: Indiana University Press.

Erickson, G.
1977 "The Enigmatic Metamorphosis: From Divine Possession to Demonic Possession." *Journal of Popular Culture* 11:656–681.

Fischer, J. L.
1963 "The Sociopsychological Analysis of Folktales." *Current Anthropology* 4:235–295.

Fraade, S. D.
1988 "Ascetical Aspects of Ancient Judaism," 253–288. In *Jewish Spirituality*. Edited by Arthur Green. New York: Crossroad.

Gaster, M.
1971 *Studies and Texts in Folklore, Magic, etc*. New York: Ktav.

Ginzberg, L.
1913 *The Legends of the Jews*. Philadelphia: Jewish Publication Society of America.
1960 *On Jewish Law and Lore*. Tel-Aviv: Dvir (Hebrew).

Grossman, A.
1988 *The Early Sages of Ashkenaz*. Jerusalem: The Magnes Press.

Gurevich, A.
1988 *Medieval Popular Culture: Problems of Belief and Perception*. Cambridge: Cambridge University Press.

Guttman, J.
1964 *Philosophies of Judaism*. London: Routledge.

Hartman, D.
1978–79 "Maimonides' Approach to Messianism and its Contemporary Implication." *Daat* 2–3:5–33 (Hebrew).
1989 *Crisis and Leadership: Epistles of Maimonides*. Tel-Aviv: Hakibbutz Hameuchad (Hebrew).

Horowitz, E.
1989 "The Eve of the Circumcision: A Chapter in the History of Jewish Nightlife." *Journal of Social History* 23:45–69.

Ibn Yahya, G.
1866 *Shalshelet Ha-Kabbala (The Chain of Tradition)*. Lemberg: Druck und Verlag von B. L. Necheles (Hebrew).

Isambert, F. A.
1977 "Religion populaire, sociology, histoire et folklore." *Archives des Sciences Sociales des Religion* 43:161–184.

Jakobson R. and P. Bogatyrev.
1929 "Die Folklore als eine besondere Form des Schaffens." In *Donum Natalicum Schrijnen,* 900–913. Nijmegen-Utrecht.

Klar, B., ed.
1974 *Megillat Ahimaaz (The Chronicle of Ahimaaz)*. Jerusalem: Tarshsish (Hebrew).

Lachs, S. T.
1973 "The Alphabet of Ben-Sira: A Study in Folk-Literature." *Gratz College Annual of Jewish Studies* 2:9–28.

Lauterbach, J.
1925 "The Ceremony of Breaking a Glass at Wedding." *Hebrew Union College Annual* 2:351–380.
1935 "The Ritual for the Kapparot Ceremony." In *Jewish Studies in Memory of George A. Kohut,* 413–422. New York: Kohut Memorial Foundation.

Le Goff, J.
1980 *Time, Work and Culture in the Middle Ages*. Chicago and London: University of Chicago Press.

Lerner, M. B.
1988 "The Story of the Tana and the Dead." *Assuppot* 2:29–70 (Hebrew).

Lévi, I.
1891 "La Nativité de Ben Sira." *Revue des Etudes Juives* 23:197–205.
1896–97 "Un recueil de contes juifs inédits." *Revue des Etudes Juives* 33:47–63, 233–254; 35:65–83.

Leviant, C.
1969 *King Artus. A Hebrew Arthurian Romance of 1279.* New York: Ktav Publishing House.

Lévi-Strauss, C.
1963 *Structural Anthropology.* New York: Basic Books.

Lewis, I.
1966 "Spirit Possession and Deprivation Cults." *Man* 1:307–329.

Lüthi, M.
1982 *The European Folktale: Form and Nature.* Trans. from the German by John D. Niles. Philadelphia: Institute for the Study of Human Issues.
1984 *The Fairytale as Art Form and Portrait of Man.* Trans. from the German by Jon Erickson. Bloomington: Indiana University Press.

Malachi, Z., ed.
1982 *The Loving Knight. The Romance Amadis De Gaula and its Hebrew Adaptation.* Lod: The Habermann Institute for Literary Research.

Manselli, R.
1975 *La Religion populaire au moyen age. Problemes de méthode et d'hitoire.* Montréal: Institute d'études médiévales.

Marmorstein, A.
1950 *Studies in Jewish Theology.* Oxford: Oxford University Press.

Marx, A.
1926 "The Correspondence between the Rabbis of Southern France and Maimonides about Astrology." *Hebrew Union College Annual* 3:311–358.

Muchembled, R.
1985 *Popular Culture and Elite Culture in France 1400–1750,* Trans. Lydia Cochrane. Baton Rouge: Louisiana State University.

Nigal, G.
1983 *Dybbuk Tales in Jewish Literature.* Jerusalem: Rubin Mass (Hebrew).

Oesterreich, T. K.
1930 *Possession, Demoniacal and other among primitive races in antiquity, the Middle Ages and Modern Times.* Trans. D. Ibberson. New York: Kegan Paul.

Oppenheimer, A.
1977 *The 'Am ha-Aretz'. A Study in the Social History of the Jewish People in the Hellenistic-Roman Period.* Leiden: Brill.

Olrik, A.
1965 "Epic Laws of Folk Narrative." In *Dundes* 1965: 129–141.

Pagis, D.
1962 "The Eternal Bird. The Phoenix Motif in Midrash and Haggadah." In *Sepher Hyovel La Gimnasia Ha-Ivrit,* 74–90. Jerusalem: Ha-Gimnasia Ha-Ivrit (Hebrew).

Prince, R., ed.
1968 *Trance and Possession States.* Montreal: R. M. Bucke Society.

Pritchard, J. B., ed.
1974 *Solomon and Sheba.* London: Phaidon.

Propp, V.
1984 *Theory and History of Folklore.* Trans. Ariadna Y. Martin and Richard P. Martin. Ed. Anatoly Liberman. Minneapolis: University of Minnesota Press.

Razahbi, Y.
1940 "The Birth of Rashi in the Yemenite Legend." *Bamishor* 1:27–28 (Hebrew).

Sadan, D.
1957–58 "The Legend of the Weasel and the Well." *Molad* 15:367–381, 467–476 (Hebrew).
1973 "The Way of the Eagle in the Sky." *Hauniversita* 18:88–91 (Hebrew).

Salzman, M., trans.
1924 *The Chronicle of Ahimaaz.* New York: Columbia University Press.

Scholem, G.
1989 *Explications and Implications. Writings on Jewish Heritage and Renaissance.* Tel-Aviv: Am Oved (Hebrew).

Sepher Hassidim.
1924 *Sepher Hassidim according to the Parma Ms.* Ed. J. Wistinetzki and J. Freimann. Frankfurt a.M.: M. A. Wahrmann Verlag.

Shamir, Z.
1991 *Love Unveiled . . . The Legend of Three and Four.* Tel Aviv: Dvir.

Shenhar, A.
1984 *Kokha Shel Tashtit,* 15–32 Tel-Aviv: Eked. (Hebrew).

Suhr, E. G.
1976 "The Phoenix." *Folklore* 87:29–37.

Thompson, S.
1955–58 *Motif Index of Folk-Literature.* Bloomington: Indiana University Press.
1977 *The Folktale.* Berkeley and Los Angeles: University of California Press.

Toelken, B.
1986 "The Folklore of the Academe." In *The Study of American Folklore*. Ed. Jan H. Brunvand, 502–528. New York and London: Norton.

Urbach, E. E.
1969 *The Sages: Their Concepts and Beliefs*. Jerusalem: The Magnes Press (Hebrew).
1973 "The Legend of the Three and Four." *Hauniversita* 18:58–71 (Hebrew).
1988 *The World of the Sages. Collected Studies*. Jerusalem: The Magnes Press (Hebrew).

Utley, F. L.
1965 "Folk-Literature: An Operational Definition." In *Dundes* 1965:7–24.

Wesselski, A.
1925 *Märchen des Mittelalters*. Berlin: Herbert Stubenrauch.

Yassif, E.
1979 "The Tale of Joab's Heroism: The Jewish Heroic Story in the Middle-Ages." *Yeda-Am* 19:17–27 (Hebrew).
1980 " 'Toldot Ben Sira': The Interpretation and Ideological Background of a Medieval Work." *Eshel Beer-Sheva* 2:97–118 (Hebrew).
1984 " 'Sepher ha-Maasim'. The Character, Origins and Influence of a Collection of Folktales from the time of the Tosaphists." *Tarbiz* 53:409–429 (Hebrew).
1985 *The Tales of Ben Sira in the Middle-Ages: Critical Edition and Literary Studies*. Jerusalem: The Magnes Press (Hebrew).
1987 "What is a Folk-Book?" *International Folklore Review* 5:20–27.
1988–89 " 'Leisure' and 'Generosity': Theory and Practice in the Creation of Hebrew Narratives in the Late Middle-Ages." *Kiriat Sepher* 62:887–905 (Hebrew).
1992 (in press) *Rashi Legends and Jewish Popular Culture in the Middle Ages*. Proceedings of the Rashi conference in Troyes, 1991.

Zaretsky I. and C. Shambough.
1979 *Spirit Possession and Spirit Mediumship in Africa and Afro-America: An Annotated Bibliography*. New York: Garland.

9

The Jewish Body: A Foot-note

Sander L. Gilman

The construction of the Jewish body in the West is absolutely linked to the underlying ideology of anti-Semitism, to the view that the Jew is inherently different. But different from what? We must fill in the blank. The difference of the Jewish body is absolute within the Western tradition; its counterimage (from the comments of Paul, Eusibius, and Origen on the "meaning" of circumcision) is the "Christian" body that eventually becomes secularized into the "German" or "English" body with the rise of the modern body politic. Thus it is of little surprise that the image of the Jewish body shifts from the rhetoric of religious anti-Judaism to the rhetoric of the pseudoscience of anti-Semitism. By the nineteenth century, with the establishment of the absolute hegemony of "science" within European (and colonial) culture, there is no space more highly impacted with the sense of difference about the body of the Jew than the public sphere of "medicine." No aspect of the representation of the Jewish body in that sphere, whether fabled or real, is free from the taint of the claim of the special nature of the Jewish body as a sign of the inherent difference of the Jew.*

The very analysis of the nature of the Jewish body, in the broader culture or within the culture of medicine, has always been linked to establishing the absolute difference (and dangerousness) of the Jew. This scientific vision of parallel and unequal "races" is part of the polygenetic argument about the definition of "race" within the scientific culture of the eighteenth century. In the nineteenth century it is more strongly linked to the idea that some "races" are inherently weaker, "degenerate," more at risk for certain types of disease than others. In the world of nineteenth-century medicine, this difference becomes labeled as the "pathological" or "pathogenic" qualities of the Jewish body. What this paper will examine is a "footnote" to the general representation of the pathophysiology of the Jew: the meaning attributed to the Jewish foot in the general and medical culture of the late nineteenth century.

The idea that the Jew's foot is unique has analogies with the hidden sign of difference attributed to the cloven-footed devil of the Middle Ages (Trachtenberg 1943). That the shape of the foot, hidden within the shoe (a sign of the primitive and corrupt masked by the cloak of civilization and higher culture), could reveal the difference of the devil was assumed in early modern European culture. By the nineteenth century the relationship between the image of the Jew and that of the hidden devil is to be found not in a religious but in a secularized scientific context. It still revolves in part about the particular nature of the Jew's foot—no longer the foot of the devil but now the pathogonomic foot of the "bad" citizen of the new national state. The political significance of the Jew's foot within the world of nineteenth-century European medicine is thus closely related to the idea of the "foot"-soldier, of the popular militia, that was the hallmark of all of the liberal movements of the mid-century. The Jew's foot marked *him* (and the Jew in this discussion is almost always the male) as congenitally unable and, therefore, unworthy of being completely integrated into the social fabric of the modern state. (That the Jewish woman had a special place in the debate about the nature of the Jewish body is without a doubt true, but it was not in regard to her role as a member of the body politic. In the context of nineteenth-century science, it was assumed that she could not function in this manner [Lazarus 1891, iii–vi].

As early as 1804, in Joseph Rohrer's study of the Jews in the Austrian monarchy, the weak constitution of the Jew and its public sign, "weak feet," were cited as "the reason that the majority of Jews called into military service were released, because the majority of Jewish soldiers spent more time in the military hospitals than in military service" (Rohrer 1804, 25–26). This link of the weak feet of the Jews and their inability to be full citizens (at a time when citizenship was being extended piecemeal to the Jews) was for Rohrer merely one further sign of the inherent, intrinsic difference of the Jews. (Berkley 1988; McCagg 1988; Oxall et al. 1987; Pulzer 1988; Witrich 1988) What is of interest is how this theme of the weakness of the Jews' feet (in the form of flat feet or impaired gait) becomes part of the necessary discourse about Jewish difference in the latter half of the nineteenth century.

There is an ongoing debate throughout late nineteenth century and well into the twentieth century that continues the basic theme which Rohrer raised in 1804. The liberal novelist and journalist

Theodor Fontane felt constrained to comment in 1870 on the false accusation that Jews were "unfitted" for war in his observations about the role that Jewish soldiers played in the Austro-Italian war of 1866 (which led to the creation of the dual monarchy and the "liberal" Austrian constitution). His example is a telling measure of the power of the legend of the Jewish foot: "Three Jews had been drafted as part of the reserves into the first battalion of the Prince's Own Regiment. One, no longer young and corpulent, suffered horribly. His feet were open sores. And yet he fought in the burning sun from the beginning to the end of the battle of Gitschin. He could not be persuaded to go into hospital before the battle" (Fontane 1870, 413). For Fontane, the Jewish foot serves as a sign of the suffering that the Jew must overcome to become a good citizen.

In 1867 Austria institutionalized the ability of the Jews to serve in the armed services as one of the basic rights of the new "liberal" constitution. This became not only one of the general goals of the Jews but also one of their must essential signs of acculturation. But, as in many other arenas of public service, being "Jewish" (here, espousing the Jewish religion) served as a barrier to status. Steven Beller points out that at least in Austria, there was "in the army evidence [that there was] a definite link between conversion and promotion." (Beller 1989, 189). Indeed, one of the legends which grew up about the young, "liberal" monarch Franz Joseph in the 1850s was that he promoted a highly decorated corporal from the ranks when he discovered that he had not been promoted because of the fact that he was a Jew, with the remark: "In the Austrian army there are no Jews, only soldiers, and a soldier who deserves it becomes an officer" (Grunwald 1936, 408). Evidently it was difficult but not impossible to achieve the rank of officer. And the Jews wanted to be officers. Theodor Fontane observed that "it seemed as if the Jews had promised themselves to make an end of their old notions about their dislike for war and inability to engage in it" (Grunwald 1936, 177). The status associated with the role of the Jew as soldier was paralleled by the increasingly intense anti-Semitic critique of the Jewish body as inherently unfit for military service. This critique became more and more important as the barriers of Jewish entry into the armed services in Germany and Austria were lessened in the closing decades of the nineteenth century. What had been an objection based on the Jew's religion came to be pathologized as an objection to the Jewish body. Images of Jewish difference inherent within the sphere of religion become metamorphosed into images of the Jew within the sphere of public service.

In 1893, H. Nordmann published a pamphlet on "Israel in the Army" in which the Jew's inherent unfittedness for military service is the central theme (Nordmann 1893). At the same time a postcard showing a ill-formed "little Mr. Kohn" showing up for his induction into the military was in circulation in Germany (Bering 1987, 211). And in the Viennese fin-de-siècle humor magazine, *Kikeriki,* the flat and misshapened feet of the Jew served as an indicator of the Jewish body almost as surely as the shape of the Jewish nose (Fuchs 1921, 200). By the 1930s the image of the Jew's feet had become ingrained in the representation of the Jewish body. The Nazi caricaturist Walter Hofmann, who drew under the name of "Waldl," presented a series of images of the construction of the Jewish body in a cartoon strip ironically entitled "What can Sigismund do about the fact that he is so pretty?" (Hofmann, n.d., [23]). The Jewish body is literally constructed, like that of Adam, from wet clay, but the Jew disobeys the divine order and arose before his body was truly formed: "Since the clay was still damp and soft, the smarty developed after the first few steps extraordinary bandy legs, but also flat feet." The foot became the hallmark of difference, of the Jewish body being separate from the real "body politic." These images aimed at a depiction of the Jew as unable to function within the social institutions, such as the armed forces, that determined the quality of social acceptance. "Real" acceptance would be true integration into the world of the armed forces. Thus Arthur Schnitzler has his "royal and imperial" officer, *Leutnant* Gustl, in the 1901 novella of the same name, mull the "nasty business" of what Jews were doing in "his" world (Politzer 1967, 45).

The Jewish response to the charge that the Jew cannot become a member of society as he cannot serve in the armed services becomes one of the foci of the Jewish response to turn-of-the-century anti-Semitism. The "Defense Committee against Anti-Semetic Attacks in Berlin" published its history of "Jews as soldiers" in 1897 in order to document the presence of Jews in the German army throughout the nineteenth century. (*Juden als Soldaten* 1897) After the end of World War I, this view of Jewish nonparticipation became the central topos of political anti-Semitism. It took the form of the "Legend of the Stab in the Back" (*Dolchstosslegende*) that associated Jewish slackers (war profiteers who refused to serve at the front) with the loss of the war (Petzold 1963; Proctor 1988; Weingert, Kroll, Bayertz 1988; Weindling 1989). In 1919 a brochure with the title "The Jews in the War: a Statistical Study using Official Sources" was published by Alfred Roth that accused the Jews of having systematically avoided service during the war in order to undermine the war effort of the home front (Armin 1919). On the part of the official Jewish community in Germany, Jacob Segall in 1922 provided a similar statistical survey to the 1893 study in which he defended the role of the Jewish soldier during the First World War against the charge of feigning inabilities in order to remain on the home front (Segall 1922). In the same year, Franz Oppenheimer drew on Segall's findings in order to provide an equally detailed critique of this charge, a charge that by 1922 had become a commonplace of anti-Semitic rhetoric (Oppenheimer 1922).

There were also attempts on the part of Jewish physicians to counter the argument of the weakness of the Jewish body within the body politic. Their arguments are, however, even more convoluted and complicated because of the constraints imposed by the rhetoric of science. As Jewish *scientists* they needed to accept the basic truth of the statistical arguments of medical science during this period. They could not dismiss these "facts" out of hand and thus operated within these categories. Like Segall and Oppenheimer, who answer one set of statistics with another set of statistics, the possibility of drawing the method of argument into disrepute does not exist for these scientists as their status as scientists rested upon the validity of these positivistic methods. And their status as scientists provided a compensation for their status as Jews. As Jews they were the object of the scientific gaze; as scientists, the observing, neutral, universal eye.

In 1908 Dr. Elias Auerbach of Berlin undertook a medical rebuttal, in an essay on the "military qualifications of the Jew," of the "fact" of the predisposition of the Jew for certain disabilities that precluded him from military service. Auerbach begins by attempting to "correct" the statistics which claimed that for every 1,000 Christians in the population, there were 11.61 soldiers, but for 1,000 Jews in the population, there were only 4.92 soldiers. His correction (based on the greater proportion of Jews entering the military who were volunteers and, therefore, did not appear in the statistics) still finds that a significant portion of Jewish soldiers were unfit for service (according to his revised statistics, of every 1,000 Christians there were 10.66 soldiers; of 1,000 Jews, 7.76). He accepts the physical differences of the Jew as a given but questions whether there is a substantive reason that these anomalies should prevent the Jew from serving in the military (Auerbach 1908). He advocates the only true solution that will make the Jews of equal value as citizens: the introduction of "sport" and the resultant reshaping of the Jewish body.

More directly related to the emblematic nature of the Jewish foot is the essay by G. Muskat, a Berlin orthopedist, that asks the question of "whether flat feet are a racial marker of the Jew." (Muskat 1909; cf. Dagnall 1980). He refutes the false charge that "the clumsy, heavy-footed gait of the semitic race made it difficult for Jews to undertake physical activity, so that their promotion within the military was impossible." While seeing flat feet as the "horror of all generals," he also refutes the charge that Jews are particularly at risk as a group from this malady. Like Auerbach, Muskat sees the problem of the weaknesses of the Jewish body as a "real" one. For him it is incontrovertible that Jews have flat feet. Thus the question he addresses is whether this pathology is an inherent quality of the Jewish body that would inherently preclude the Jew from becoming a full-fledged member of secular (i.e., military) society. For Muskat the real problem is the faulty development of the feet because of the misuse of the foot. The view that it is civilization and its impact on the otherwise "natural" body that marks the Jew becomes one of the major arguments against the idea of the sign value of the Jewish foot as a sign of racial difference. The Jew is, for the medical literature of the nineteenth century, the ultimate example of the effect of civilization (i.e., the city and "modern life") on the individual (Mosse 1987, 14–15). The Jew is both the city dweller par excellence as well as the must evident victim of the city (Gilman 1986, 1988; cf. Larson et al. 1989).

For nineteenth-century medicine (following the views of Rousseau) cities are places of disease and the Jews are the quintessential city dwellers. Richard Krafft-Ebing remarks that civilization regularly brings forth degenerate forms of sexuality because of the "more stringent demands which circumstances make upon the nervous system" and which manifest themselves in the "psychopathological or neuropathological conditions of the nation involved" (Krafft-Ebing 1965, 24). For him the Jew is the ultimate "city person" whose sensibilities are dulled, whose sexuality is pathological. It is also the city that triggers the weakness hidden within the corrupted individual (cf. Binswanger 1904, 82). It is the city's turbulence, its excitement, what August Forel in his *The Sexual Question* calls its "Americanism," that leads to "illnesses" such as degenerate neurasthenia (Forel 1925, 331–32). This image of the corrupt and corrupted city dweller is seen by physicians of the period as "Jewish" in its dimensions. Jews manifest an "abnormally intensified sensuality and sexual excitement that lead to sexual errors that are of etiological significance" (Krafft-Ebing 1905, 143). The diseases of civilization are the diseases of the Jew. The shape of the Jew's foot is read in this context as the structure of the Jewish mind. As late as 1940, Leopold Boehmer can speak of the "foot as the helpless victim of civilization" (Boehmer 1940, 180; cf. Swann 1988).

Muskat's argument is a vital one. He must shift the argument away from the inherited qualities of the Jewish body to the social anomalies inflicted on the body (and feet) of all "modern men" by their lifestyle. He begins his essay with a refutation of the analogy present within the older literature that speaks about the flat foot of the black (and by analogy of the Jew) as an atavistic sign, a sign of the earlier stage of development (in analogy to the infant who lacks a well-formed arch). Muskat notes that flat feet have linked the black and the Jew as "throw-backs" to more primitive forms of life. He quotes a nineteenth-century ethologist, Karl Hermann Burmeister, who in 1855 commented that "Blacks and all of those with flat feet are closest to the animals." Muskat begins his essay by denying that flat feet are a racial sign for any group, but rather a pathological sign of the misuse of the feet. (But he carefully avoids the implications that the misuse is the result of the urban location of the Jew or the Jew's inability to deal with the benefits of civilization.) He cites as his authorities a number of "modern" liberal commentators such as the famed Berlin surgeon/politician Rudolf Virchow, who had examined and commented on the feet of the black in order to refute the implication that flat feet were as a sign of racial difference. Like other Jewish commentators, Muskat is constrained to acknowledge the "reality" of the "flat feet" of both the Jew and the black but cites the renown orthopedist Albert Hoffa to the effect that only 4 percent of all flat feet are congenital.[†] Flat feet are not a racial sign, they are "merely" a sign of the abuse of the foot. That 25 percent of all recruits in Austria and 30 percent in Switzerland were rejected for flat feet is a sign for Muskat that the Jewish recruit is no better nor worse than his Christian counterpart. (He never cites the rate of the rejection of Jewish recruits.) Muskat's rebuttal of the standard view that sees the foot as a sign of the racial difference of the Jew still leaves the Jew's foot deformed. What Muskat has done is to adapt the view of the corruption of the Jew by civilization (and of civilization by the Jew) to create a space where the Jew's foot has neither more nor less signification as a pathological sign than does the flat foot in the general population. This attempt at the universalization of the quality ascribed to the Jewish foot does not however counter the prevailing sense of the specific meaning ascribed to the Jew's foot as a sign of difference.

This view is repeated by M. J. Guttmann in his 1920 dissertation that attempted to survey the entire spectrum of charges concerning the nature of the Jewish body (Guttman 1920, 38). Guttmann dismisses the common wisdom that " 'all Jews have flat feet' as excessive." He notes, as does Muskat, that Jews seem to have a more frequent occurrence of this malady (8 percent to 12 percent higher than the norm for the general population). And his source, like that of Muskat, are the military statistics. But Guttmann accepts the notion that Jews have a peculiar pathological construction of the musculature of the lower extremities.

In a standard handbook of eugenics published as late as 1940, the difference in the construction of the musculature of the foot is cited as the cause of the different gait of the Jew (Just 1940, 39). The German physician-writer Oskar Panizza, in one of the most extraordinary works depicting the nature of the Jewish body written in the fin de siècle, observed that the Jew's body language was clearly marked: "When he walked, Itzig always raised both thighs almost to his mid-riff so that he bore some resemblance to a stork. At the same time he lowered his head deeply into his breast-plated tie and stared at the ground. Similar disturbances can be noted in people with spinal diseases. However, Itzig did not have a spinal disease, for he was young and in good condition" (Panizza 1980, 64; see also Zipes 1980; and Bauer 1984). This image of the pathological nature of the gait of the Jews is linked to their inherently different anatomical structure. Flat feet remain a significant sign of Jewish difference in German science through the Nazi period. And it is always connected with the discourse about military service. According to Baur, Fischer, and Lenz in 1936: "Flat feet are especially frequent among the Jews. Salaman reports during the World War that about a sixth of the 5000 Jewish soldiers examined had flat feet while in a similar sample of other English soldiers it occurred in about a fortieth" (Baur, Fischer, Lenz 1936, 396). In 1945, Otmar Freiherr von Verschuer can still comment without the need for any further substantiation that great numbers of cases of flat feet are to be found among the Jews (Verschuer 1945, 87).

The debate about the special nature of the Jew's foot and gait enters into another sphere, that of neurology, which provides a series of links between the inherent nature of the Jew's body and his psyche. This view, too, has a specific political and social dimension. Elias Auerbach's evocation of sport as the social force to reshape the Jewish body had its origins in the turn-of-the-century call of Max Nordau, a physician trained by Jean-Martin Charcot in Paris and the vice-president of the first six Zionist Congresses (1897–1903), for a "new muscle Jew" (Nordau 1909, 379–81). This view became a common place of the early Zionist literature, which called upon sport, as an activity, as one of the central means of shaping the new Jewish body (Jalowicz 1901). His desire was not merely for an improvement in the physical well-being of the Jew but rather an acknowledgement of the older German tradition that saw an inherent relationship between the healthy political mind and the healthy body. It was not merely "mens sano in corpore sane" but the sign that the true citizen had a healthy body which provided his ability to be a full-scale citizen, itself a sign of mental health. Nordau's cry that we have killed our bodies in the stinking streets of the ghettos and we must now rebuild them on the playing fields of Berlin and Vienna is picked up by M. Jastrowitz of Berlin in the major Jewish newspaper devoted to gymnastics in 1908. For Jastrowitz the real disease of the Jews, that which marks their bodies, is a neurological deficit that has been caused by the impact of civilization. Jastrowitz, like all of the Jewish physicians of the fin de siècle, accepts the general views that Jews are indeed at special risk for specific forms of mental and neurological disease. He warns that too great a reliance on sport as a remedy may exacerbate these illnesses. For Jastrowitz, the attempt to create the "new muscle Jew" works against the inherent neurological weaknesses of the Jew. This is the link to the general view of organic psychiatry of the latter half of the nineteenth century which saw the mind as a product of the nervous system and assumed that "mind illness is brain illness." Thus the improvement of the nervous system through training the body would positively impact on the mind (so Nordau). Jastrowitz's view also assumes an absolute relationship, and he fears that, given the inherent weakness of the Jewish nervous system, any alteration of the precarious balance would negatively impact on the one reservoir of Jewish strength, the Jewish mind. The Jew could forfeit the qualities of mind that have made him successful in the world by robbing his brain of oxygen through overexercise. For Nordau and Jastrowitz the relationship between the healthy body, including the healthy foot and the healthy gait, and the healthy mind is an absolute one. The only question is whether it is alterable. This debate is played out within European neurology in the discussion of one of the more widely discussed neurological syndromes created in the late nineteenth century, that of intermittent claudication.

"Claudication intermittente" was created by Max Nordau's teacher (as well as the inspiration of Sigmund Freud), the Parisian neurologist Jean Martin Charcot in 1858 (Charcot 1858; Erb 1898; cf. Rosenbloom et al. 1989). This diagnostic category was described by Charcot as the chronic recurrence of pain and tension in the lower leg, a growing sense of stiffness and finally a total inability to move the leg, that causes a marked and noticeable inhibition of gait. This occurs between a few minutes and a half-hour after beginning a period of activity, such as walking. It spontaneously vanishes only to be repeated at regular intervals. Like flat feet, "claudication intermittente" is a "reality," i.e., it exists in the real world, but, like flat feet, it was placed in a specific ideological context at the turn of the century.

Charcot determined that this syndrome seemed to be the result of the reduction of blood flow through the arteries of the leg and led to the virtual disappearance of any pulse from the four arteries which provide the lower extremity with blood. The interruption of circulation to the feet leads to the initial symptoms and can eventually lead to even more severe symptoms such as spontaneous gangrene. Charcot's diagnostic category was rooted in work done by veterinarians, such as Bouley and Rademacher, who observed similar alterations in the gait of dray horses. The image of the Jew's foot as an atavistic structure, similar to the flat feet of the horse (an argument refuted by Muskat), reappears in the very antecedent of this syndrome.

What is vital is that this diagnostic category soon became the marker in neurology for the difference between the Jewish foot and that of the "normal" European. This diagnostic category becomes central to the description of the pathological difference of the Jew. And it is, itself, differentiated from other "racially" marked categories that have the impairment of gait as part of their clinical presentation. Charcot clearly differentiates "claudication intermittente" from the chronic pain associated with the diabetic's foot (a diagnostic category so closely associated with Jews in nineteenth-century medicine that it was commonly called the "Jewish disease" (Singer 1904; cf. Kretzmer 1901; and Hoppe 1903). In 1911 Dejerine also differentiated this syndrome from "spinal intermittent claudication" (Steiner 1929, 230). This is one of the syndromes associated with syphilis, a disease that also has a special relationship to the representation of the Jew in nineteenth-century medicine (Gilman

1989). What is clear is that the sign of the "limping Jew" is read into a number of diagnostic categories of nineteenth-century neurology.

Very quickly "claudication intermittente" becomes one of the specific diseases associated with Eastern European Jews. H. Higier in Warsaw publishes a long paper in 1901 in which he summarizes the state of the knowledge about "claudication intermittente" as a sign of the racial makeup of the Jew. The majority of the twenty-three patients he examined were Jews, and he found that the etiology of the disease was "the primary role of the neuropathic disposition [of the patients] and the inborn weakness of their peripheral circulatory system." (Higier 1901). By the time Higier publishes his paper at the turn of the century, this is a given in the neurological literature. The debate about the flat feet of the Jews as a marker of social stigma gives way to the creation of a scientific discourse about the difference of the Jew's feet that does not merely rely on the argument of atavism, which had been generally refuted in the medical literature of the fin-de-siècle, but on the question of the relationship between the Jew's body and the Jew's mind through the image of the deficits of the neurological system. "Claudication intermittente" becomes a sign of inherent constitutional weakness so that it is also to be found as a sign for the male hysteric (Olivier and Halipré 1896). Hysteria is, of course, also a neurological deficit that is primarily to be found among Eastern European Jewish males. Maurice Fishberg states the case boldly in 1911: "The Jews, as is well known to every physician, are notorious sufferers of the functional disorders of the nervous system. Their nervous organization is constantly under strain, and the least injury will disturb its smooth workings." (Fishberg 1911, 6, 324–25; cf. Dagnall 1987). But it is not all Jews, according to Fishberg, quoting from Tobler's 1889 study of mental illness in Russia: "The Jewish population of [Warsaw] alone is almost exclusively the inexhaustible source for the supply of specimens of hysterical humanity, particularly the hysteria in the male, for all the clinics of Europe." It is the male Jew from the East, from the provinces, who is most as risk for hysteria. And the symptom of the hysteric that most characterizes the Eastern Jew is his impaired gait. This remains a truism of medical science through the decades. The hysterical and the limping Jew are related in the outward manifestation of their illness: both are represented by the inability of the limbs to function "normally," by the disruption of their gait, as in Sigmund Freud's case of "Dora" (1905 [1901]) (Freud 1955–74, 7:16–17, n. 2; Ellenberger 1970; cf. Baker and Silver 1987; and Keane 1989).

The link between the older discussion of "flat feet" and the new category of "claudication intermittente" is examined by a number of sources. H. Idelsohn in Riga makes the association between the Jews, Charcot's category of "claudication intermittente," and flat feet overt when he examines his Jewish patients to see whether there is any inherent relationship between the fabled Jewish flat feet and inherent muscular weakness. He places the discussion of the special nature of the Jewish foot into the context of a neurological deficit. While he does not wish to overdetermine this relationship (according to his own statement), he does find that there is reason to grant flat feet a "specific importance as an etiological moment" (Idelsohn 1903). He describes the flat foot, citing Hoffa, as "tending to sweat, often blue colored and cold, with extended veins . . . People with flat feet are often easily tired, and are incapable of greater exertion and marches." (300) He sees in this description a visual and structural analogy to Charcot's category of "claudication intermittente." This view is echoed by G. Muskat in a paper of 1910 in which he makes the link between the appearance of "claudication intermittente" and the preexisting pathology of flat feet (Muskat 1910).

One of Idelsohn's major sources for his views is a paper by Samuel Goldflam in Warsaw (Goldflam 1901a, 1901b). Goldflam is one of the most notable neurologists of the first half of the century and the co-discoverer of "Goldflam-Oehler sign" (the paleness of the foot after active movement) in the diagnosis of intermittent claudication (Herman 1963, 3:143–49). While Goldflam does not make any overt mention of race in this context, Idelsohn argues that since all of his patients were Jews, it is clear that "claudication intermittente" is a Jewish disease and that this is proven by the relationship between the evident sign of the difference of the Jewish foot, the flat foot, and its presence in a number of his own cases. Its absence in the clinical description given by Goldflam (and others) is attributed by him to its relatively benign and usual occurrence, which is often overlooked because of the radical problems, such as gangrene, which occur with "claudication intermittente."

In a major review essay on the "nervous diseases" of the Jews, Toby Cohn, one of the leading Berlin neurologists, included "claudication intermittente" as one of his categories of neurological deficits. While commenting on the anecdotal nature of the evidence, and calling on a review essay by K. Mendel (1922) (who does not discuss the question of "race" at all), he accepts the specific nature of the Jewish risk for this syndrome while leaving the etiology open. Two radically different etiologies had been proposed: the first, as we have noted in Higier, Idelsohn, and Mendel, reflected on the neuropathic qualities of the Jewish body, especially in regard to diseases of the circulatory system (hemorrhoids, another vascular syndrome, are cited as another "Jewish" disease). The other potential etiology noted by Cohn does not reflect on inherent qualities of the Jewish foot but on the misuse of tobacco and the resulting occlusion of the circulatory system of the extremities. Indeed, the social dimension that Cohn provides in his discussion of the evils of tobacco misuse is an answer to the image of the neurological predisposition of the Jew's body to avoid military service (cf. Waller, Solomon, and Ramsay 1989). But the misuse of tobacco is for Cohn is sign of the Eastern Jew, not of the Western Jew. The Eastern Jew's mind is that of a social misfit and his body reifies this role, but this is not a problem of Western Jewry except by extension.

Here the parameters are set: Jews walk oddly because of the form of their feet and legs. This unique gait represents the inability of the Jew to function as a citizen within a state that defines full participation as military service. Jewish savants, rather than generally dismissing the statistical evidence as nonsense, seek to "make sense" of it in a way which would enable them (as representatives of the authoritative voice of that very society) to see a way out. The "way out" is, in fact, the acceptance of difference through the attribution of this difference to social rather than genetic causes and its projection on to a group labeled as inherently "different," the Eastern Jews. This is an important moment in the work of these scientists—for the risk that they see lies in the East, lies in the "misuse" of tobacco by Eastern Jews. It is not accidental that the major reports on the nature of the Jew's gait come from Eastern Europe and are cited as signs of the difference in social attitudes and practices among Eastern European Jews. The rhetorical movement that these scientists undertook implied an inherently different role for the Western Jew serving in the armed forces of the Empire, whether German or Austrian. This movement was important because the clean line between "nature" and "nurture" was blurred in nineteenth-century medicine. The physician of the nineteenth and early twentieth century understood that the appearance of signs of degeneration, such as the flat foot, may have been triggered by aspects in the social environment but was, at its core, an indicator of the inherent weakness of the individual. The corollary to this is the inheritance of acquired characteristics—that the physiological changes which the impact of environment triggers become part of the inheritance of an individual. This view can be found in the work of the neurologist C. E. Brown-Séquard, who, as early as 1860, had argued that there were hereditary transmissions of acquired injuries, as in the case of "animals born of parents having been rendered epileptic by an injury to the spinal cord" (Brown-Séquard 1875). The damage rendered by environmental factors ("tobacco") to the Jewish foot thus mark the next generation. The loop is thus complete: whether hereditary or environmental, the qualities of "poor citizenship" are marked by the Jewish foot. For non-Jewish scientists of the late nineteenth century, this marker exists as a sign of the Jewish body. For Jewish scientists, whose orientation is Western (no matter what their actual geographic locus), these qualities are a sign of the atavistic nature of the Eastern Jews and serve as a boundary between the degenerated Jews in the East and the Western Jew.

Notes

*In this paper I am not interested in determining the line between "real" and "fabled" aspects of the Jewish body. This can be done only by ignoring the fact that *all* aspects of the Jewish body, whether real or invented, are the locus of difference (see Mourant, Kopec & Domaniewska-Sobczak 1978; Goodman 1979). My argument is not merely one of "labeling," as Edward Shorter (1989) claims. Rather, I am interested in the ideological implications associated with the image of the Jews (and other groups) as "diseased." This says nothing at all about the "realities" of the disease. Indeed, I have consistently claimed that all of the disease patterns I have examined are rooted in some type of observable phenomenon which is then labeled as "pathological." Some of these phenomena may well be "pathological" responses to stress, as Shorter claims. But it is not the "reality" of the phenomenon that is central to my own examination but its representation. Compare the work of Armstrong 1983, Dodier 1986, and Labisch 1986. On the general background of the idea of the Jewish body within the rhetoric of nineteenth- and twentieth-century eugenics in Germany and Austria, see Proctor 1988; Weingart, Kroll and Bayertz 1988; Weindling 1989. An extended version of this paper has appeared in *The Bulletin of the History of Medicine* 64 (1990):588–602.

†Hoffa is the author of the authoritative study *Die Orthopädie im Dienst der Nervenheilkunde* (Hoffa 1900) and the compiler (with August Blencke) of the standard overview of the orthopedic literature of the fin-de-siècle (Hoffa and Blencke 1905).

Bibliography

Armin, O. [i.e., Alfred Roth]. 1919. *Die Juden im Heere, eine statistische Untersuchung nach amtlichen Quellen.* München: Deutsche Volks-Verlag.

Armstrong, D. 1983. *The Political Anatomy of the Body: Medical Knowledge in Britain in the Twentieth Century.* Cambridge: Cambridge University Press.

Auerback, E. 1908. "Die Militärtauglichkeit der Juden." *Jüdische Rundschau.* 50 (11 December 1908):491–92.

Baker, J. H. & Silver, J. R. 1987. "Hysterical paraplegia." *Journal of Neurology, Neurosurgery and Psychiatry* 50:375–82.

Baldwin, P. M. 1980. "Liberalism, nationalism, and degeneration: The case of Max Nordau." *Central European History* 13:99–120.

Bauer, M. 1984. *Oskar Panizza: Ein literarisches Porträt.* Munich: Hanser.

Baur, E., E. Fischer, F. Lenz, eds. 1936. *Menschliche Erblehre und Rassenhygiene: I. Menschliche Erblehre.* München: J. F. Lehmann.

Beller, S. 1989. *Vienna and the Jews 1867–1938: A Cultural History.* Cambridge: Cambridge University Press.

Bering, D. 1987. *Der Name als Stigma: Antisemitismus in deutschen Alltag 1812–1933.* Stuttgart: Klett/Cotta.

Berkley, G. E. 1988. *Vienna and Its Jews: The Tragedy of Success, 1880–1980s.* Cambridge Mass.: Abt/Madison.

Binswanger, O. 1904. *Hysterie.* Wien: Deuticke.

Boehmer, L. 1940. "Fußschäden und schwingedes Schuhwerk." In *Zeiss & Pintschovius* 1940, 180.

Brown-Séquard, C. E. 1875. "On the hereditary transmission of certain injuries to the nervous system." *The Lancet* (January 2):7–8.

Charcot, J. M. 1858. "Sur la claudication intermittente." *Compte rendus de séances et mémoires de la societé de biologie (Paris) Mémoire* 1859, 2 series, 5:25–38.

Dagnall, J. C. 1980. "Feet and the military system." *British Journal of Chiropody.* 45:137.

——— 1987. "The diabetic foot." *British Journal of Chiropody* 52:63.

Dodier, N. 1986. "Corps fragiles. La construction sociale des evénements corporels dans les activites quotidiennes des travail." *Revue français de sociologie* 27:603–28.

Ellenberger, H. F. 1970. *The Discovery of the Unconscious: The History and Evolution of Dynamic Psychiatry*. New York: Basic Books.

Erb, W. 1898. "Über das 'intermittirende Hinken' und andere nervöse Störungen in Folge von Gefässerkrankungen." *Deutsche Zeitschrift für Nervenheilkunde* 13:1–77.

Fishberg, M. *The Jews: A Study of Race and Environment*. New York: Walter Scott.

Fontane, T. 1870. *Der deutsche Krieg von 1866*. Band 1: *Der Feldzug in Böhmen und Mähren*. Berlin: Verlag der königlichen geheimen Ober-Hofbuchdruckerei.

Forel, A. 1925. *The Sexual Question: A Scientific, Psychological, Hygienic and Sociological Study,* trans. D. F. Marshall. New York: Physicians and Surgeons Book Co.

Freud, S. 1955–74. *The Standard Edition of the Complete Psychological Works of Sigmund Freud,* ed. and trans. J. Strachey, A. Freud, A. Strachey, and A. Tyson. 24 vol. London: Hogarth.

Fuchs, E. 1921. *Die Juden in der Karikatur*. München: Langen.

Gilman, S. L. 1986. *Difference and Pathology: Stereotypes of Sexuality, Race, and Madness*. Ithaca, N.Y.: Cornell University Press.

——— 1988. *Disease and Representation: Images of Illness from Madness to AIDS*. Ithaca, N.Y.: Cornell University Press.

——— 1989. " 'I'm down on whores': Race and gender in Victorian London." *Whitewalls: A Journal of Language and Art* no. 23: *Regarding An/Other,* 100–26.

Goldflam, S. 1901a "Weiteres über das intermittierende Hinken." *Neurologisches Centralblatt* 20:197–213.

——— 1901b. "Über intermittierende Hinken ('claudication intermittente' Charcots) und Arteritis der Beine. "Deutsche medizinische Wochenschrift 21:587–98.

Goodman, R. M. 1979. *Genetic Disorders among the Jewish People*. Baltimore: Johns Hopkins University Press.

Grunwald, M. 1936. *Vienna*. Philadelphia: Jewish Publication Society of America.

Guttmann, M. J. 1920. *Über den heutigen Stand der Rasse- und Krankheitsfrage der Juden*. München: Rudolf Müller & Steinicke.

Herman, E. 1963. "Samuel Goldflam (1852–1932)." In *Kolle* 1963, 3:143–49.

Higier, H. 1901. "Zur Klinik der angiosklerotischenn paroxysmalen Myasthenie ('claudication intermittente' Charcots) und der sog. spontanen Gangrän." *Deutsche Zeitschrift für Nervenheilkunde* 19:438–67.

Hoffa, A. 1900. *Die Orthopädie im Dienst der Nervenheilkunde.* Jena: Gustav Fischer.

——— and Blencke, A. 1905. *Die orthopädische Literatur.* Stuttgart: Enke.

Hofmann, W. n.d. *Lacht ihn tot! Ein tendenziöses Bilderbuch von Waldl.* Dresden: Nationalsozialistischer Verlag für den Gau Sachsen.

Hoppe, H. 1903. "Sterblichkeit und Krankheit bei Juden und Nichtjuden." *Ost und West* 3: 565–68, 631–38, 775–80, 849–52.

Idelsohn, H. 1903. "Zur Casuistik und Aetiologie des intermittierenden Hinkens." *Deutsche Zeitschrift für Nervenheilkunde* 24:285–304.

Jalowicz, H. 1901. "Die körperliche Entartung der Juden, ihre Ursachen und ihre Bekämpfung." *Jüdische Turnzeitung* 2:57–65.

Judassohn, J. et al. 1929. *Handbuch der Haut- und Geschlechtskrankheiten.* Vol. 17, 1, ed. G. Alexander. Berlin: Springer.

Die Juden als Soldaten. 1897. Berlin: Sigfried Cronbach.

Just, G. (Ed.) 1940. *Handbuch der Erbbiologie des Menschen: I. Erbbiologie und Erbpathologie Körperlicher Zustände und Funktionen: Stützgewebe, Haut, Auge.* Berlin: Julius Springer, 1940.

Keane, J. R. 1989. "Hysterical gait disorders: 60 cases." *Neurology* 39:586–89.

Kolle, K. (Ed.) 1963. *Grosse Nervanärzte.* 3 vol. Stuttgart: Thieme.

Krafft-Ebing, R. v. 1905. *Text-Book of Insanity,* trans. C. G. Chaddock. Philadelphia: F. A. Davis.

——— 1965. *Psychopathia Sexualis: A Medico-Forensic Study,* rev. trans. H. E. Wedeck. New York: Putnam.

Kretzmer, M. 1901. "Über anthropologische, physiologische und pathologische Eigenheiten der Juden." *Die Welt* 5:3–5.

Labisch, A. 1986. "Die soziale Construktion der Gesundheit und des Homo Hygienicus." *Österreichische Zeitschrift für Soziologie* 3/4:60–82.

Larson, D. B. et al. 1989. "Religious affiliations in mental health research samples as compared with national samples." *Journal of Nervous and Mental Disease.* 177:109–11.

Lazarus, M. [1891]. Introduction to Remy [1891].

McCagg, W. O., Jr. 1989. *A History of Habsburg Jews, 1670–1918*. Bloomington: Indiana University Press.

Mendel, K. 1922. "Intermitterendes Hinken." *Zentralblatt für die gesamt Neurologie und Psychiatry* 27:65–95.

Mosse, G. L. 1987. *Germans and Jews: The Right, the Left, and the Search for a "Third Force" in Pre-Nazi Germany.* Detroit: Wayne State University Press.

Mourant, A. E., A. C. Kopec, and K. Domaniewska-Sobczak. 1978. *The Genetics of the Jews.* Oxford: Clarendon.

Muskat, G. 1909. "Ist der Plattfuß eine Rasseneigentümlichkeit?" *Im deutschen Reich.* 354–58.

——— 1910. "Über Gangstockung." *Verhandlungen des deutschen Kongresses für innere Medizin* 27:45–56.

Naudh, H. [i.e., H. Nordmann]. 1893. *Israel im Heere.* Leipzig: Hermann Beyer.

Nordau, M. 1909. *Zionistische Schriften.* Köln: Jüdischer Verlag.

Olivier, P. & Halipré, A. 1896. "Claudication intermittente chez un homme hystérique atteint de pouls lent permanent." *La Normandie Médicale* 11:21–28.

Oppenheimer, F. 1922. *Die Judenstatistik des preußischen Kriegsministeriums.* München: Verlag für Kulturpolitik.

Oxaal, I., M. Pollak, G. Botz, eds. 1987. *Jews, Anti-Semitism and Culture in Vienna.* London/New York: Routledge & Kegan Paul.

Panizza, O. 1980. "The Operated Jew." Trans. J. Zipes. *New German Critique* 21:63–79.

Petzold, J. 1963. *Die Dolchstosslegende: Eine Geschichtsfälschung im Dienst des deutschen Imperialismus und Militarismus.* Berlin (Ost): Akadmie Verlag.

Proctor, R. 1988. *Racial Hygiene: Medicine under the Nazis.* Cambridge: Harvard University Press.

Pulzer, P. 1988. *The Rise of Political Anti-Semitism in Germany and Austria.* Revised Edition. London: Peter Halban.

Remy, N. [i.e. Nahida Ruth Lazarus] [1891]. *Das jüdische Weib.* Leipzig: Gustav Fock.

Rohrer, J. 1804. *Versuch über die jüdischen Bewohner der österreichischen Monarchie.* Wien: n.p.

Rosenbloom, M. S. et al. 1989. "Risk factors affecting the natural history of intermittent claudication." *Archive of Surgery* 123:867–70.

Segall, J. 1922. *Die deutschen Juden als Soldaten im Kriege 1914–1918*. Berlin: Philo Verlag.

Shorter, E. 1989. "Women and Jews in a private nervous clinic in late nineteenth-century Vienna." *Medical History* 33:149–83.

Singer, H. 1904. *Allgemeine und spezielle Krankheitslehre der Juden*. Leipzig: Benno Konegen.

Steiner, G. "Klinik der Neurosyphilis." In Judassohn et al. 1929, 230.

Swann, J. 1988. "Nineteenth-century footwear and foot health." *Cliopedic Items* 3:1–2.

Trachtenberg, J. 1943. *The Devil and the Jews: The Medieval Conception of the Jew and Its Relation to Modern Antisemitism*. New Haven, Conn.: Yale University Press.

Verschuer, O. Frhr. v. 1945. *Erbpathologie: Ein Lehrbuch für Ärtzte und Medizinstudierende*. Dresden/Leipzig: Theodor Steinkopff.

Waller, P. C., S. A. Solomon, and L. E. Ramsay. 1989. "The acute effects of cigarette smoking on treadmill exercise distances in patients with stable intermittent claudication." *Angiology* 40:164–69.

Weindling, P. 1989. *Health, Race and German Politics between National Unification and Nazism, 1870–1945*. Cambridge: Cambridge University Press.

Weingart, P., J. Kroll, and K. Bayertz. 1988. *Rasse, Blut und Gene: Geschichte der Eugenik und Rassenhygiene in Deutschland*. Frankfurt a. M.: Suhrkamp.

Wistrich, R. S. 1989. *The Jews of Vienna in the Age of Franz Joseph*. Oxford: The Littman Library of Jewish Civilization/Oxford University Press.

Zeiss, H. & Pintschovius, K. (Eds.) 1940. *Zivilizationsschäden am Menschen*. München/Berlin: J. F. Lehmann.

Zipes, J. 1980. "Oskar Panizza: The operated German as operated Jew." *New German Critique* 21:47–61.

10

(G)nos(e)ology: The Cultural Construction of the Other

Jay Geller

> Artists tell us that the best way to make a caricature of the Jewish nose is to write a figure 6 with a long tail.
>
> —*The Jewish Encyclopedia* (1905 ed.)

> *Die Judennase ist die Figur sechs (= Sex) mit einem langen Schwanz.*
>
> —a German paraphrase

Since its formation in the late eighteenth century, the political culture of bourgeois society may best be characterized as an exclusively masculine order, a *Männerbund* (Baeumler 1934; Blüher 1917; Mayer 1982, 103; Mosse 1982b, 1985; Rosenberg 1930; Thalmann 1982, esp. chap. 2), forged preeminently by Christian heterosexual men.[1] The masculinist and binary ideology pervading this society privileged sexual difference as the one opposition grounded in nature and hence as universally valid. Upon this foundation individual identities and social institutions were determined, maintained, and legitimated. The opposition between a male-coded public sphere characterized by rationality (i.e., freedom from desire), autonomy, and activity (i.e., aggression) and a female-coded private sphere of emotionality, dependence, and passivity exemplified the economy of sexual difference; their separation enforced it (Poovey 1988, esp. 1–23, 79–80, 199; also see Brittan 1989; Swan 1974). Consequently, in the last instance sexual difference adjudicated the threats to the hegemony of the *Männerbund* posed by deviance or otherness: judged unmanly or effeminate, the other was relegated to the private sphere. To question gender identity—to allow the unmanned or unmanly into the public sphere—was in turn to question the legitimacy of the entire order.

Facilitating the administration of sexually differentiated bourgeois society was the development of scientific disciplines and their allegedly objective epistemic discourses (gnosiology). These sciences provided a grammar of truth that treated the reproductive system as the language by which "natural" difference was expressed (Poovey 1988, 6 and chap. 2; Laqueur 1987; also see Foucault 1973, esp. pt. 2). The primacy granted to reproduction increasingly biologized the representation of the other (cf. Foucault 1978; Turner 1984; Weeks 1981; among many). Further, the body of the Jew, the revolutionary (cf. Goldstein 1985, 524), the homosexual, the black, the woman became, by the ascription of disease (nosology), the site for the medical regulation of the other and for the maintenance of sexual identity. The others were put in their place—the textbook and the clinic. In the process, the *Männerbund* and its representative disciplines articulated their own position and authority.

Complementing nosological classification was the teleological theory of evolution, exemplified by Ernst Haeckel and his apothegm "ontogeny recapitulates phylogeny." The others had their chapter in the story of "the ascent of man" (cf. Vogt 1864). Just as the different stages of the embryo recapitulated the evolutionary process, so races and genders represented different stages of human development (cf. Gilman 1987, 300–301; Haller 1975). That is, the biologization of the other entailed a hierarchization of the other which legitimated the domination of white, heterosexual men. Moreover, grounding sexual difference in the complementary discourses of descent and of development revealed another facet of the masculinist ideology: the male expropriation of reproduction and its language from women and women-associated others (cf. O'Brien 1981 and Jay 1985). The self-made autonomous man authored and authorized himself in discipline and discourse formation. Yet their ideology of reproduction also mandated increasing the population of the dominant class; their disciplines and discourses betrayed the anxieties of bourgeois, heterosexual men about the demographic threat posed by the other to their hegemony. They feared their position atop the evolutionary and social hierarchies would be overrun (Hull 1982).

Mirroring these race- and gender-determined distinctions was a sensory hierarchy. In contrast to the cognitive and hygienic superiority of vision, smell characterized the sexual, the primitive, the animal. On the one hand, the degeneration of smell was *civilized man*'s mark of biological difference: "Among most mammals . . . smell is certainly the most highly developed of the senses . . . in man it has become almost rudimentary giving place to the supremacy of vision" (Ellis 1928, 45; cf. Horkheimer and Adorno 1972, 184;

Berillon 1908–9, 264; and Lowe 1982). On the other hand, the metaphorics of smell and its organ, the nose, became the mark of class and cultural difference (cf. Ellis 1928, 59–61; Corbin 1986; Stallybrass and White 1986, 139–40). With these nostrums, the other, in particular, the Jew, was constructed (noseology).

The masculinist ideology, the "objective" authority of knowledge, the labeling power of nosology, the expropriation of reproduction, and the telltale signs of the nose converge on 24 July 1895. Sometime early that morning Freud dreamed that he and his wife are receiving numerous guests; among them is his patient Irma. Taking her aside, he becomes alarmed by her symptoms, in particular the "extensive whitish grey scabs upon some remarkable curly structures which were evidently modelled on the turbinal bones of the nose [*Nasenmuscheln*]" (Freud 1900, 4:107). He calls in his male colleagues. After examining her body, the doctors diagnose her infection and nonsensically predict that the toxin (*Gift*) will be (rather odorously) eliminated through the supervention of dysentery. They then identify the cause of Irma's ailment: one of Freud's consulted colleagues had used an unclean syringe to inject Irma. The dirty *Spritze* contained a preparation that reeked, according to Freud, of associations to strong smelling substances. Among these chemical preparations was trimethylamin, whose formula he visualized in heavy type ($\mathbf{N[CH_3]_3}$) and whose role in sexual chemistry had been pointed out by his friend and confidante Wilhelm Fliess. Fliess "had drawn scientific attention to some very remarkable connections between the turbinal bones [*Nasenmuscheln*] and the female organs of sex" (Freud 1900, 4:117).

The origin of Irma's plaint is also the source of the dream's familiar designation: "the dream of Irma's injection." In the *Interpretation of Dreams* Freud would employ it as a "specimen dream" (*Traummuster*) to exemplify his method of interpretation. It is both the first thoroughly analyzed dream of Freud's groundbreaking text and the first of his own dreams that Freud subjected to a "detailed" (*eingehend,* thorough) analysis (Freud 1900, 4:106n).[2] As a consequence of its significant placement in his text and life, it is also perhaps the dream most thoroughly analyzed by Freud's later commentators (cf. Anzieu 1986; Eissler 1985; Elms 1980; Erikson 1954; Gay 1988, 80–86; R. Greenberg and C. Pearlman 1978; Kuper and Stone 1982; Mahony 1977, 1979; Masson 1985, 57, 60, 213 n. 1, 213–14 n. 4; Schur 1966; Swan 1974; Van Valzen 1984). Further enticing readers to continue Freud's own dream work is his confession at its conclusion: "I will not pretend that I have completely uncovered the meaning of this dream or that its interpretation is without a gap" (1900, 4:120–21). The text of his analysis confirms this incompleteness. Thus, while Freud's analysis elicits from the dream a wide array of associations, the final interpretation is restricted to the motifs of professional rivalry and guilt. He concludes that the dream represents his wish both to absolve himself of responsibility for Irma's condition and to stick the onus on his colleagues.

The dream text and Freud's accompanying commentary have generated a number of controversies—particularly about the identity of Irma—and many other interpretations: these range from Freud's valorizing his theory of the sexual etiology of neurosis (Kuper and Stone 1982) to his confronting a life-stage crisis of generativity (Erikson 1954), from his own problematic identification with a neurotic woman patient (Van Velzen 1984) to his efforts to restore his idealized relationship with Fliess that had been jeopardized by the latter's botched operation upon Freud's own patient Emma Eckstein (Schur 1966).

My discussion takes as its lead the recognition by Didier Anzieu (1986, 155) that "the Irma dream makes a kind of inventory of the body . . . [It] spells out the identity of both the body of the dream and the dream of the body." In particular, I isolate one item of that inventory, the repeatedly mentioned nasal turbinal bones, the *Nasenmuscheln*. These body parts generate associations with a number of the motifs and alluded-to individuals noted by Freud and his successors: personal responsibility and scientific authority, creativity and sexuality, Wilhelm Fliess and Emma Eckstein. The *Nasenmuscheln* also call attention to the nose. The prominent role the nose plays as an interpretive key to the dream has been pointed out by Mahony (1977, 93; cf. his remarks in Derrida 1985, 59–67) in his thorough analysis of Freud's visualization of the formula for trimethylamin:

> the N, the hetero-atom that Freud reflected on orthographically, olfactorily, medically and symbolically establishes crucial links, extending from Fliess the rhinologist and his all-embracing theories about the nose, to the nasal operation of Emma, Freud, and Fliess, to the smelly bottle of liquor. Or, said somewhat differently, the letter N, the chemical sign for nitrogen, which also orthographically represents the first consonant of the word *Nase* ('nose'), significantly enough represents a sound the linguistic decoding of which inevitably constitutes a kinesthetically nasal performance.

But the *Nasenmuscheln* do not allude to just any nose; rather, they evoke the Jewish nose. *Muscheln*'s near homophones—*Mauscheln* and *Muskeljuden,* both turn-of-the-century figurations of (male) Jews[3]—resonate with ethnic as well as sexual overtones. This Chapter pursues the curly trail of the *Nasenmuscheln* from the metaphorical, scientific, and sexological determination of the (Jewish) nose and smell, through Charcot's Salpêtrière, President Schreber's asylum, and Emma Eckstein's apartment, to a significant subtext of both Freud's dream and his Vienna: the construct of the feminized (male) Jew whose presence in the public sphere threatened the sexual difference sustaining the *Männerbund.*

The *Judennase* and the *foetor Judaicus*

According to Dennis Showalter (1983, 61) "the 'Jewish type' . . . only emerged during the seventeenth century. Before that the Jews were identified symbolically rather than physically: by tall hats, money bags, and similar items. The creation of physical forms of caricature began with giving all male Jews beards—a pattern reflecting accurate observation as much as anti-Semitism. The process of distortion began with the nose" (cf. Fuchs 1921, esp. 161–65). This shift from symbolic to physical identification was not the consequence of any increased Jewish presence; rather it signaled both the erosion of feudal-aristocratic society, in which identity and status were symbolically indicated, and the shift from a theological to a rational/natural ground of meaning (cf. Habermas 1962). Characteristic of this period was the widespread belief in physiognomy. This "science," advanced by Johann Caspar Lavater in 1776, discerned people's true natures by their features. For Lavater "the moral life of man discovers itself principally in the face" (1792, 1:17; cf. Gilman 1981, 56). In the late eighteenth century, physiognomic verities became commonplace and, despite either the universalistic intent of Lavater or the radical empiricism of many of his scientific disciples, they were employed in the social stereotyping of the dominant culture's others. The Jews became categorized by their physiognomy—their noses. As the leading chronicler of Jewish caricature remarked: "It is impossible to deny that the extraordinarily big, and usually also conspicuously [*auffällig*] formed, namely hooked [*hakenmässig*], nose is characteristic of the Jews as a whole" (Fuchs 1921, 161–62).

That the nose should become so prominent in representations of a person or a people is no surprise. The nose, generally, is considered "the physiognomic *principium individuationis,* the symbol of the specific character of an individual, described between the lines of his countenance" (Horkheimer and Adorno 1972, 184). It is "the most conspicuous body part as well as, at the same time, the one most capable of expression" (*ausdrucksfähigste;* Fuchs 1921, 163). For Lavater (1792, 3:363), the nose was "the fulcrum of the brain"; 120 years later, Wilhelm Fliess (1977, 17) begins his 1897 work on the relation between the nose and the genitals by also calling attention to its central location: "In the middle of the face, between the eyes, the mouth, and the osseous formations of the fore- and midbrain, there is the nose. Connected to the rhinopharyngeal space, it communicates with the ear and the larynx." Moreover the German language is rife with idioms, proverbs, and superstitions about the nose as a visual index—without any original Jewish context; for example, "*In einer kleinen Stadt kennt einer den anderen an der Nase*" (In a small town one knows the other by his nose), "*Man kann's ihm an der Nase ansehen*" (you can read his character in his face [nose]), "*sich an der Nase fassen*" (to confess one's guilt, to reprove one's self; lit. "fix [it] on one's nose oneself"), "*die Nase hochtragen*" (to hold up one's nose) (Küpper 1984, s.v. "*Nase*");[4] and the traditional belief that the possessors of large noses also possess large penises (cf. Hoffman-Krayer and Bächtold-Stäubli 1934–35, 6:970; cf. e.g., Ellis 1928, 67). Yet, while the so-called Jewish nose is not universally characteristic of Jews—as not only the *Jewish Encyclopedia* (1905, s.v. "nose," 9:338–39) endeavors statistically to demonstrate, but even the racist anti-Semite Houston Stewart Chamberlain (1969, 1:375–76) concedes, "The nose alone is no reliable proof of Jewish descent"[5]—it remains ever present in the popular imagination.

In one of the most popular novels of the nineteenth century, Gustav Freytag's 1855 *Soll und Haben* (Debit and Credit), the main antagonist, the Jew Veitel Itzig, "had a curious preference for crooked (*krumme*) alleys and narrow pavements. Here and there behind the back of his travel companion he beckoned with brazen familiarity to the dolled-up young girls who stood in the doorways or to the young fellows with crooked (*krummer*) noses and round eyes who hands in their pockets loitered about the streets" (1977, 40).[6] Freytag's description hooks Itzig into a tradition of anti-Semitic representations exemplified by Wilhelm Busch's notorious depiction of the Jews (in the first chapter of *Die fromme Helene* [1872]): Freytag's "harmless appearing, doubtless ironically intended indication, loses its harmlessness, when one recognizes with what prejudice the adjective '*krumm*' is bound: 'And the Jew with crooked (*krummer*) back,/crooked (*krumme*) Nose and crooked (*krummer*) legs/snakes his way to the stock market/profoundly corrupted and soulless' " (Hubrich 1974, 91). Jacob Burckhardt, the great historian and one of Freud's favorite authors, was no less caught up in the nasal representation of the Jews. In a letter to his friend, the architect Max Aliot, he describes his visit to Frankfurt where "Kalle and Shickselchen and Papa with their famous noses, appear on the balcony between females borrowed from the Pandroseion" (Burckhardt 1955, 169 [letter of 24 July 1875]; cited by Mosse 1970, 58–59).

Jewish writers were quite aware of the identification of the Jews with their noses. Moses Hess, in his 1862 proto-Zionist tract *Rome and Jerusalem,* undercuts the belief held by many Jewish Reformers that the German perception of the Jewish religion as ritualistic and atavistic was the primary obstacle to emancipation. He writes: the German "objects less to the Jews' peculiar beliefs than to their peculiar noses. . . . Jewish noses cannot be reformed" (Hess 1943, 52). Heinrich Heine also ironically identifies the nose with the Jewish people. In his 1840 *Denkschrift* for Ludwig Börne, Heine recalls Börne describing Jewish converts to Christianity: old daughters of Israel who wear crosses that are "even longer than their noses." Later, he recounts Börne's comment that "The renegades [*Abtrünnigen*] who deserted to the new covenant need only smell a *tsholent* to feel a certain homesickness for the synagogue" (Heine 1971, 183; cf. Loewenthal 1947; Rainey 1975, 60). In a similar vein, Heine's contemporaneous prose fragment *The Rabbi of Bacharach* has the apostate courtier Don Isaak Abarbanel declaim, "My nose has kept the faith" (*abtrünnig geworden;* Heine 1969–72, 2:550; cf. Rainey 1975, 22).[7]

The passages from Heine shift the focus on the *Judennase* from form to function, from shape to smell, and reflect a metonymic broadening of its symbolic field.[8] For the European cultural imagination, however, the earmark of the Jews was not so much their sense of smell as it was their smell. The Jewish scent, the noxious *foetor Judaicus,*[9] betrayed the Jew, and the physiognomics of caricature were joined by a metaphysics of scent (Nietzsche 1969, 233):[10]

> My instinct for cleanliness is characterized by a perfectly uncanny sensitivity so that the proximity of—what am I saying?—the inmost parts, the 'entrails' of every soul are physiologically perceived by me—*smelled.*
>
> This sensitivity furnishes me with psychological antennae with which I feel and get a hold of every secret: the abundant *hidden*

> dirt at the bottom of many a character—perhaps the result of bad blood, but glossed over by education—enters my consciousness almost at the first contact.

The most celebrated modern[11] disseminator of the *foetor Judaicus* was perhaps Arthur Schopenhauer,[12] who talks repeatedly of being overcome (*übermannt*) by it. Even Spinoza, one of his favorite philosophers, does not escape its taint: "Here [Spinoza in part 4 of the *Ethics*] speaks even as a Jew understands it, following Gen. 1:9, such that the *foetor Judaicus* thereby overcomes [*übermannt*] the rest of us who are so accustomed to purer and worthier theories" (Schopenhauer 1974, 1:73). Indeed, "Spinoza . . . could not get rid of the Jews: *quo semel est imbuta recens servabit odom*" ([A smelling bottle] long retains the smell of that which filled it; Schopenhauer 1958, 2:645). In Schopenhauer's essay sequence "On Religion" (1974, 2:375; cf. 1972, 4:240) a most telling and repeated phrase appears: "A man must be bereft of all his senses or completely chloroformed by the *foetor Judaicus,* not to see that, in all essential respects, the animal is absolutely identical with us and the difference lies merely in the accident, the intellect, and not in the substance, which is the will." This last utterance suggests two interrelated implications of the association of the Jew with the nose: the animalistic (sexual) Jew and the Jewish threat to gender identity.

First, even as Schopenhauer rails against the Jews' presumption of their superiority to the animal kingdom, he reduces them to animal-like status.[13] By ascribing odorousness to the Jews, he expels them from the confines of civilized humanity (cf. Corbin 1986). This ascription simultaneously binds the Jews to the "primitive" and atavistic sense of smell in word and deed: on the linguistic level, in German (as in English) *riechen* (to smell) signifies both the emission and the perception of an odor;[14] and, from a phenomenological perspective, a smell and its perceiver become united (cf. Howes 1987). And olfaction, like its object, is tied to animality. Whereas smell is highly developed in animals, it has become almost rudimentary in the human, a biological fact that nineteenth-century comparative brain anatomy proved—at least for the European. According to G. Eliot Smith, "sometimes, especially in some of the non-European races, the whole of the posterior rhinal fissure is retained in that typical form which we find in the anthropoid apes" (cited by Ellis 1928, 46). Smell lies in a "most ancient. . . . a remote and almost disused storehouse of our minds" (Ellis 1928, 55). Consequently, to attend to smells inordinately is to resort to primitive processes; it is a sign of biological degeneration.

Preoccupation with smells is a sign of cultural degeneration. According to Max Nordau's anatomy of fin-de-siècle culture *Entartung* (*Degeneration*), "Even the nose, hitherto basely ignored by the fine arts, attracts the pioneers, and is by them invited to take part in aesthetic delights" (1895, 14). Obsessions about odors gripped the French representatives of this "degenerate" epoch, such as the novelist Huysmans and the defender of Dreyfus Zola (cf. Corbin 1986, 198–99, 205–6; Ellis 1928, 73; Nordau 1895, 541ff). Nordau (1895, 209) also notes that the followers of a particular German variant of degenerate culture—anti-Semitism—have nightmares about body odor.[15] Despite infusing the self-proclaimed antitheses of Jewry with the odorous stigmata of *Entartung*, Nordau and his contemporaries implicitly render, by this connection of smell with degeneration, the Jews as fallen from the evolutionary pinnacle embodied by the representatives of the *Männerbund*.

The association of the Jews with the primitive sense of smell also entailed an association with sexuality. Since for animals smell is an essential ingredient of that most animalistic of activities, sexuality, the sexologists of the late nineteenth century added that "a certain histological conformity [exists] between the nose and the genitals, for both have erectile tissue." The "intimate association" (Ellis 1928, 46, 55, 67–70) of nose and genitals was also observed in the relationship between source and sensation. Ellis (1928, 64) cites Gustav Klein, who "argues the special function of the glands at the vulvar orifice . . . is to give out an odorous secretion to act as an attraction to the male, this relic of sexual periodicity." Ellis's reference to the *odor di feminina* indicates that the primary focus of discussions of odor and sexuality was feminine odor and sexuality. Although sexologists usually conceded that "Much of what has been said concerning the *parfum de la femme* applies to the sexual exhalation or scent of men" (Bloch 1934, 74), the vast preponderance of attention was directed toward women's odors. Hence to speak of a particular Jewish odor was to evoke the primitive, the sexual, the feminine.

As the sexological literature attests, the connection of scent to sexuality was subject to biological and medical investigation. Various embryological and evolutionary theories were proposed: "As early as G. Valentin's 1835 handbook of human development, the chronological parallels in the development of soft-tissue areas and cavities of the fetus had been noted" (Gilman 1987, 300). Through the evolutionism propounded by scientists like Haeckel, the common and early development of nasal cavities and genitalia in the fetus were signs both of their mutual implication and of their comparative primitivism. Haeckel himself expounded upon the connection between smell and sexuality. He "theorized in his *Anthropogenie oder Entwickelungsgeschichte des Menschen* that 'erotic chemotropisms'—that is to say, chemically based sex stimulants affecting taste and smell—were phylogenetically the 'primal source' of all sexual attraction in nature" (Haeckel 1874, 656–57; cited by Sulloway 1979, 150). Haeckel's theory of primal smells was hailed by the sexologist and author of *Odoratus Sexualis* Iwan Bloch in his 1902–3 *Beiträge zur Aetiologie der Psychopathia sexualis* (cf. Sulloway 1979, 150; Bloch 1909, 15). Even the commonplace association between a large nose and a large penis got tied into smell: large noses smell more and hence are sexually more excitable (Bloch 1934, 24–25). The increased attention directed at matters nasal led the *Gazette hebdomodaire des sciences médicales de Bourdeaux* to conclude, if half facetiously, in its report of Dr. Oméga's letter to the editor of *Archivii italiani di laryngolia:* "a new science is in the process of being born: who knows if in the twentieth century we will not have chairs of comparative rhinography in our universities?" (*Revue de l'hypnotisme* 1890, 124)

Out of this scientific focus on sexuality, smell, and, by implication, the nose, emerged the work of Wilhelm Fliess and that of his predecessor, the American laryngologist John Noland Mackenzie (Sulloway 1979, 148–49):

> Mackenzie believed that all such afflictions of the nasal mucous membranes were probably 'the [phylogenetic] connecting link between the sense of smell and erethism of the reproductive organs exhibited in the lower animals' (1898:117–18). It was in this implicit phylogenetic connection that Mackenzie specifically attributed perversions of smell to pathological reversions to 'the purely animal type.' Summing up the phenomena on nasal pathology in general, and those of the 'nasal reflex neuroses' specifically, Mackenzie suggested that such disturbances are probably a direct result of the major reduction in olfactory acuity that has accompanied human evolution and the advent of civilized life (1898: 118).

Freud, in a letter to Fliess (11 January 1897 [Freud 1985, 223]), provides a similar summary of the connection among smell, animality, perverse sexuality (cf. Bloch 1934, 120; Koestenbaum 1988), and psychopathology (cf. Ellis 1928; Iribane 1912; Krafft-Ebing 1965; Mackenzie 1887):

> Perversions regularly . . . have an animal character. They are explained . . . by the effect of erogenous sensations that later lose their force. In this connection one recalls that the principal sense in animals (for sexuality as well) is that of smell, which has been reduced in human beings. As long as smell . . . is dominant, urine, feces, and the whole surface of the body, also blood, have a sexually exciting effect. The heightened sense of smell in hysteria presumably is connected with this.

From this miasma of biological speculation about the relationship between smell and animality arose an implicit connection among Jews, their noses, and "primitive," ergo degenerative, sexuality (cf. Gilman 1985); that is, between Jews and a sexuality which did not support or which threatened male heterosexual gender identity.

This conclusion suggests that for his readers Schopenhauer's references to the *foetor Judaicus* associate Jews not only with the animalistic but with questions of gender identity as well. The phrasing out of which the *foetor* emanates echoes this second connection. Schopenhauer employs gender-indicative language. The evocation of gender identity in being "über*mann*t" (lit. overmanned) by the *foetor Judaicus* is obvious. But his other preferred term, "chloroformiert," and his comparison of Spinoza with a smelling bottle are no less so. Ellis (1928, 64) notes that "During menstruation girls and young women frequently give off an odor which . . . may smell of chloroform."[16] Moreover, as the sexological literature (Bloch 1934, 69–70; citing Jaeger 1884, 1912) reports, "It is known to all that during her menses woman gives off an idiosyncratic repulsive odor." Thus, through the chloroformlike, repulsive *foetor Judaicus,* the Jew again becomes associated with women.[17] "Chloroform" moreover provokes other questions about gender identity that were a matter of much discussion during the late 1840s when Schopenhauer was composing the essays (1974) in which "*chloroformiert*" appears.[18] At this time, chloroform became the anaesthetic of choice for women in labor (cf. Poovey 1988, chap. 2). Comparing Spinoza to a smelling bottle has a complementary connection with women. Whereas chloroform puts the soon-to-be mother—a dominant nineteenth-century stereotype of women—to sleep, the smelling bottle restores the fainted hysteric—another dominant stereotype—to her senses. The *foetor Judaicus* put its male victim in a female role; it put male gender identity in jeopardy. To be "overmanned" by the *foetor Judaicus* was to be unmanned. Consequently, noses—and their bearers—would become an object of nosological classification and medical administration.

In addition to iconic and olfactive indices, the *Judennase* had a more sanguine connection to sexuality, gender identity, and the biologization of the Jew: the bloody nose as male menstruation. Sander Gilman (1987) has recently chronicled the traditional Christian calumny of Jewish male menstruation that continued at least into the eighteenth century.[19] Interest in the subject rekindled toward the end of the nineteenth century, especially in the work of Magnus Hirschfeld, for whom it "came to hold a very special place in the 'proofs' for the continuum between male and female sexuality" (Gilman 1987, 302–3). The link between the medieval theory that Jews needed Christian blood to replace the blood lost in (male) menstruation and the contemporary theory of bisexuality was found in the study of nosebleeds. In his *Beziehungen zwischen Nase und weiblichen Geschlechtsorganen,* Fliess argued that nosebleeds in prepubescent and postmenopausal as well as in pregnant women are not merely vicarious menstrual discharges; rather, they demonstrate that "the process of monthly uterine bleeding is only a link in the chain" (1977, 26, cf. 19) of human periodicity. He goes on to cite, as proof of his theory that men like women have menstrual periods, the case of a man who had periodic nosebleeds that his friends referred to as his "menstruation" (1977, 242; case 147, Dr. L . . . n). Indeed, Freud, ever ready to provide his friend Fliess with evidence for his theory of periodicity, informs him (1985, 256; letter of 20 July 1897) of Freud's own "menstruation with occasional bloody nasal secretion before and after." Cases like this were, according to Fliess, "consistent with our bisexual constitution" (1977, 10).[20] They were also consistent with the threat to gender identity posed by menstruation and, implicitly, by those who menstruate: "Menstrual blood, on the contrary, stands for the danger issuing from within the identity (social or sexual); it threatens the relationship between the sexes within a social aggregate and through internalization, the identity of each sex in the face of sexual difference" (Kristeva 1982, 71). These permutations of the *Judennase,* the *foetor Judaicus,* and male menstruation combined to question sexual identity in a society that at least since the 1860s had endeavored to force individuals through legal, medical, and administrative means to have an unambiguous sexual identity (Foucault 1980, viii; cf. Turner 1984, 21). For a man to be bisexual, or to have a "strong homosexual current" (Freud 1985, 464; letter of 23 July 1904), that is, to share qualities characteristic of the ideological construct "woman," threatened the sexual difference which undergirded masculinist bourgeois society. The bleeding Jewish nose with its suggestion of male menstruation and bisexuality stigmatized the male Jew as feminine. Yet the scientific exploration of bisexuality implicit to the representation of Jewish nasality threatened to universalize Jewish difference—and therefore undermine sexual difference (cf. Gilman 1987, 301). The psychiatric appropriation of the other familiar image of the Jew, the Wandering Jew, would endeavor to limit the damage.[21]

The *ewige Jude*

Paralleling the biologization, medicalization, and sexualization of what in the popular imagination was the most prominent Jewish physical characteristic, the nose, was a similar process applied to the "most tenacious" (Champfleury 1886, 1) popular image of the Jews: the Wandering Jew. Although the figure of the Wandering Jew underwent a series of metamorphoses during the nineteenth century (cf. Knecht 1974–77), one leitmotif identified the Wandering Jew with the entire Jewish people: "Ahasverus, the Wandering Jew, is nothing but the personification of the whole Jewish race" (Schopenhauer 1974, 2:261). A variation on this theme was adopted by Charcot and his students at the famous Salpêtrière clinic: Henry Meige's 1893 "Le Juif-errant à la Salpêtrière. Essai nosographique sur les névropathes voyageurs." Personifying the new science of psychiatry and given the authority granted scientific pronouncements, Charcot and his school had through psychiatric nosology the "power to define the collective identity of the Jews" (Goldstein 1985, 523). Meige's study was the culmination of a century of discussion about the existence of a specifically Jewish psychopathology. The alleged propensity of Jews for epilepsy or insanity, although buttressed by statistics (albeit fallaciously employed ones), more or less had been dismissed. Still there arose a general consensus of a Jewish predisposition (i.e., an inherited defect as a consequence of inbreeding) for neurasthenia and neurosis (cf. *Revue de l'hypnotisme* 1893, 147; Gilman 1984)—diseases associated with increased sensitivity to odors (cf. Ellis 1928, 70, 74). In his medical thesis, Meige made a particular psychiatric malady, "ambulatory neurosis," specifically Jewish by combining the clinical study of five Jewish patients with legendary accounts. Meige gives extensive verbal descriptions of his patients' faces, including their noses "sometimes long and sharp, more often large, flat, as one sees frequently in the German [Jewish] race" (1893, 347). In detailing a series of representations of the Wandering Jew collected from 1816 to 1850 at the Bibliothèque Nationale, he finds iconic reproductions of his patients: "the person is indeed typical of German and Polish Jews: the nose, the beard, and the hair are classic" (1893, 201–2). These resemblances betray a theory of legend which, following Goldstein (1985, 542; cf. *Revue de l'hypnotisme* 1893, 149–50), assumed that:

> The bulk of [almost all legends'] content comes from straightforward 'observations of material facts,' but these are then 'disguised' by a touch of 'superadded miraculousness,' indicative of the primitive mode of reasoning of their anonymous popular authors. . . . The traditional woodcuts of the Wandering Jew sold in the countryside were not some 'fantastic composition,' but were rather the 'exact' if naïve 'reproduction of a model which the artist had before his eyes'—as point-by-point comparisons with the drawings and photographs of living Jewish *névropathes voyageurs* at the Salpêtrière really showed. Stripped of his religious import, Meige concluded, the Wandering Jew 'still exists today.'

The base for European representation of the Jew had shifted from theology to pathology.

The psychopathology of the Wandering Jew would take a curious turn a year later in Dr. Paul Emil Flechsig's Psychiatric Clinic at the University of Leipzig. Residing there was Daniel Paul Schreber, who following the publication of his *Denkwürdigkeiten eines Nervenkranken* (Memoirs of My Mental Illness) in 1903 and the appearance eight years later of Freud's study of that work, "Psychoanalytic Notes upon an Autobiographical Account of a Case of Paranoia (Dementia Paranoides),"[22] retains even today a certain notoriety. In early 1894, Schreber had a series of hallucinations about the "Eternal Jew" (*ewiger Jude*). He recalls how voices informed him that in the event of world catastrophe (Schreber 1988, 73–74),

> in order to maintain the species, one single human being was spared—perhaps the relatively most moral—called by the voices that talk to me the '*Eternal Jew.*' This appellation has therefore a somewhat different sense from that underlying the legend of the same name of the Jew Ahasver; one is automatically reminded of the legends of Noah, Deucalion and Pyrrha, etc. . . . The Eternal Jew (in the sense described) had to be *unmanned* (transformed into a woman) to be able to bear children [*Der ewige Jude (in dem angegebenen Sinne) mußte entmannt (in ein Weib verwandelt) werden, um Kinder gebären zu können*]. . . . A regression occurred therefore, or a reversal of that developmental process which occurs in the human embryo in the fourth or fifth month of pregnancy, according to whether nature intends the future child to be of male

> or female sex. It is well known that in the first months of pregnancy the rudiments of both sexes are laid down and the characteristics of the sex which is not developed remain as rudimentary organs at a lower stage of development, like the nipples of the male[23]. . . . The Eternal Jew was maintained and provided with the necessary means of life by the 'fleeting-improvised-men'. . . .

Although in his memoirs Schreber never explicitly identifies himself as the unmanned Eternal Jew, his account suggests otherwise.[24] "During the latter part of my stay in Flechsig's Asylum [i.e., early 1894] I thought this period [i.e., the last 212 years allotted the earth] had already expired, and therefore thought I was the last real human being left, and that the few human shapes whom I saw apart from myself . . . were only 'fleeting-improvised-men' created by miracle" (Schreber 1988, 85; cf. 107 n. 56, 125). Schreber describes his body in the process of being transformed into a female body at this same time. Later "I could see beyond doubt that the Order of the World imperiously demanded my unmanning, whether I personally like it or not, and that therefore it was *common sense* that nothing was left to me but to reconcile myself to the thought of being transformed into a woman. Nothing of course could be envisaged as a further consequence of unmanning but fertilization by divine rays for the purpose of creating new human beings. My change of will was facilitated by my not believing at that time that apart from myself a real mankind existed; on the contrary I thought all the human shapes I saw were only 'fleeting and improvised' " (Schreber 1988, 148; cf. 212). The unmanned body of bourgeois, heterosexual (i.e., he was married), and male Schreber was the object of the gnosiological discourse of medical, here psychiatric, nosology and epitomized the inscribed bodies of those other than bourgeois, heterosexual, and male. Schreber's hallucinations also call attention to the primacy of reproduction within the regnant masculinist ideology and at play in the popular and scientific discussion of inherited predispositions and male menstruation. Finally, they point out an apparent association, despite his disclaimer, between Jews and the problematizing of sexual identity. These hegemonic practices, beliefs, and associations that formed about Schreber's body also suppurate from the noses of Freud, Fliess, and Eckstein.

Emma's *Foetos*

After riding some curls of nineteenth-century cultural and scientific history, we return to Freud's Vienna and to a series of events that began almost six months before the dream of Irma's injection: Fliess's operation on Emma Eckstein's *Nasenmuscheln* to remedy her gastric distress[25] and its aftermath. These events both anticipate many of the elements[26] of Freud's dream and recapitulate much of the preceding discussion of noses, smells, gender identity, and reproduction.

By the time Fliess journeyed to Vienna in February 1895 to operate on Eckstein and Freud, he and Freud had already been meeting, corresponding, and exchanging research for almost eight years. The preceding two years had marked an intensification of their relationship; both men were increasingly involved in comparing notes and noses. Leaving aside Fliess's rhinological specialization, their correspondence revealed, between their shared nose-related ailments and involvement with cocaine, a virtual obsession with the nose and nasality. Freud endeavored to incorporate Fliess's insights about the nose into his own psychological theory. He had already at the end of 1892 treated a patient suffering from olfactory hallucinations. Indeed, his discussion of the case of Lucy R. (Freud and Breuer 1895, 106–24) is where Freud clearly describes the active process of repression for the first time (cf. Jones 1953–57, 1:252; Gay 1988, 72–73; David-Menard 1989, 67–70). From this early recognition of smell as a possible sign of repressed ideas, Freud's theory of repression acquired an increasingly olfactive air: "To put it crudely, the memory stinks just as in the present the object stinks; and in the same manner as we turn away our sense organ (the head and nose) in disgust, the preconscious and the sense of consciousness turn away from the memory. This is repression" (Freud 1985, 280; letter of 14 November 1897; cf. Freud 1909, 247–48; Freud 1930, 100n., 106n.).[27] And just as smell betrayed the conflicts within Lucy R.'s situation of employment, so too did Fliess and Freud's professional preoccupation with noses and psychopathology betray their shared fate as Jews within the Central European medical establishment. Jews like Freud and Fliess who sought status and upward mobility by pursuing a medical career were generally confined to the lower rungs of the medical academic hierarchy. Rhinolaryngology, dermatology, syphilology, psychopathology, sexology, all of the specializations that dealt with primitive sense organs and sensations, all of the subdisciplines that had contact with the socially unacceptable, all of the vocations that were not marked by the objective, disinterested, technical mastery which characterized surgery or neurology, were the preserve of the Jews (Gilman 1987, 299–305). Yet Fliess and Freud's revaluation of the importance of nasality would restructure the strictures on Jewish medical mobility. By restoring the nose to an important role in the makeup of civilized modernity, Freud and Fliess would redeem the nose bearers as well.[28]

Other factors than this common quest for medical respectability led to the intensification of their relationship. Fliess's charisma, his comparative professional success, and Freud's feeling of isolation and corresponding need for an audience ("Without such an audience I cannot work" [Freud 1985, 243; letter of 16 May 1897]), for an "Other" (Freud 1985, 374; letter of 21 Sept. 1899; cf. 73; letter of 21 May 1894: "you are the only other, the *alter*"), led to a "transferencelike relationship" in which Freud idealized his Berlin friend (Schur 1972, 77 and *ff.*; Mahony 1978, 68). In their correspondence, and outside as well,[29] Freud assumed the role of patient. Considering the predominance of female patients in Freud's practice as well as the general and gendered structure of medical relationships—masculine subject—feminine object—he thereby took on an all but "feminine" persona (cf. Swan 1974, 24). Freud continuously yielded to the opinions of his "Daimonie" (Freud 1985, 134; letter of 24 July 1985, i.e., the morning after the dream of Irma's injection). He would come to describe their relationship in terms of "homosexual cathexis" (Freud to Ferenczi, 6 October 1910, cited in Jones 1953–57, 2:83; cf. Freud to Jones, 8 December 1912, cited in Jones 1953–57, 1:317; also see Gay 1988, 274–83; Heller 1981). This relationship between two Jewish men recapitulated the shared belief in human bisexuality. But in ideologically heterosexual, gender-differentiated Vienna, any intimation of male-to-male intimacy rendered the offending parties unmanly (cf. Baeumler 1934, 6–9, 30–42, 166–67; Mosse 1982b). Within the binary logic of masculinist ideology, they were feminized. Freud's male relationships—with their inherent potential for feminization—would play a large role in the dream of Irma's injection and Freud's later theories and relationships (cf. McGrath 1986; Koestenbaum 1988).

Freud's theoretical formulations at this juncture—he was working through his theory of the sexual etiology of hysteria as well as completing his *Studies on Hysteria* with Breuer—were guided by the hegemonic ideology of reproduction. Reproduction, neurosis, and its treatment were intimately connected. Freud hypothesized that the so-called actual neuroses were caused by the impairment of normal sexual activity, defined as heterosexual intercourse for the purpose of reproduction. Anxiety and neurasthenia arose not only from too much sex, exemplified by masturbation, or too little, the fate of unmarried women, but also from contraceptive sexual practices such as *coitus interruptus* and *coitus reservatus,* i.e., with condums (see, e.g., Freud 1985, 57–58, 90–91, 92–94, 98, 101–2; letters of 6 October 1893; 18 August 1894 (Draft F); 23 August 1894; 7 January 1895 [Draft G]).[30] He also knew that Breuer had ended his therapeutic relationship with Anna O., the most famous study on hysteria, when she confronted him with the claim that she was hysterically pregnant with his child (cf. Gay 1988, 66–67). Freud's concern with reproduction extended to the metaphors employed in describing his work: for example, in his 12 June 1895 letter to Fliess, Freud states that "Reporting on [the psychological construction of defense] now would be like sending a six-month fetus of a girl to a ball" (Freud 1985, 131).[31] On a more personal level, Freud was ever concerned about the effects of pregnancy on Martha's health, on their sex life, and on his ability to support a family. Epitomizing how the ideology of reproduction impinged upon both his theoretical and his personal life is a comment in his 25 May 1895 letter to Fliess: "I felt like shouting with excitement when I got your news. If you really have solved the problem of conception, just make up your mind immediately which kind of marble is most likely to meet with your approval. For me you are a few months too late, but perhaps it can be used next year. In any event, I am burning with curiosity about it" (Freud 1985, 129). Fliess's solution to unwanted pregnancy was to induce labor by stimulating the *Nasenmuscheln.*

His answer to Emma Eckstein's gastric distress was the partial removal of those same *Nasenmuscheln.* Several weeks later (4 March 1895) Freud wrote to Fliess that "Eckstein's condition is still unsatisfactory" (Freud 1985, 113). Freud convinces himself to call in another physician to Eckstein's apartment, who diagnoses that access to the site of the operation is impeded, thus making drainage difficult. "To judge by the smell [*Geruch*]" (Freud 1985, 114) emanating from her, Freud accepts his conclusion. According to the letter of 8 March 1895 (Freud 1985, 116–18), Eckstein's condition had seriously deteriorated. Freud begins the letter by summing up his previous correspondence: "I wrote you that the swelling and the hemorrhages would not stop, and that suddenly a fetid odor [*Foetos*] set in, and that there was an obstacle upon irrigation (or is the latter new [to you]?). . . ." The *Foetos,* this bearer of bad tidings, suddenly makes an appearance, like an actor entering on stage (Freud writes "*auftrat*"), a stage upon which Freud would soon play out the problem of gender identity.

Two days later, he adds, he had to call in Dr. Rosanes, an ear, nose, and throat specialist like Fliess. "There still was moderate bleeding from the nose and mouth; the fetid odor [*Foetos*] was very bad." Smell remains the key index of the severity of the situation. "Rosanes . . . suddenly pulled at something like a thread, kept on pulling. Before either of us had time to think, at least half a meter of [iodoform] gauze had been removed from the cavity. The next moment came a flood of blood [*Verblutung*]." Following this nasal hemorrhaging, there is no more discussion of the smell: with the removal of the gauze comes a corresponding elimination of the *Foetos* as well as the implication that an alternative scene is being enacted. That is, *Foetos* is a virtual homophone for *Foetus* or *fetus*. Through this phonetic connection the *Verblutung*, by definition a scene of (nearly) bleeding to death, also suggests a scene of birthing or rather, of miscarriage, of abortion. This symbolic depiction conforms with Fliess's contention that both nosebleeds and labor were forms of "transformed menstruation"; birthing is described as a "magnified version of menstrual flow" (Fliess 1977, 111, 69). Freud and Fliess shared the "shibboleth" (Fliess 1977, 111) that allowed them to recognize these relationships among nose, sexuality, and birth. Further contributing to the impression that Eckstein's nasal hemorrhaging represents a birthing is the iodoform gauze left in by Fliess, the source of the *Foetos*.[32] Iodoform is closely related chemically to that other strong-smelling substance frequently present in birthing rooms—chloroform.

Freud continues to describe the scene: "At the moment the foreign body came out and everything became clear to me—and I immediately afterward was confronted by the sight of the patient—I felt sick. After she had been packed, I fled to the next room. . . . The brave Frau Doktor [*tapfere Doktorin*] then brought me a small glass of cognac and I became myself again. . . . " In this scene Freud was less than manly or professional, in stark contrast to the *tapfere Doktorin*. Masson's decision (and Schur's before that [1966, 57]) to translate *Doktorin* as "Frau Doktor" is curious, since the identity of the individual is unknown (Freud 1985, 118 n. 2). Although professional women were extremely rare in 1895 Vienna, their assumption that the *Doktorin* must be the spouse of a doctor undercuts the gender inversion which Freud—unconsciously—suggests. That gender roles are at stake in this aborted birth scene becomes clear when Freud, after describing Eckstein's subsequent care, returns to recount what happened after "I became myself again." Eckstein "had not lost consciousness during the massive hemorrhage; when I returned to the room somewhat shaky, she greeted me with the condescending remark, 'So this is the strong sex' [*Das ist das starke Geschlecht*]." Freud becomes very defensive in his commentary on her remark: "I do not believe it was the blood that overwhelmed [*überwältigt*] me—at that moment strong emotions were welling up in me." He endeavors to restore his professional—and masculine—status. Yet his alternative explanation, the surge of affects, undercut his defense. The source of this welled-up emotion is his relationship to Fliess, and he situates himself in a "feminine" position: irrational, dependent, passive, powerless. "That this mishap should have happened to you [i.e., Fliess]; how you will react to it when you hear about it; what others would make of it, how wrong I was to urge you to operate in a foreign city where you could not follow through on the case; how my intention to do my best for this poor girl ['my child of sorrows'] was insidiously thwarted and resulted in endangering her life—all this came over me simultaneously." Fliess, by leaving the gauze in the wound, is the father of the *Foetos;* Freud is the mother or midwife. Freud's "feminine" defensiveness, however, had to be itself defended against: "I only want to add that for a day I shied away from letting you know about [the scene]. . . . " Yet once again he was overcome by a feeling ascribed to women, shame:[33] "then I began to feel ashamed [*mich zu schämen*], and here is the letter." In the aftermath of Fliess's surgery, Emma Eckstein's hemorrhaging nose becomes the stage upon which problems of gender identity are played out.

Through the end of May, Freud continues to report on Eckstein as well as endeavors to absolve Fliess of all responsibility for her condition. His letters are filled with accounts of his cocainization, case histories to validate Fliess's nasal theories, and discussion of the impending births of both Freud's last child and Fliess's first. When 24 July comes, Freud queries Fliess about the entire inventory of his concerns: "What is happening to the nose, menstruation, labor pains, neuroses, your dear wife, and the budding little one?" (Freud 1985, 134) But there is no mention of Eckstein, nor is there any mention of the dream of the preceding night—the dream of Irma's injection.

The Dream of Sigmund's *Nasenmuscheln*

The role of the *Nasenmuscheln,* the significant presence of strong odors, the medical intervention, the casting (out) of toxic substances, and the questioning of gender identity all find their parallel in the dream of Irma's injection. Was Irma Emma? In the course of his analysis, Freud associates her with a number of people, including a governess; Irma's friend whom he would have preferred to treat; a patient who has the same name as his eldest daughter, Sophie; an old woman who has the same name as his middle daughter, Mathilde; and his wife. When he takes up the analysis of the dream again in the *Interpretation of Dreams,* he refers to Irma as a "collective figure" (Freud 1900, 4:292) and adds a few more associations. Emma Eckstein is not mentioned in either account. Some later investigators have found a clue to Irma's identity in the word "Ananas," which appeared on the bottle of liqueur whose foul smell Freud credited with initiating the series "propyl . . . propyls . . . proprionic acid." Freud appended a note to his mention of the word: "I must add that the sound of the word 'Ananas' bears a remarkable resemblance to that of my patient Irma's family name" (Freud 1900, 4:115n). Since none of Freud's patients is known to have a last name in any way close to this, it has been assumed that Freud was merely diverting attention from the patient whose first name would bear a "remarkable resemblance": *Anna* Lichtheim. She was the daughter of Freud's beloved teacher Samuel Hammerschlag, a current patient, family friend and widow like Irma, and the person for whom Freud would name his last child, the child Martha was carrying at the time of the dream.[34] When this identification is made, however, Irma's identity tends to be downplayed in the interpretation.[35] She is merely the occasion for other dream thoughts to be represented. Another school of thought takes its cue from Schur (1966) and identifies Irma with Emma. These interpreters cite among other clues Freud's comment that "I had had Irma examined by [Fliess] to see whether her gastric pains might be of nasal origin" [Freud 1900, 4:117). For this school, the identity of Irma is the interpretive key and the dream a way for Freud to work through the trauma Fliess's botched surgery caused to their relationship (cf. Gay 1988, 83–87).

Irma clearly has a composite identity, inclusive of Emma, but the identification process that this dream enacts and that brings together the earlier scene of Freud's apparent unmanning with the motif of questioned gender identity is Freud's own conflicted identification with a woman. This analysis occurs during his analysis of dream elements that deal with particular body locales. When discussing the passage in his dream account Freud writes that "a portion of the skin [*Hautpartie*] on the left shoulder was infiltrated. (I noticed this, just as [my colleague] did . . .)." Freud thus recognizes the shoulder infiltration as his own rheumatism and further specifies that "I noticed it in my own body" (Freud 1900, 4:113). The doctor and, by extension, his colleague detect this *Hautpartie* on Freud's body. Freud has become the patient: "he, the doctor and man, fuses with the image of the *patient* and *woman*" (Erikson 1954, 33). By fusing with Irma, Freud confirms as well that he had relinquished male authority by calling upon other men to examine and help his patient.[36] Yet this identification with Irma is a conflicted one. Freud is struck by the dream wording that refers to the body (i.e., the "left shoulder") rather than to abstract coordinates "left upper posterior." His puzzlement over the use of nontechnical language, on the one hand, acknowledges the objectification of the female patient by medical examination and its "objective" discourse. On the other hand, the omission of medical body topography indicates Freud's wish to distinguish himself from the traditional object of medicine and therefore manifests his resistance to the implications of being identified with a woman patient, namely, being subjected to "homosexual submission and humiliation before male authority" (Swan 1974, 34). The surface of Freud's body that is observed and contested over is also the skin of a Jew; and what infiltrates the *Hautpartie* is Freud's isolation within a Jewish medical preserve, like neurology. That is, the locus of medical treatment and Freud's professional concerns converge on dermatology, a field nicknamed *Judenhaut* (Jew-skin; cf. Gilman 1987, 299).[37]

Freud's Jewish- and gender-coded identification with Irma through the spot on her shoulder hooks into two other body sites mentioned in the analysis. In the dream segment he writes: "She then opened her mouth properly and on the right I found a big white patch; at another place I saw extensive whitish grey scabs upon some remarkably curly structures which were evidently modeled on the turbinal bones of the nose." According to Freud, Irma's friend "would have yielded sooner [*würde also eher nachgeben*]"—a clearly feminine position—and "would then have *opened her mouth properly,* and have told me more than Irma." Following this scene of yielding and confessing, Freud notes that he had curtailed his analysis; he then adds, "There is at least one spot (*Stelle*) in every dream at which it is unplumbable—a navel, as it were, that is its point of contact with the unknown" (4:111 n. 1). It is also the male fetus's point of contact with the mother: they are fused together. At this junction distinctions, gender distinctions, blur; the male is passive and dependent—"feminine." Identification with woman is something that cannot be known or let be known.[38]

Discussion of this spot is immediately followed by discussion of another one, the so-called genital spots (*Genital*stellen), the turbinal bones or *Nasenmuscheln*. Here too Freud associates Irma's body with his own: "The scabs on the turbinal bones recalled a worry about my own state of health. I was making frequent use of cocaine at that time to reduce some troublesome nasal swellings. . . . " The implications of the *Nase* in *Nasenmuscheln* in cultural and gender terms have already been explored. But *muscheln* resonates as well with two diametrically opposite images of turn-of-the-century Jews: Theodor Herzl's *Mauscheln* and Max Nordau's *Muskeljuden*. For Herzl, "*Mauschel* [pl. *Mauscheln*] is the curse of the Jews." *Mauschel* is antithetic to, if tragically confused with, his idealized image of the *Jew*. *Mauschel,* derived from the derogatory term for nasally Jewish-accented German and its purported content, deceptive economic dealmaking, is the cringing, mocking, arrogant, selfish, mendacious *Schnorrer,* ever on the lookout for an underhanded deal and quick profit (Herzl 1973, cit. 165).[39] Nordau's *Muskeljuden,* his muscle-Jews, are for their part physically different from their confrères. They engage in gymnastics in order to "straighten us in body and in character" (Nordau 1980, 435); they seek to differentiate themselves from the unmasculine Jews pictured by Walter Rathenau in "Höre Israel": "unathletic build," "narrow shoulders," "clumsy feet," "sloppy roundish shape" (Rathenau 1980, 232). Arousing the anxieties of Herzl, Nordau, and Rathenau were the consequences, for all Jews, of the entry into the public sphere of the now-emancipated, perceived-as-feminized Jew. Freud's turbinal bones evoke his feminization, not just as a late-nineteenth-century male, but as a late-nineteenth-century Jewish male.

The reference to the *Nasenmuscheln* also evokes one other intrinsically "feminine" body process: birthing. Again, according to Fliess, these "genital spots" were intimately related to the birthing process: "an important connection . . . close and reciprocal rapports" (1977, 17). The process of conception is alluded to at both the beginning and end of the dream. When the dream opens, Freud and his wife are receiving guests. The German term for "receive," "*empfangen,*" is rife with associations to conception; for example, the "*unbefleckte Empfängnis*" is the Immaculate Conception. Unfortunately in Irma's mouth, a traditional womb/vagina symbol, is "a big white patch," "*einen großen weißen Fleck.*" The other allusions to birthing are no less maculate. The elimination of the "toxin"[40] through the supervention of dysentery clearly evokes parturition. Freud would later write to Fliess that birthing—or miscarrying—is dirty, diarrhetic: "everything related to birth, miscarriage, [menstrual] period goes back to the toilet via the word *Abort* [toilet] (*Abortus* [abortion])" (Freud 1985, 288; letter of 22 December 1897).

And the cause of the conception, the unclean syringe, is a dirty squirter or penis [*Spritze nicht rein*].

These images of befouled or failed birth conflict with Freud's desires to create. His works are his creations, his children with Fliess: Fliess is introduced into the chain of associations as "another friend who had for many years been familiar with all my writings during the period of their gestation [*meine keimenden Arbeiten*]" (4:116). And he wishes to re-create himself; such is the goal of his self-analysis, which may be said to have begun with this dream. Yet in this dream, when Freud assumes the woman's role, conception is no longer scientific; it becomes dirty, if not aborted. The imagery of conception is both modeled after and distinguishes itself from women's fertility.

There is a conflict in this dream between Freud's desire to be a member of the *Männerbund,* represented by the authoritative, probing male medical examiners, and his identification with woman, the neurotic, nasal, victimized—Jewish—patient. He wishes to (re)join his confrères. According to the dream such men, on the one hand, assert their socially sanctioned male aggressiveness against women and the unmanned and, on the other hand, desire to usurp from women the ability to reproduce: they desire to create themselves as independent individuals. And through *his* analysis of the dream he succeeds: he willingly confesses his aggression (4:120; cf. Swan 1974) and applauds his own new production, "the achievement of this one piece of new knowledge" (4:121). Yet, Freud remains plagued by the impossibility of desire within the *Männerbund;* male intimacy is overlaid with a socially encoded feminine role: yielding, passive, desiring of men.[41] The dream reveals the fragile nature of the gender identities supporting the Vienna of the late nineteenth century. The dream's focus on Irma's/Freud's body shows how the body became the field upon which the various disciplines and institutions sought to construct gender identity necessary to sustain the *Männerbund.*[42] The *Nasenmuscheln* and related nasal imagery point out how the feminized body of the male Jew, as an individual and as a group, threatened that construct.[43]

Notes

*A briefer version of this chapter was presented before the Religion and the Social Sciences Section session on the Psychosocial Construction of the body at the November 1989 annual meeting of the American Academy of Religion in Anaheim. The research for this paper was performed under the auspices of the American Council of Learned Societies. I would also like to thank Amy-Jill Levine, Scott Gilbert, and Hans-Jakob Werlen for their helpful comments.

1. This is not to suggest that the public sphere formed either simultaneously or uniformly among the various populations of Europe; on the public sphere see Landes 1988; following Habermas 1958.

2. This dream only assumed its central role in *The Interpretation of Dreams* because Fliess advised against Freud's employing his only completely analyzed dream—Irma was merely "thoroughly" analyzed—as a frame upon which he would construct his text. That original dream has never turned up. Cf. Freud 1985, 315, 316 n. 1, 317; letters of 9, 20 June 1898.

3. See discussion of these figures below. On the propensity of dreams to take advantage of the ambiguity of the pronunciation as well as of the meaning of words, see Mahony 1977 and Freud's discussion of the "Considerations of Representability" (1900, 5:339*ff.*). Freud (1985, 295; letter of 22 January 1898) also punned with other of Fliess's nose-related terms when awake; for instance he jokingly refers to the "reflex new-roses [*Reflexneurosen*]," a play on the nasal reflex neuroses [*Reflexneurosen*].

4. Küpper's lexicon lists more idioms under *Nase* than under either *Auge* (eye), *Ohr* (ear), or *Mund/Maul* (mouth). On the influence of proverbs on Freud's thought, cf. Freud to Fliess, 14 November 1897 (Freud 1985, 279): "(. . . the notion [of organic repression] was linked to the changed part played by sensations of smell: upright walking, nose raised from the ground, at the same time a number of formerly interesting sensations attached to the earth becoming repulsive—by a process still unknown to me.) (He turns up his nose = he regards himself as something particularly noble.)"

5. Conversely its presence/absence is indication of Jews as mongrel race, cf. Chamberlain 1968, 1:389.

6. Curiously the English translation (Freytag 1855) omits this passage.

7. *The Rabbi of Bacharach* is rife with nasal imagery: the gatekeeper to the Frankfurter ghetto is Nasenstern (Nose-Star) whose "fast unglaublich lange Nase" facetiously substitutes for the key to the ghetto gate; the voluptuous and promiscuous Schnapper-Elle "hat sich in seine Nase verliebt"; together because of his (i.e., Nasenstern's) imagined reproductive prodigality, in 300 years Frankfurt would be hidden beneath the numerous Nasensterns; odors just pour out of Schnapper-Elle's kitchen (motivating

Don Issac's comment); Nasenstern's partner is Jäkel the fool who has a "näselnde Stimme" and is "krummbeinig."

8. This "regression to a very early interchangeability of the container and the contents, in other words to a mechanism of primary thought" (Anzieu 1966, 153) may also reflect the psychopathology of a dominant group that seeks to deny its dependence on the other for its own self-determination.

9. On the medieval origin of the notion of a *foetor Judaicus,* see Trachtenberg 1943, 47–50.

10. Despite Nietzsche's olfactory sensitivity and his alleged anti-Semitism, Nietzsche does not contribute significantly to the dissemination of the *foetor Judaicus;* however, he does remark in the *Anti-Christ* (Nietzsche 1968, 161): "One would no more choose to associate with 'first Christians' than one would with Polish Jews. . . . Neither of them smell very pleasant." Also see Bloch 1934, 10–11: "In the act of olfaction it seems that a real contact of the psyche with the material world has taken place, a penetration into the sensed matter and an immediate perception of its essence. . . . the sublimated thing-in-itself."

11. On the medieval and early modern origins of this attribution see Poliakov 1965, 142–43 and n. 14; the tradition of a scent peculiar to the Jews goes back at least as far as Marcus Aurelius, cf. Jaeger 1884, 113.

12. Others vying for this honor include Richard Wagner (cf. Weiner 1989); Jaeger (1884, 6–7, 10, 64, 113 [citing Andrée 1876, 246–47]); Berillon (1909, 266); Günther (1930, 260–68, chap "Geruchliche Eigenart"); and Hitler (1943, 57), who writes: "The cleanliness of [the Jews], moral and otherwise, I must say, is a point in itself. By their very exterior you could tell that these were no lovers of water, and, to your distress, you often knew it with your eyes closed. Later I often grew sick to my stomach from the smell of these caftan wearers."

This last passage in retrospect perversely evokes the depiction of the Davidic Messiah in B. Sanhedrin 93b—"And further it is written, *And He will let him have delight in* [lit. 'will let him scent'] *the fear of the Lord* [Isa. 11:3; Luther's Bible reads 'mein Riechen wird sein bei der Furcht des Herrn']. R. Alexandri said: 'This teaches us that they burdened him with commandments and sufferings like millstones' [assuming *hariho,* which literally means 'he will let him scent', derives from *rehayim,* millstones]. Rava said: '[This teaches us that] he will scent [the truth] and will adjudicate, as it is written, *and he shall not judge after the sight of his eyes, neither reprove after the hearing of his ears, yet with righteousness shall he judge the poor'* [Isa. 11:3–4]" (cf. Patai 1979).

13. Horkheimer and Adorno are perhaps referring to Schopenhauer when they write in their "Elements of Anti-Semitism" (1972, 184): "The multifarious nuances of the sense of smell embody the archetypal longing

for the lower forms of existence, for direct unification with circumambient nature, with the earth and mud. Of all the senses, that of smell—which is attracted without objectifying—bears clearest witness to the urge to lose oneself in and become the 'other.' As perception and the perceived—both are united—smell is more expressive than the other senses. When we see we remain what we are; but when we smell we are taken over by otherness. Hence the sense of smell is considered a disgrace in civilization, the sign of lower social strata, lesser races and base animals. The civilized individual may only indulge in such pleasure if the prohibition is suspended by rationalization in the service of real or apparent practical ends. The prohibited impulse may be tolerated if there is no doubt that the final aim is its elimination—this is the case with jokes or fun, the miserable parody of fulfillment. As a despised and despising characteristic, the mimetic function is enjoyed craftily. Anyone who seeks out 'bad' smells, in order to destroy them, may imitate sniffing to his heart's content, taking unrationalized pleasure in the experience. The civilized man 'disinfects' the forbidden impulse by his unconditional identification with the authority which prohibited it; in this way the action is made acceptable. If he goes beyond the permitted bounds, laughter ensues. This is the schema of the anti-Semitic reaction. Anti-Semites gather together to celebrate the moment when authority permits what is usually forbidden. . . . "

14. On the primitiveness of language which does not distinguish between objective and subjective perspectives, cf. Jaeger 1884, 108.

15. Nordau cites the anti-Semites' fascination with the work of Gustav Jaeger (1884, 1912), which identified the individuality of each soul with the totality of odors released in the breakdown of protein molecules and the natural differences between the race with the correspondingly different—and incompatible—scents.

16. Bloch (1934, 70) cites a different odor, that of trimethylamin, which appears in the dream of Irma's injection and which Freud associates with Fliess.

17. On the other hand, Bloch (1934, 74) notes: "In strong, vigorous men this *odeur de l'homme* is considerably sharper than among effeminate and weak ones."

18. The association between chloroform and questions of gender identity also played a role in Freud's early career; the Viennese psychiatrist, former teacher of Freud, and chloroform addict Theodor Meynert, objected strenuously to Freud's contention that men can suffer from the archetypal woman's neurosis, hysteria. In *Interpretation* Freud reports on Meynert's deathbed confession that he was a male hysteric (1900, 5:438). This conflict, which was implicitly about gender identity, led to Freud's foreclosure from the neurological institute at the University of Vienna and severely limited his opportunities within Viennese medical circles; cf. Kris 1954, 20.

On Meynert's addiction to drinking chloroform, see Freud 1985, 293; letter of 4 January 1898.

19. On Jewish male menstruation and the blood libel, see Trachtenberg 1943, 50–51, 149; and Hsia, esp. his discussions of Johannes Eck and Andreas Osiander (1988, 4, 134, 138).

20. Translation in Kris (1954, 7). Cf. Freud 1985, 212; letter of 6 December 1896: "I avail myself of the bisexuality of all human beings"; and Gilman (1987, 304): "Jews show their inherent difference through their damaged sexuality [i.e., their implicit bisexuality], and the sign of that is, in the popular mind, the fact that males menstruate. . . . The hidden sign, the link between the homosexual, the woman, and the Jew is the menstruation of the Jewish male."

21. Cf. Freud, "Draft M. The Architecture of Hysteria" (1985, 246): "What men essentially repress is the pederastic element."

22. Freud (1911); this case history is Freud's most extensive discussion of paranoia as repressed homosexuality. His consideration of the homosexual content of Schreber's *Memoirs* was inextricably bound with his relationship with Fliess: "I am unable to judge [the Schreber case history's] objective worth as was possible with earlier papers, because in working on it I have had to fight off complexes with myself (Fliess)"; Freud and Jung (1974, letter to Jung, 18 December 1910), cited by Mahony (1979, 87). On learning from Fliess that paranoia was dependent on repressed homosexuality, cf. Jones 1953–57, 2:250, 268; letters to Jung [27 January 1908] and Abraham [3 March 1911].

23. Interestingly, they are motivated by some of the same embryological hypotheses about human bisexuality that undergird the theories, such as those of Fliess, of the connection between nose and genitalia.

24. Questions arise, ones that cannot be dealt with here: why was Schreber silent about his apparent identification with the "Eternal Jew"? did Schreber, despite his disclaimer that the "Eternal Jew" was not Jewish, find being transformed into a Jew more difficult to accept than being turned into a woman? and why have the later commentators ignored (with the exception of Lukacher [1981] and Prado de Oliveira [1979]) discussion of the "Eternal Jew"? I have addressed these issues in "The Unmanning of the Wandering Jew" (Geller 1991).

25. Fliess (1977, 135–36) had theorized that there were "stomach ache spots" adjacent to the nasal genital spots (*Nasenmuscheln*). The cocainization, cauterization, and extirpation of the offending parts were among the operative procedures to which Fliess would subject his patients who suffered from any number of possible nasal reflex neuroses.

26. Greenberg and Pearlman (1978, table 1) list some twenty correlations—some of which are rather tenuous—between elements in the dream and those in Freud's letters to Fliess.

27. For Sulloway (1979), Freud's theory of organic "repression and the sense of smell were to become paradigmatic for all of his subsequent attempts to resolve the problem of repression in phylogenetic terms" (359). Indeed, the tie of smell and repression, " 'the corner-stone' in Freud's theory of psychoneurosis" (368) is the cornerstone of Sulloway's claims of both Freud's continued biologism and his extensive theoretical dependence upon Fliess. Interestingly, Schopenhauer (1958, 2:31) refers to smell as "the sense of memory."

28. An extensive literature has developed during the last fifteen years that addresses Freud's position as a Jew in a Christian society; cf. the annotated bibliography in Gay 1987, 157–77.

29. In addition to the operation that occurred during the same period as the operation on Eckstein, Freud regularly consulted him on his cardiac condition and cigar addiction. Cf. Freud 1985, 129; letter of 25 May 1895: "I hope to bring enough with me to Berlin so that I can amuse you and hold your interest for the entire time I am your patient."

30. At this juncture Freud more or less accepts the general hysteria about the dangers of masturbation. Fliess (1977, 238) also remarks that "The sexually mature man, who to the extent that he can satisfy entirely the reproductive instinct, does not have anxiety. The excitation finds its normal expression and thereby its equilibrium." On the relations among the ideology of reproduction, normative sex, and health, see Hull 1982, 256–58; and Mosse 1982, 226 [citing the depiction of contraception use as "conjugal onanism" in the British medical journal *Lancet*], 232.

31. The manner in which the ideology of reproduction channels Freud's desire into the desire to sublate woman's reproductive power finds its most blatant expression in his ode to celebrate the birth of Fliess's second son and his father's calculation of the exact birthdate: "Hail/To the valiant son who at the behest of his father appeared at the right time,/ . . . /But hail to the father, too, who just prior to the event found in his calculations/the key to restraining the power of the female sex/And to shouldering his burden of lawful succession;/ . . . /He calls upon the higher powers to claim his right, conclusion, belief, and doubt;/ . . . /May the calculation be correct and, as the legacy of labor, be transferred from father to son . . . " (Freud 1985, 393–94; letter of 29 December 1899); cf. Koestenbaum 1988, 73–74.

32. Schur (1966, 57 n. 13) comments: "There is hardly a more sickeningly foetid odor than that of iodoform gauze left in a wound for fourteen days."

33. In "Draft K. The Neuroses of Defense"—is this perhaps the fully matured "six-month-old fetus" of 12 June 1895—enclosed in the letter of 1 January 1896, Freud (1985, 163) writes "Where there is no shame (as in a male person). . . ."

34. Cf. Anzieu 1986, 134; Eissler 1985; and others. Anzieu (1986, 134, 140) also suggests that Anna O. is one of the individuals condensed onto the figure of Irma. Surprisingly, although Masson makes much of the significance of Emma Eckstein for both Freud's seduction theory and his relationship with Fliess, he accepts the Anna Lichtheim hypothesis (1985, 57, 60, 213 n. 1, 213–14 n. 4).

35. Thus Eissler (1985), like Elms (1980) before him, focuses on Freud's relationship with and the pregnancy of Martha. Anzieu (1986, 153) does tie Anna in with the motif of smell: "Ananas is pronounced in German in exactly the same way as *Anna nass* (wet Anna); so she stinks."

36. Both Erikson (1954) and Swan (1976) focus on the male medical confraternity, the *Männerbund,* formed by Freud's colleagues in his dream and on Freud's inclusion/exclusion from this group as a consequence of his shifting relationship to Irma. Erikson's model is, in Swan's formulation, "the religious brotherhood [which] forms and perpetuates itself through rites in which a group of men assimilate for themselves symbolically the powers of feared, envied and excluded women. That is, the model adopted by Erikson is the social institution which, historically, has offered a patriarchal and homosexual resolution to masculine anxiety about weakness and passivity" (1974, 28–29). Swan's model is historically specific to late-nineteenth-century European bourgeois society that was marked by separate gender-coded spheres.

37. And by relinquishing medical authority to his colleagues, he is no longer the ***Partieführer,*** the foreman of the medical examination team.

38. Writing in response to Freud's explanation of his latest in a series of fainting spells as a "bit of neurosis that I ought to really look into," Jung proposes: "may I draw your attention to the fact that you open *The Interpretation of Dreams* with the mournful admission of your own neurosis—the dream of Irma's injection—identification with the neurotic in need of treatment. Very significant" (Freud to Jung, 29 November 1912, and Jung to Freud, 3 December 1912; in Freud and Jung 1974, 524 [#329 F], 526 [#330 J]). Freud apparently recognized the significance. Soon after the receipt of Jung's missive, Freud wrote to Jones. He first discusses his recent fainting spell in terms of "some piece of unruly homosexual feeling"—that Jones surmises relates to Fliess (Jones 1953–57, 1:317; cf. Schur 1972, 264–72)—and then describes how he deflected Jung's parry, when "in [Jung's] last letter [he] again hinted at my 'neurosis' " (Freud to Jones, 8 December 1912; cited in Jones 1953–57, 1:317). Freud, who seven years earlier had written of "the necessary universality of the tendency to inversion in psy-

choneurotics," hints at his own feminization (1905, 166n; Freud concedes here that Fliess had first drawn his attention to this universal). Jung rubbed Freud's nose in this "hint." His letter of 3 December 1912 opens with "my very best thanks for one passage in your letter, where you speak of a 'bit of neurosis' you haven't got rid of. This 'bit' should in my opinion, be taken very seriously indeed because, as experience shows, it leads 'usque ad instar voluntariae mortis.' I have suffered from this bit in my dealings with you . . . " (Freud and Jung 1974, 525 [#330J]).

39. Cf. the extensive researches on Jewish language as a figure of the Jew in Gilman (1986).

40. The toxin [*Gift*] is also a sign of the (anticipated) consummation of a marriage, the dowry [***Mitgift***].

41. Thus in a later letter to Fliess (Masson, *Complete Letters,* 447 [7 August 1901]) Freud wrote: "I do not share your contempt for friendship between men, probably because I am to a high degree party to it. In my life, as you know, woman has never replaced the comrade, the friend. If Breuer's male inclination were not so odd, so timid, so contradictory . . . it would provide a nice example of the accomplishments into which the androphilic current in men can be sublimated." In this letter Freud finally realizes that "there is no concealing the fact that the two of us have drawn apart to some extent."

42. Swan (1974, 5) writes: "In Freud's work, the contradictions of late-nineteenth century bourgeois society appear in the form of unresolved conflicts about masculine and feminine identification." I would amend Swan's formulation to read "entail" rather than "appear in the form of."

43. On the implications of the merger of "viraginous woman and the effeminate Jew," see Djikstra (1986, especially the last paragraph, 401).

References

Andrée, Richard
1876 "Völkergeruch." *Korrespondenzblatt der Anthropologischen Gesellschaft* 5:246–47.

Anzieu, Didier
1986 *Freud's Self-Analysis.* Trans. P. Graham. Madison, Conn.: International Universities Press. Orig. Fr. ed. 1975.

Arendt, Hannah
1958 *The Human Condition.* Chicago: University of Chicago Press.

Baeumler, Alfred
1934 *Männerbund und Wissenschaft.* Berlin: Junker und Dünnhaupt.

Berillon, Edgar
1908–09 "Psychologie de l'olfaction: La fascination olfactive chez les animaux et chez l'homme." *Revue de l'hypnotisme et de la psychologie physiologique* 23:98–103, 135–38, 167–69, 196–200, 235–39, 263–67, 303–7.

Bloch, Iwan
1909 *The Sexual Life of Our Time in Its Relations to Modern Civilization.* Trans. M. E. Paul from 6th Germ. ed. London: Rebman.
1934 *Odoratus Sexualis.* New York: Panurge Press.

Blüher, Hans
1917 *Die Rolle der Erotik in der männlichen Gesellschaft.* 2 vols. Jena: Eugen Diederichs.

Brittan, Arthur
1989 *Masculinity and Power.* Oxford: Basil Blackwell.

Burckhardt, Jacob
1955 *The Letters of Jacob Burckhardt.* Ed. and trans. A. Dru. New York: Pantheon.

Chamberlain, Houston Stewart
1968 *Foundations of the Nineteenth Century.* Trans. J. Lees. New York: Howard Fertig, 1968. Orig. Eng. ed., 1910. Orig. Germ. ed., 1899.

Champfleury
1886 *Histoire de l'imagerie populaire.* New ed. Paris: E. Deutu.

Corbin, Alain
1986 *The Foul and the Fragrant. Odor and the French Social Imagination.* Cambridge: Harvard University Press. Orig. Fr. ed. 1982.

David-Menard, Monique
1989 *Hysteria from Freud to Lacan. Body and Language in Psychoanalysis.* Trans. C. Porter. Ithaca: Cornell University Press. Orig. Fr. ed. 1983.

Derrida, Jacques
1985 *The Ear of the Other: Otobiography, Transference, Translation: Texts and Discussions with Jacques Derrida.* Ed. C. V. McDonald. Trans. P. Kamuf. New York: Schocken.

Djikstra, Bram
1986 *Idols of Perversity. Fantasies of Feminine Evil in Fin-de-Siècle Culture.* New York: Oxford University Press.

Eissler, K. R.
1985 "A Farewell to Freud's *Interpretation of Dreams.*" *American Imago* 42:111–29.

Ellis, Havelock
1928 *Studies in the Psychology of Sex*. Vol. 4: *Sexual Selection in Man*. Rev. and enl. ed. Philadelphia: F. A. Davis.

Elms, Alan C.
1980 "Freud, Irma, Martha: Sex and Marriage in the 'Dream of Irma's Injection.'" *Psychoanalytic Review* 67:63–109.

Erikson, Erik H.
1954 "The Dream Specimen of Psychoanalysis." *Journal of the American Psychoanalytic Association* 2:5–56.

Fliess, Wilhelm
1977 *Les relations entre le nez et les organes génitaux féminins. Présentées selon leurs significations biologiques*. Trans. P. Ach and J. Guir. Paris: Seuil. Orig. Germ. ed., 1897.

Foucault, Michel
1973 *The Order of Things*. Trans. A. M. S. Smith. New York: Random House. Orig. Fr. ed., 1970.
1978 *History of Sexuality*. Vol. 1: *An Introduction*. Trans. R. Hurley. New York: Random House. Orig. Fr. ed. 1975.
1980 "Introduction." *Hercules Barbin*. Ed. M. Foucault. Trans. R. McDougall. New York: Pantheon.

Freud, Sigmund
1900 *The Interpretation of Dreams. The Standard Edition of the Complete Psychological Works (=S.E.)*. Trans. and ed. J. Strachey. vols 4–5. London: Hogarth Press, 1953–74.
1905 *Three Essays on the Theory of Sexuality*. *S.E.* 7:123–243.
1909 "Notes upon a Case of Obsessional Neurosis." *S.E.* 10:151–249.
1911 "Psychoanalytic Notes upon an Autobiographical Account of a Case of Paranoia (Dementia Paranoides)." *S.E.* 12:1–79.
1930 *Civilization and Its Discontents*. *S.E.* 21:57–145.
1985 *The Complete Letters of Sigmund Freud to Wilhelm Fliess*. Ed. and trans. J. M. Masson. Cambridge: Harvard University Press.

Freud, Sigmund, and Josef Breuer
1895 *Studies on Hysteria*. *S.E.* 2:48–305.

Freud, Sigmund, and C. G. Jung
1974 *The Freud/Jung Letters. The Correspondence between Sigmund Freud and C. G. Jung*. Ed. W. McGuire. Trans. R. Manheim and R. F. C. Hull. Princeton: Princeton University Press.

Freytag, Gustav
1855 *Debit and Credit*. Trans. L. C. C. New York: Harper and Brothers.
1977 *Soll und Haben*. Munich: Hauser.

Fuchs, Eduard
1921 *Die Juden in der Karikatur. Ein Beitrag zur Kulturgeschichte*. Munich: Albert Langen.

Gay, Peter
1987 *A Godless Jew: Freud, Atheism, and the Making of Psychoanalysis*. New Haven: Yale University Press.
1988 *Freud. A Life for Our Time*. New York: Norton.

Geller, Jay
1991 "The Unmanning of the Wandering Jew." Lecture delivered at Syracuse University, 11 April.

Gilman, Sander L.
1981 "What Looks Crazy. Towards an Iconography of Insanity in Art and Medicine in the Nineteenth Century." In *The Turn of the Century: German Literature and Art 1890–1915*. Ed. G. Chapple and H. H. Schulte. Bonn: Bouvier Verlag.
1984 "Jews and Mental Illness: Medical Metaphors, Anti-Semitism, and the Jewish Response." *Journal of the History of the Behavioral Sciences* 20: 150–59.
1985 "Sexuality, Psychoanalysis, and Degeneration: From a Theory of Race to a Race to Theory." In *Degeneration: The Dark Side of Progress*. Ed. J. E. Chamberlin and S. L. Gilman. New York: Columbia University Press.
1986 *Jewish Self-Hatred. Anti-Semitism and the Hidden Language of the Jews*. Baltimore: Johns Hopkins University Press.
1987 "The Struggle of Psychiatry with Psychoanalysis: Who Won?" *Critical Inquiry* 13:293–313.

Goldstein, Jan
1985 "The Wandering Jew and the Problem of Psychiatric Anti-Semitism in Fin-de-Siècle France." *Journal of Contemporary History* 20: 521–51.

Greenberg, R., and C. Pearlman
1978 "If Freud Only Knew: A Reconsideration of Psychoanalytic Dream Theory." *International Review of Psycho-Analysis* 5:71–75.

Günther, Hans
1930 *Rassenkunde des jüdischen Volkes*. Munich: J. F. Lehmann.

Habermas, Jürgen
1962 *Strukturwandel der Öffentlichkeit. Untersuchungen zu einer Kategorie der bürgerlichen Gesellschaft*. Neuwied: Luchterhand.

Haeckel, Ernst
1874 *Anthropogenie oder Entwickelungsgeschichte des Menschen: Keimes- und Stammes-Geschichte*. Leipzig: Wilhelm Engelmann.

Haller, John S., Jr.
1975 *Outcasts from Evolution. Scientific Attitudes of Racial Inferiority, 1859–1900.* New York: McGraw-Hill.

Heine, Heinrich
1947 *The Rabbi of Bacharach. A Fragment.* New York: Schocken.
1969–72 *Der Rabbi von Bacharach.* In *Sämtliche Werke.* Ed. J. Perfahl. Munich: Winkler.
1971 *Ludwig Börne. Ein Denkschrift.* In *Beiträge zur deutschen Ideologie.* Frankfurt/M.: Ullstein.

Heller, Peter
1981 "A Quarrel over Bisexuality." In *The Turn of the Century. German Literature and Art.* Ed. G Chapple and H. H. Schulte. Bonn: Bouvier.

Herzl, Theodor
1973 *"Mauschel."* In *Zionist Writings.* Vol. 1: *January 1896–June 1898.* Trans. H. Zohn. New York: Herzl Press. Orig. *Die Welt.* 15 October 1897.

Hess, Moses
1943 *Rome and Jerusalem. A Study in Jewish Nationality.* Trans. Meyer Waxman. New York: Bloch. Orig. Germ. ed. 1862.

Hitler, Adolph
1943 *Mein Kampf.* Trans. R. Manheim. Boston: Houghton Mifflin.

Hoffman-Krayer, E., and H. Bächtold-Stäubli (eds.)
1934–35 *Handwörterbuch des deutschen Aberglaubens.* 10 vols. Berlin/Leipzig: Walter de Gruyter.

Horkheimer, Max, and Theodor W. Adorno
1972 *Dialectic of Enlightenment.* Trans. J. Cumming. New York: Seabury Press.

Howes, David
1987 "Olfaction and Transition: An Essay on Ritual Uses of Smell." *Canadian Review of Sociology and Anthropology* 24:390–416.

Hsia, R. Po-chia
1988 *The Myth of Ritual Murder. Jews and Magic in Reformation Germany.* New Haven: Yale University Press.

Hubrich, Peter Heinz
1974 *Gustav Freytags 'Deutsche Ideologie' in 'Soll und Haben.'* Kronberg, Czech.: Scriptor.

Hull, Isabel V.
1982 "The Bourgeoisie and Its Discontents: Reflections on [Mosse's] 'Nationalism and Respectability.'" *Journal of Contemporary History* 17:247–68.

Jaeger, Gustav
1884 *Entdeckung der Seele*. Vol. 1. 3d ed. Leipzig: W. Kohlhammer.
1912 *Entdeckung der Seele*. Vol. 2. 4th ed. Leipzig: W. Kohlhammer.

Iribarne, J.
1912 "Névropathies réflexes d'origine nasale." *Revue de psychothérapie et de psychologie appliqué* 26:236–42.

Jay, Nancy
1985 "Sacrifice as Remedy for Having Been Born of Woman." In *Immaculate and Powerful: The Female in Sacred Image and Social Reality*. Ed. C. W. Atkinson, C. H. Buchanan, and M. R. Miles. Boston: Beacon Press.

Jones, Ernest
1953–57 *The Life and Work of Sigmund Freud*. 3 vols. New York: Basic Books.

Knecht, Edgar
1974–77 "Le mythe du Juif errant." *Romantisme* 8, 9, 12, 16:103–16, 84–96, 95–112, 101–15.

Koestenbaum, Wayne
1988 "Privileging the Anus: Anna O. and the Collaborative Origin of Psychoanalysis." *Genders* 3:57–81.

Krafft-Ebing, Richard von
1965 *Psychopathia Sexualis. A Medico-Forensic Study*. Trans. H. E. Wedeck. New York: Putnam. Orig. 1887–.

Kris, Ernst
1954 "Introduction." In *The Origins of Psychoanalysis. Letters to Wilhelm Fliess*. Ed. M. Bonaparte, A. Freud, and E. Kris. Trans. E. Mosbacher and J. Strachey. New York: Basic Books.

Kristeva, Julia
1982 *Powers of Horror. An Essay on Abjection*. Trans. L. S. Roudiez. New York: Columbia University Press.

Küpper, Heinz
1984 *Illustriertes Lexicon der Deutschen Umgangssprache*. Vol. 6. Stuttgart: Klett.

Kuper, Adam, and Alan A. Stone
1982 "The Dream of Irma's Injection: A Structural Analysis." *American Journal of Psychiatry* 139:1225–34.

Landes, Joan B.
1988 *Women and the Public Sphere in the Age of the French Revolution*. Ithaca: Cornell University Press.

Laqueur, Thomas
1987 "Orgasm, Generation, and the Politics of Reproductive Biology." In *The Making of the Modern Body. Sexuality and Society in the Nineteenth Century.* Ed. C. Gallagher and T. Laqueur. Berkeley: University of California Press.

Lavater, J. C.
1792 *Essays on Physiognomy. Designed to Promote the Knowledge and the Love of Mankind.* Trans. H. Hunter. 4 vols. London: for J. Murray, H. Hunter, and T. Holloway. Orig. Germ. ed, 1776.

Lowe, Donald M.
1982 *The History of Bourgeois Perception.* Chicago: University of Chicago Press.

Loewenthal, Erich
1947 "Epilogue." In Heinrich Heine. *The Rabbi of Bacharach. A Fragment.* New York: Schocken.

Lukacher, Ned
1981 "Schreber's Juridical Opera: A Reading of the *Denkwürdigkeiten eines Nervenkranken.*" *Structuralist Review* 2,2.

McGrath, William J.
1986 *Freud's Discovery of Psychoanalysis: The Politics of Hysteria.* Ithaca, N.Y.: Cornell University Press.

Mackenzie, John Noland
1887 "The Pathological Nasal Reflex. An Historical Study." *New York Medical Journal* (August 20):199–205.
1898 "Physiological and Pathological Relations between the Nose and the Sexual Apparatus in Man." *The Journal of Laryngology, Rhinology, and Otology* 13:109–23. Also appeared in *Johns Hopkins Hospital Bulletin* 82 (January):10–17.

Mahony, Patrick
1977 "Towards a Formalist Approach to Dreams." *International Review of Psycho-Analysis* 4:83–98.
1979 "Friendship and Its Discontents." *Contemporary Psychoanalysis* 15:55–109.

Masson, Jeffrey M.
1985 *The Assault on Truth. Freud's Suppression of the Seduction Theory.* New York: Penguin.

Mayer, Hans
1982 *Outsiders. A Study in Life and Letters.* Trans. D. M. Sweet. Cambridge: MIT Press.

Meige, Henri
1893 "Le Juif-errant à la Salpêtrière. Essai nosographique sur les névropathes voyageurs." *Nouvelle Iconographie de la Salpêtrière* 6.
1986 "The Wandering Jew in the Clinic." In *The Wandering Jew. Essays in the Interpretation of a Christian Legend.* Ed. G. Hasan-Rokem and A. Dundes, 190–94. Bloomington: Indiana University Press.

Mosse, George
1970 *Germans and Jews. The Right, the Left, and the Search for a "Third Force" in Pre-Nazi Germany.* New York: Grosset & Dunlap.
1982a "Nationalism and Respectability: Normal and Abnormal Sexuality in the 19th Century." *Journal of Contemporary History* 17:221–46.
1982b "Friendship and Nationalism: About the Promise and Failure of German Nationalism." *Journal of Contemporary History* 17:351–67.
1985 *Nationalism and Sexuality: Nationalism and Abnormal Sexuality in Modern Europe.* New York: Fertig.

Nietzsche, Friedrich
1968 *The Anti Christ.* In *Twilight of the Idols/The Anti-Christ.* Trans. R. J. Hollingdale. Harmondsworth, U.K.: Penguin.
1969 *Ecce Homo.* In *On the Genealogy of Morals/Ecce Homo.* Trans. W. Kaufmann. New York: Random House.

Nordau, Max
1895 *Degeneration.* New York: D. Appleton & Co.
1980 "Jewry of Muscle" In *The Jew in the Modern World. A Documentary History.* Ed. P. R. Mendes-Flohr and J. Reinharz. New York: Oxford University Press. Germ. orig.: *Jüdische Turnzeitung* (June 1903).

O'Brien, Mary
1981 *The Politics of Reproduction.* Boston: Routledge & Kegan Paul.

Patai, Raphael
1979 *The Messiah Texts.* Detroit: Wayne State University Press.

Poliakov, Leon
1965 *The History of Anti-Semitism.* Vol. 1: *From the Time of Christ to the Court Jews.* Trans. R. Howard. New York: Vanguard Press.

Poovey, Mary
1988 *Uneven Developments. The Ideological Work of Gender in Mid-Victorian England.* Chicago: University of Chicago Press.

Prado de Oliveira, Eduardo
1979 "Trois études sur Schreber et la citation." *Psychanalyse à l'université* 4:245–82.

Rainey, Reuben M.
1975 *Freud as Student of Religion.* Missoula, Mont.: American Academy of Religion.

Rathenau, Walter
1980 "Höre Israel!" In *The Jew in the Modern World. A Documentary History.* Ed. P. R. Mendes-Flohr and J. Reinharz. New York: Oxford University Press. Germ. orig.: *Zukunft* 18 (16 March 1897).

Revue de l'hypnotisme
1890 "Étude médico-sociale sur le nez," *Revue de l'hypnotisme* 4:122–24.
1893 Review of Meige, "Le Juif errant à la Salpêtrière." *Revue de l'hypnotisme* 8:146–50.

Rosenberg, Alfred
1930 *Der Mythus des 20. Jahrhunderts.* Munich: Hoheneichen-Verlag.

Schopenhauer, Arthur
1958 *World as Will and Representation.* Trans. E. F. J. Payne. 2 vols. Clinton, Mass.: Falcon's Wing Press.
1972 *Die beiden Grundprobleme der Ethik. Über das Fündament der Moral.* In vol. 4 of *Sämtliche Werke.* Ed. Arthur Hübscher. Wiesbaden: Brockhaus.
1974 *Parerga and Paralipomena.* Trans. E. F. J. Payne. 2 vols. Oxford: Clarendon Press.

Schreber, Daniel Paul
1988 *Memoirs of My Mental Illness.* Trans. and ed. I. Macalpine and R. A. Hunter. Cambridge: Harvard University Press. Orig. Eng. ed., 1955. Orig. Germ. ed., 1903.

Schur, Max
1966 "Some Additional 'Day Residues' of 'The Specimen Dream of Psychoanalysis.' " In *Psychoanalysis: A General Psychology. Essays in Honor of Heinz Hartmann.* Ed. R. M. Loewenstein, L. M. Newman, M. Schur, and A. J. Solnit. New York: International Universities Press.
1972 *Freud: Living and Dying.* New York: International Universities Press.

Showalter, Dennis E.
1983 *Little Man, What Now?* Der Stürmer *in the Weimar Republic.* Hamden, Conn.: Archon.

Stallybrass, Peter, and Allon White
1986 *The Politics and Poetics of Transgression.* Ithaca, N.Y.: Cornell University Press.

Sulloway, Frank
1979 *Freud, Biologist of the Mind. Beyond the Psychoanalytic Legend.* New York: Basic.

Swan, Jim
1974 "*Mater* and Nannie: Freud's Two Mothers and the Discovery of the Oedipus Complex." *American Imago* 31:1–64.

Thalmann, Rita
1982 *Etre femme sous le IIIᵉ Reich.* Paris: Editions Robert Laffont.

Trachtenberg, Joshua
1943 *The Devil and the Jews. The Medieval Conception of the Jew and Its Relation to Modern Antisemitism.* New Haven: Yale University Press.

Turner, Bryan S.
1984 *The Body and Society. Explorations in Social Theory.* Oxford: Basil Blackwell.

Van Velzen, H. U. E. T
1984 "Irma at the Window: The Fourth Script of Freud's Specimen Dream." *American Imago* 41:245–93.

Vogt, Carl
1864 *Lectures on Man. His Place in Creation and in the History of the Earth.* London: Longman, Green.

Weeks, Jeffrey
1981 *Sex, Politics, and Society. The Regulation of Sexuality since 1800.* White Plains, N.Y.: Longman.

Weiner, Marc A.
1989 "Wagner's Nose and the Ideology of Perception." *Monatshefte* 81:62–78.

11

Zionism as an Erotic Revolution

David Biale

In February 1932, Magnus Hirschfield, the German-Jewish "sexologist" and campaigner for homosexual rights visited Palestine and reported admiringly on the young socialist Zionist pioneers.

> In their simple dress—hatless, bare-necked and with bare legs—in the ingenuousness of their manner . . . [they] seem so full of joy, strength and affirmation of life that they seem to have overcome all the repressions and unconscious feelings of erotic inferiority frequently found at this age.[1]

In their new attitude toward the body, Hirschfeld believed that these young people had overcome centuries of traditional sexual repression as well as bourgeois reticence. During his visit, Hirschfeld investigated with great curiosity the prevalent rumors that in the communal settlements of the Yishuv, marriage partners were freely exchanged and promiscuity and polygamy were common, a kind of Jewish version of the nineteenth-century Oneida experiment in sexual utopia. Although Hirschfeld rejected these rumors as pure fiction, his report is revealing evidence of the myth of Zionism as a utopian movement of erotic liberation.

One of the central claims of Zionism was that the Jews lived a disembodied existence in exile and that only a healthy national life could restore a necessary measure of physicality or materiality. What I shall argue here is that this political ideology was not only based on the body as metaphor, but, in addition, also sought to transform the Jewish body itself, and especially the sexual body. Zionism meant not only the physical rooting of "people of the air" (*Luftmenschen*) in the soil of Palestine, but also the reclamation of the body. Zionism promised an erotic revolution for the Jews: the creation of a virile New Hebrew Man as well as rejection of the inequality of women in traditional Judaism in favor of full equality between the sexes in all spheres of life. Among the socialist pioneers, a new sexual ethic opposed bourgeois marriage and affirmed a healthy sensuality.

This erotic vision was closely bound up with images of the land of Israel as a lover, a kind of materialistic transformation of the old allegory of love between God and Israel. For the early Zionists, Oriential Palestine promised liberation of the senses from the suffocation of Europe, a suffocation at once traditional and bourgeois. The image of the Arab as a sensual savage played a key role in this mythology; later, when the national struggle between Zionism and the Palestinians became sharper, the Arab was frequently seen as effeminate as opposed to the virile modernism of Jewish nationalism. The image of the impotent Diaspora Jew was now projected on to the Palestinian, who, like the Galut Jew, refused to free himself from medieval traditions.

Yet, the story of Zionism as an erotic revolution is by no means so straightforward. The new nationalism was accompanied by a strong sense of respectability, if not exactly the respectability of the bourgeoisie, then the equally powerful asceticism of a fanatical movement dedicated to goals higher than the happiness of the individual. Doctrines of "free love" and "puritanism" coexisted in a peculiar dialectic, similar in many ways to the status of sexuality in the Soviet Union after the revolution.[2] In the Zionist case, the tension between sexual liberation and asceticism channeled erotic energies into the tasks of nation building, a form of sublimation reminiscent of traditional Jewish culture.[3] Out of its own inner dynamic, Zionism, which had sought a radical break with the Jewish past, often ended up returning unwittingly to traditional patterns. The conflicts within the erotic ideology of Zionism can therefore serve as a set of signs for the tensions within Zionism as a whole between revolution and continuation.

The Zionist Polemic Against Degeneration

Like other nationalist movements of the end of the nineteenth century, Zionism was preoccupied by the physical and emotional degeneration of the nation and by the threat of demographic decline.[4] Prominent in this general fin d'siecle diagnosis was a conception of the physical body as a mirror of emotional disease and the prescription for curing the disturbed soul involved exercise and physical labor: a healthy body would make for a harmonious psyche, not only for the individual, but for the nation as a whole. In this nationalist thought, the individual body became a microcosm for the body politic of the nation. To create a new image of the Jewish body became a symbol for creating a new Jewish nation.

The name most commonly associated with this doctrine was Max Nordau, whose cultural critique *Degeneration* had created a sensation in the 1890s. Within a few years, Nordau was to become Theodor Herzl's main Western European collaborator, and in his Zionist writings, one can find direct links to his general theory of degeneration. For Nordau, degeneration is both a physiological and psychological condition; to be precise, it is a disease of the nervous system, corresponding to the fashionable diagnosis of "neuresthenia."[5] Of all the components of degeneration, sexual pathology is perhaps the most pervasive. The "sexual centers" rule the "erotomaniacal" degenerate: "He feels that he cannot resist the exciting influences proceeding from the woman, that he is her helpless slave . . . He necessarily, therefore, sees in woman an uncanny, overpowering force of nature, bestowing supreme delights or dealing destruction."[6] Obsessed by women, the degenerate either falls into promiscuity or flees to the opposite extreme of celibacy.

Nordau's Zionism reflected this diatribe against degeneration. In an important article in 1900 in the journal of the German Zionist sports association, he popularized the already bourgeoning nationalist idea of a "Judaism with muscles."[7] As he suggested in *Degeneration,* exercise was able to adapt the organs to stress and the Jews, thought by many physicians to be the quintessential neuresthenics, could overcome their hereditary nervousness by developing their bodies. As George Mosse aptly put it, Jews, according to Nordau, must become "men of muscle instead of remaining slaves to their nerves."[8]

The journals of the Zionist sports societies repeated Nordau's arguments in issue after issue, often with learned medical "proof."[9] Return to nature and return to the body were part of the same revolutionary continuum. The iconography of the postcards published by the early Zionist congresses typically featured virile young farmers in Palestine contrasted with old, frail Orthodox Jews in the Diaspora.[10] Physical strength, youth, nature, and secularism were the constellation of Zionist symbols set against the degeneracy, old age, urban and religious signs of the Exile.

To build a "Judaism with muscles" meant to create a sexually healthy Judaism; indeed, the two went together because, in Nordau's account, their opposites, physical and erotic degeneracy, were linked. Nordau in his essay from 1900, glorified the modern Jewish sportsmen who proudly proclaim their physical connection to their people and contrasted them with those Jews in ancient times who would only engage in sports after surgically hiding their circumcisions. By implication, the Zionist Jews of the sports associations—the readers of his article—are not only proud of their bodies as a whole, but also have a healthy attitude toward their sexuality: they no longer need to hide the physical sign of Jewish sexual difference.

For Nordau—and for those Zionists who wrote more explicitly than he did on the subject—such sexual health did not demand libertine permissiveness. On the contrary, excessive sexual desire, just as excessive abstinence, were signs of degeneration. Stable and sober marriage was evidently the cure, as Nordau had argued in *Degeneration*. And Nordau's ideas were known among the Zionist pioneers. As the Hebrew novelist Y. H. Brenner has one of his characters put it ironically in *Breakdown and Bereavement,* his novel of sexual frustration from the Second Aliya, to which we shall return:

> "If only these tender souls could be married off, they'd get over their tragic tears soon enough." That was how he'd phrased it . . . almost another Max Nordau . . . and he'd actually underlined the words "married off." . . . "Married off"—ergo, they could never find a woman by themselves. . . .[11]

It scarcely escapes us that this "cure" is, of course, not that far from the bourgeois European model out of which Zionists like Nordau came.

Nordau was less specific about Zionism as an erotic revolution than were others who wrote in the same vein. In 1918 and 1919, Rafael Becker, a Swiss Jewish doctor who was a committed Zionist, wrote two essays about the nervous diseases of the Jews.[12] Becker admits that the Jews suffer more than others from a variety of psychological abnormalities—a common belief at the time—but he argues that this is not a result of some racial disposition. Rather, it is a consequence of their political status as a minority and their skewed occupational structure. As a result, they tend to marry late, much later than in traditional Jewish society and also later than their Gentile neighbors. Late marriage then becomes the cause of degeneration since the period when sexual desire is greatest is spent in frustration. In sounding this attack on late marriage, Becker was echoing a very widespread theme in Zionist thinking, as we shall see. But what is most striking is that this concern with late marriage, which had become prevalent among Central European

Jews as early as the eighteenth century, reversed the preoccupation with *early* marriage among the nineteenth-century Eastern European Jewish disciples of the Enlightenment. For Becker and others, sexual dysfunction comes from delayed gratification, while for their Eastern European predecessors, it is a result of premature sexuality.

At the end of one of his essays, Becker offers some homey medical advice for Jewish sexual frustration. He prescribes the elimination of the strong spices so beloved in Jewish kitchens, as well as coffee, tea, and alcohol, since they "promote" sexual lust, especially in the young. But he hastens to add that such remedies are mere palliatives. The cure for the sexual neurosis of the Jews must be radical: "the creation of our own home and land. Only this will brings us a healthy body and a free and untroubled spirit."[13]

Becker and many other Jews of his time were obsessed with the problem of diminished Jewish fertility.[14] This problem, which was particularly acute in Central Europe, reflected a general concern in Germany, France, and elsewhere with the low birth rate resulting from modern urban life and, after World War I, with the loss of population caused by the war. Yet, low Jewish fertility was exacerbated by intermarriage. The Jewish sexologist Max Marcuse argued in a small monograph entitled "On the Fertility of Christian-Jewish Intermarriage,"[15] that the low birthrate of such marriages was a result of cultural rather than biological factors; in principle, intermarriage could actually contribute to Jewish population growth. Marcuse's statistical analysis concealed a polemical attempt to justify intermarriage. This was, to be sure, a minority position; most Jewish writers lamented intermarriage as a cause of the decline in fertility. These writers were not only Zionists, although Zionists were perhaps among the most vocal. Even an opponent of Zionist, like the philosopher Franz Rosenzweig, appears to have been motivated by the demographic decline of his community. His great work of theology, the *Star of the Redemption,* is, in fact, an argument for defining the Jews as a "blood" community of procreation, as opposed to Christianity, which is a faith community of proselytism. In emphasizing blood and procreation as the defining essence of Judaism, Rosenzweig was engaged in a desperate polemic against the mounting assimilation and intermarriage of the Weimar Jews.[16]

Among the Zionist writings from Central Europe, perhaps the most comprehensive discussion of the connection between Zionism, Jewish fertility, and sexuality is a monograph by Hans Goslar (1889–1945) entitled *The Sexual Ethic of Jewish Rebirth: A Word to*

Our Youth.[17] Like others writing on this subject, Goslar was influenced by the movement of sexology. In this essay, Goslar quotes other sexologists like Max Marcuse, Iwan Bloch as well as Sigmund Freud in an effort to ground the erotic ideology of his Zionism on ostensibly scientific premises. If Zionism was to transform the sexual life of the Jews, along with all its other revolutionary goals, it must do so on rational grounds, much as Theodor Herzl, in his *Jewish State* had tried to show on the basis of technological metaphors that Zionism is practical and must not to be confused with romantic utopianism. This attempt to argue for an erotic revolution in scientific terms was to be one characteristic of Zionism. Yet, such a sober, scientific approach coexisted uneasily with more romantic, libertine notions that some young Zionists, whom we shall encounter presently, borrowed from the sexual revolution of the 1920s.

Like Becker, Goslar decries late marriage among the Jews and urges a return to early marriage, as it had existed in traditional Jewish society. In modern Europe, marriage is late, which results in a double standard: women are required to remain chaste, while men are encouraged to engage in premarital sex for physical and psychological reasons. Following Nordau, he holds that urbanization has only served to increase the sexual drive and has brought about all kinds of sexual ills, especially prostitution. Jewish youth has succumbed to all these ills, particularly since Jews mature sexually earlier than Germans. Here, Goslar—unlike Becker—resorts to something like a racial argument not so distant from that of some of the anti-Semites: since the Jews come originally from the warm Mediterranean climate, their sexual urges develop at an early age. Although he does not say it, Goslar comes periously close to the myth of Jewish hypersexuality.

Yet, the Jews are capable of controlling these urges. Goslar opposes those who think that sexual abstinence is bad. On the contrary, not only is it the foundation for moral development, but, he argues, quoting the sexologist Iwan Bloch,[18] the ancient Israelites were the first to discover it. Despite this celebration of the virtues of chastity, however, Goslar favors early marriage for the Jews as a better solution than voluntary abstinence. Since such a shift in the age of marriage is impossible in Germany, only Zionism holds out the promise of curing the sexual frustrations of the Jews. Adopting the general Zionist romanticization of agriculture, Goslar believed that the creation of a rural, peasant society will cool the overheated erotic drives caused by urban life. More practically, Zionist land and taxation policy will make it economically feasible to marry young and to restore high fertility. Thus, like Becker, Goslar saw Zionism as the only possible solution to the endemic sexual and demographical diseases of Jewish life in modern Europe.

In addition to attacking sexual degeneracy, many Zionist writers were also highly critical of Jewish women in the Diaspora. Goslar denounced what he called the "cult of women" (*Frauenkult unseres Zeitalters*) that turns them into sexual objects and materialistic "luxury animals" (*Luxustierchen*), rather than treating them as comrades, wives, and mothers.[19] Martin Buber, in an essay entitled "The Zion of the Jewish Woman,"[20] took a similar position. Like Goslar, he idealizes women in traditional life in contrast to their contemporary degeneration (Buber uses Nordau's *Entartung*). In past times, the family was the cornerstone of the Jewish world, the substitute for the lost Jewish state, and women were its main guardians. Given women's central role, the Jewish family's decline in modern times is largely their fault, as they have become slaves to their Christian servants. The "regal beauty" of Jewish women in earlier times has become ostentatious materialism. Zionism calls upon Jewish women to return to the virtues of motherhood, which will help them overcome the nervous disorders of their lives. To be fair to the German Zionists, not only these male voices were heard. In a thoughtful article in *Jerubbaal,* Marie Popper analyzed the problems of growing up female in the bourgeois Jewish world.[21] Although Popper castigated the structure of the bourgeois Jewish family for the distorted development of its daughters, she echoed the male critique of Jewish women. Yet, the curious advocacy of female liberation, while returning women to their traditional roles as wives and mothers, was to characterize much of Zionist thought, including even the more radical sexual ideologies of the socialist pioneers, to whom we now turn.

Sexual Experimentation in the Second and Third Aliyot

Between the years 1903 to 1914 and 1918 to 1924, two waves of immigration to Palestine, primarily from Eastern Europe, known as the Second and Third Aliyot, established the elite culture of the Zionist movement. These agricultural pioneers, or *haluztim,* were a very small minority among the population in the Yishuv (the Zionist community in Palestine), yet, because their experience or, better, their construction of their experience, became so formative for the cultural ethos of Israeli society, their importance outweighs their actual numbers. Their memoirs and literary efforts created a collective memory that serves as Israel's myth of its own origins.

The evidence available to us suggests that many of these idealistic young people typically had great difficulty establishing mature erotic relationships. There were, of course, objective difficulties: men far outnumbered women in many of the settlements and this demographic fact created enormous sexual frustrations. But there were other deeper and more complex reasons. In order to understand the experience of these pioneers, we need first to look at their ideologies, which contained a contradictory mix of hostility to both traditional and bourgeois marriage together with affirmation of the family, and of sexual liberation together with fanatical puritanism. These conflicted ideas both reflected and shaped their experiences in that same tangled web that always characterizes the relationship between texts and life. Indeed, there are many cases where we might suspect that written texts became a kind of substitute for experience, a way of representing that which was most absent, yet most devoutly desired.

Let us begin with Aharon David Gordon (1856–1922), the father figure and perhaps chief ideologue of the Second Aliya who had joined the young pioneers at the settlement of Kinneret when he was forty-eight. In 1918, Gordon wrote an essay decrying the lack of family life among his young comrades.[22] Echoing themes prevalent in Zionist writings from Europe, Gordon argued that the failure of the *halutzim* to marry and have children was not only a result of economic conditions in Palestine, but was, much more importantly, a continuation of the pattern in Europe of marrying at a late age. Since Jews had traditionally married early, says Gordon, the sudden shift to a late age of marriage, which was adopted from non-Jewish society, had had catastrophic physical and psychological effects, from excessive nervousness to poor eyesight, bad teeth, and early balding! Gordon laments the loss of youth, perhaps reflecting a sense of his own approaching death: as a result of the failure to find sexual release, the young people with whom he lived and worked had become old while still in their youth.

Gordon called for new forms of family life as the only true basis for creating a Jewish nation. Gender relations must be based on pure "naturalness." Consistent with his overall philosophy of work and nature, Gordon envisioned an almost mystical new form of marriage that would meld human forces with the forces of nature.

Out of intense disillusionment with marriage and family life in the Diaspora, many of the members of the Second and Third Aliyot agreed with Gordon that a new form of male-female relations was necessary as an integral part of their Zionism. One of the most interesting of these was the Second Aliyah poet and novelist Zvi Shatz (1890–1921), who developed the idea of an intimate commune or *kevutzah*.[23] For Shatz, the commune had to resurrect the family on the basis of love linked to a religion of nature:

> The family is collapsing and religion is dying, but eternal life values are still valid; they will only change their forms, because the need for family is deep and organic and the religious relation to life and nature will yet become strong within us and be resurrected in our return to the land and to nature. For these are our true Messiah. Thus, a new family on the basis of a new religion will establish the laboring nation on its soil. The family will be resurrected not on the basis of blood relations, but on the basis of spiritual intimacy.

Here was a veritable religion of the family, which, like Gordon, Shatz saw as a manifestation of a new, secular messianic religion of nature. The return to the soil would revolutionize erotic relations. We will see again and again how appropriation and transformation of traditional language was crucial to many of these attempts to construct a new sexual ethos.

While still in Russia, Shatz become intimately friendly with Joseph Trumpeldor, the one-armed Jewish hero of the Russo-Japanese War who was to become a Zionist icon after his death at the hands of the Arabs in 1920. A devout socialist, Trumpeldor played a role in organizing a number of Zionist settlements and self-defense groups. In letters, the eighteenth-year-old Shatz poured out his heart to the older Trumpeldor about his yearnings for love and the correspondence between the two has an almost homoerotic flavor. Trumpeldor refers to Shatz's preoccupation with the "question of sexuality":

> This question, the question of relations between the sexes, is the most difficult and acute one of our day. What is the difference between our relations with a woman we love and a man we love? Why, among all the many, do we see one, respond to her, bow down to her, pray to her and also pray for her? . . . It is the sexual question and not friendship which has struck you, Grisha, which has swept you to the depths of your soul as a storm sweeps a boat in the ocean.[24]

Shatz's struggle with the "sexual question" preoccupied him in the years after he came to Palestine. In his two works of prose fiction, one of which was published in 1920 just before his death and the other after, Shatz left a literary reflection of the struggle for new forms of love in the setting of the intimate commune.[25] In both of these awkward stories, complicated love triangles lead to unsatisfactory conclusions. The characters are adolescents in every respect, groping for ways of expressing love while remaining true to their ideological pretensions. Shatz captures the erotic tensions in the communes, the interminable ideological discussions followed by tentative and usually abortive attempts at sexual relations. Shatz's Hebrew style was in many ways quite artificial since he had only begun to write in his adopted language, but the almost tongue-tied quality of the dialogue accurately reflects the psychological immaturity of his characters. The literary inadequacies of Shatz's stories expressed not only his own sexual confusion but also that of his generation, which evidently received his meager efforts with great enthusiasm.

Shatz's own life reflected his art. After he settled for the third time in Palestine in 1913, he married Rivka Shatz. But within a few years, he fell in love with another woman, Nechama Avrunin. In the letters that have been published, it appears that he tried to work out a kind of *menage a trois* with the two women, based on his radical ideas of an intimate commune.[26] At the same time, it seems that Rivka became involved with another man, Eliezer Braun. Shatz sought Braun out in Gan Shmuel and sought now to create a *menage a quatre*. From one letter that he wrote to Rivka at the time, it would appear that he himself developed very strong erotic feelings for Braun! After Shatz was killed, both his wife Rivka and his lover Nechama moved to Kibbutz Ein Harod. Nechama married and had a child but then became romantically involved with another man, Aharon Rosen. She ended the affair by shooting Rosen and herself; they are buried side-by-side in the old graveyard of Ein Harod. Like the conclusion to I. B. Singer's *Enemies: A Love Story,* Rivka Shatz raised Nechama's child.[27] As lurid as this convoluted soap opera sounds, it was by no means unique, but Shatz was original in trying to give his experience and that of his circle an ideological veneer.

Shatz's attempts to put in writing a theory of erotic liberation were unusual for the members of the Second Aliya, who tended to be quite reticent in speaking about sexual matters. Even though they were committed to new forms of family life, they were typically unwilling to articulate them fully and, as Gordon's essay indicates, neither were they able to fulfill them. Indeed, most of their memoirs touch only briefly, if at all, on the subject. A kind of self-censorship suggests the degree to which they remained ambivalent about their own inchoate ideology.

The Third Aliya was different. The Zionist youth movements were deeply influenced by the ideas of the *völkisch* German *Wandervogel,* although the *Wandervogel* itself was frequently anti-Semitic. One of the theoreticians of the *Wandervogel* was Hans Blüher, and his book, *Die deutsche Wandervogelbewegung als eroticisches Phänomen,* had an important impact on the Jewish youth movements of Central Europe, even though Blüher himself was anti-semitic. Blüher's almost mystical celebration of the youth culture of the *Wandervogel* emphasized the strong homoerotic bonds between the male members, and it is no surprise that Magnus Hirschfeld, the leading campaigner in Germany for homosexual rights, wrote the introduction to the book. This aspect of Blüher's book evidently held little appeal for the young Zionists, but his contrast between the revolutionary erotic spirit in the youth movements and the conventions of bourgeois society had very strong resonance.[28]

The period immediately after World War I saw the sexual experimentation and frankness that characterized Weimar Germany and Soviet Russia, as well as the impact of sexually explicit writers like D. H. Lawrence. Freud's psychology of sexuality had become a cultural commonplace, and his writings were widely read by young European Jews, as were, probably to a lesser extent, the writings of "sexologists" like Magnus Hirschfeld and Iwan Bloch. As a consequence of all these influences, some of the young Zionists of the Third Aliya developed much fuller reflections on the connection between Eros and Zion. Many in the Third Aliya came to Zionism through the new Jewish nationalist youth movements such as the Blau-Weiss in Germany and the Hashomer Ha-Tzair, or Young Guard, that began in the Austro-Hungarian portion of Poland in 1913. In the 1930s, this latter movement was to become avowedly Marxist, but in the decade after World War I, it was imbued primarily with a romantic ideology of nature and the cult of youth.[29]

One of the most important ideological leaders of the early Hashomer Ha-Tzair was Meir Yaari (1897–1987) who joined the movement in his native Galicia and immigrated to Palestine after World War I. Already in his early twenties and a veteran of the war, Yaari quickly became the guru of the younger Hashomer pioneers. In August 1920 he led a small group of these to the settlement of Bitania Elite overlooking the Jordan Valley. Although the settlement disbanded a half year later, the experience of the group became a kind of mythic crucible of the Third Aliya, an attempt to create Zvi Shatz's intimate commune. Writing to his comrades in Europe from Bitania, Yaari laid out the erotic ideology of the commune:

> The commune is not based only on economic cooperation, but also on the erotic. Bourgeois domestic eroticism is the enemy of the commune. The commune cannot exist without a deeper connection between its members.[30]

In terms redolent of Nietzsche, but also of Jewish mysticism, he declares:

> We felt that the person who is suffocating in the private stiffling framework . . . of mechanical civilization must destroy first and foremost the husks (*kelipot*) that weigh on his natural personality . . . What will be gained by this destruction is the wild and free communalism of a nation that rules its elemental forces, that answers to them but is not enslaved to them.

The elemental force that needs to be freed is the sexual, and the result will be a virile New Man, as opposed to the neurotic Jews of the Exile:

> [Hashomer Ha-Tzair puts an end to sexual hypocrisy and removes that instinctual impotence . . . that characterizes the conventional type of Jew from the developmental path of the youth. . . . We love the naked youth who remains a child when he matures, who sanctifies his instinct and the pleasure of his instinct and does not pollute it. I see before me the man who demolishes the walls that generations have put up between spirit and flesh and between reason and instinct. In this way, in an instinctual way, we will create a man who is at once the most primitive and the most cultured, who will unite with his wife and his comrades. . . .

The New Man is a naked child, which raises questions about whether he is sexually mature: no real distinction is made between sexual union with one's wife and one's comrades. This, then, is primarily the eroticism of a youth culture rather than a doctrine of free love between men and women. It is also important for the emerging culture of secular Zionism how Yaari assaults the Jewish tradition by using its own language: he seizes the rabbinic concept of "sanctification" of the sexual act and presses it into the service of a Dionysian religion of nature.

Yaari's erotic Zionism was based on a cascade of masculine images contrasted to the "feminine" weakness of the Diaspora. For example, in a letter written to a convention of Hashomer leaders in 1918, he asserts, again, with Nietzschean bombast:

> We want to educate this generation to be tough and strong and not soft and wallowing in their imaginations. Only the [strong] arms of heroes will accomplish this work and not poets . . . I view with great trepidation the groups of Hashomer which are dominated not by men but by angels of beauty and love.

In his letter from Bitania, he castigates the women in the group who were not ready to undertake the new erotic life of the commune: "Eroticism for them is only inflated words and, in addition, something that is private for each person. In the final analysis, [the women] say, you cannot change your nature and your instincts."[31] This ill-concealed misogyny was not uncommon in the overheated writings of this circle.[32]

That some women were unhappy with this secondary role is an important and complex story in its own right. One woman from the Second Aliya bitterly complained in her diary that the men expect the women to exhibit conventional standards of beauty and their only interest in their female comrades is sexual.[33] Another woman of the same time rejected all advances and demanded that every man regard her as a "sister."[34] In 1921, Ada Fishman, one of the leaders of the movement for equality for women workers, argued that women in Palestine are too much identified with the private realm and that they must take equal part in work in order to break out of the private sphere.[35] Her essay is an explicit attack on patriarchy and on the way the quest for equality is undermined when the pioneering women become mothers. Yaari himself later came to renounce his initial position and those of others like him as degrading to women.

But the women of the Second and Third Aliyot should not be seen anachronistically through the eyes of contemporary feminism. It is significant, it seems to me, that none of the testimonies of women from the Bitania group reflect at all on sexual relations. Although a movement for equality in work existed, few women systematically resisted the maternal role that Zionist ideology gave them.

The problematic status of women and the role of sexuality in general become especially clear in the extraordinary collection of documents from the Hashomer group entitled *Kehilyateinu* (Our Community). Two are of particular interest, one by the editor, Nathan Bistritsky and the other by Eliahu Rapoport. Bistritsky evidently believed that the new family in Zion would move somehow beyond patriarchy, but he regarded the present state of sexuality as chaotic and unformed: "We have not sufficiently matured to raise the erotic power within us to a sexual power, one that can create a new relationship to woman." What did he envision as the new relationship to woman? Here, Bistritsky reveals the profoundly conservative nature of his erotic philosophy: mature sexuality must have procreation as its primary end. But since Zionist eroticism is still immature, "we are not yet able to see in woman a sister and mother." Despite the desire for sexual liberation that permeates his writing—and that of others—Bistritsky sees women less as sexual partners than as potential mothers of children.

This attitude found even more extreme expression in Bistritsky's novel, *Days and Nights,* first published in 1926. The novel is clearly based on *Kehilyateinu,* consisting, as it does, of interminable speeches by members of a utopian Zionist commune. One speech in particular captures not only Bistritsky's position, but that of the *Kehilyateinu* circle as well. His character, Alexander Tsuri, denounces bourgeois romantic love and demands a community that includes women as equals. But once again, the need for these women stems from the need to procreate. Women preserve the essence of humanity, while men are the force for change. In an extraordinary piece of mythology that harkens back to the blood symbolism of the biblical priestly code, he predicts that at the end of history, matriarchy will return. In messianic times, Abraham will suckle from the breasts of Sarah his wife, alternating with his son, Isaac. Here is how he describes the role of women:

> She—the mother—stands outside of our circle, the circle of history, and a strip of blood stands red behind her like a holy, terrifying shadow. She wallows in the blood, her holy blood, the blood of virginity, the blood of her first sacrifice, the blood of childbirth. Humanity washes in the blood of its heroes, but the dove of the holy spirit descends only on the fountain of blood that flows from the woman. I want to see the face of a young girl, to see in her the mother of my children, to see in her my mother. Mother! What am I and who am I, a man, without my mother . . . ?[36]

This confusion between woman as one's mother or as the mother of one's children or as one's sister, but never, it would seem, as a full equal, was by no means limited to Bistritsky. Instead, it reflects a deep confusion among many of the men of the Second and Third Aliyot. Might it be that the premature abandonment of their own mothers had left these teen-age boys still uncertain about just what they expected from women? Or perhaps even earlier separation issues were at stake, traumatic separations that we know of from the nineteenth-century Haskalah critique of traditional Jewish childhood.

The language of blood is also fascinating in this passage. Early Zionism often used the German *völkisch* language of "blood and soil," before it became irretrivably corrupted by the Nazis. Here, Bistritsky specifically attributes procreative blood to women and his allusions to the famous passage in Ezekiel 16 suggest that this blood has a nationalist dimension: in that chapter, Ezekiel describes how God weds Israel, metaphorically portrayed as a girl "wallowing" in the blood of childbirth. So, for Bistritsky, female blood will be the force for national renewal.

Eliahu Rapoport's copious contributions to *Kehilyateinu* reflect a similar confusion about women and the role of sexuality. Unlike the younger members of the group, Rapoport (1889–1952) had married in 1910 and had studied philosophy and mathematics at the University of Göttingen; he was a disciple of Martin Buber and his writings suggest something of Buber's influence. Like Bistritsky, Rapoport saw the ultimate value of sexuality in procreation. He concludes his elegy to eroticism with a feverish appeal to biblical women who broke conventional morality in order to procreate:

> This is what today's generation demands of me: liberate me from the burden of morality; redeem me from the curse of barrenness; redeem me towards the distant image of a blood community. . . . Tamar, Tamar, you who generations from Israel kneel before in fear and respect, were are you? . . . And you, the heroines, the daughters of Lot, who dared and thus gave life to nations of the world, where are you? And you, the divine poet who wrote the Song of Songs, were you writing about love or morality when you asked anxiously: 'We have a little sister and she has no breasts . . .'? I swear to you, community of Israel in the name of the sacrifice of your love and your oath: We have grown sisters and their breasts are like towers and walls built upon them and they are barren and their breasts are hidden and sealed between the thighs of fanatical priests. Redeem me from the curse of barrenness—such is the cry to me of today's generation.[37]

In this extraordinary passage, the Bible has become a Nietzschean manifesto against conventional morality and religion. The biblical Tamar, who seduced her father-in-law in order to give birth to the ancestor of King David,[38] and the daughters of Lot who committed incest with their father to create the nations of Moab and Amon,[39] are models for revolutionary women who are prepared to shatter bourgeois respectability. The Song of Songs becomes a broadside for sexual liberation against the priests of traditional religion. Only the liberation of eroticism, suggests Rapoport, will restore fertility to the impotent Jews; only an eroticized Zionism will return them to the glory of the Bible and recreate a mystical, *völkisch* "blood community."[40]

It was not only the left wing of the Zionist movement that indulged in such erotic fantasies. Vladimir Jabotinsky (1880–1940), the leader of the right-wing Revisionist Movement, celebrated virile masculinity, expressed in military metaphors, as the answer to Jewish impotence.[41] Like Eliahu Rapoport, Jabotinsky saw the Bible as a model for the sexual liberation of the Jews, which he considered as part and parcel of national liberation. In his fascinating novel, *Samson,* first written in Russian and published in 1927, Jabotinsky portrays the Philistines as models of both national pride and sexual health. In one astonishing passage describing a Philistine mass ceremony, the Philistine women are provocatively bare-breasted, their nudity evidently a sign of their vigor. Samson, who is revealed at the end to be the son of an Israelite mother and a Philistine father, becomes the bridge between the still-stunted Israelites and the virile Philistines. His intermarriages with Philistine women represents Israel breaking the chains of sexual bondage in favor of a new, liberated national life.

Internal Contradictions

The ideology of erotic liberation that became explicit in the Third Aliya was, however, only one side of the story. The inflated sexual rhetoric of the Hashomer group was not without its critics.[42] Within the movement itself, there were dissenters, notably David Horowitz, who broke with Yaari at Bitania and was later to become one of the leading figures in creating Israel's modern economy. Horowitz charged that what Yaari thought was erotic, was really "neurotic," a sublimation of natural instincts.[43] Yaari himself fell out with his former comrades, in part, it seems, as a result of his marriage to one of the women from Bitania. He refused to allow his contribution to *Kehilyateinu* to appear in the collection and, instead, he published a scathing denunciation of *Kehilyateinu* under the title "Alienated Symbols,"[44] an essay that might be considered a self-criticism as well. Among his objections to the bombastic philosophizing of his former comrades, he decried the failure of women's liberation in the movement; women had been turned into "holy mothers," but in reality were no more than servants.[45]

The ideology of erotic liberation was always a means to realize the broader nationalist goals of Zionism; hence, in part, the repeated insistence on the need for procreation. Sexual liberation might be necessary as part of a revolt against the bourgeois, assimilationist culture of the Diaspora, but not as a means toward individual fulfillment. Instead, a very widespread notion prevailed that one must sacrifice family life and erotic relations in order to fulfill national goals, which led A. D. Gordon to protest against what he called the artificial division between "life" and "work."[46] One example of this attitude is a story of a young woman of the Second Aliya who denied the sexual overtones of her relationships with the men in her commune and insisted on referring to all of them as "brothers." One of them fell in love with her to such an extent that he threatened to kill himself if she would not marry him. Her response is revealing:

> She didn't understand how it was possible to concern oneself with matters of love at a time when the land needed workers, Hebrew labor . . . She said to him: "you are my brother, so how can you love me as a woman?' She finally persuaded him that he should only regard her as a sister.[47]

The sublimation of sexual desire in the service of national ideals was a common theme, then, in the ideologies of the Second and Third Aliyot and it was often expressed in the notion that the *halutzim* were creating a new family in which they were all brothers and sisters. To have an erotic relationship with a comrade in such circumstances was both akin to incest and a betrayal of the national ideal. It may well be that the strong sense of having left families in far-away Russia created the profound need among these adolescents for recapturing what they had lost. Indeed, the memoirs of the pioneers are filled with homesickness and longing for parents in the Old Country.[48] Unable to see themselves yet in the role of parents, they could only envision themselves as children in need of siblings.

Even among the Hashomer Ha-Tzair proponents of an erotic Zionism, there was a strong tendency toward abstinence and restraint. In his 1921 polemic for liberating the "instincts," Meir Yaari nevertheless expressed concern about those who were enslaved to their sexual drives: "they are not able to be victorious by conquering their instincts and to overcome chaos with the strength of a dominant will."[49] Eliahu Rapoport also celebrated the virtues of sexual restraint. In a very self-revealing confession, he reports that when he was still a youth, his sexual urge had caused him to repeatedly fall in love with girls who, because of their devotion to ideals, rejected his advances. Thanks to these virtuous women, he was once again able to experience shame, and now in Palestine, work on the land had brought him back to a state of purity. For Rapoport, women are not only mothers but also the buffers of men's dangerous sexuality, both notions that he might well have borrowed from Jewish tradition.

In their educational doctrines, as well, the utopian youth movements were often fanatically puritanical. The Tenth Commandment of Hashomer Ha-Tzair's secular decalogue read: "The Shomer is pure in his thoughts, words and deeds. He does not smoke or drink alcohol and he guards his sexual purity." In one illustrated version of the Ten Commandments of Hashomer, the words "sexual purity" are highlighted and are framed by a chaste boy and equally chaste girl shaking hands while he holds the flag of the movement.[50] The iconography scarcely differs from the socialist realism of soviet Russia.

This attitude was also reflected in the child-rearing philosophy of the kibbutz movement, especially, but not exclusively, in the settlements of Hashomer Ha-Tzair.[51] One of the chief theorists of this philosophy was Shmuel Golan, an early disciple of Meir Yaari at Bitania.[52] In Golan's writings and those of other educational theorists, one senses the almost irreconcilable tensions between utopianism and puritanism, although these contradictions are papered over with "scientific" jargon.[53] On the one hand, they understood psychoanalysis to teach the necessity of freeing the child from sexual neurosis. Under the influence of such disciples of Freud as Wilhelm Reich, Herbert Marcuse, and Erich Fromm, they held that patriarchal, capitalist society must repress the sexual instinct since the child is an extension of the father's private property. The kibbutz would create a sexual utopia by freeing sexuality from the constraints of property. Yet sexual utopia did not mean anarchism, for Golan; sex as a source of transient physical pleasure was no less pathological than bourgeois repression. A utopian educational system must be based not on the instincts, but on scientific rationality. Borrowing from the behavioralist interpretation of Freud, Golan insisted that parents exhibit little physical affection, such as hugging and kissing, toward their children.

In order to liberate the child from guilt over sex, it was necessary to neutralize sexual attraction during all periods of childhood. Children must sleep apart from their parents since they are traumatized by any exposure to adult sexuality. But the main instrument for neutralizing sexual obsession was overexposure, the exact opposite of traditional Jewish or, for that matter, bourgeois repression. Nudity was thought to lessen sexual stimulation, rather than encourage it. Communal, coeducational showers, which, in some settlements, continued through high school, were based on the theory that constant exposure to the naked bodies of the opposite sex would create a more natural attitude toward sexuality. The underlying assumption of this theory was that children should not regard the genitals as having any different meaning than any other organ of the body, a view that thoroughly contradicted the biblical concept according to which sexual transgression is called "uncovering nakedness."

The child-rearing philosophy of the kibbutz movement therefore tried to create a sexual utopia by utterly demystifying eroticism, yet the often intended consequence was to suppress sexuality altogether. Adolescents were expected to refrain from any sexual experimentation since their education made it ostensibly unnecessary. Under the guise of eliminating guilt and sublimation, the new philosophy found its way to a different form of repression, in which sexual openness became the instrument for suppression of sexuality. In its educational philosophy, then, the kibbutz movement captured the larger contradiction in its attitude toward eroticism: the more explicit and verbose the discourse around sexuality, the greater the repression. The proclamation of an erotic ideology of Zionism undermined itself by turning Eros into an neutralizing discourse.[54]

Romances Without Solution

What, then, can we conclude about Magnus Hirschfeld's view of the scantily dressed *halutzim* as erotically liberated, their bodies freed from the clothing of bourgeois and traditional repression? As a Dionysian erotic revolution, Zionism must be judged a failure. Like the antihero Hefetz, which means desire, in Brenner's novel of the Second Aliya, *Breakdown and Bereavement,* that generation judged its erotic strivings to have been in vain. Brenner significantly captures this failure in the symbolism of Hefetz's hernia that causes him to abandon the pioneering collective and return to the Orthodox community in Jerusalem where, erotically frustrated, he sinks back into the swamp of traditional Judaism. The failure of Hefetz's body represents the failure of Zionism to achieve both erotic liberation and liberation from the Jewish tradition. One veteran woman of the Second Aliya reflected on

> the celibacy, distortion of life, waste of energy and hastening of the end, the end of life. The men continued, in effect, the life of yeshivah students from the Diaspora, without any thought to their private lives, as if it was a sin to think of one's own life. In this way, emerged the phenomenon of "romances without solution," that lasted for decades, which characterized the Second Aliya. This was the cause of families without children, of the many cases of infertility and failure to marry.[55]

All the sexual neuroses of the Diaspora had come to roost in Palestine, but without the solutions dictated by tradition. It is this sense of personal failure which strikes me as one of the most remarkable characteristics of this generation that created the Zionist revolution. Perhaps never has a revolution been accompanied by such a feeling of inadequacy and despair, what this memoirist called "romances without solutions." This was a generation that cultivated personal tragedy as almost a necessary component of nation building.

A figure who became emblematic of the tragedy of erotic Zionism was the Second Aliya poetess, Rachel Blubstein (1890–1931). Rachel was one of the pioneers at Kinneret before World War I but left for France in 1912 to study agronomy. She returned to Russia during the war and only made her way back to Palestine in 1918. Having contracted tuberculosis, she was rejected from membership in Kibbutz Degania and wandered, ill, from place to place until her untimely death in 1931. With her death, she became a romantic figure in the pantheon of the Second Aliya, a "femme fatale" who had captured the hearts of half the men of her generation but who died alone.[56] Zalman Shazar, A. D. Gordon and other lesser known figures are among those mentioned as her flames.[57] What is interesting about Rachel is less whether she had lovers than the way the question itself continues to haunt the myth of the Second and Third Aliyot. It is as if for those generations themselves and for subsequent memory, the only true romance must have been doomed to tragedy.

Indeed, the refraction of the twin myths of erotic liberation and romantic failure in contemporary Israeli culture—a subject unto itself—reveals much about the problematic nature of Israeli self-identity since the creation of the state. As Yehoshua Sobel's "Twentieth Night," a play based on the Bitania commune, reveals, those who see themselves as dwarfs on the shoulders of giants are obsessed with the sexual history of their ancestors, as if a romantic myth of erotic liberation might serve to liberate a culture whose own dreams have turned sour.

The life of Rachel had great paradigmatic resonance for the members of her generation. For the same reasons, they found an echo of their feelings in the romantic poems of Hayyim Nachman Bialik, whose melancholy Hebrew verses were set to music and, already in the first decade of the century, became the love songs with which the members of the Second Aliya wooed each other.[58] In one of his most popular poems, written in 1905, Bialik mourns the loss of youth and the failure of love.[59] The poem is addressed ambiguously to a woman in terms reminiscent of a Jewish mystic's prayer to the *shekhinah,* the female aspect of God. Lamenting the impossibility of erotic love, Bialik appeals to this woman to care for him instead:

Place me under your wing
And be a mother and sister to me.
Let your lap be a shelter for my head,
A nest for my rejected prayers.

Beset by personal and ideological contradictions, mature erotic love with an equal from the opposite sex seemed to Bialik's audience tragically unattainable. Having escaped from the ambivalent embrace of their parents' homes, the young people of the Second and Third Aliyot remained adrift between the search for autonomy and a return to parental affections, between erotic liberation and a return to traditional sexual patterns. So, too, the national movement they created was torn between revolution against the Jewish past and some form of continuation. One might therefore say that the ambiguities of Zionism as a erotic revolution for the bodies of Jews prefigured the larger political question, which remains with us today, of how to constitute a Jewish national body in the modern world.

Notes

1. Magnus Hirschfeld, *Men and Women: The World Journey of a Sexologist,* English trans. (New York, 1935), 275–76. See also Charlotte Wolf, *Magnus Hirschfeld: A Portrait of a Pioneer in Sexology* (London, 1986), 358.

2. See Vera S. Dunham, "Sex—From Free Love to Puritanism," *Soviet Society,* eds. A. Inkeles and K. Geiger (Boston, 1961), 540–46.

3. See S. Diamond, "Kibbutz and Shtetl," *Social Problems,* 5 (1957), 71–99.

4. See Robert A. Nye, "Degeneration and the Medical Model of Cultural Crisis in the French Belle Epoque" and Anson Rabinbach, "The Body without Fatigue: A Nineteenth-Century Utopia," in *Political Symbolism in Modern Europe: Essays in Honor of George L. Mosse,* ed. Seymour Drescher, David Sabean, and Allan Sharlin (New Brunswick, 1982), 19–62. See also George Mosse, *Nationalism and Sexuality* (New York, 1985), 48–65.

5. On neuresthenia, see Anson Rabinbach, *The Human Motor: Energey, Fatique and the Origins of Modernity* (New York, 1990), chap. 6.

6. Max Nordau, *Degeneration,* 1895 Eng. trans of 2nd ed., intro by George Mosse (New York, 1968), 167–68.

7. Max Nordau, "Muskeljudentum" in Jüdische Turnzeitung (June 1900) 10–11 and "Was bedeutet Turnen für uns Juden?" ibid (July 1902) 109–112.

8. George Mosse, "Introduction," *Degeneration,* xxvii.

9. See, for example, "Jüdische Erziehungsprobleme," *Jüdische Turnzeitung* 2:1 (January 1901), 5–8, and "Diskussionen über die Frage der körperlichen Hebung der Juden," ibid, 3:1 (January, 1902), 1–5.

10. Michael Berkowitz, " 'Mind, Muscle and Men': The Imagination of a Zionist National Culture for the Jews of Central and Western Europe, 1897–1914" (Unpublished Ph.D. diss., University of Wisconsin, 1989), 219–220.

11. Y. H. Brenner, *Breakdown and Bereavement,* trans. Hillel Halkin (Ithaca, N.Y., 1971), 158.

12. Rafael Becker, *Die jüedische Nervosität: Ihre Art, Enstenhung und Bekämpfung* (Zurich, 1918) and *Die Nervosität bei ben Juden: Ein Beitrag zur Rassenpsychiatrie füer Aertzte und gebildete Laien* (Zurich, 1919). On these essays, see Sanford Gilman, *Difference and Pathology,* 159–61.

13. Becker, *Judische Nervosität,* 26–27.

14. See, for example, Max Besser, "Der Einfluss der ökonomischen Stellung der deutschen Juden auf ihre physische Beschaffenheit," in *Körper-*

liche Renaissance der Juden (Berlin, 1909), 6–13. Besser argues that lack of physical work by Jews and urban conditions cause diminution of marital fertility and decrease in Jewish population. One of the oft-quoted studies was by Felix Theilhaber, *Der Untergang der deutschen Juden.*

15. Max Marcuse, *Ueber die Fruchtbarkeit der christlich-jüdischen Mischehe* (Bonn, 1920)

16. *The Star of Redemption,* trans. William Hallo (Boston, 1971), 298, 326, 341–42.

17. Hans Goslar, *Die Sexualethik der jüdischen Wiedergeburt. Ein Wort an unsere Jugend* (Berlin, 1919). I am grateful to Professor Paul Mendes-Flohr for bringing this important work to my attention.

18. Iwan Bloch, *Das Sexualleben unserer Zeit,* 737.

19. Goslar, *Die Sexualethik,* 5 and 10.

20. Martin Buber, "Das Zion der juedischen Frau" *Die jüedische Bewegung,* 1st ed. (Berlin, 1920), 28–38.

21. Marie Popper, "Jüedische Mädchen," *Jerubbaal* 1 (1918), 391–96.

22. A. D. Gordon, *Ha-Umma ve-ha-Avodah* (Tel Aviv, 1962), 475–76. See also his letter to Shlomo Tzemach on the problem of celibacy among the hired workers in Shmuel Dayan, *'Im avot ha-hityashvut* (Givatayim, 1967).

23. On Shatz, see Menachen Poznansky in Zvi Shatz, *Al Gevul ha-Demamah,* ed. Muki Tsur (Tel Aviv, 1990), 13–22, and Muki Tsur, *Aviv Mukdam: Zvi Shatz ve-ha-Kevutzah ha-Intimit* (Tel Aviv, 1984)

24. Trumpeldor to Shatz, 20 December 1908 in Menachem Poznansky (ed), *Me-Hayye Joseph Trumpeldor* (Tel Aviv, 1945), 63. For letters from Shatz to Trumpeldor from the same period, see *Al Gevul ha-Demamah,* 113ff.

25. The two novellas or short stories are "Be-Lo Niv," first published in *Ha-Adamah* 7 (1920) and "Batya," which was published in *Ha-Adamah* 12 (1923). Both were reprinted in *Al Gevul ha-Demamah.*

26. Tsur, *Aviv Mukdam,* 64–75.

27. Muki Tzur relates the story in *Aviv Mukdam,* 87.

28. On Blüher's influence on the Zionist youth movements, see Margalit, *Hashomer ha-Tzair,* 32, Shlomo Rekhev, *Hashomer Ha-Tzair: Mi-Tenuat ha-Noar le-Kibbutz ha-Artzi* (Tel Aviv, 1952/53), 54ff and Muki Tsur, "Introduction," *Kehilyateinu* (Jerusalem, 1988), 11.

29. For a history of Hashomer Ha-Tzair, see Elkana Margalit, *Hashomer Ha-Tzair: Mi-Edat Ne'urim le Marxism Ma'hapkhani (1913–1936)* (Tel Aviv, 1971).

30. *Kehilyateinu,* 276.

31. *Kehilyateinu,* 276.

32. See also Benjamin Dror in ibid., 28–31.

33. Quoted in Muki Tzur, Ta'ir Zevulun and Hanina Porat (eds), *Kan al Penei Adamah* (Tel Aviv, 1981), 70.

34. Ibid., 71.

35. Ada Fishman, "The Question of the Female Worker," *Ha-Po'el Ha-Tzair* 15:1–2 (11 November 1921), 12–14. For a study of the question of women and labor in the Zionist movement, although with a particular focus on the cities, see Deborah Bernstein, *The Struggle for Equality: Urban Women Workers in Prestate Israeli Society* (New York, 1987).

36. Ibid., 1st ed. (Jerusalem, 1926), 197.

37. Ibid.

38. Gen. 38.

39. Gen. 19:30–38.

40. In using this term, Rapoport was drawing from the strain of German *völkisch* thought described by George Mosse in *The Crisis of German Ideology*. Martin Buber, with whom Rapoport studied also used the language of "blood and soil" (*Blut und Boden*) in his prewar writings. It is striking how even a non-Zionist like Franz Rosenzweig resorted to such language: the term "blood community" is a central one in his vocabulary of Judaism in *The Star of Redemption*.

41. See Shlomo Avineri, "Jabotinsky: Integralist Nationalism and the Illusion of Power" in his *The Making of Modern Zionism* (New York, 1981), 159–86.

42. Yaari's manifesto in *Ha-Po'el Ha-Tzair* from 1921 was a reply to an earlier article in the same publication by A. Zioni that attacked the romanticism of Hashomer Ha-Tzair.

43. David Horowitz, *Ha-Etmol Sheli* (Jerusalem, 1970), 106.

44. "Semalim Telushim," first published in *Hedim* (1923); reprinted in Yaari, *Ba-Derekh*.

45. *Ba-Derekh,* 29–30.

46. See Gordon, "An Irrational Solution" in *Ha-Umma ve-ha-Avo-dah,* 99.

47. Ibid.

48. See the diary of Rivka Mahnimit, *Haverot ba-Kibbutz,* vol. 1 (Ein Harod, 1943), 35–48, entries from 1911 to 1917. She speaks much more

about her family of origin than about her husband, whom she mentions only in passing. Zvi Shatz captured this homesickness in "Batya," *Al Gevul ha-Demamah,* 39.

49. Yaari, *Ba-Derekh,* 13.

50. The illustrations are by Shraga Weill. The booklet is undated but is probably from the late 1930s.

51. See Melvin Spiro, *Children of the Kibbutz,* 2nd ed. (Cambridge, Mass. 1975), and Yonina Talmon-Garber, *Yahid ve-Hevrah ba-Kibbutz* (Jerusalem, 1970). For an excellent critique of the psychoanalytic assumptions of this philosophy, see Immanuel Berman, "Communal Education in the Kibbutz: The Attraction and Dangers of Psychoanalysic Utopia," (Hebrew), *Ha-Hinukh ha-Mishutaf* (1990), 64–77; English version in *Psychoanalytic Study of the Child* (1988).

52. See Horowitz, *Ha-Etmol Sheli,* 107.

53. See, for example, the set of principles laid out by a committee led by Golan, "Principles of Sex Education in the Kibbutz Artzi of Ha-Shomer Ha-Tzair," (Hebrew), *Ha-Hinukh ha-Mishutaf* 1 (1937) 28–32, and Golan, "On the Means for Communal Education," (Hebrew), *Ofakim* 3:4 (1946), 51–52. See also Ha-hinukh ha-Shomri (Warsaw, 1939), 72–75.

54. This analysis obviously owes much to Michel Foucault in his *History of Sexuality,* vol. 1, trans. Robert Hurley (New York, 1980), but Foucault makes, in essence, the opposite argument. He claims that the belief of the Victorians that they were sexually repressed was the result of its opposite: a new public discourse about sexuality. In the case of the Zionists, an explicit discourse of sexual liberation reinforces an actual culture of repression.

55. Quoted in *Kan al-Penei ha-Adamah,* 70.

56. See *Rahel: Shirim, Mikhtavim, Reshimot, Korot Hayyeha,* ed. Uri Milstein (Tel Aviv, 1958), 46–47. See further, Dan Miron, "Founding Mothers, Step-Sisters: On the Phenomenon of Hebrew 'Women's Poetry'," (Hebrew) *Alpayim* 1 (1989), 31–32.

57. The Shazar connection is fairly well attested from the 1920s when he was already married to Rachel Katznelson. It seems less likely than an actual affair took place between Rachel Blubstein and A. D. Gordon, who was already in his fifties when they met. But his letters to her bear the unmistakable mark of a man deeply infatuated. See A. D. Gordon, *Mikhtavim* (Jerusalem, 1954), 53–62. The letters are from 1913–1914.

58. See, for example, Katznelson-Shazar, *Adam Kemo She'hu,* 53.

59. "Hakhnisini takhat knafekh," *Kol Kitve Bialik* (Tel Aviv, 1945), 41.

12

Menstruation and Identity: The Meaning of Niddah for Moroccan Women Immigrants to Israel

Rahel Wasserfall

I did not have a particular interest in the laws of purity (niddah) when beginning my fieldwork.[1] Rather, I began with an interest in understanding how women of Moroccan origin shape their identity and how they construe their sense of self. In other words, I was interested in grasping how these women understand what it means to be a Moroccan Jewish woman.[2] But I quickly realized that it was impossible to deal with this question without taking account of the meaning of niddah (menstruation) for these women. Indeed, I discovered that religious identity and gender are inextricably entangled in practices related to the female body, specifically to menstruation.

Niddah means "separation" and "seclusion" and refers to the woman who is menstruating and who has been separated for a specified period after her menstrual flow has ended. In Jewish law, niddah refers to a whole complex of regulations concerning the behavior of the menstruating woman, including, perhaps most importantly, the prohibition on sexual relations during this period.[3] But niddah has a very different set of meanings from the perspective of the women whom I interviewed, women who immigrated from Morocco to Israel in the 1950s and who did not have a formal religious education. Their conceptions of niddah differ from the meanings encoded in classical religious sources. This analysis, then, allows women to speak for themselves on a fundamental set of Jewish regulations. It shows how those regulations of the female body are taken up by women themselves and become part and parcel of their own identity that is in turn demarcated in contrast to other identities.

The importance of niddah first came home to me at the very outset of my fieldwork when I was conversing with a young woman (35) born in Fez but educated from childhood in a large town in Israel; with some reticence she told me of her problems with her mother-in-law, problems that influenced her decision to build a separate household and to leave the common roof of the extended family. She urged her husband who was the first born in his family to build a new house, near the common house. The point of contention in this dispute was the mother-in-law's insistence that her daughter-in-law obey the laws of niddah and go to the miqve (the ritual bath that ends the period of separation following menstruation).

There are a number of ways of interpreting this argument. Quite plausibly these two women were in conflict for influence in the house, love of the son or husband, the division of common labor, and so forth. Yet it is interesting to note that the dispute crystallized around the issue of niddah. The laws of purity, then, served as the institutionalized, and hence legitimate means, of channeling the tensions between mother-in-law and daughter-in-law.

This incident intrigued me, and I looked for an opportunity to ask the older women about niddah. Given my own background as a French born, Ashkenazi Jew, I regarded these matters as personal and intimate, and hence difficult to approach. I therefore tried to approach the subject circuitously, by framing my questions as question of Jewish law and by asking them what mitzvot (commandments) they actually perform. To my surprise, they mentioned only education and charity. No one mentioned the laws of purity or kashrut (the dietary rules). It was as if niddah had nothing to do with Jewish law. After circling around the subject, I realized that without a direct question the subject would never be broached.

But as soon as I put the question directly, the women cried out, "You are not Jewish" 'F'[4] (don't you know that for us niddah is essential?) or "Are we Arabs?" 'F' (for not obeying the laws of niddah). From these reactions it was obvious to me that niddah occupies a central place within these women's thinking about themselves as Jewish women.[5] It also turned out that niddah was a subject about which these women felt entirely comfortable speaking. Among women, niddah was not intrinsically a shameful or private subject. It became shameful, as in the case of the mother- and daughter-in-law incident, when sexual relations were at issue. For example, I was told that "it is shameful" 'F' and "it is not honorable" 'F' for a mother to educate her daughter on sexual relations that included the teaching of laws of niddah. Because the subject of niddah is relatively public, it is available as a symbol through which personal and communal identity can be expressed. Before exploring the various significations of niddah, I will first introduce the basic data on my informants.

Portrait of the Moshav[6]

My fieldwork was carried out on a Moshav (a small agricultural community) that was founded in 1955 by immigrants of Moroccan origin. In the early fifties a nucleus of ninety-four families (ninety from towns in the North-Fez and Sifrou and four from Gilmama in the South) bought a plot of land and a house from the Jewish Agency. The first settlers had enough money to change the standard architectural housing plans. A majority of the immigrants were merchants who were for the most part financially secure enough to invest a large sum of money in the early fifties, immigrating to Israel only in 1955.[7]

The nucleus of settlers from Fez, who were traditionalists, had established criteria of religious observance as a precondition for candidacy to the group. For example, families were not accepted when the head of the family shaved. The severe criteria of observance made it difficult to assemble the one hundred families required for the formation of the moshav (only a third were found); For this reason, the Jewish Agency envoys turned to the township closest to Fez, Sifrou.[8] The two communities maintained constant family, economic, and religious relations.[9] Of the moshav population today, one third originates in Fez, nearly two-thirds from Sifrou, and four families from Gilmama.

A number of families left the moshav at the start of the settlement, but members of established families bought out their shares and replaced them. The beginning of the moshav was not without political rivalry between the two groups. Today, two synagogues stand side by side in the center of the village, relics of past problems. For a variety of reasons, including problems of ideology and farming, the settlers abandonned their first occupation in favor of trade. In the words of my informants, Jews from the towns of Morocco were not accustomed to the hard physical labor of agriculture, which was linked in their minds with low-grade Arab labor.[10]

In 1981, the time of this fieldwork, the moshav[11] had a population of six hundred, comprised of 120 families. The average number of children per family was 7.8. In the early 1980s, twenty families were engaged in farming full time or part time, fifteen families in market gardening of vegetables, and five families in rose-growing export. Most of the settler population had established a variety of businesses in the small town some ten minutes drive from the moshav. Among the settlers we find occupations such as bank employees, bureaucrats, and career officers. From an Israeli point of view, the architecture and interiors of the new houses are luxurious since one can find a great variety of household appliances.

For analytical purposes, I classified my informants in two age groups, 1) fifty to seventy-five years of age and 2) thirty-five to forty-nine years of age. The great majority of women had never worked for a salary. In the first group, not a single woman had worked outside her home, while among those originating from Fez, two women had been employed as secretaries before marriage. As for the second group from Sifrou, one woman had been employed before her marriage as an embroiderer. Among those coming from Fez only one woman worked outside her house as a nurse; another told me of having taught dressmaking before her marriage. A majority of women received a formal education. In the first group, six out of the seven women from Fez received a formal education while only four out of the ten from Sifrou had that advantage. All the women in the second group originating from Fez and Sifrou reported receiving formal education.[12]

Niddah and Jewish Identity

In this community, the observance of niddah was not primarily considered a mitzvah (religious obligation) but helped articulate and was entangled in what it meant for these women to be both female and Jewish. These women described menstruation as "*our* way" (*haderech shelanou*) 'H' (i.e., the way of women). The use of the Hebrew idiom "our way" is significant. It indicates that they understood the observance of niddah not only as a distinguishing mark of being a woman but also as a sign of their being Jews. The use of the Hebrew idiom "our way" is apparently the same expression used by Jewish women of Algeria at the start of the century. According to M. Cohen (1912), Algerian Jews used this expression of Hebrew origin, even though in everyday life they spoke Arabic. This linguistic peculiarity illustrates the way in which niddah observance was construed as a specifically Jewish practice rooted in Jewish tradition and distinctive in the Muslim host cultures.[13] In fact, niddah observances perform a crucial role in the articulation of Jewish identity.

Niddah is a complex cultural symbol through which women interpret a specific bodily process, namely, menstruation. It is thus a symbolic process referring to 1) the flow of menstrual blood, "our way" in the words of these women, 2) the seven-day period of purity following the cessation of the menstrual flow, an interim period during which spouses refrain from sexual relations; and 3) the miqve or ritual bath, an institution marking the resumption of relations between the spouses. In what follows, I will explore the meaning of each of these three dimensions of niddah.

The Menstrual Flow

During their period of menstrual flow, older women had tended to neglect their physical appearance, did not wash, but had continued to fulfill their other obligations as housewives (cooking, education of the children). The majority of prohibitions during this period are connected with abstinence from relations between the spouses. The woman does not pass any object directly to her husband but instead places it on a table so that the latter should not come into physical contact with her, a contact that could arouse a husband's sexual desires. She must not speak "too much" with him, nor enter into either the bathroom when he is present there or their bedroom to arrange the beds, wipe his face, and so forth. During the first three days of their menstrual period, older women also tend to refrain from kneading or blessing the hallah (bread used for the ritual meals on the Sabbath). They will recite the blessing only if there are no other women in the house. The blessing over the Sabbath loaf and the Friday night candles as well as the laws of niddah are the only religious observances that apply exclusively to women.[14]

Days of Purity

As soon as a woman's menstrual flow ends, she must daily verify that no blood-colored flow is seen.[15] According to Jewish law, if she discovers no blood, she must count seven days and then take her ritual bath. All the older women referred to the days of purity as a "safety period" 'H', a period that ensured her purity when she took her ritual bath. In other words, this period ensures "that she had nothing left" 'H', that the woman no longer had any flow of blood and therefore that sexual relations with the husband would take place at the legitimate time. Guarding the purity of sexual relations is believed to protect any fetus that might be conceived. The women of the second group spoke of observing only three to four days as a period of safety. In practice, matters are even more complicated when one considers that women of both age groups do not automatically go to the ritual bath after having counted the specified period of time.[16] The woman's going to the bath also depends on the husband's involvement. He is expected "to send" his wife when he deems it appropriate. In other words, not all of the responsibility devolves on the wife. If for various reasons the husband does not send her, the woman remains in a state of limbo, during which sexual relations are forbidden but women can otherwise perform their other functions.

A woman's visit to the ritual bath is thus dependent on informal negotiations between the spouses. Significantly, then, the religious obligation that is par excellence a woman's responsibility is dependent on the husband's intervention. This would seem to confirm the public authority of the husband in Judeo-Moslem culture. But further study of niddah symbolism will significantly alter the perception of how niddah observances are actually negotiated.

Miqve, the Ritual Bath

A certain proportion of the water in the miqve must be rainwater. In Morocco, it was not heated because in the Judeo-Moroccan cultural system only cold water in considered to have purifying powers while hot water is reserved for hygiene (Bruno and Malka 1939, 338). In the moshav, the miqve is heated to attract the younger women. After counting the seventh day, the woman must wash herself in her home before nightfall and then go to the miqve. The miqve is open daily at nightfall and is kept by an old woman (who a few years ago had tried unsuccessfully to persuade the young women of the importance of the miqve). The miqve is set back, its architecture the most banal possible. It is near the school that is empty in the evening when the women arrive. The women go to the miqve by indirect routes, hiding their towels so that their own children and the neighbors would not guess from the behavior that sexual relations would take place between the couple that night. Older women relate that if on leaving the ritual bath their eyes would fall on an Arab or a donkey, they must again purify themselves. S. Deshen (1981) writes that during the last century this belief caused the closure of a Jewish store in a mellah (Moroccan Jewish quarter). This store was located next to the miqve and the returning women would bump into Arab customers. The community exerted pressure on the storekeeper to close his stall. Malka (1946) recounts that a Jewish rabbi was in the habit of coming to recite psalms in front of the miqve so that the women's first glance would fall on his person. These attitudes are linked to the belief that the first glance after the bath affects the conception of the potential child.[17]

Meanings of Niddah

The women I interviewed ascribed three distinctive kinds of meanings to niddah observances. Niddah plays a role in 1) the construction of religious/ethnic identity 2) is embedded in ideas about the physical and spiritual well-being of the Jewish people and 3) is strongly linked to matters of public honor.

Identity/Religion

Like all mitzvot (religious obligations), the practices of niddah may or may not be observed. Religious commandments, by definition, are characterized by the possibility of nonperformance. If nonperformance were not possible, then the obligations could not be commandments, since there would be no choice or will involved on the part of the religious actor. However, when a commandment, such as niddah, becomes constitutive of identity, the actor ceases to recognize the possibility of refusing or failing to perform the commandment in question. As an element of one's identity, the failure in its performance necessary implies the failure of the actor to implement his or her identity, that is, to be who he or she is. As noted earlier, women in this community did not include niddah among the religious commandments they perform. Women mentioned only child rearing and charity as religious duties. The observance of niddah, therefore, was so deeply connected to their identities that its performance was simply taken for granted.

The niddah practices distinguish Jewish from non-Jewish women. This is evident in the way in which the miqve serves as a sign of female Jewish identity. I am not suggesting that the miqve has completely lost its status as a mitzvah (religious duty) but that in the minds of these women its primary importance is its ability to differentiate them from their neighbors. Consider the following quotations from my informants that illustrate the way in which an ideology of identity is linked to the niddah observances: ". . . what! we are Arabs (for not going to the miqve)" 'F' ". . . You are not Jewish? (for asking such a question and showing your lack of knowledge) 'F' ". . . in Fez, in Sifrou, the rabbi does not have to ask for a proof that the bride has been to the miqve, no woman would think of marrying without going to the miqve" 'F'.

It is only possible to understand this transformation, whereby the practices of niddah become not only a religious duty but in fact a marker of identity if we consider the way in which the institution of miqve is symbolically linked to the physiological processes of women's bodies. Menstruation is considered essential to female identity; it is what makes a woman out of a girl. But the miqve not only signifies this developmental change. The miqve, as these women see it, is also what makes a Jewish woman out of a menstruating woman. To understand this point, I will explore the ways in which women describe and feel about their menstrual blood and the ritual of going to the miqve.

Blood, Miqve and Feminine identity

The appearance of blood is "their way," the feminine way of being. ". . . she must have blood to become a woman, it is nature, so that she should give birth" 'H'. "Blood is natural for the woman. It was usual not to touch the husband. That is how it was" 'H'. Menstrual blood, then, is considered to be an expression and symbol of the feminine essence. It signifies the potential of conception, the construction of the Jewish household and the continuity of the Jewish people; all of which are central values in Judeo-Moroccan culture. A woman who does not menstruate is considered to be an outstanding anomaly. In this community, which cares deeply about the fertility of couples, the absence of menstruation, like sterility, becomes a personal and family tragedy.

The blood that appears each month[18] symbolizes the capacity to reproduce and thus transforms a young girl into a woman. But in going to the miqve, these women understand that their behavior stems directly from their identity as Jews. According to my informants, in Morocco Moslems did not institutionalize any observances with regard to menstruation. As understood by my informants, then, menstruation involves two processes that are linked but assume different meanings. Menstruation is simultaneously a personal yet universal symbol of a girl's transformation into a woman.

But this physiological event has become institutionalized in a set of practices such as the ritual bath that superimposes on these personal meanings a reference to Jewish identity. It is the ritual bath that enables the women to identify collectively as not just women, but Jewish women. If blood turns a girl into a woman, the miqve turns the woman into a Jew. Niddah then provides the link between personal identity (I am a woman) and collective identity (I am a Jew).

It is incumbent upon the mother-in-law and the sisters-in-law to convey to the young bride the normative behavior prescribed by the niddah observances. The Jewish mother has no role in that education.[19] In traditional Judeo-Moroccan culture, the interaction between mother and daughter around matters pertaining to niddah is more than problematic. Mothers do not guide their daughters when they first menstruate and a number of firstborn daughters were inclined for several months to conceal from their mothers their new state of womanhood. Mothers, like daughters, felt embarrassed to discuss this subject with each other. This reticence in fact signifies that the daughters have entered a new state of being in which their potential fertility could become a reality through sexual relations. Mothers are reticent to intervene in anything concerning their daughters' sexual relations.[20] And menstruation and sexuality are deeply entwined.[21] Miqve, we recall, is itself a sign that sexual relations have resumed between husband and wife. And menstruation itself is a sign of a woman's reproductive potential. In a culture where sex is essentially regarded as a means to procreation, the ability to menstruate is regarded as making women desirable. Before menopause, women regard themselves as sexual beings because of their potential fertility. The period in life when niddah observances must be observed thus represents women's active sexual period when they are desired by their husbands.

Personal Health and the Well-Being of the Jewish People

Proper observance of niddah practices is critical for the health of a woman and her loved ones. For the women, menstruation is a sign that she is cleansed. The flow of the blood is regarded as very beneficial for the women, and some men said that because of this monthly cleaning, women live longer lives. Menstruation is regarded as a potential danger to a husband who may become ill if he comes in contact with this blood. Miqve is the means of preventing menstruation from "soiling" the husband and making him ill. More importantly, the health of a potential child is also endangered unless a woman immerses in the ritual bath. Only with the protection of the miqve is the child born pure and healthy. And without the miqve, the child risks "sullying" (toomha) the whole Jewish people when it in turn matures and has its own children. Because husbands are perceived as being more interested in sex than their wives, it is therefore the responsibility of husbands to abstain from all relations with their wives during the period of menstrual flow.

Women referred to all of these different "perils" of niddah in the same interviews. It is important to note that it is only the anticipated Jewish community of the future that is in danger of being defiled by menstrual blood. The actual Jewish community in its present concrete form is apparently not endangered by menstruation. Thus women sit beside other men in the community while they withdraw from their husbands.[22] For the Moroccan community studied, niddah is only institutionalized as a matter of importance between spouses. This I believe is because there niddah conceals a sexual preoccupation between spouses and so belongs in the domain of sexual modesty. It is not about protecting the community from impurity. This contrasts with the behavior of men and women in orthodox communities, such as Mea Shearim, where every woman is potentially a niddah and so must be avoided.

Personal and Communal Health

Why is menstrual blood simultaneously conceptualized as "sick" and as a process of cleansing and gaining potential longevity? I suggest that there is a connection between the restrictions on menstrual blood and the prohibition against Jews eating blood, a prohibition that also finds its first articulation in biblical sources. As some interpreters have suggested, the origin of this latter prohibition presupposes that blood is the vehicle of life. Swallowing blood thus constitutes a mixing of life and death, since the blood from a dead animal is being used as nourishment. It is this mixing of life and death that is prohibited and regarded as repugnant. Analogously, the blood of menstruation signifies that an opportunity for conception has been missed and that the potential for new life has been lost. One must be on guard regarding this ambiguous blood, which while once potentially life giving, now signifies loss of life.

This is why sexual intercourse is regarded as dangerous to the potential infant.[23] To have intercourse while the woman is menstruating is to potentially mingle menstrual blood, which is linked to death, with the potential blood of the infant. According to the writings of Aristotle (Barnes 1973), a fetus is created when blood is coagulated by the sperm. When conception does not take place, unfertilized blood runs off as menstrual blood. This understanding of conception is found in the rabbinic Midrashim (Feldman 1974, 133) and seems to underlie the statements of my female informants:[24] ". . . the blood of menstruation is the blood of a dead" 'F' (Le sang des regles c'est le sang d'un mort); ". . . death is in your belly" 'F' (la mort est dans ton ventre).

Although the women knew that from the perspective of modern medicine the chances of becoming pregnant at the time of the flow were infinitesimal, they continued to think that sexual relations were prohibited so as to prevent the blood of the potential child from becoming impure. The flow of menstrual blood signifies that the potential for this blood to be transformed into a fetus had passed and that this blood, previously available for life, had become a symbol of death. Menstruation, then, appears both to a woman and her husband as a blatant sign that conception has not taken place. Yet at the same time menstruation is an agent of the woman's health for through this process her blood is cleaned. Here again we see the dual life/death symbolism operating in the menstrual blood. For this reason, women would appear in this culture as ambiguous beings, bearing symbols of death and life within. Menstruation is the point of convergence for two sets of concerns: concerns about women's personal health and the larger concern with the Jewish people's well-being.

On Public Honor

Older and younger women speak of honor in relation to the miqve. By fulfilling the laws of niddah, women are in fact preserving their honor vis-a-vis their husbands. Why is honor, a central element of the culture of the Magrheb, linked to the practices of Niddah generally and to the ritual of the miqve specifically? Fertility in this culture brings honor, and firstborns are generally called by the women "my honor." By performing the ritual of the miqve, the women not only help their husbands and themselves reproduce the Jewish people but maintain the purity of the Jewish people by preventing the child from "turning out a mamzer."[25] On the night of women's return from the miqve, they or their mother-in-laws used to prepare a festive meal, a kind of symbolic wedding ceremony. As the menstrual blood renews the woman's body, the miqve renews the relationship between the couple. Going to the miqve symbolizes the end of sexual abstinence and revives desire in the couple. Sexual intercourse is incumbent on husbands the night the woman returns from the miqve. In this way too the couple renews their marriage contract that they understand as their potential to build a house in Israel, to "reproduce" the Jewish people.

Interaction between Marriage Partners

Thus far, I have interpreted the meanings of niddah from the perspective of Jewish women. But as I will now suggest, niddah also is the symbolic site where the division of power between husband and wife is enacted. As previously mentioned, the task of sending his wife to the miqve is incumbent on the husband. Women say that in cases of conjugal fights, husbands would delay sending them. In such cases, sending one's wife to the miqve is the means of reconciliation between husband and wife. Women, I was told, sometimes insist that men "beg" them before they actually go to the miqve. Expressing interest in going to the miqve is in fact a way of indicating interest in sexual relations, and sex is an important area of bargaining power between husbands and wives. My informants agreed that if the men do not ask their wives to go to the miqve, a woman can remain in this state for an indefinite period, which in no way prevents her from carrying out her other tasks of housewife duties. One woman described how her husband would prevent her from going if on the night she was permitted to go, he came home and found her still at home. That day, he would declare, did not count as one of her clean days, and thus he would establish himself as the expert.

The visit to the miqve is thus not automatic and the husband exercises a great deal of control. But at the same time going to the miqve is fraught with symbolic significance. A woman who goes to the miqve without the instruction of her husband is regarded as declaring her sexual desire. Women talked with pride of their spouses waiting impatiently for their return from the miqve, representing them as more sexually desirous than they themselves felt. It is interesting to note that the men with whom I talked described the opposite state of affairs; for them it is the women who were more sexually desirous. The visit to the miqve then is a kind of game of power in which the one who is labeled as more sexual desirous is perceived as the loser.

Miqve and Strategies of Power

The husband may manipulate the niddah observances in one of three ways: 1) he can make his wife have sexual relations before going to the miqve; 2) he can insist that his wife cut short the days of safety and go to the miqve before the completion of the seven obligatory days; and 3) the husband can "forget" to send his wife.

Of these three possibilities, the second is the most common. The others, though possible, are not very common for specific reasons. Were a man to have sexual intercourse without his wife going to the miqve, he would have to be willing to ignore the conception that niddah can make him ill. At least in theory, this possibility is recognized, as illustrated by a woman who said: "the husband was kind; he knew how to wait" 'H'. Her statement implies that if he were not kind, he could have taken her by force. But fear of personal illness and concerns over the well-being of the Jewish people act as important deterrents against this kind of behavior.[26] As one of the men expressed it, "if anything would happen to the child, I would feel guilty, I would think it was because of that" [the infraction of the laws of niddah] 'H'.

The third possibility, of not sending his wife to the miqve, may occur in one of several situations: a) sexual intercourse is seen by the man as a "service" he provides to his wife; b) his virility is not in question because he already has a large number of children; c) he presents himself as a religious expert and is a stickler for the regulations. In this case, he may insist that his wife delay the miqve one or two days.

What is interesting to note here, is the symbolic manipulation of sexuality; both partners present the other as more desirous of sexual relations. As one of my male informants put it, "if one could do without it, everyone would feel better" 'H'. "It would take away honor and contribute nothing to it" 'H', said another. Whoever wins in portraying the partner as having more interest in sex thus appears to be doing their spouse a service. The denial of desire, therefore, conceals a desire for symbolic and social power. To deny one's own desire is to accrue symbolic capital, to win in the game of distributing power.

Women play this game as well. The women I interviewed consider the Jewish Moroccan woman to be without social power. "The Moroccan woman is a zero" 'H', several women cried out. Thus women have a variety of strategies for gaining and exercising power in their relationships. Since a man's virility lies in the number of children he has fathered, women can render their husbands a service by shortening the "days of security." While it is ultimately the husband's decision as to when the wife should go to the miqve, women accrue symbolic capital by agreeing to go early.

The concept of impurity enters in a critical way into this ongoing negotiation over who is pleasing whom more. By going to the miqve before the end of the period of safety, the wife exposes herself to a risk; As one informant put it, "if any [blood, impurity] is left, it is my illness" 'H'. To go to the miqve early is to risk becoming ill. But in taking this risk, she has accrued a significant gain in the distribution of power. Women are willing to take this risk because they gain what they could not acquire by other means. Thus this manipulation of wives by men, which at first glance exhibits their social power, proves in fact to be a feminine gain.[27] And women would capitalize on this gain in arguments with their husbands.

But there is a second strategy by which women seek to exercise power in their relationships. Women tell of putting off their visits to the miqve and not paying heed to the constant demands of the husband to go to the ritual bath. Indeed, delaying the miqve and thereby sexual relations seem in the eyes of these women to be the principle source of feminine power (Deshen 1981). The man waits with impatience and brings his wife presents on the evening of the miqve. Since masturbation is prohibited, men have no other outlets. By delaying the miqve, then, women make the desires of their husbands more obvious and thereby emerge victorious in the game of power relations.

Conclusion

The niddah observances are both symbolic representations and cultural practices. As representations, they help articulate what it means to be a woman and a Jew. Niddah is one of the core symbols of women's identity. It serves as the link between women's personal identity as a woman and their collective identity as Jews. Niddah is also what links the Jewish couple to the Jewish tradition. As practices, they are the sites in which men and women seek to develop and exercise power in their marital relations. As this analysis has suggested, although social authority is represented as masculine, it is in fact moderated by informal female power. Women see themselves as dominated by their husbands, yet they are not completely subordinated. Niddah remains one of the importance contexts in which women can finesse their husbands in the game of authority. Therein may perhaps lie one of the causes for the profound attachment to niddah by these women who viewed it as one of the main symbols of womanhood.

Notes

1. I would like to thank Harvey Goldberg and Madeleine Adelman for their comments. The fieldwork on which this article is based was funded by a scholarship of the Ben-Zvi Institute of Jerusalem.

2. The interviews were conducted in French or Hebrew. The older women from Fez speak French and Hebrew. One single woman born in Sifrou had troubles speaking Hebrew. For the younger ones the use of French was difficult and the interviews were generally conducted in Hebrew.

3. Niddah is a Hebrew word meaning "a menstruating woman." The rules concerning Niddah are compiled in a number of legal codes including the Shulkhan Arukh (yoreh de'ah 18–31–200) and in tractates Niddah in the two Talmuds. Jewish law prohibits sexual relations between husband and wife while the woman is menstruating and seven days after the end of the period. A woman must count five days for menstruation and add seven days of purity. After that period, the woman must immerse in the ritual bath, the miqve, before resuming conjugal relations. Similar restrictions apply at childbirth (Lev. 12:1–8). For the birth of a boy, a woman is in a severe state of impurity for seven days and a lesser state of impurity for another thirty-three days. Both of these periods are doubled after the birth of a girl. One who had several relations with a menstruating woman was subject to karet (being cut off from the community). These biblical restrictions were primarily focused on preserving the purity of the temple cult, yet they remained in force even after the destruction of the second temple in 70 C.E. For a more detailed discussion, see "Niddah" in *Encyclopedia Judaica* (1972) and Eilberg-Schwartz 1990:177–194.

4. When the quotations are translated from Hebrew, they are followed by a 'H', when they are translated from French, they are followed by a 'F'.

5. Kashrut (the Jewish dietary restrictions) also play a similar role that is beyond the focus of the present inquiry.

6. The moshav is registered with the list of moshavim aligned with religious groups of the center (Hapoel Hamizrahi) of the NRP, the National Religious Party.

7. The settlers were sufficiently well-to-do not to be under economic pressure at the start of their settlement. As distinct from Moshav Romema studied by M. Shokeid where economic problems formed one of the causes that forced the women to redefine their traditional role and relations with husbands. The economic independence of the settlers under study perhaps strengthened the traditional role of the women I interviewed.

8. Sifrou is one of the Moroccan towns that, after the emigration, has been studied by several American anthropologists (Geertz and Geertz [1979]) and Rosen (1984). These interpreters make allusion to the important economic situation occupied by the Jewish population.

9. The Department of Folklore of the Jerusalem Museum treats both towns as a single ethnographic complex. The ethnographic research on which this article is based supports the contention that at the level of gender ideology, the same conclusions may be made. Evidently, it is not easy to answer the question of ideology of identity; did it come from Morocco or from the contiguity of the two groups on the moshav itself? For the use of the concept of gender ideology in the Moroccan setting see Dwyer (1978).

10. Shokeid (1971, 178) in his work on immigrants from Southern Morocco describes the beliefs that physical agricultural work is Arab labor. Such labor in the eyes of the villagers is a symbol of poor education and lack of humanity.

Women did not want to be photographed in the fields and said, "Don't take our photographs when we are working like Arabs." The expression "like Arabs" is a common idiom used to condemn a person's manners.

11. I studied two age groups, 1) 50 to 75, and 2) 35 to 49 years of age. Average number of children according to the family's origin and the mother's age group.

	Fez	Sifrou
Years of Age		
1) 50 to 75	6.5	9.4
2) 35 to 49	5.4	6.4

The data presented in the statistical inquiry represent the replies of twenty-seven women, while thirty-one settlers were interviewed in "in depth-interviews." Four persons were not interviewed for technical reasons (two women from Fez, age group number 2 and two from Sifrou, age group number 1.

12. Women were not particularly precise about their years of schooling. One woman born in 1908 in Fez received a bachelor's degree.

13. Donath (1962, 113) wrote that "a study in depth of structures of the Jewish family and their evolution in contact with different host nations remains to be made."

14. Women do not generally participate in synagogue services and after menopause very few even follow religious services on the Sabbath and High Holidays. Some women mentioned that they refrained from going to the cemetery while menstruating.

15. The color of the flow is one of the problematic subjects discussed in the Mishnah.

16. This seems to be the case with orthodox Ashkenazi Jewish women from Mea Shearim, who go to the miqve even when their husbands are absent. Verbal communication from R. Berger-Sofer who spent a year in the field in the community.

17. See Verdier (1979) for a discussion of beliefs in the power of the glance and the effects on the menstruating woman. Beliefs in the evil eye is also very common in Jewish Moroccan populations settled in Israeli Moshavim (Wasserfall 1987).

18. B. B. Harrel (1981, 817) argues that during the pre-industrial period, menstruation was uncommon because women passed from one pregnancy to the next. She interprets menstruation as a borderline period that is also symbolic of feminine fertility and sexual attractiveness. "Menstrual flow would thus symbolize the height of female sexual capacity via-a-vis the male as well as the female's liminal freedom from biological and culturally mandated intensive infant parasitism."

19. In Mea Shearim the role is incumbent on the mother just before the marriage ceremony (Berger-Sofer 1979, 149). In Algeria the mother avoids connection with the procedure of miqve. Briggs and Guede (1964, 5) wrote that the bride goes to purify herself toward noon on the day of her wedding and is not accompanied by her mother. "It would have been considered shameful for her mother to take part in such physically intimate proceedings." In the research I conducted in 1983–84 in a Moroccan moshav in Israel, the mother indeed took part in the miqve procedure before the wedding (Wasserfall 1987).

20. For an interpretation of the mother's role in the marriage ceremony that supports this argument see (Wasserfall), Rosen (1981, 65), "The rite of the table."

21. I would like to point to the difference existing here between my Moroccan Jewish informants and traditional Jewish Ashkenazi women of Mea Shearim. It seems that the Ashkenazi women would interpret the miqve in direct relation to their state of purity. Those women would go to the miqve even if their husbands were not in town. The Moroccan Jewish woman of my research would have abstained in that case (verbal communication from Berger-Sofer).

22. It seems that worries about keeping the community pure direct the behavior of women in Mea Shearim. For example, they do not go to public ceremonies such as circumcisions while they are observing niddah (verbal

communication from Jayanti who conducted a field study in Mea Shearim). One may argue that the differences in the observances of niddah between the communities derive from their understanding of how severe the possibility of contagion from a woman observing niddah.

23. Though women knew that according to modern medicine the chances of becoming pregnant at the time of the flow were infinitesimal, they continued to think that the prohibition of sexual relations were for the purpose of preventing impurity of the blood in the potential child.

24. There is conflicting opinions in rabbinic literature on the role of the woman in conception. The Talmud reflects a view different from that of Aristotle. It suggests that the woman as well as the man together contribute to the body of the child. In the midrash, however, the Aristotelian idea is reflected. The occasion for this comment is the verse from Job 10:10–22, "Hast thou not poured me out like milk and curdled me like cheese." The Midrash comments: "A mother's womb is full of standing blood, which flows there from menstruation. But at God's will, a drop of whiteness enters and falls into its midst and behold a child is formed. This is likened unto a bowl of milk. When a drop of rennet falls into it, it congeals and stands, if not it continues as liquid" (Leviticus Rabbah 14:9; Yalkut to Job 10:10 cited in Feldman 1974).

25. "Mamzer" refers to a the status of a child born of an illegitimate union, such as an adulterous union between a man and a married woman. The women of the moshav apply this term to a child conceived before the woman has been to the miqve.

26. In another moshav (Wasserfall 1987), I was told by a Tunisian woman that once she complained to her mother that her husband wanted her to shorten the days and send her to the miqve before she was due. Her mother said that her husband was behaving "nicely" and told her that her own father did even worse and had intercourse when she was menstruating. Gilad (1989) notes the use of a specific ritual by Yemenite women used when defiled by their husbands, as for example when their husbands force them to have intercourse while still in a state of niddah.

27. This woman's choice to shorten the "security days" may be linked to the fact that in Jewish tradition the days of purity have not always been seven days. The period of seven days was institutionalized at a later date, at the time of the Mishnah (see *Encyclopedia Judaica*).

References

Barnes, J. A (1973): "Genetrix, Genitor; Nature Culture?" in (ed) Goody, J. *The Character of Kinship*. Cambridge University Press.

Berger-Sofer, R. (1979): "Pious women: A study of women's roles in a Hassidic and Pious community, Mea Shearim". Ph.D. dissertation. Rutgers, New Jersey, New Brunswick.

Briggs, L. and Guede, M. (1964): *No more Forever: A Saharian Jewish Town*. Peabody Museum, Cambridge, U.S.A.

Brunot, L. and Malka, E. (1939): *Textes Judeo-Arabes*. Fes, Rabat.

Cohen, M. (1912): *Le parler arabe des juifs d'Alger*. Paris

Deshen, S. (1981): *Responsa du 19e Siecle*. Bar Ilan University (in Hebrew). Israel.

Donath, D. (Bensimon) (1962): *L'evolution de la femme Israelite a Fes*. Aix-en-Provence.

Dwyer, D. (1978): *Images and self images, Male and Female in Morocco*. New York, Columbia University Press.

Dwyer, D. (1978): "Ideologies of Sexual inequality and Strategies for change in Male-Female relations" *American Ethnologist*. 5:227–240.

Eilberg-Schwartz, H. (1990) *The Savage in Judaism* (Bloomington: Indiana University Press).

Encyclopedia Judaica (1972): Jerusalem, vol. 12, Keter Publishing, LTD.

Feldman, D. M. (1974): *Marital Relations, Birth control and Abortion in Jewish Law*. New York, Schocken Books.

Geertz, C. Geertz, H. and Rosen, L. (1979): *Meaning and Order in Moroccan Society*. Cambridge University Press, Cambridge.

Gilad, L. (1989): *Ginger and Salt; Yemeni Jewish Women in an Israeli Town*. Westview Press, Boulder, San Fransico & London.

Harrell, B. B. (1981): "Lactation and Menstruation in Cultural Perspective" *American Anthropologist* Vol. 83:4.

Malka, E. (1946): *Essai d'Ethnographie traditionnelle des Mellahs*. Rabat.

Pitts-Rivers, J. (1977): *The Fate of Schem or the Politics of Sex*. Cambridge University Press, Cambridge.

Rosen, R. (Wasserfall) (1981): "Le symbolisme feminin ou la femme dans le systeme de representation judeo-marocain dans un moshav en Israel". These de MA, Departement de Sociologie et d'Anthropologie Sociale, Jerusalem, Septembre 1981 (en Hebreu).

Wasserfall, R. (1987): *Gender Identification in an Israeli Moshav*. Unpublished Ph.D dissertation, Hebrew University of Jerusalem.

13

Why Jewish Princesses Don't Sweat: Desire and Consumption in Postwar American Jewish Culture

Riv-Ellen Prell

Desire is central to the relationship between men and women in the Bible. The rabbis, in turn, understood it as a motivational force in human life. The biblical text that frames relations of desire results from the primal human disobedience of eating forbidden fruit in the Garden of Eden.

> And to the woman He said
> I will make most severe
> Your pangs in childbearing;
> In pain shall you bear children.
> Yet your urge shall be for your husband,
> and he shall rule over you. (Genesis 3:16)

Desire and power are linked by the biblical and rabbinic traditions. Women are ruled by men because of their desire, and men's desire constantly threatens their religious lives, resulting in a view of women as possessing a power frequently beyond their control (Biale 1984; Adler 1973).

The centrality of desire, power, and sexuality to ancient Jewish life might be seen as an invisible counterpoint to contemporary American depictions of Jewish male and female relationships. As preoccupied as the rabbis were with women's sexuality and male and female desire, innumerable forms of contemporary American Jewish culture—film, literature, and humor—portray women as precisely the opposite—desexualized and nonerotic. The same popular culture and literature often portray Jewish men as powerless, dominated, and uninterested in Jewish women as objects of or for sexual desire.

This contrast represents more than the historical loosening of sexual repression because these constructions of desire describe far more than passion. Each encodes an entire system of attitudes toward the place of male and female in social and sacred space. Rabbinic texts make these attitudes overt and explicit (Eilberg-Schwartz 1990). Females as polluting and less able to control their desire, as well as male obligations for sexual satisfaction of their wives and prohibitions on pleasure, are among only a small number of consequences of these gender encodings in rabbinic law and texts.

When we move beyond the study of these texts, it is considerably harder to understand what becomes of gender in Jewish culture. While we read from texts to the complexities of life at our peril, we can assume that these texts had some normative significance. As we follow Jews into the Diaspora, where many of the social norms described in these crucial works can no longer be enforced, we find ourselves less able to understand the effect of these regulations on the lives of Jewish men and women, or how gender served as a system of classification. Historians of the European Jewish experience, and to a lesser extent American Jewish life, have increasingly paid attention to links between gender and Jewish life. The Jewish family and its relationship to modernization has proven to be particularly fertile ground for these concerns (Cohen and Hyman 1986).

However, this work does not explore what historian Joan Scott described as an entire system of gender (1986). She defines gender as a "constitutive element of social relations" (1986, 1067–1068). Gender is constitutive because it is particularly amenable to signifying difference. The normative explanations of these symbolic meanings also limit how gender can signify, and "naturalize" its ability to do so (1986, 1067–1068). Gender, then, is tied to relations of power and control where such symbolic representations are used to make claims and counter claims about authority and standing in a polity. In rabbinic conceptions, for example, purity and pollution were associated with both genders under various circumstances, and the regulation of pollution and its dangers gave men regulative power over women. Gender, the body, and a code of behavior, as well as a system of regulation, were all encompassed within a system of differentiation between men and women.

It is with good reason, then, that gender falls away from analyses of Jewish life in the Diaspora. The task is daunting. Jews are and have been embedded within a larger social system in which they participate. At the same time, issues such as the formation of the family, regulation of morals, and attitudes about the body have often been the media through which Jews resisted, or at least held the larger culture at bay. We are aware, of course, that the Enlightenment made these separations problematic and that ultimately no domain was immune from the refiguring of gender, citizenship, world view, and knowledge which it introduced. We will never find a Jewish gender system comparable to the rules laid out in the Bible and rabbinic documents. However, without understanding the ways gender differentiation both reflects and creates the ways Jews live, we must risk simplifying our knowledge of Jewish culture in the Diaspora. Any reading of culture which leaves out gender, and with that ideas about the body, fails to grasp not only central ideas about differentiation of human experience but about one of the most potent symbolic systems of society.

The study, then, of eroticized and deeroticized Jewish women, and authoritative and powerless Jewish men, provides equally appropriate cultural phenomena to explore. When a minority community such as American Jews marks gender and sexuality as overtly "Jewish" in their popular culture and literature, we have an opportunity to explore the wider significance of a partial gender system, embedded within the larger culture's, but uniquely differentiated from it.

Portraits of American Jewish Women

I pursue the study of gendered American Jewish experience through representations of Jewish women that developed shortly after World War II. These portraits are consistent and ubiquitous, and they are created by Jewish comics, novelists, and film makers. They circulate throughout American Jewish life, not only in the media, but in ordinary conversations as well.

The Jewish woman is represented through her body that is at once exceptionally passive and highly adorned. She simultaneously lacks sexual desire and abundantly lavishes attention on her desire to beautify herself. She attends to the needs of no one else, exerting no labor for others, and expending great energy on herself instead. This popularly constructed Jewish woman performs no domestic labor and gives no sexual pleasure. Rather, her body is a surface to decorate, financed by the sweat of others.

This representation of the Jewish woman emerged specifically within the postwar period. She is preceded in time by the "Jewish mother" and the "Jewish wife." Wives were a dominant subject of Jewish humor for both Europeans and immigrant Americans. Mothers appeared later in American-Jewish humor, dominating it until the 1970s (Rothbell 1986, 114). All of these Jewish women "types" can be found in Jewish humor today. However, each representation emerged in different periods and remained dominant until she was replaced by another. Jewish Princesses do not grow into Jewish Mothers necessarily, and Jewish Mothers in no sense began their lives as princesses. The genesis of the representations makes clear the points and absences of overlap between these images. One of the great differences in these representations is the extent of aggression directed at them. If the wives and mothers of Jewish humor were wished dead by their male relatives, the contemporary jokes come perilously close to rendering Jewish women as adorned corpses. This new construction of the Jewish woman's body is crucial to understanding why the image emerged at the beginning of the postwar era.

According to the contemporary humor, the Jewish wife and daughter are infamous for their indifference to domestic caretaking and nurture of their husbands. For example, a recently circulating joke asks, "What is a JAP pornography film? Debbie does dishes." A variant of the joke asks, "Did you hear about the new JAP horror movie? It's called Debbie Does Dishes" (Allen 1990, 21). The joke plays on the title of a pornographic film of the 1980s, *Debbie Does Dallas,* substituting for the male fantasy of a woman's sexual availability to a city of men a Jewish woman's purported disgust at the thought of laboring over dishes.

This, and a host of jokes about a Jewish woman's refusal to clean or cook—"What does a Jewish American Princess make best for dinner? Reservations"—casts her as an unwilling participant in any form of domestic labor. One joke asks, "What does a JAP like most about being married? Having a maid" (Allen 1990, 15). Domesticity in all forms is repulsive. An unusually long joke on the subject underlines her refusal.

> To her family's delight, the JAP landed a prize husband, the son of an English duke. After the honeymoon, the couple came to the United States to live. The JAP began to instruct her husband, who had grown up on a huge country estate, on more informal ways of life in the USA.
>
> On the second day back she took her husband to a supermarket. "Darling," she said, "I'll push this cart. You walk along and put all

your favorites into the cart." He trotted off ahead of her, then returned with an armful of packages.

She inspected them, pointing. "Drop this in the cart. And this. And this." Suddenly, she spied a large steak. Her face formed an expression of deep disgust, and she said "No. You must never buy anything like that."

"But why?" her husband asked.

"It needs to be cooked." (Allen 1990, 13).

The punch line underlines *the* crucial quality of this young Jewish woman; she does not engage in any domestic labor. Groceries are to be bought that require no preparation; these Jewish women do not transform the raw into the cooked, or nature into culture. If the domestic realm belongs to women, then this Jewish woman defies her gender because she cannot be domesticated. Whether the jokes concern food, dishes, or cleaning, the humor rests on the JAP's rejection of any work.

Another related series of jokes represents women refusing another activity parallel to domestic labor. They do not participate actively in sex. Jewish women are portrayed as either indifferent to sex or inactive when they participate.

"How do you get a J.A.P. to stop having sex? Marry her."

"What's the definition of a Jewish nymphomaniac? A woman who makes love once a year."

"What is the difference between a JAP and jello [or spaghetti]? Jello moves when you touch [eat] it."

The Jewish woman does not have an active, sexual body. A number of jokes, in fact, cast her as dead or comatose, so extreme is the construction of her body as nonactive. The point is illustrated by a longer joke.

A prince enters a castle, and finds a beautiful woman lying on a bed. He tiptoes into her room and ravishes her. As he leaves, he is approached by the lord of the castle.

Lord of the Castle: "Have you seen my poor daughter? She's been in a coma since her horse threw her last week."

Prince: "In a *coma!* I thought she was *Jewish*" (Schneider 1979, 5).

Less elaborate versions of the story also play on the woman as a corpse and the man as the corpse's partner. A popular story attributed to Woody Allen includes the following dialogue:

> A many sees his ex-wife and asks if they can't make love again. She responds, "Over my dead body." He rejoins, "Isn't that how we always used to do it?"

Another joke recently found its way into the tape of a rap group called Two Live Jews, a sendup of the rappers Two Live Crew, who were accused of obscenity. One song on the album is called "Jokes." A rapper tells the following joke,

> Mildred and I had doggie sex last night. I sat up and begged and she rolled over and played dead.[1]

The alternative to the Jewish woman's deathlike passivity is her active refusal to participate in sexual relations. Another joke portrays this rejection in the following way.

> "What is Jewish foreplay? Twenty minutes of begging."[2]

The Jewish woman's profound reluctance to participate in sex, or to be an animated partner who experiences or gives pleasure is central to her cultural representation. She is inactive in the domestic realm—both the kitchen and the bedroom.

Domestic and sexual "labor" are parallel because each ties women to reciprocal relationships with men. If men support women, then women provide for men through a range of domestic services. Women withhold their part in the contract generated by postwar American middle-class life. Their morbid bodies allows them the power to refuse to participate. Men are reduced to necrophilia or humiliation in the humor in order to experience pleasure.

The Jewish woman's refusal of the relationship is made even clearer in her lack of activity in another form of labor—active participation in childbirth. Joan Rivers, an American Jewish comedienne, describes a Jewish labor as follows:

> "I had a Jewish delivery. They knock you out with the first pain and wake you up when the hairdresser shows" (Rivers, n.d.).

The Jewish woman is so inactive that she will not even participate in the one form of labor unique to her sex. She avoids the labor required for the production of life itself. According to these caricatures and stereotypes, the Jewish woman neither labors to produce nor reproduce. As a result, all of the characterizations rest on an inactive body, fundamentally defined as nonproductive or nonreproductive.

Jewish women, then, do not sweat. Their cultural representation as inactive results in this central transformation of their bodies. *Mad Magazine*'s description of campus "types," lists the princess (discretely dropping the Jewish descripter) "wish(ing) scientists would hurry up to find a cure for perspiration (*Mad Magazine* 1987, 22–23). The sweatless Jewish woman possesses a body that is less than human, incapable of exertion, and withholds pleasure.

These representations are not peculiar to jokes alone. A similar portrait of a Jewish woman appeared in the 1974 film *The Heartbreak Kid,* based on the Bruce Jay Friedman short story, "A Change of Plans" (1966, originally 1962). In this film, although not in the original short story, it is the classically passive Jewish woman's body that brings her disaster. The film concerns the brief marriage of Lila Kolodny and Lenny Cantrow, and his subsequent pursuit of another woman, whom he meets on his honeymoon. Neither Lenny nor Lila is affluent, nor is their Judaism portrayed through elaborate Jewish rituals or symbols. They are physically typed as Jews (dark hair); they live in New York; their wedding includes the words "Mazel Tov" as a glass is broken at its conclusion. These minimal clues seem sufficient to alert the viewer to the film's backdrop of middle class Jewish life.

The new groom grows increasingly unhappy and even repulsed by his wife during their first few days together. She talks during sex. She eats sloppily and disgusts him. But it is her inactivity that allows his distaste to blossom into passionate pursuit of another woman. Lila cannot swim, and she is so badly burned by her first day in the sun that she must spend her subsequent honeymoon days lying immobile in their hotel room. It is on the very beach where Lila's pale and inactive body was burned that Lenny, now free of ailing Lila, meets Kelly Corchran, the embodiment of a beautiful WASP woman. Kelly swims, runs, and moves gracefully. Her class and culture in every way oppose Lila's. Kelly's athletic body is especially desirable in contrast to Lila's inactive body and its other associated unattractive qualities.[3] By the third day of the honeymoon, Lenny has abandoned Lila to begin his pursuit of Kelly, which will take him to the WASP heartland of Minnesota, leaving behind his ethnicity, religion, and class in pursuit of the embodiment of its opposite. The Jewish woman's passive body is inadequate and leaves her cut off from relationships with men.

The inactive, deathlike body of Jewish women is only one side of her representation, however. Her passive and sweatless body exists to be adorned. The Jewish woman's body is less a vessel to contain energy or passion than a surface for self-display of wealth and style. Her lack of reciprocation with males who she will not serve or please is most apparent in her self-adornment. She depends upon men in order to adorn herself. Her lack of productivity requires the sweat of others who labor for her. Her excessive adornment is not portrayed as reflecting male success but only the Jewish woman's self-directed pleasure. She does not desire men in the caricature, rather she decorates and indulges herself. Desire is not only embodied in adornment, it is essential to the Jewish woman's sexuality.

The connection between the Jewish woman's passive body and adorned body is complex. The Jewish woman's body can be constructed as the site of adornment only if it is passive. Her sexual feelings are both created and canceled by adornment. In neither case, however, is mutuality part of the Jewish woman's representation. Paradoxically, the Jewish woman is entirely dependent upon and indifferent to her male partner.

The Jewish woman is represented more frequently through her adorned body than through her passive one. Stereotypes multiply upon the foundational image of the adorned body. Wealth, bargains, self-indulgence, designer clothes, and many forms of consumer excess are all associated with the Jewish woman.

A series of jokes emphasize that the Jewish woman is capable of erotic feelings but they are inseparable from shopping and consumption. A widely circulated joke asks, "How do you give a J.A.P. an orgasm? Scream 'Charge it to Daddy'." Or from Joan River's album (n.d.), a related joke, "Jews get orgasmic in department stores. They scream 'Charge it, charge it,' and they start to shake." An interesting variant places the source of the orgasm on adornment itself. "How do you know when a JAP is having an orgasm? She drops her nail file." In this joke adornment is simultaneous with sexuality. Sexuality, however, is also opposed to adornment. A common joke of the genre presents the following dialogue,

> The scene is in bed: He: "Can I do anything?" She: "Sure, as long as you don't touch my hair" (1976, 226)[4]

A sexualized image of consumption in the person of a Jewish young woman was also offered in the early days of the Saturday Night Live television program in the 1970s. Gilda Radner, one of the original members of the company, frequently portrayed a newly married, suburban Jewish woman. She also performed a mock commercial for a product called "Jewess Jeans," a sendup of French designer jeans. She is dressed for the commercial in tight jeans with the star of David embroidered on the rear pocket. She is covered with many gold chains, a gold star of David, chews gum, and wears dark glasses. She sings, backed up by a multiracial chorus of women wearing identical tight jeans, through glossy red lips that appear on the screen before her entire body is revealed.

> Jewess jeans.
> They're skin tight, they're out of sight.
> Jewess jeans.
> She's got a life style uniquely hers,
> Europe, Nassau, wholesale furs . . .
> She shops the sales for designer clothes
> She's got designer nails and a designer nose.
> She's an American princess and a disco queen
> She's the Jewess in Jewish jeans.

If the viewer has any doubts about the meaning of the commercial the narrator's voice announces, "You don't have to be Jewish to wear Jewess Jeans," and Radner responds, "But it doesn't hurt" (in the archive of the Jewish Video Archives, Jewish Museum, New York).[5] The inseparability of her clothes, nails, and cosmetically produced nose focus our attention quite clearly on the body of the "Jewess," representing both her gender and Jewish affluence.

In humor above all, but also in film and fiction, the Jewish woman is portrayed as self-adorning through shopping and maintaining an unmovable and impermeable appearance. Whether she fakes an orgasm by pretending she is shopping or achieves it by a similar fantasy, this woman's polysemic body is the site of elaborate adornment. She is not a producer, but a consumer. When the Jewish woman of popular culture might be expected to be productive—in the domestic sphere for example—her body exerts no labor. She passively resists the desires of others. When her body is presented as a site for adornment, her desire is voracious. She must have it all. The passive body is one of consuming desire with no object of desire other than the self.

The humor and representations that I have described are easily placed in an historical context. These are not the jokes of immigrants. Jewish women appeared in literature written by Jewish men and women as greedy, bourgeois, and even uncouth as early as the 1920s. These women were, however, always contrasted to an idealized mother capable not only of perfect love, but inhuman, slavish labor. These Jewish mother representations are predicated upon an exceptionally active woman's body. Her subsequent, no longer idealized role as suffocater/nurturer also depends on her activity and power. For example, in the English version of the song "My Yidishe Momme," introduced by Sophie Tucker in 1925 and an international success, the lyrics describe the *momme* in the following way:

> I see her at her daily task in the morning's early light
> Her willing hands forever toiling far into the night.

Toil is not mentioned in the Yiddish version, but the Yiddish lyrics emphasize sacrifice—"She would have leaped into fire and water for her children" (Slobin 1982, 198, 204). The English language version portrays an extraordinarily physically active person who never rests. Elizabeth Stern's memoir, *My Mother and I,* (1917) reflects a similar portrait. She writes:

> I can never remember my mother in my childhood in any other than one of two positions, standing in the corner; her foot rocking the cradle, and her hands stitching, stitching. Mother eked out the family income by making aprons—by hand. (212)

Her labor and activity are central to her representation in the work of songwriters, film makers, and novelists of the period.

The sentimentalized Yidishe Momme is transformed in the 1940s, and for decades thereafter, into a symbiotic martyr. Her activity is increasingly portrayed in terms of her capacity to induce her children's guilt or repress her husband's activities. Nevertheless, her early cultural portrait of physical exertion is directly inverted in the subsequent representation of the "princess's" passive body.

Women's Bodies

This range of portraits of Jewish women in popular culture asks us to consider why their bodies are a site of symbolic elaboration. What forms of differentiation and what ideas about American-

Jewish experience are constructed upon this body, which is at once passive and elaborately decorated? If, after all, American Jews more frequently encounter themselves in film, jokes, and family gatherings than in synagogues or sacred study, these representations are ubiquitous and consistent clues to American Jewish life. If cultures provide us with models and mirrors for experience, then we must explore this representation of the body.

Why is the woman's passive body such a powerful feature of American Jewish humor and popular culture? The passive body is a surprising representation of women in Western culture, where portrayals of women's unbridled sexuality and their intimate link to the natural world are far more common. Western culture's deeply Christian roots are evident in the dualist representations of women as virgins and whores. Women are frequently portrayed as either without desire and sexuality, or they are nothing other than their sexuality. A passive body that is still an object of sexual desire is unusual. The passive body may be most closely connected to the idealized Victorian woman who, though married, found activity in general, and sexuality in particular, distasteful. Queen Victoria is rumored to have given her daughter, the evening before her marriage, the same advice she received, "Lie still and think of England." The Victorian woman, no less than its monarch, understood the importance of duty and virtue, even in the service of sexuality. The Jewish woman appears to have no sense of duty, but is nevertheless still and passive. The image, then, is unique, but lays claim to middle class respectability embodied in Victorian visions of womanhood and the family. The representation of the Jewish woman both inverts and borrows from Victorian domesticity.

That legacy creates a representation full of contradictions, not within womanhood itself, but within a single woman. The Jewish woman is passive but voracious, (sometimes) sexual, but unavailable, dependent upon men but inaccessible to them, and capable of great pleasure, but incapable of it in the "natural" world of mutual sexuality.[6] Cultural critic John Fiske argues that "the struggle over the meaning of the body and validation of its pleasure is a power struggle in which class, gender and race form complexly intersected axes" (1989, 50). Any study of the body, then, depends on developing its social contexts. For Jews, gender, race, and class are each symbolized by and experienced through the Jewish woman's body, which specifies a Jewish ethnicity situated in middle class affluence and dependent on the male as a producer. This contradictory body, with its demand for and denial of pleasure, suggests powerful conflicts that circle around Jewish gender relations embedded within the middle class.

Fiske's view of the study of the body is widely supported by a growing literature that recognizes its cultural representation as an important and largely neglected site for understanding how human experience is regulated and represented, as well as how humans resist domination. He suggests that the middle class and the dominant culture have long felt threatened by the exercise of pleasure, by men's and women's refusal to regulate their sexuality along narrow and church-controlled norms. "Unruliness" was characterized by the middle class as "immoral, disorderly and economically improvident," which Fiske argues is also potentially subversive, and a venue for participation in cultural forms outlawed by those in power (1989, 75, 97).

Pleasure, however, in the case of Jewish women, is a complex matter because they are neither portrayed as lusty nor are they dominated by sexual desire. They are portrayed in the more purely aesthetic terms of seeking beauty—the point of their consumption. Beauty, however, is typically associated with subordination and a class-defined and regulated aesthetic. The images of the perfectly coiffed woman wearing very expensive, stylish clothing is both a critique of excess and praise for beauty, success, and aesthetics. Ironically, these representations of Jewish women do not symbolize subordination or control, but precisely their opposite. Their passive bodies cannot be regulated. They resist by their passivity because they lack the capacity for productivity. The representation denies the women represented a sense of embodied power, at the same time that they are cast as passively voracious and capable of inducing others to produce. The link between body and pleasure in particular is what is convoluted and disassociated in this representation.

The sociologist Bryan Turner writes in *The Body and Society* that "every mode of production has a mode of desire" (1984, 249). Every society must reproduce its existence and its members, and these processes are linked to desire, which is socially controlled. These representations of women can be pinpointed to the entry of the American Jews, particularly descendents of Eastern European Jews, into the consumer culture at the very same time that the consumer culture came to dominate the American economy. The representation, as I suggested, took on particular force after World War II. The distorted mode of desire embodied by the Jewish woman's representation is linked, then, to the consumer society that depends on insatiable and unmeetable desires for its future.

The centrality of consumption to the American economy began before 1935, that is, before the time American Jewish humor and literature began portraying wives as voracious leeches. The seeds of such economic relations developed much earlier in the century, and Jews played important entrepreneurial roles in their emergence (May, 1983, originally, 1980; Heinze 1990). Scholars have recently begun to debate precisely how acculturating consumerism was for American ethnics from 1890–1930 (Heinze 1990; Cohen 1989). Some argue that consumerism emphasized ethnic ties until 1930, and others that it hastened acculturation as early as 1890. The consumer economy alone cannot be the foundation for this view of the body. Rather, the distorted pleasures so central to this image are best understood in the social relationships that surround consumption—family, work, and ethnic ties—that developed after World War II.

The representation of the Jewish woman as young, demanding, and withholding appears to be particularly associated with the period of unprecedented affluence for white Americans, including their mass migration to the suburbs. Jews shared in these middle class developments, participating in both the economic opportunities and the move into single-family homes beyond the city and urban ethnic communities. Suburban parents produced children whose life experiences differed dramatically from their own. A psychiatrist writing at the time, Joseph Adelsen, carefully spelled out the causes of and dreams for suburban life.

> We had as a nation emerged from a great war, itself following upon a long and protracted Depression. We thought, all of us, men and women alike, to replenish ourselves in goods and spirit, to undo, by exercise of collective will, the psychic disruptions of the immediate past. We would achieve the serenity that had eluded the lives of our parents. The men would be secure in stable careers, the women in comfortable homes, and together they would raise perfect children. It was the zeitgeist, the spirit of the times. (cited in May 1988, 58).

The vast majority of Jews realized this very dream. What they probably did not anticipate was how dramatically their own children's lives would differ from theirs. Both the experience of this suburban dream and the way its children differentiated themselves from their parents created the social relationships which generated the popular culture that depended on the Jewish woman's body.

Through the 1950s, for example, Jewish males were far more likely to be in business than professions. A Jewish federation study of Boston Jews reported in 1965 that nearly 75 percent of the heads of households (overwhelmingly men) were in business and 23 percent were in the professions. About a third of those queried owned their own businesses (S. Cohen 1983, 87). Sociologist Marshall Sklare learned from his study of a Chicago suburb that 61 percent of the Jewish household heads (again overwhelmingly males) were self-employed in business (1979, 25–27). The Boston and Chicago studies examined men of about the same age. The greater percentage of self-employed in Chicago is obviously related to the smaller number of people in the survey, all of whom are situated in a more economically homogeneous and affluent town than the greater Boston area.

The children of the suburbs differ markedly from their parents. The Boston survey was repeated in 1975. Household heads between the ages of 25 and 54 at that point were more likely to be in a profession than in business, especially for the 25 to 34-year-old baby boom cohort who were born between 1941 and 1950. Fifty-four percent of its members were employed in a profession, and of the 38 percent who were in business, 11 percent were self-employed. Even the 45 to 54 age group (born 1921 to 1932) were more likely to be in professions than in 1965. Thirty-seven percent of this cohort was professional as against 62 percent in business and 40 percent self-employed as either professionals or in business. Similarly, in 1975, 91 percent of both the 25 to 34 and the 35 to 44 age cohort attended college and graduate school. In 1965, 79 percent of the 25 to 34 age group attended college and graduate school, and 57 percent of the 35 to 44 age group did the same.

Those whose young lives were shaped in the immediate postwar period were more educated and more often directed toward professions than business. Like the mainstream society, they had a vast array of consumer items available to them as well and experienced neither the Depression years nor the Second World War. This younger group continued to have a small number of occupations, as Jews have since their arrival in the United States. However, its members held different occupations, had more education, and were less likely to be self-employed or in business than the older cohort. The daughters of these families also came of age during the second wave of feminism in the United States and anticipated staying in the work force even when they had children, a pattern that differed dramatically from their mothers.

This demographic information, drawn from a major northeastern city but typical of American Jewish experience, suggests that the uniqueness of the humor and other forms of popular culture of the 1970s arises from the experiences of the generation that first expressed it. Men and women are both more likely to be employed. Wage earners probably have less autonomy than did their fathers or parents, and they are more firmly entrenched as white collar professionals whose success depends on education and formal training. At the same time these American Jewish children were the products of unprecedented suburban affluence. Their childhoods must have been somewhat paradoxical, as they were simultaneously expected to enjoy life and their parents' indulgences, and to be self-disciplined, hard working, and capable of the deferred gratification that produces middle class success.

In short, these children fell prey to a common problem in the life of the American middle class, only exacerbated by an economy that began to weaken in the 1970s. Barbara Ehrenreich argues in *Fear of Falling* (1989) that the middle class keeps its children in the same class position not by passing on land and capital, but primarily by instilling self-denial and self-discipline in them. It's capital, in contrast to the upper class's real capital, is skill and knowledge earned at a high price that demands quite systematically foreswearing the rewards of a consumer society (1989, 15, 84). The American Jewish middle class, then, entered the affluent society with a vengeance, enjoying the fruits of postwar affluence and working to keep their children firmly entrenched in it by investing in their education and encouraging success and consumption. These children were provided a narrow path to travel. Their achievements were predicated on denial, but their indulgence was proof of their mothers' and fathers' success. They were urged to have both and to reward their parents by creating a duplicate middle-class life predicated on endogamous Jewish marriage, affluence, and children to be further indulged by grandparents.

There is no question that these children followed suit, but not as clones of their parents. With the hindsight of the 1990s we now know that the economic success that awaited them required two incomes to their parents' one and a diminished sense of independence and autonomy that came from entering the corporate world and corporate models of medicine, law, and accounting, rather than self-employment. Even consumption items became impossible to control, and the clear sense of what was appropriate to own in the 1950s and 1960s was supplanted by an infinite variety of possibilities. By the

1980s, for example, both men and women began new consumer roles; for example, women buying cars and men buying clothes. After 1960 Jews began to intermarry until, by the late 1980s, the percentage of intermarriage has been placed at about 30 percent of all Jews. The suburban family hardly exists any longer given the widespread employment of women and the advent of not only American feminism, but a specific Jewish feminism that began in the 1970s. The "ideal" family and "normal" sex roles have been criticized by Jewish women for their oppression of them (Schneider 1984; Baum et al., 1975). From the 1970s on, this young adult generation began to enter different professions, different marriages, and different forms of consumption than their parents. With these differences came the new, very antagonistic, and deadly representations of Jewish women's bodies, and the somewhat more persistent Jewish men's self-portraits as weak and dominated.

The period's representation of the Jewish woman as inactive and unproductive, as an impermeable consumer, bears an uncanny alikeness to the role of the entire middle class in the consumer economy. Jew's close association with the middle class, not surprisingly, is central to this representation. The middle class increasingly found itself anxious, passive, and preyed upon as postwar affluence began to decline in the 1970s. Unlike the producers or "self-made men" of earlier days, the middle class is now professional and technocratic. Its members must work to produce affluence, but the nature of the work, dependent on denial and abstraction, is difficult to measure other than by what can be bought by the income it produces. Encoded in the Jewish woman's passive and adorned body is the very paradox of middle class work. The highly decorated surface rests upon an unproductive foundation. Indeed, the woman's body absorbs labor and investment without, in the parodied image, production or reproduction.[7]

The suburbs promised happiness, ease, companionate marriage, and loving families (May 1988). According to Ehrenreich, it produced men so burdened by supporting their families that multiple subversions developed—the Playboy philosophy, the Beat generation, and humanistic psychology—all dedicated to rationalize men's lack of responsibilities to women and children (1983). The children of that era, the male ones in particular, assumed a nurturing environment that placed their needs first, as males and children. Not only did the nature of middle class life change by the 1970s, but its promises of pleasure did not include women single-mindedly devoted to the needs of husbands who provided them support.

If, as Turner suggests, modes of production and desire/sexuality are linked, then Jews' active participation in *both* the consumer culture and its professional/managerial class is reflected in this representation of the woman's body that does not sweat. Jews have negotiated their passage into the mainstream of American culture through the middle class. Gender, embodied by the woman, symbolizes Jewish American experience. The woman's body, freed from labor, but depicted as requiring others to work, certainly reveals the anxiety that is the patrimony of the middle class. The passive body, and the bitterness that creates the representation, incorporate this anxiety. Driving its "keepers" to continue to work, the "bodies" cannot, however, be controlled. The humor casts men as victimized by women and their insatiable wants. But what drives men is only symbolized by Jewish women. "Embodied" in that passive female body is a consumption-driven economic system in which men are rendered unproductive as surely as women are. Work is abstract, its products difficult to identify. Consumption is almost infinitely variegated and as such, inevitably disappointing. Sweat evaporates. Women's sexuality is, in the humor, subsumed by her consumerism because she embodies the economic system that depends on manipulation rather than manufacture, consumption rather than production. In the popular culture the Jewish male is portrayed as shackled to a ferocious taskmaster who drives him toward financing what he cannot enjoy as he continually works to satisfy her. Work cannot seem to satisfy or succeed as it once did, and it results in a sense of loss.

The close tie between American Jewish life and culture and membership in the middle class is embodied in the Jewish woman who does not sweat. Her father's daughter and her husband's wife, she is the consumer in the family economic unit. Like hunters and gatherers whose ideal woman is the young wife rather than the mother, the withholding young Jewish woman, rather than the yielding mother, "energizes" the entire "social-economy" of the consumer society for Jewish men (Collier and Rosaldo 1981). In hunting and gathering societies, the young woman is the prize for successful productivity. To marry her, rather than to have children with her, establishes adulthood and relations with men throughout the camp. The Jewish American Princess appears to be a "prize." She is beautifully adorned and the realization of all aspirations for success. But unlike hunters and gatherers, Jewish men, like so many men of the middle class, not only resent and reject their place in the economy but portray themselves as failing to reap the rewards of sexual satisfaction. They construct marriage and marriage partners as the dark side of the social world. Jewish women "energize" nothing. Instead, they absorb energy, leading men to experience their disappointment and their success as the same thing. Marriage and work cannot establish manhood and yet manhood is impossible without them.

Therefore, it is their relationship to women and within the family that best came to symbolize for fathers, and particularly sons, the disappointment with middle class suburban life. The life that promised pleasure, leisure, security, and satisfaction is inverted in a popular culture of withholding women. Elisa New, reviewing a recent book about the murder of a suburban Arizona Jewish woman by her husband whose successful defense was that his wife behaved like a Jewish Princess, writes,

> Indeed, what Veblen did not anticipate—though Henry James did when he noted the "growing divorce between the American women (with her comparative leisure, culture, grace) and the male American immersed in the ferocity of business"—was that, in a country without a landed class, it would fall to women to exercise the tastes their husbands labored to support; that the leisure class in America could only be a female class whose lifestyle was preserved through intrafamilial class warfare. It is this warfare that we see explode in the comedy of the fifties, where the American man as Provider is a disgruntled or bemused prole, shackled to supporting his wife's conspicuous spending. And it is this warfare that is, not incidentally, so standard in the repertoire of those Borscht Belt comics who are our mainstream American comics. When Rodney Dangerfield, Shecky Green, and Alan King pillory their wives, it is not to reveal that the wrangling over the Visa card is unique to the Jewish marriage. It is rather to point with rueful humor, to the Americanization of that marriage. (1989, 114).

Americanization was virtually indistinguishable from suburban affluence. As Jews successfully entered the mainstream, abandoning much of their unique ethnic culture by the 1930s, their spending habits and consumption patterns as well as their types of employment all hastened their Americanization. The tension between men and women symbolized through their family division of labor is further proof, as New contends, of this complete Americanization and, with it, the benefits and disappointments of middle class life embodied in affluent women, a sign of poisoned success. Work, family relations, and rampant Americanization are each expressed in the Jewish woman's passive and adorned body. The humor of the 1950s comics was to escalate, with American Jewish affluence, into the 1970s humor of the Jewish American Princess.

I have described a popular culture that envisions women as symbols of men's economic and cultural experiences. As such, women appear largely as a representation of male experience. Women are, nevertheless, actors in this drama of middle class life. I described as a central part of the transformation of suburban life both women's employment and their dissatisfaction with the suburban family. In particular, Jewish women created a Jewish feminism that addressed quite specifically their rejection of the narrow range of roles idealized by their community. Jewish mothers came in for considerable discussion in the 1970s.[8] The Jewish American Princess humor developed in precisely this period. Many Jewish women rejected male dominance of every aspect of Jewish life—prayer, ritual, higher Jewish education, secular boards, the rabbinate, and cantorate—and an unabashed cultural preference for male children. As Jewish women, supported by the larger feminist movement, abandoned their role as "Jewish mothers," fundamentally defined as self-sacrificing, they were portrayed more frequently as "princesses." Jewish women's widespread entry into the paid labor force, at a much younger age than their mothers, was translated as continuing symbiosis and the denial of men's desires.

What form a Jewish American popular culture of young Jewish comediennes, film makers, novelists, and writers will take remains to be seen because this work is only now being produced. Film maker and humorist Elaine May and comedienne Joan Rivers, who gained attention and popularity in the 1960s and 1970s, have echoed many of the views of Jewish women and consumption of their male age-mates. There is little question that different voices and images will soon emerge that will address the issues which remain central to middle class American Jewish life.

The consumer culture, the middle class path to Americanization, the economic and cultural upheavals that developed in the 1970s, and second wave American feminism, can all be traced to the sweatless body of the Jewish woman. The convoluted desire that locates pleasure in consumption but not mutual sexuality is the product of postwar America's pains and disappointments anesthetized by the devouring pleasures of the consumer society.

Sweating Princesses

I have suggested that the passive body cannot sweat for lack of exertion and that passivity is tied to a new form of labor and economy in which Jewish males found themselves at the onset, and then more fully, at the end of World War II. Ironically, these women, in the eyes of men, are both passive and powerful because they consume without either producing or reproducing. I would, however, be misleading if I did not acknowledge the existence of a prominent Jewish princess who did sweat, one who may have defined the very contours of the representation itself. It is the very nature of her sweat that may best demonstrate my point because her sweat is a metaphor for leisure and consumption.

Brenda Patimkin is the central character of Philip Roth's novella *Goodbye Columbus*. First published in 1959, this story, and Herman Wouk's *Marjorie Morningstar* (1955), are the source of the two first postwar Jewish princesses. *Goodbye Columbus* is a far richer text for analysis with more complex emotions than one finds in jokes and much of the popular culture I have described here, and yet, there are uncanny similarities between them. Roth's novella—it appears in retrospect—symbolized the Jewish woman's body in a way that anticipated its power to represent economic, social, and cultural transformation.

When Neil Klugman, son of the lower middle class in Newark, New Jersey, first sees Brenda it is at an upper class suburban country club where his cousins are members. Drawn to Brenda's beauty, he calls her for a date. She is at the country club exerting herself at tennis and golf. When he inquires if he can meet her after tennis, Roth writes,

> "I'll be sweaty after," Brenda said.
> It was not to warn me to clothespin my nose and run in the opposite direction; it was a fact, it apparently didn't bother Brenda, but she wanted it recorded. (1989, 8)

And when Neil slyly inquires "how will I know you," as they make their first date, Brenda responds, "I'll be sweating" (1989, 18).

Thus begins a passionate romance between a Jewish lower-middle class male, out of college, working in a library, and "not a planner," with the daughter of a family that epitomizes American Jewish success. Brenda's father is a transitional figure between prewar and postwar American Jewish life. His manufacturing business, Patimkin Kitchen and Bathroom Sinks, transformed the Patimkins into the nouveau riche when the War Department installed his sinks in all American barracks. They can "live on stocks alone," Brenda tells her mother. And to Neil she says, "Money! My father's up to here with it" (1989, 26).

In this suburban world of the 1950s, upperclass success is associated with all sorts of physical exertion. Brenda's brother is a large, successful athlete, a "crewcut proteus" who appears to Neil to be a giant as capable of drinking the country club pool water as of swimming in it. Brenda is good at every sport. Even her mother was a New Jersey tennis champion as a girl. However, none of this sweat is productive. The only producer, Brenda's father, is portrayed as "sweet," "not too smart," and crude. His business is located in the "Negro section" of Newark, once home of Jewish immigrants, including Neil's grandparents. His work and its location attach Ben Patimkin to an older order. The Patimkin children and wife sweat the sweat of leisure, locating them in the suburban world of postwar affluence.

Neil, always the outsider to this Short Hills suburban rambler, notes the artificiality of their environment. The air, he says, is "by Westinghouse," (1989, 22) in contrast to his aunt and uncle's apartment in Newark where they escape the heat by sitting in the alley. Looking out the Patimkin's picture window, he describes their oaks:

> I saw oaks, though fancifully, one might call them sporting-goods trees. Beneath their branches, like fruit, dropped from their limbs, were two irons, a golf ball, a tennis can, a baseball bat, basketball, a first baseman's glove, and what was apparently a riding crop. (1989, 21–22)

When Neil discovers their basement refrigerator—brought from Newark—completely full of fruit, he wonders that the trees produce sporting equipment and the machines yield fruit. Through the eyes of a Jewish man who remains exceptionally ambivalent about the climb up the social class ladder, everything in the Patimkin's world is artificial. The sweat, the fruit, and the sporting equipment are all produced through leisure and artificiality. Even Brenda's nose, a topic of discussion at their first meeting, was artificially created by plastic surgery.

Unlike latter-day Jewish princesses, Brenda *is* erotic and physically and sexually active. But in the end, she fails Neil by her loyalty to her parents, and one must assume, to her social class. In their final fight, precipitated by her mother's discovery of the diaphragm Neil insisted Brenda buy, she says,

> Neil, you don't understand. They're still my parents. They did send me to the best schools, didn't they? They have given me everything I've wanted, haven't they? (1989, 134)

This love story is sundered by social class. In the mid-1950s these are not lovers separated by religion or culture but instead Jews differentiated by upward mobility. Each time Brenda evokes Newark as the place her family left behind, Neil, whose life is still rooted there, is stung. As he learns of the conflicted, angry relationship between Brenda and her mother, Neil feels an "unfaithful" identification with Mrs. Patimkin. Brenda believes that "money is a waste" for her mother who "still thinks we live in Newark" (1989, 26). Brenda's struggle for cashmere sweaters and Bonwit Teller coats against her mother's anxiety about money draws her closer to her father and his generosity. Neil finds Brenda's desire for "fabrics that felt soft to the skin" (1980, 26) distasteful and wonders at the fact that she understands her fights about them with her mother to be of "cosmic" significance.

Mrs. Patimkin, surrounded by affluence and housekeepers, irrationally accuses Brenda of "laziness," condemning her for not working, not doing dishes, and above all for believing that "the world owes you a living" (1989, 65). Mrs. Patimkin's harsh accusations evoke a work ethic that no longer makes sense. Mr. Patimkin, without condemnation, also calls on that ethic in a conversation with Neil when he begins to appear to be a marriage prospect for Brenda.

> 'A man works hard he's got something. You don't get anywhere sitting on your behind, you know . . . The biggest men in the country worked hard, believe me. Even Rockefeller. Success don't come easy.' He was not a man enamored of words. I only knew that these few words he did speak could hardly transmit all the satisfaction and surprise he felt about the life he had managed to build for himself and his family. (1989, 93–93)

Their conversation concludes as Mr. Patimkin hands Neil the silver patterns his wife will peruse for their son, who is soon to wed.

> 'When I got married we had forks and knives from the Five and Ten,' Mr. Patimkin muses. 'This kid needs gold to eat off,' but there was no anger; far from it. (1989, 95)

Through the novelist's eye we see the contours of both the "mode of production" and the "mode of desire" that will come to dominate postwar America, and American Jews in particular. The producer's work ethic rings hollow in this world of consumption and leisure. And what lies beneath the sweet passions of Neil and Brenda's affair is a fundamental differentiation by social class in their attitude toward how firmly love is embedded in consumerism, adornment, and the decorated body. Their passion is an illusion, incapable of cementing real ties. As it wanes, so sexuality will soon disappear from representations of Jewish women, and all that will remain will communicate the world of leisure and consumption. People who produced without words will be replaced by those whose living depend on words and abstractions directed toward purchasing finer and finer discriminations of consumer items to mark their success.

Neil is consistently drawn and repulsed by the affluent world of Short Hills, New Jersey. He imagines joining "the business." He contrasts the Newark of his family—its craziness, incivility, and discomfort—with the leisure of the suburbs. He calls his aunt's life, and by extension, his childhood a "throwing off," a maniacal desire to feed, to empty the shelves and refrigerators, and to fill others, but to take nothing. Brenda, by contrast, along with the other two Patimkin children, are "gathered in." They are given and served, and they counted on having everything. Brenda's younger sister is always allowed to win at every game because she constantly is given second chances. Neil observes, "Over the years Mr. Patimkin had taught his daughters that free throws were theirs for the asking; he could afford to" (1989, 29).

Neil cannot locate himself in either world and is pursued by fear of "numbness" in his work and his life. The sweat of leisure and sexuality are inviting, but he is uncertain of where it will lead him. He is drawn by security and protection embodied in Brenda's beauty, sexuality, and affluence, and repulsed by a world rendered unappealing by Roth. Its sterility, sociability, denominational Judaism, and entitled children, all associated with one another, put him off.[9]

Initially, he believes that Brenda is singular and different from the young matrons, his former classmates in high school, he observes one summer afternoon.

> They looked immortal sitting there. There hair would always stay the color they desired, their clothes the right texture and shade; in

> their homes they would have simple Swedish modern when that was fashionable, and if huge ugly baroque ever came back, out would go the long midget-legged marble coffee table and in would come Louis Quatorze. These were the goddesses, and if I were Paris I could not have been able to choose among them, so microscopic were the differences. Their fates had collapsed them into one. Only Brenda had shone. Money and comfort would not erase her singleness—they hadn't yet, or had they? (1989, 96)

What ultimately perplexes Neil is what is the source of his attraction to Brenda. He finds in her affluent suburban world two types of pleasure and desire—sex and affluence. Brenda is only one of many to tell Neil that when he loves her he will never have to worry again. As he waits to meet Brenda after her appointment to be fitted for a diaphragm, he contemplates this relationship. He is sitting in St. Patrick's Cathedral to escape the heat. He finds himself making a silent speech that might pass for a prayer directed to an audience he calls God. He asks:

> 'What is it I love, Lord? Why have I chosen?' 'If we meet You at all, God, it's that we're carnal and acquisitive, and thereby partake of You. I am carnal and I know You approve, I just know it. But how carnal can I get? I am acquisitive. Where do I turn now in my acquisitiveness? Which prize is You?' (1989, 100)

Neil Klugman continues:

> 'Which prizes do you think, schmuck? Gold dinnerware, sporting-goods trees, nectarines, garbage disposals, bumpless noses, Patimkin sinks, Bonwit Teller. . . .' (1989, 100).

Neil finds it difficult to separate his various desires and does not know which to trust. His desire for Brenda depends on her uniqueness, but he finds it difficult to assure himself that she is different from the women and world he believes are created by new Jewish affluence.

Matters are resolved when Brenda finally cannot join her sexual relationship with Neil and her loyalty to her family and its affluence. Neil is about to propose marriage just as he learns that Brenda's parents have discovered their sexual liaison. She remains loyal to her parents and all that they have given her. Her mother's final words to Brenda in the letter revealing her discovery of Brenda's sexual relationship, "this is some thank you for all we gave you," (1989, 129) seem definitive. Brenda will reject Neil, her right to sexuality, and her independence in order to stay in the orbit of affluence and leisure. Roth has constructed a Jewish princess against whom Neil can rebel, rejecting his rightful inheritance as the next male generation. Neil asserts his independence and perhaps "manhood" against the Jewish woman, who is made to embody the modes of production and desire.

Neil identifies at the margin of social life throughout the book.[10] He sometimes identifies with Mr. or Mrs. Patimkin's Newark roots against Brenda's easy affluence. He identifies with the family housekeeper Carlotta against the Patimkins, and with impoverished and desolate Leo Patimkin, against Brenda's successful and affluent father, Leo's half brother. Above all, Neil identifies with the "colored kid" who comes to the library each day to look at Gaugin prints in an expensive art book. Neil alone appears to understand the search for beauty that compels the boy to look at a book he will not take to a home Roth represents as noisy and unsafe. Neil dreams, one night of his summer vacation at the Patimkins, that he and the boy are on a pirate ship moored to a Tahitian island where they are enjoying the beauty of naked native women. Suddenly, they are cut loose and sail away, slipping farther and farther from the beauty of the island women. Neil is unmoored throughout the story, unable to find himself in anything other than his opposition to the suburbs and his passions for Brenda. The outsider to Brenda's insider, Neil knows who he is by opposing himself to Short Hills, New Jersey, to the banalities of suburban Judaism, and to desire for affluence. Neil wonders at the novella's conclusion, "If she had only been slightly not Brenda . . . but then would I have loved her" (1989, 136)? It is as if he asked whether he could have experienced "carnal" love without "acquisitiveness?" His freedom from want allowed him to equate Brenda's family and Jewish culture with mobility and directed him on a path where passion and lust would never be linked to affluence.[11]

Goodbye Columbus provided the outline of a set of relations that would generate the American Jewish humor of the 1970s. The manufacturers' wealth of the war years created the children whose enlarged vistas promised affluence and professionalization. Their (almost always male) success was marked by their ability to maintain the affluence of their fathers and fathers-in-law. The consumer culture generated an unceasing and insatiable set of demands. American Jewish men, inheritors of a long tradition of "overdemanding wife" jokes, translated the frustrations of their class and epoch into the Jewish woman, whose body became a surface reflecting affluence, purchased at a high price. Even Brenda's sexual and physical exertions cannot allow her to transcend her overdetermined role as the "glittering prize" of male success. Her sweat of leisure will soon evaporate, leaving Jewish women with passive bodies. Neil, who rejected this world, foreswears not just a social class but an American Judaism that he inseparably linked to the synagogue, organizations, and empty ritual observances of the Patimkins' suburban life. Neither Neil, nor Philip Roth for that matter, cease to be Jews. But their sense of American Jewish life as inseparable from middle class consumerism defines their rite of passage to adulthood and with it the rejection of American Jewish women who will rarely again appear as a source of erotic desire in Roth's work.[12]

American Jewish Gender Systems

I have argued that gender systems persist in American Jewish culture, particularly as we recognize that American Jewish life is fully embedded in the economy and culture of middle class American life. And yet Jewish ethnicity persists, and one of its most potent forms is the popular culture and literature that American Jews produce through characterizations of American Jewish men and women and their lives. Jewish women are represented in these media in terms of a passive and repressed body, but one often beyond the control of men. This representation focuses very powerfully on the body because the woman's body is made to symbolize forces of both production and reproduction, consumption and deferred gratification, repression and the fulfillment of desire. In short, whether the Jewish woman is portrayed as sweating in sports, or not sweating at all, playing sports, or refusing to move, desire for her and her desire are always frustrated by the lack of the active body or physical productivity. Understanding these images and how desire is linked to economy stand to tell us a great deal about the elusive American Jewish culture.

Notes

Versions of this chapter were presented in 1989 at the Conference on Social Scientific Approaches to Judaism, Toronto, and The American Studies Association meeting, New Orleans. I benefited from discussions of the chapter at these conferences. I would like to acknowledge the very thoughtful comments of the following colleagues on an earlier draft of this article: Harry Boyte, Howard Eilberg-Schwartz, Sara Evans, Steven Foldes, Amy Kaminsky, Rebecca Mark, Elaine May, Lary May, Cheri Register, and Naomi Scheman. I was assisted by Nicole Pineda's thorough library research and wish to acknowledge her help. This chapter was written in the months of mourning immediately after the death of my mother, Mary Prell. Though it would cause her chagrin, with the deepest love I dedicate this chapter to her memory for reasons so numerous that they are impossible to detail.

Notes

1. This rap, a song string of Jewish jokes, is framed by responses between the two rappers. On some occasions one laughs and on others there are attempts to silence the jokes. As Irving tells this joke, Moishe continues to say, "don't say it; it's not funny." The rap also ends with a string of obscene words in Yiddish, with parenthetical comments about "talking dirty" and "getting arrested," references to the fate of Two Live Crew's music being censored. Two Live Jews both represent Jewish women in stereotyped fashion and resist the interpretation throughout the album.

2. Folklorist Alan Dundes suggests that such jokes are part of a larger ethnic slur tradition that criticizes insensitive males who are oblivious to female sexual needs. He includes in the genre, jokes such as "What is Irish foreplay? Brace yourself Bridget." "What is Italian foreplay? Hey you awake?" or "Slamming the front door and announcing, "Hey Honey, I'm home" " (1987).

3. The "shikse" is a representation of the non-Jewish woman closely linked to the Jewish woman. They reflect one another through contrasts and depend upon one another to create either stereotype. See Prell 1990. On the shikse in literature, see Jaher 1983.

4. This joke was printed in Leslie Tonner's book, *Nothing But The Best: The Luck of the Jewish Princess* (1975), and reprinted in her article for *Cosmopolitan Magazine* (1976). The joke is described as a warning to Jewish princesses who want to marry and may be overly interested in their appearance to the detriment of their ability to "catch" a husband by being sexually available.

5. Levi rye bread produced a popular advertisement in the 1970s that showed a variety of ethnic groups eating rye bread sandwiches. The caption announced, "You don't have to be Jewish to eat Levi's rye bread." Radner's line punctures the artificial pluralism of the Levi's commercial.

6. Bartky argues that women's pleasure and agency are part of her embodiment. Women also play a role in the styles they wear. They are not simply victims of patriarchal culture. Nevertheless, she argues that though women tend to respond to men's desire, style may allow for certain forms of resistance against patriarchy. She wants to explore the "dialectic of the image" at work in women's pleasure in self-display (1989, 79–80).

7. George Lipsitz (1990) links early television to the transformation to a consumption economy. "The Goldbergs," the popular program that made the switch from radio to television, abounds with examples of growing affluence directed toward transforming these immigrant Jews into people of civility and self-conscious consumers.

8. See Prell 1990 for a discussion of this stereotype.

9. In Roth's preface to the thirtieth anniversary edition of *Goodbye Columbus,* he singles out *Commentary Magazine* for providing models and inspirations for critiques of American Jewish life. He found in *Commentary* of the forties and fifties an attitude of "ineluctably Jewish self scrutiny" in fiction that examined everyday lives of Jews—their passions, customs, and family relations. Roth's depiction of Short Hills Jewish life is intended to do more than draw on local color. He clearly understood himself to be offering a critique of American Jewish life that he accomplishes through his depictions of men and women in the Patimkin family (1989, xii).

10. Critical attempts to understand *Goodbye Columbus* in light of American Jewish life may be found in Rockland 1975 and Walden 1978. A feminist critique of Roth may be found in Cohen 1975.

11. L. S. Dembo also underscores the significance of this "prayer" in his study *The Monological Jew.* He takes the prayer by a Jew in a Catholic church to an invented God as an example of the carnivalesque that characterizes American Jewish fiction. Yet, Dembo ignores the content of the "prayer," missing the crucial relationship between the erotic and the social that Roth and Neil Klugman do resolve. Therefore, this is not the fiction of the topsy turvey but a rejection in favor of desire at the expense of Jewish women. Dembo, in addition, in the same chapter, perhaps not surprisingly makes a strange defense of the accuracy of Jewish fiction's depictions of the stereotypical Jewish mother (1988, 68–75).

12. Baum et al. (1975) also consider Roth and Wouk in their study. My interpretation is in basic agreement with theirs, but they use the texts for different purposes.

References

Adler, R. 1973. "The Jew who Wasn't There: Halacha and the Jewish Woman," *Response: A Contemporary Jewish Review* 3 (18) 77–83.

Allen, J. 1990. *500 Great Jewish Jokes.* New York: Signet.

Bartky, Sandra 1989 "Women, Bodies and Power: A Research Agenda for Philosophy." Newsletter on Feminism and Philosophy. American Philosophical Association 89 (1) 78–90.

Baum, C., P. Hyman, S. Michel. 1975. *The Jewish Woman in America.* New York: Dial Press.

Biale, R. 1984. *Jewish Woman and Jewish Law.* New York: Schocken Press.

Cohen, L. 1989. "Encountering Mass Culture at the Grassroots: The Experience of Chicago Workers in the 1920's," *American Quarterly.* Vol. 41 (1) 6–33, March.

Cohen, S. B. 1975. "Philip Roth's Would-be Patriarchs and Their Shikses and Shrews," *Studies in American Jewish literature,* Vol. 1 (1) Spring, 16–29.

Cohen, S. 1983. *America Modernity and Jewish Identity.* New York: Tavistock.

Cohen, S., and P. Hyman eds. 1986. *The Jewish Family: Myths and Realities,* New York and London: Holmes and Meier.

Collier, J. and M. Rosaldo. 1981. "Politics and Gender in Simple Societies." In *Sexual Meanings: The Cultural Construction of Gender and Sexuality.* Ed. S. B. Ortner and H. Whitehead, 275–329. London and New York: Cambridge University Press.

Dembo, L. S. 1988. *The Monological Jew: A Literary Study.* Madison: University of Wisconsin.

Dundes, A. 1985. "The J.A.P. and the J.A.M. in American Jokelore." *Journal of American Folklore.* Vol. 98 (390) 456–475.

Ehrenreich, B. 1989. *Fear of Falling: The Inner Life of The Middle Class.* N.Y.: Pantheon Books 1989.

——— 1983. *The Hearts of Men: American Dreams and The Flight From Commitment.* New York: Anchor Books.

Eilberg-Schwartz, H. 1990 *The Savage In Judaism: An Anthropology of Israelite Religion and Ancient Judaism.* Bloomington: Indiana University Press.

Fiske, J. 1989. *Understanding Popular Culture.* Boston: Unwin Hyman.

Friedman, B. J. 1966. "A Change of Plans." In *Black Angels: Stories By Bruce Jay Friedman.* 80–90. New York: Simon and Schuster.

Heinze, A. 1990. *Adapting To Abundance: Jewish Immigrants, Mass Consumption, and the Search for American Identity.* New York: Columbia University Press.

Jaher, F. C. 1983. "The Quest for the Ultimate Shiksa." *American Quarterly.* Vol. 35, Winter 518–541.

Lipsitz, G. 1990. "The Meaning of Memory: Family, Class, and Ethnicity in Early Television." In *Time Passages: Collective Memory and American Popular Culture,* 39–76. Minneapolis: University of Minnesota Press.

———. 1987. *Mad Magazine,* 268.

May, E. 1988. *Homeward Bound: American Families in the Cold War.* New York: Basic Books.

May, L. 1983. *Screening Out The Past: The Birth of Mass Culture and the Motion Picture Industry.* Chicago: University of Chicago Press.

New, E. 1988. "Killing the Princess: The Offense of a Bad Defense." *Tikkun* Vol. 4, no. 2, pp. 17–18.

Prell, R. 1990. "Rage and Representation: Jewish Gender Stereotypes in America." In *Uncertain Terms: Negotiating Gender in American Culture.* Ed. Faye Ginsburg and Anna Lownhaupt Tsing, 248–268. Boston: Beacon Press.

Rivers, J. n.d. *What Becomes a Semi Legend Most?* Geffen Records.

Rockland, M.A. "The Jewish Side of Philip Roth," *Studies in American Jewish Literature,* Vol. 1 (1) Spring 1975, 29–37.

Roth, P. 1989. (First published 1959). *Goodbye, Columbus and Other Short Stories.* Boston: Houghton Mifflin.

Rothbell G. 1986. "The Jewish Mother: Social Construction of A Popular Image." In *The Jewish Family: Myths and Realities,* 1986. Ed. Steven Cohen and Paula Hyman. New York and London: Holmes and Meier.

Scott, J. 1986. "Gender: A Useful Category of Historical Analysis." *American Historical Review,* Vol. 91 (5), 1053–1075.

Schneider, S. W. 1984. *Jewish And Female: Choices and Changes in Our Lives Today.* New York: Simon and Schuster.

———. 1979. "In a Coma! I thought she was Jewish: Some Truths and Some Speculations about Jewish Women and Sex." *Lilith: The Jewish Women's Magazine.* 5–8.

Sklare, M. and J. Greenblum. 1979. *Jewish Identity on the Suburban Frontier: A Study of Group Survival in the Open Society.* 2d ed. Chicago: University of Chicago Press.

Slobin, M. 1982. *Tenement Songs: The Popular Music of the Jewish Immigrants.* University of Illinois Press: Urbana.

Stern, E. G. 1917. *My Mother and I.* New York: McMillan.

Tonner, L. 1975. *Nothing But the Best: The Luck of the Jewish Princess.* New York: Coward, McCann and Geoghegan.

———. 1976. "The Truth About Being a Jewish Princess." *Cosmopolitan Magazine,* September.

Turner, B. 1984. *The Body and Society: Explorations in Social Theory.* Oxford and New York: Basil Blackwell.

Walden, D. 1977–1978 "Goodbye Columbus, Hello Portnoy—And Beyond: The Ordeal of Philip Roth." *Studies in American Jewish Literature,* Vol. III (2) Winter.

Waxman, Barbara Frey. 1988. "Jewish American Princesses, Their Mothers, and Feminist Psychology: A Rereading of Roth's "Goodbye, Columbus." Studies in American Jewish Literature, Vol. 7 (1) 90–104.

Wouk, Herman. 1955. *Marjorie Morningstar.* New York: Doubleday and Company.

14

Challenging Male/Female Complementarity: Jewish Lesbians and the Jewish Tradition

Rebecca Alpert

In 1982 Evelyn Torton Beck published her ground-breaking anthology, *Nice Jewish Girls.* This book challenged the Jewish community to acknowledge a developing Jewish lesbian feminist consciousness. The past several years have witnessed the growth of that consciousness, as many women have begun to take the risk of identifying ourselves publicly as lesbians and as Jews. We have become a visible presence in the Jewish community, taking public leadership roles, developing communal structures and rituals, searching the tradition for role models, and challenging discrimination against us.[1]

Making lesbians visible in the Jewish community has meant creating an awareness in the Jewish community of who we are and how we define ourselves. Lesbians have been defined by others exclusively in relationship to our sexuality. What distinguishes us by this definition is that we are women who have sexual relationships with persons of our own gender. Lesbians are anomalous only because we do not practice procreative, heterosexual sex.

To the lesbian community, however, sexuality is only one element of lesbian identity. While contemporary definitions of lesbianism vary, lesbian identity can include genital sex and erotic passion, nonconformity to gender roles, romantic friendship, as well as an affiliation with a political and cultural community of women (Duberman, Vicinus, Chauncey 1989). Lesbian cultural identity incorporates other dimensions of our embodiedness including, for example, speech, dress, and ornamentation (Grahn 1984). Only when others are aware of the complete range of lesbian cultural identity will we be understood as fully embodied, fully visible in the Jewish community.

Lesbian visibility is an important first step toward creating a Judaism that affirms our existence. But lesbian feminism poses a deeper, more fundamental challenge to Judaism. Lesbians will never become truly integrated into the Jewish community without challenging the norm of complementarity between men and women in Jewish tradition and contemporary Jewish culture.

Complementarity is the notion that to be whole, women must be partners with men (Ross 1989). Complementarity does have a biological component—it is supported by the idea that men and women "fit" together anatomically. Heterosexual, procreative sex is natural because penises fit into vaginas. But complementarity goes beyond the issues of anatomy, influencing every dimension of the cultural relationships between men and women.

Complementarity is embedded deeply within the structure of biblical and ancient Judaism. Much of Judaism is based on the understanding that women exist only in relationship to men and primarily for the purpose of enabling the continuity of the species through childbearing. Unlike other traditions, Judaism has no role for the autonomous woman who has not in some way fulfilled her role as companion to a man.[2]

Lesbianism as it has come to be understood in contemporary times is women's claim of independence from complementarity. Lesbians are by definition women who choose to define central aspects of our identity in relation to other women, not to men. All these definitions of contemporary lesbian identity pose a fundamental challenge to Judaism in regard to the ways in which it defines women in relationship to men.

In all probability, the lesbian feminist challenge to complementarity will be experienced in liberal Judaism. While liberal Judaism defines itself in continuity with ancient Judaism, it has in fact excised much of Jewish tradition that does not conform to contemporary ethical standards. For example, Reform, Reconstructionist and some Conservative Jews are strongly committed to equal rights for women and civil rights for gay men and lesbians. Liberal Judaism for the most part ignores the traditional Jewish sex ethic that permits sexual expression only within the context of heterosexual, monogamous marriage. Liberal Jewish women are not expected to dress modestly or refrain from touching men. But these attitudes have not led to an affirmation of women's autonomy or women's primary connections to one another rather than to a man as positive values.

Of course, lesbians do not present the only challenge to complementarity in Judaism. Both feminism and the gay liberation movements question male-female complementarity. Yet the questions raised by lesbians both incorporate and complicate the challenges posed by gay men and feminists.

Much of Jewish feminism challenges the dominance of men (androcentric patriarchy) in Judaism.[3] These feminists question the nature of the relationships of power between men and women. But heterosexual feminists assume the centrality of male/female relationships. Their goal is to change the dynamics of male/female relationships, not to question their primacy. Feminists also have to combat the invisibility of women in male-dominated Judaism. But lesbians are rendered invisible not only as women but also as a sexual minority (Rubin 1984). In fact, liberal Jewish feminists have contributed to the invisibility of lesbians because of their own fears of being labeled as lesbian (Rogow 1990). While lesbians and heterosexual feminists share a desire to change complementarity, their struggles are not synonomous.

Gay men do challenge the centrality of heterosexual relationships in Judaism. But they do not face exclusion from Jewish tradition on the basis of gender and often fail to recognize the problems all women face gaining access to Jewish tradition. Because they are accepted as men, they often lose sight of the necessity to change Jewish tradition so that women can be full participants.[4] Lesbians are in the unique situation of having to contend both with issues of gender and sexuality in combination.

To understand the dimensions of the problems facing Jewish lesbians as we confront the issue of complementarity, we must closely examine Jewish tradition and contemporary communal life. Virtually every aspect of Jewish life assumes the centrality of complementary relationships between men and women. This chapter will look at complementarity in myth, law, sexuality, gender roles, and theology in ancient and contemporary Judaism and propose ways to change the current structures.

Complementarity in Jewish Tradition

Myth

The so-called "curse of Eve" ("And your desire shall be for your husband, and he shall rule over you." Gen. 3:16) forms the basis for male-female complementarity in Judaism. While feminism questions the relationship of dominance described—"and he shall rule over you"—lesbianism also questions the prior assumption that women desire men. For lesbians to be included in Jewish life, the idea that women desire men must not be assumed to be universal. To include lesbians means that contemporary Judaism must acknowledge boldly that there are women who desire women in much the same way that other women desire men.

Judith Plaskow's contemporary midrash on the Garden story, "Applesource" (1979, 206–207), at least points the way to other possibilities. Here, Plaskow ruminates on the friendship between Eve and Lilith, usually viewed as Eve's rival for Adam's affection. In the end, however, Lilith and Eve return to a chastened God and Adam. For lesbian reality to become part of Judaism, this midrash would have to include the possibility of an erotic attraction between Eve and Lilith and examine its implications.

The Hebrew Bible does not provide stories of women who are independent of men. Of course there are stories that suggest close friendships between women, such as the declaration of commitment offered by Ruth to Naomi (Ruth 1:16), or the strange final request of Jephthah's unnamed daughter: to spend the month with her women friends in isolation before being killed as fulfillment of her father's vow (Judg. 11:37). But even these women's lives revolve around men. Ruth will ultimately desire Boaz, not Naomi. Jephthah's daughter goes away to mourn dying before she has been with a man sexually or given birth to her father's heir.

Law

While myth serves an important role, the legal tradition of biblical and ancient Judaism provides the structural basis for complementarity of male-female roles. With its passion for structure and abhorrence of ambiguity, Jewish law designates strict categories for all things in the world, including men and women (Eilberg-Schwartz 1990). Because of the essential androcentric bias of Jewish law, men are the central category and women are other (Plaskow 1990). Being other constructs women's reality only in relationship to men. This has several implications for lesbians.

In Jewish law there is no such thing as an autonomous woman. All issues related to women are delineated in terms of their relationship to men. Heterosexuality is of course assumed. Until the modern era the nature of the heterosexual relationship was one of ownership. A man (father or husband) possessed the rights to a woman's sexuality and to her procreative capabilities. The writers of rabbinic law dealt with women only around the times of transition (marriage, widowhood, divorce) between ownership of one man and another to ensure her safe passage (Neusner 1980). In theory, this structure allowed for the possibility of the autonomous woman in rare instances—the widow who had given her husband a male heir, the legally emancipated daughter who did not marry, the divorcee (Wegner 1988). It would be erroneous to conclude however that many autonomous women survived within the culture without the protection and financial support of a man.

All other considerations of women in rabbinic Judaism reinforce the existence of the centrality of the heterosexual relationship. Most prohibitions on women's behavior (modesty in dress, abstention from public rituals, menstrual taboos) involve controlling women's demeanor toward their husbands and their circumscribed role with other men in the culture. The tradition remains silent about primary relationships between women, including one as basic as the mother-daughter bond. What women did outside of men's control was simply not of interest.

Even the rare references to lesbian behavior arise in relationship to men. There is no mention of sexual activity between women in the Hebrew Bible. Some discussion of lesbian behavior occurs in the Talmud[5] (Biale 1984) where there is a disagreement over whether women who are *mesolelot* are nonetheless eligible to marry priests. While it is clear from the context that *mesolelot* has a sexual connotation, no definition is given in this text. The medieval scholar Rashi (1040–1105) suggests a definition in his commentary on this passage (Yebamot 76a), "Like in intercourse of male and female, they rub their femininity [the genitals] against one another." The text raises questions about the consequences of this behavior. The Talmud concludes that although one scholar (Rav Huna) would prohibit *mesolelot* from marriage to a priest, the majority considers the behavior *pritzut,* mere licentiousness, a trivial offense and therefore not a disqualification. The only other mention of *mesolelot* is in a similar context. In Shabbat 65a we are informed that a certain scholar did not permit his daughters to sleep together. The question is raised as to whether this is a support for the opinion of Rav Huna that they would be tempted to sexual behavior and thus disqualified from marriage into the priesthood. The response is no; the prohibition is so that they would not become accustomed to sleeping together and then have problems after marriage sleeping separately from their husbands in observance of the menstrual taboo (*niddah*).

Both of these texts clearly show an awareness of the possibility of women's erotic interest in one another. Yet the texts define this as a specific behavior of otherwise heterosexual women, not to be taken too seriously. The assumption of the text is clear—while women may engage in lesbian behavior, this is not an indication that they do not desire men. Also inherent in the comment in Shabbat 65a is that the purpose of prohibiting lesbian behavior is to further the observance of *niddah* in heterosexual marriage.

Another reference to lesbian sexual practice is found in the legal code *Mishneh Torah,* written by Moses Maimonides (1135–1204).[6] In his codification, however, Maimonides obviously takes these practices more seriously and sees them as potentially threatening to the heterosexual norm:

> Women are forbidden to engage in *mesolelot* with one another, these being 'the doings of Egypt' against which we have been warned, as it is said: 'You shall not copy the practices of the land of Egypt . . .' (Lev. 18:3) Our Sages have said: 'What did they do? A man would marry a man, or a woman a woman, or a woman would marry two men.'[7] Although such an act is forbidden, the perpetrators are not liable for a flogging, since there is no specific negative commandment prohibiting it, nor is actual intercourse of any kind involved. Consequently, such women are not disqualified from the priesthood on account of prostitution, nor is a woman prohibited to her husband because of it. It behooves the court, however, to administer the flogging prescribed for rebelliousness since they performed a forbidden act. A man should be particularly strict with his wife in this matter and should prevent women known to indulge in such practices from visiting her and her from visiting them. (Issurei Bi'ah 21:8)

Lacking legal precedent, Maimonides could do no more than recommend the most stringent possible punishment for rebelliousness for lesbian sexual behavior. Nonetheless it is obvious from his comments that by the Middle Ages lesbian sexual behavior was recognized as something women did, that women who engaged in such practices could be identified, and that men were admonished to be sure that their wives were not involved with other women known to engage in this behavior. Once again, lesbianism is understood as a challenge to the norm that women exist only for men. The law is specifically addressed to men, and admonishes them to keep their wives under control. The women involved could have performed any act of rebelliousness and been treated in this manner; there is no specific interdiction of lesbian behavior per se.

Pleasure and Procreation

Jewish legal tradition recognizes that there are two crucial aspects of sexuality in marriage—pleasure and procreation. Sexual relations between married men and women are strictly regulated while at the same time viewed in a positive light. The commandment of *onah* demands that a man must satisfy his wife sexually. The underlying assumption of this commandment is that women have a natural sexual desire for men, but that they are unable to communicate that desire. Therefore it is the man's obligation to be sexual with his wife. The commandment of *onah* makes clear that the heterosexual act is designed for pleasure as distinct from procreation.

Heterosexual pleasure is also reaffirmed by contemporary feminists who write about the erotic love between man and woman in the Songs of Songs and the passionate eroticism between God and humans in the Jewish mystical tradition (Plaskow 1990). The same passion of women for one another finds no expression. Nor is its absence lamented by those who praise the erotic passion expressed in elements of Jewish tradition. In fact, heterosexual pleasure is taken by some as evidence to prove that lesbian love is unnatural.

While Judaism acknowledges heterosexual pleasure, the main goal of sexual relations between men and women is procreation. The laws of *niddah,* the rules governing separation of women from their husbands during the time of menstruation and for a week following, are constructed to ensure sexual relations during the time when women are fertile and to prohibit them when women are not.

Lesbian sexuality calls into question the fundamental purpose of marriage, species continuity, by establishing the complete independence of sexual pleasure and procreation. It eliminates both the possibility of pregnancy as an outcome of the sexual encounter and the necessity of engaging in heterosexual sex to procreate, as pregnancy can be achieved through alternative insemination. These factors combine to challenge Judaism to see pleasure and procreation as independent of one another.

Gender

In biblical and ancient Judaism, gender roles were rigidly defined and directly related to biological functions.[8] In societies that define sex and gender roles as inseparable, there is little room for gender fluidity. Men and women remain in separate spheres and have clear and distinct roles assigned to them. Experimentation with gender roles is prohibited. (Note the prohibition against men and women wearing clothes designated for the other sex in Deut. 22:5, the later prohibition against mixing between the sexes, and the rigid divisions between men's and women's religious obligations.)

The absence of gender fluidity in ancient Judaism contributed to the complementarity between men and women by making absolute the definition of what it meant to be male and female. No deviation from that norm was permissible. Women were unable to explore what it felt like to take on roles not assigned to them by gender. All women's gender assigned roles were based on their biology and relationships to men.

While rigid gender roles are the hallmark of ancient Judaism, they have not been completely erased in liberal Judaism. There is a strong cultural taboo against men taking on the "woman's commandment" of lighting candles, for example. While women have begun to wear traditionally male ritual garb, they have characteristically "feminized" it, creating ritual objects such as lace kippot and multicolored tallesim.

At the same time, much of contemporary Jewish feminism has also focused on a new respect for women's biological roles at the expense of a clear analysis of the relationship between social and biological roles. New ceremonies have been introduced that focus on pregnancy, childbirth, lactation, and menstruation. Rosh Hodesh (new moon) ceremonies focus on the cycles of a woman's body and its relationship to nature. Of course, asserting the value of women's biological roles is an important feminist concern. But it is too often the dominant concern in Jewish feminist circles and renders invisible those women who do not see biological roles as central to defining themselves as women.[9]

Lesbian gender nonconformity raises profound questions about how men and women define themselves in relation to one another. There is a common misconception that lesbians are women who want to be men. In fact, the truth is quite the contrary—many lesbians seek to broaden the concept of what it means to be a woman and sometimes behave in ways that do not conform to rigid notions of gender (Grahn 1984). Lesbians may seek traditionally male prerogatives, (e.g., the right to wear comfortable clothing, the right to move freely in public, the right to love other women). They may decide that women's biological roles are not central in their lives. This does not imply an identification with men so much as the right of women to define ourselves without preconceived notions of biologically determined roles and behaviors. For the Jewish community to come to terms with this dimension of lesbian existence requires the celebration of women in ways unrelated to biologically determined definitions.

Homorelationism

Ancient Judaism defined separate spheres for men and women. Complementarity did not have the same effect on men as it did on women. While women were defined in relationship to men, men were defined as autonomous selves and also in relationship to one another. As in all patriarchal cultures, men's sphere was defined as public space, and relationships between men were valued. To be sure, men were obligated to marry and have children. But unlike women, they were not expected to devote their lives to their families.

Women, on the other hand, were kept out of public space. The lives of women were meant to be lived privately, not in relationship to one another. Their lives were circumscribed by the necessities of bearing and raising children and maintaining a household. Significant relationships between women must have existed even in these contexts. But Jewish society was not designed to promote relationships between women, and patriarchal history certainly left no records of significant female bonding.

One need only contrast the stringent biblical prohibition on male homosexual behavior with the lenient rabbinic interdiction against lesbianism (Alpert 1989) to see the attention given to bonding between men and the disinterest in bonding between women. Male homosexuality was more threatening to the existing order because it was more plausible given the nature of the society.

One byproduct of the rigid gender role division in Judaism is the male bonding that occurs as men transfer passion from sexual temptation with women to the Torah they study and consequently to the men with whom they study Torah. While affection between women is unnoticed and made difficult through the privatization of their lives, male bonding through Torah is elevated to holiness. Study partners and teachers are spoken of in the most loving ways and honored above parents and wives. Descriptions of relations between rabbis boast of their unending love (Adler 1988, Eilberg-Schwartz 1990).

The rigid gender roles and the dualism they imply support male prerogatives and male bonding. The positive evaluations of maleness and of Torah study reinforce the otherness of women. Passion is reserved for God and Torah. Heterosexuality must be enforced to guard against men's disinterest in connecting to women they were taught to devalue (Harrison 1985). Women are kept from male prerogatives, and from female bonding given the structure of the culture that privatized women's lives.

Lesbianism offers the possibility of female bonding as an alternative to complementarity. The male homorelationism of the tradition leaves Judaism open to the possibility of the power of same-sex relations for women as well.

The Relatively Genderless Male Deity

The God of the Bible was distinguished from other gods of the Ancient Near East by the absence of sexuality. Although sexless, Yahweh was undoubtedly described metaphorically as a male-gendered God. He [sic] was described with male pronouns as well as with the attributes of masculine body parts and personality characteristics, as contemporary feminist Jewish scholars have illustrated so eloquently (Gross 1981, Plaskow 1990). The maleness and sexlessness of God is a major factor in the devaluation of women and of sexuality in a Jewish context (Eilberg-Schwartz 1990).[10]

The efforts of Jewish feminists to begin to think of God in female pronomial and attributive terms and to reclaim sources in ancient Near Eastern Goddess worship have met with strongly negative reaction within the Jewish community, more so than any other feminist contribution (Dresner 1988).

There are several reasons for this reaction. God's maleness is traditionally understood as asexual. Because women do not exist without men, imagining God as woman threatens both the asexuality and maleness of God at the same time. Additionally, if God is to be thought of in sexual metaphors, the very powerful nonsexual relationship between men and the relatively genderless male deity must be reevaluated as well.

But there is likely an additional reason. Some have suggested an association between women worshiping images of women and women loving women (Dresner 1988). The association between Goddess worship and fears of lesbianism is borne out in other cultures. The cultic prostitution associated with sexual acts in sacred temples is often thought to be connected to lesbianism (Raymond 1986).

For lesbians to be included in Jewish life in the fullest measure, the fear that female images of God are related to lesbianism must be faced directly. If lesbians, too, are made in God's image, there must be room to explore images of God that support the divinity of erotic love between women.

The Yentl Syndrome

When Isaac Bashevis Singer (1904–) created the character "Yentl The Yeshiva Boy," he did not do so in order to create a symbol for feminism. Singer himself was fascinated by the rigid gender-role divisions and issues of sexuality in Jewish life. He created many characters who pushed the boundaries of ambiguities between men and women, the traditional and modern worlds, and this world and the next.

In American Jewish feminist circles, Yentl became a symbol of the exclusion of women from the world of Torah. Singer, and Barbara Streisand who produced a contemporary screen version of Yentl, ridiculed the traditional assumption that only a man could study Torah by turning a woman into a man. Yentl was portrayed to have the soul of a man within her because of her love of male things, of Torah. When she asked her father why she was born a woman, he replied, "Even heaven makes mistakes." For Yentl, taking on the male prerogative of study and dressing as a man to gain entrance to the study house did not pose a problem. Yentl's masquerade became problematic when she fell in love with her (male) study partner, Anshl. Although the homorelational love of study partners is certainly looming here beneath the surface, it is never dealt with. Yentl then reverted to being a woman, her "desire for her man" so strong that she gave up dressing like a man and entering the Yeshiva. In the contemporary version by Streisand, Yentl does not give up Torah study, although she must give up the male prerogative of entering the Yeshiva to study.

The story of Yentl provides us with a model for what needs to be changed and eradicated for lesbians to be at home in the Jewish world. For lesbians to be affirmed within Judaism today, the Yentl story must be presented in yet another version. Yentl must ask herself in a self-conscious way what it means to desire those prerogatives from which women were traditionally excluded—not only Torah study but the possibility of loving women.

Yentl would have to explore her relationship to Hadass, the woman in the story to whom Yentl was "married" and ultimately to question the desirability of traditional gender roles within the context of their relationship.[11] She would see her dressing as a man not as becoming a man but as a further exploration of what it means to be a woman. She would have to understand that the possibilities of changing roles for women also includes an exploration of sexuality and female bonding.

Whatever Yentl decided to do with her life, the possibility that she would be aware of and open to the option of lesbian existence would provide an opening for the affirmation of lesbian choices with the Jewish community.

Challenging Complementarity in Judaism

Of course, for changes to take place within the Jewish community, we need to begin to tell new stories and to retell old ones. There is no doubt to the value of sharing personal stories and writing midrash about lesbian themes in biblical and ancient stories.[12]

But for lesbians truly to become part of the Jewish community, we must begin to face some of the theological and ethical challenges that lesbianism poses to Judaism. Most of the changes that are necessary have to do with the ways in which the human body in general and the female body in particular have been denigrated in Judaism.

A new respect for the human body and its interconnections with the mind and spirit must be developed. Christian feminist Beverly Harrison, African-American lesbian feminist Audre Lorde, and Jewish feminist Judith Plaskow, among others, have begun to work on these redefinitions. They include a new understanding of the erotic as a power that infuses our lives, that derives from but is not limited to genital sexuality. It is this sense of the erotic that forms the basis of a new understanding of sexuality. In this new understanding, sexuality is not a frightening, unmanageable energy that needs to be controlled. Rather, sexuality is a potential source of human creativity and enormous joy.

Based on this orientation to the sexual, Harrison (1988, xviii) describes a new religious sexual ethic. Although she writes for a Christian audience, her ideas are clearly applicable in the Jewish context. She argues for the reconnection of bodies and emotions as sources of moral data, a respect for the rights of bodily integrity as the foundation of moral well-being, a celebration of bodies and sexuality, an end to sex-role rigidity, and an honoring of all expressions of mutual sexual communication. She also emphasizes the importance of touch (including genital touch) as a way of conveying bonds of feeling rather than of control, viewing intense touch as a source of spiritual power (149).

The ethic described above will enable a new understanding of the positive power of women's bodies and touch and sexuality to emerge and will be part of the process that will enable lesbians to find positive experiences within Judaism.

In a Jewish context, this theology can be grounded in a new configuration of the divine image, which will allow lesbians, too, to see in ourselves the image of God. It will make holy our connections to one another, enabling us to understand that if we are made in God's image then sexual relationships between women are part of the divine plan.

New sources of holiness will arise in women's connections with one another. As Adrienne Rich (1980, 83) proclaimed the passion of debating ideas with women to be an erotic passion, so a new Torah that combines mind and body will emerge from women. It will mean affirming that what women do apart from men is integral to the process of Jewish renewal.

There will also be a new understanding of women as sexual beings unrelated to men. Without the notion that a woman is complementary to a man, lesbian sexuality will have to be affirmed. This will mean making room for a lesbian version of the Songs of Songs that proclaims the joy and power of women loving women in a sexual way. It will mean creating new poetry and images that suggest the positive qualities of women's bodies as they intertwine with one another. Sexual attraction between women will be seen as holy, valued, and meant to be celebrated.

There will also be a new understanding of the relationship between women and their procreative capacities. Affirming lesbian alternative insemination will enable us to separate the role of childbearing for women as something distinct and unrelated to our sexuality and our parenting, as men's procreative and parental capacities are generally understood. This will enable us to understand the childbearing role in a new light and to offer fresh insights about the meanings of pregnancy for women.

At the same time, we need to honor those lesbians (and all women) who do not choose or are unable to be pregnant. A new understanding of the body requires that women's bodies be respected for roles other than that of bearing children. Clearly in our contemporary society, pregnancy has taken on a more limited role even for those women who follow more traditional life paths. We must come to terms with the implications of the fact that most women are pregnant or nursing during a very limited part of their lives. We must celebrate and create rituals to express the value of women's bodies for the capacity to love, to work, to think, and to act creatively.

This new orientation to the body will incorporate a more fluid concept of gender, enabling women and men to experiment with the range of roles and behaviors open within a Jewish context, and leaving open the possibility of creating new ones. Women who choose to take on roles traditionally assigned to men will be able to do that without their womanhood being questioned.

Finally, as Harrison and Plaskow point out, the challenge we set forth must be linked to the struggle for economic justice, for no one's body can be liberated without the satisfaction of basic human needs of food, clothing, and shelter.

Our bodies are the medium through which we are in touch with the world (Ross 1989). The changes described here will enable us to connect physical dimensions of ourselves long neglected in a Jewish context. We will celebrate our sexuality and connect it to our intelligence and our spirituality. Ultimately, this perspective will not only enable lesbians to be at home in a Jewish context but create possibilities for men and women of all sexual orientations to find deeper and richer meanings in Judaism.

Notes

I would like to thank Christie Balka and Sharon Cohen for their thoughtful comments on earlier drafts of this manuscript.

1. Much of this history is detailed in *Twice Blessed: On Being Lesbian, Gay and Jewish* (Balka and Rose 1989). See especially the introduction and articles by Faith Rogow and Linda Holtzman. An additional article by Faith Rogow (1990) chronicles the history of the lesbian feminist movement of the past decade.

2. Christian tradition did allow women to choose a celibate life style.

3. Of course, for some women who define themselves as Jewish feminists, this is not a central issue. They believe that the main goal is gaining equal rights within the Jewish tradition that have been denied them as women.

4. The gay synagogue movement has been committed to incorporating feminist elements in the liturgy and working toward women's full participation (Kahn 1989). In many gay synagogues, feminist influences are strongly felt, but there are exceptions.

5. According to Bernadette Brooten (1985), the first references to female homoerotic behavior in Jewish texts should be dated to the Roman

period, with prohibitions found in the pseudepigraphical text *The Sentences of Pseudo-Phocylides* and in the *Sifra*, an early legal commentary on Leviticus.

6. There is a similar passage in the code *Shulhan Arukh, Even HaEzer* 20.2, compiled by Joseph Karo a few centuries later.

7. The sages in this reference are the author of the *Sifra* commentary on Lev. 18:3.

8. That biological sex characteristics form the basis for gender roles is a common cultural assumption. Yet the relationship between sex, gender, and gender roles is vastly more complex. Often persons become socially recognized as members of a gender based on role behaviors, not biological sex, which is in fact not exposed to public view (Devor 1989, 148).

9. For a comprehensive discussion of these ceremonies, see the forthcoming article by Shulamit Magnus. Magnus also explores the significance of female bonding in these rituals in contrast to the pervasive male bonding in Judaism discussed below.

10. Elements of prophetic and medieval Judaism introduce complementarity into theological concerns. Yahweh is seen as the (metaphorical) male and Israel as his (sic) female partner. Unfortunately, this allegory did not elevate woman's role, as Israel was often described negatively, especially in the prophetic tradition, as a faithless wife.

11. Contemporary lesbians have also had to deal with the issue of rigid gender stereotyping in butch-fem relationships that were common in the lesbian community before the feminist movement. Recent scholarship has indicated that these categories were not as restrictive as originally believed and that lesbians experimented with both roles in a quest to redefine womanhood (Kennedy and Davis 1989).

12. Of course efforts to find lesbian themes in Jewish history such as those presented by Faith Rogow (1989) are to be understood as fanciful imaginings and not attempts at historical reconstruction.

References

Adler, R. 1988. "The Virgin in the Brothel: The Legend of Beruriah." *Tikkun*. 3:28–35, 102–105.

Alpert, R. 1989. "In God's Image: Coming to Terms with Leviticus." In *Twice Blessed: On Being Lesbian, Gay and Jewish*. Ed. Christie Balka and Andy Rose, 61–70. Boston: Beacon Press.

Balka, C. and Andy Rose. 1989. "Introduction." In *Twice Blessed: On Being Lesbian, Gay and Jewish*. 1–10. Boston: Beacon Press.

Beck, E. T. 1982. "Why Is This Book Different From All Other Books?" In *Nice Jewish Girls: A Lesbian Anthology.* Ed. Evelyn Torton Beck, xiii–xxxvi. Watertown, Mass.: Persephone Press.

Biale, R. 1984. *Women and Jewish Law: An Exploration of Women's Issues in Halakhic Sources.* New York: Schocken Press.

Brooten, B. 1985. "Paul's Views on the Nature of Women and Female Homoeroticism. In *Immaculate and Powerful: The Female in Sacred Image and Social Reality.* Ed. Clarissa W. Atkinson, Constance H. Buchanan, and Margaret R. Miles, 61–87. Boston: Beacon Press.

Devor, H. 1989. *Gender blending: Confronting the Limits of Duality.* Bloomington: Indiana University Press.

Dresner, S. 1988. "The Return of Paganism?" *Midstream.* 34:32–38.

Duberman, M. B. and Martha Vicinus and George Chauncey, Jr. 1989 "Introduction." In *Hidden From History: Reclaiming the Gay and Lesbian Past,* 1–13. New York: New American Library.

Eilberg-Schwartz, H. 1990. *The Savage in Judaism: An Anthropology of Israelite Religion and Ancient Judaism.* Bloomington: Indiana University Press.

Grahn, J. 1984. *Another Mother Tongue: Gay Words, Gay Worlds.* Boston: Beacon Press.

Gross, R. 1981. "Steps towards Feminine Imagery of Deity in Feminist Theology." *Judaism.* 30:183–193.

Harrison, B. 1985. *Making the Connections: Essays in Feminist Social Ethics.* Ed. Carol Robb. Boston: Beacon Press.

Holtzman, L. 1989. "Jewish Lesbian Parenting." In *Twice Blessed: On Being Lesbian, Gay and Jewish.* Ed. Christie Balka and Andy Rose, 133–140. Boston: Beacon Press.

Kahn, Y. 1989. "The Liturgy of Gay and Lesbian Jews." In *Twice Blessed: On Being Lesbian, Gay and Jewish.* Ed. Christie Balka and Andy Rose, 182–197. Boston: Beacon Press.

Kennedy, E. L. and Madeline Davis. 1989. "The Reproduction of Butch-Fem Roles: A Social Constructionist Approach." In *Passion and Power: Sexuality in History.* Ed. Kathy Peiss and Christine Simmons, 241–258. Philadelphia: Temple University Press.

Lorde, A. 1984. "Uses of the Erotic: The Erotic as Power." In *Sister/Outsider: Essays and Speeches,* 53–59. Trumansburg, N.Y.: The Crossing Press.

Magnus, S. forthcoming. "Re-inventing Miriam's Well: Jewish Feminist Ceremonials." In *The Uses of Tradition: Jewish Continuity Since Emancipation*. New York: Jewish Theological Seminary of America.

Neusner, J. 1980. "Mishnah on Women: Thematic or Systematic Description." *Marxist Perspectives*. 3:79–98.

Plaskow, J. 1990. *Standing Again at Sinai: Judaism from a Feminist Perspective*. New York: Harper and Row.

———. 1979. "The Coming of Lilith: Toward a Feminist Theology." In *Womanspirit Rising: A Feminist Reader in Religion*. Ed. Carol Christ and Judith Plaskow, 198–209. San Francisco: Harper and Row.

Raymond, J. 1986. *A Passion for Friends: Toward a Philosophy of Female Affection*. Boston: Beacon Press.

Rich, A. 1980. "Compulsory Heterosexuality and Lesbian Existence." In *Blood, Bread and Poetry: Selected Prose 1979–1985*, 23–75. New York: W. W. Norton.

Rogow, F. 1989. "Speaking the Unspeakable: Gay Jewish Historical Inquiry." In *Twice Blessed: On Being Lesbian, Gay and Jewish*. Ed. Christie Balka and Andy Rose, 71–82. Boston: Beacon Press.

———. 1990. "The Rise of Jewish Lesbian Feminism." In *Bridges* 1:67–79.

Ross, S. 1989. " 'Then Honor God in Your Body' (1 Cor. 6:20): Feminist and Sacramental Theology of The Body." *Horizons* 16:7–27.

Rubin, G. 1984. "Thinking Sex: Notes for a Radical Theory of the Politics of Sexuality." In *Pleasure and Danger: Explorations of Female Sexuality*. Ed. Carol Vance, 267–319. Boston: Routledge and Kegan Paul.

Singer, I. B. 1983. *Yentl the Yeshiva Boy*. New York: Farrar, Straus, Giroux.

Wegner, J. 1988. *Chattel or Person? The Status of Women in the Mishnah*. New York: Oxford University Press.

Contributors

Rebecca Alpert holds a doctoral degree from the department of Religion at Temple University and rabbinic ordination from the Reconstructionist Rabbinical College, where she served as Dean of Students for ten years. She currently runs the Adult Program of the Russell Conwell Educational Services Center at Temple University. She has published and lectured widely on the subjects of feminist Judaism, medical ethics, and issues in adult education.

Gary Anderson is associate professor of Hebrew Bible in Religious Studies at the University of Virginia. He is author of *A Time to Mourn and a Time to Dance: The Expression of Joy and Grief in Israelite Religion* (1991) and *Sacrifices and Offerings in Ancient Israel* (1988) and is coeditor of *Studies in Cult and Priesthood of Ancient Israel.*

David Biale is Koret Professor of Jewish History and Director of the Center for Jewish Studies at the Graduate Theological Union in Berkeley and adjunct professor in the Department of Near Eastern Studies at UC Berkeley. He is author of *Gershom Scholem: Kabbalah and Counter-History* (Harvard University 1979) and *Power and Power lessness in Jewish History* (Schocken 1986). In 1992 Basic Books will publish his new book, *Eros and the Jews: From Biblical Israel to Contemporary America.*

Daniel Boyarin is the Taubman Professor of Talmudic Culture in the Department of Near Eastern Studies at the University of California at Berkeley. His most recent book is *Intertextuality and the Reading of Midrash* (Indiana University, 1990). The present article is a chapter of a forthcoming book from University of California Press entitled *Carnal Israel: Reading*

Sex in Talmudic Culture. In addition, he has published articles in *Critical Inquiry, diacritics, The Journal of the History of Sexuality, Poetics Today, Representations,* and *The Yale Journal of Criticism.* He is currently working on a book on the constructions of gender through descriptions of the female body in talmudic literature.

Howard Eilberg-Schwartz is assistant professor of Religious Studies at Stanford University. His work on ancient Judaism is broadly interdisciplinary, drawing particularly from cultural criticism, anthropology, and gender studies. He is the author of *The Savage in Judaism: An Anthropology of Israelite Religion and Ancient Judaism* (winner of a 1990 American Academy Award for Academic Excellence) as well as *The Human Will in Judaism.* He is currently working on a book on the conflicts of masculinity in monotheism. Eilberg-Schwartz also serves as editor for the SUNY Press series "The Body in Culture, History, and Religion" in which this volume appears. When not writing, he is happily parenting his daughter Penina.

Lawrence Fine is the Irene Kaplan Leiwant Professor of Jewish Studies at Mount Holyoke College. He taught at Indiana University, and served as the Padnos Visiting Professor of Judaic Studies at the University of Michigan. Much of his work has been concerned with understanding the experiential and devotional aspects of kabbalistic life. He is author of *Safed Spirituality, Essential Papers On Kabbalah (ed.)* and numerous articles on the history of Jewish mysticism.

Jay Geller currently teaches religion at Princeton University. He has previously taught at Rutgers, Wesleyan, Swarthmore, Duke and UNC-Greensboro. In addition, he has held fellowships with DAAD, ACLS, and the Center for the Critical Analysis of Contemporary Culture. His study of how the depiction of male Jewish body parts—circumcised penises, bleeding noses—and smells led to the identification of Jewish men with the socially threatening feminine within the Central European cultural and scientific imagination, *The Nose Job: Freud and the Feminized Jew,* is forthcoming from SUNY Press.

Sander L. Gilman is the Goldwin Smith Professor of Humane Studies at Cornell University and Professor of the History of Psychiatry at the Cornell Medical College. During 1990–91, he served as the Visiting Historical Scholar at the National Library of Medicine, Bethesda, Maryland. A member of the Cornell faculty since 1969, he is an intellectual and literary historian and the author or editor of over twenty-seven books, the most recent—*The Jew's Body*—having appeared in 1991 with Routledge. He is author of the widely cited study of *Jewish Self-Hatred* which appeared with the Johns Hopkins University Press in 1986.

Naomi Janowitz is associate professor of Religious Studies at the University of California-Davis. She is author of *The Poetics of Ascent: Theories of Language in a Rabbinic Ascent Text* (SUNY) which draws on insights in linguistic anthropology to rethink our understanding of mystical ascent texts. Her writing, both historical and multidisciplinary in character, focuses on various aspects of late antique Judaism.

Riv-Ellen Prell, an anthropologist, is associate professor of American Studies at the University of Minnesota. She has done both ethnographic and historical research about American Jewish life with particular attention to ritual, gender, and popular culture. She is author of *Prayer and Community: The Havurah in American Judaism* (Wayne State University Press), and co-editor with The Personal Narrative Group of *Interpreting Women's Lives: Theories of Personal Narratives* (Indiana University Press). This essay is part of a larger work on Jewish gender relations in America, *Fighting to Become American: Jewish Women and Men in Conflict in the Twentieth Century* (Basic Books).

Chava Weissler is associate professor and chair of the Religion Studies Dept., Lehigh University. She also holds the Philip and Muriel Berman Chair of Jewish Civilization at Lehigh. She is the author of *Making Judaism Meaningful* (1989), a study of the havurah movement, and has published a number of articles on devotional literature in Yiddish for women. Her book on the tkhines, *Voices of the Matriarchs,* will be published by Beacon Press.

Rahel R. Wasserfall was born in France and moved to Israel in her late teens. She studied anthropology and philosophy at the Hebrew University of Jerusalem where she received her Ph.D. As a Fulbright post-doctoral fellow she taught courses on Gender and Women in Israel at Duke University of North Carolina, Chapel Hill. She is currently a visiting teacher at the Institute for Sociology at Eotvos Lorand University in Budapest, Hungary where she teaches classes on the impact of feminism on the Social Sciences in the West. Her articles include "Bargaining for Gender Identity: Sex, Money and Love in an Israeli Moshav" published in *Ethnology* (1990). Her main theoretical interests is the construction of identities, particularly the intersection of ethnic and gender identities. She is currently writing a book on gender identification in two Jewish Moroccan Moshavim in Israel in which she worked. Last but not least, she is the mother of a 17–month-old daughter.

Elliot R. Wolfson is currently associate professor of Hebrew and Judaic Studies at New York University and adjunct professor of Jewish History at Columbia University. His major area of research is medieval Jewish mysticism. Additionally, he has published articles in medieval and modern Jewish philosophy. He is author of *The Book of the Pomegranate: Moses de León's Sefer ha-Rimmon* (1988) and is currently completing a manuscript *Through a Speculum That Shines: Vision and Visionary Experience in Medieval Jewish Mysticism* as well as an annotated translation of ancient Jewish mystical texts called *Hekhalot Mysticism* to be published by Paulist Press in The Classics of Western Spirituality Series. He is also the editor of The Journal of Jewish Thought and Philosophy.

Eli Yassif is associate professor of Hebrew Literature at Ben Gurion University, Israel. He has published widely in the area of Jewish folklore including *The Tales of Ben Sira in the Middle Ages* and *From Folktale to Literature: Folk-Genres and the Emergence of Hebrew Narratives in the Middle Ages*. In addition, he has served as editor of *The Sacrifice of Isaac: Studies in the Development of a Literary Tradition* and *The Study of Jewish Folklore: An Annotated Bibliography*.

Index

Abba, 119, 129, 132
Abraham, 22, 24
Abstinence
  Christian vs. Jewish philosophy, 47–48
  Kabbalism and, 135
  Zionist ideology, 288
  See also Asceticism
Academia folklore, 210
Adam
  Eve's beating of, 104
  Lilith and, 205, 364
  Lurianic Kabbalah, 129–130
  Seth and, 31, 37, 62
  sexual life, 47, 49–54
Adam Qadmon, 128–130, 134
Adelsen, Joseph, 341
Aggada, 49
Ahasverus, 255, 256
Algerian Jews, 312
Alkabetz, Solomon, 122, 123
Allen, Woody, 332–334
Alpha-Beth of Ben Sira, 205–206
Alsheikh, Moses, 122
Altshuler, Moses Henoch, 102, 111
American Jewish culture
  consumerism, 340–341, 343–345
  depictions of women in, 329, 331–338, 347–354
  feminism, 342, 344
  middle class life, 341–347
  women's body in, 338–340
  "Yentl" problem, 371–372
Androgyny, 83–84
Angels, 145, 153, 163
Animals, 29, 34, 52–54
Anorexia, 18–19
Anthropomorphism, 183–185. *See also* God's body
Anti-Semitism, 223. *See also* Jewish body stereotypes
Aphrahat, 47–48
Arabs, feminization of, 284
Asceticism, 20
  Christian tradition, 117–118
  Kabbalistic atonement, 123–126
  Lurianic Kabbalism, 131–133
  Zionist erotic revolution, 284
  See also Abstinence
Austria, 224–225
Ayn shoen froen bukhlein, 101–102
Azikri, Eleazer, 122

Baal, 60
Baba Metsia, 69, 87
Bakhtin, M., 69–70, 72–73, 79
Baraita' de-Ma'aseh Bereshit, 150, 152, 160
Barr, James, 35–36
Beauty, 81–82, 84–85, 88–89, 340
Beck, Evelyn Torton, 361
Becker, Rafael, 286
Ben-Sira, 205
Berukhim, Abraham ben Eliezer ha-Levi, 122
Bialik, Hayyim Nachman, 303
Binah, 119–120
Bisexuality, 254–255, 259
Bistritsky, Nathan, 296–297
Bitania Elite, 293
Blessing
  Edenic images, 60–63
  procreation and, 23–24, 29, 48
  for wedding rites, 56–60
Bloch, Iwan, 252, 293
Blubstein, Rachel, 302–303
Bluher, Hans, 293

Bodily regulations, 20–21. *See also* *Niddah*
Body-spirit dualism, 20, 209
Body stereotypes, *see* Jewish body stereotypes
Bovine theology, 183–184
Boyarin, Daniel, 185
Brantshpigl, 102, 106, 111
Brenner, Y. H., 286, 301–302
Brown-Séquard, C. E., 236
Buber, Martin, 289, 297
Burckhardt, Jacob, 249
Burnt offering, 126
Busch, Wilhelm, 248

Celibacy, *see* Abstinence
Charcot, Jean-Martin, 231, 232, 255
Charity, 108
Chernus, Ira, 188
Cherub, 158–159
Childbirth
  blood of, 297
  Edenic origins, 110, 329
  Jewish humor, 334–335
  menstrual analogies, 261
  nose symbolism, 261, 265–266
  tkhines for, 107, 108–109, 110
Child-rearing, 300–301
Christianity
  body conceptions, 117–118
  Garden of Eden sexuality, 48–49
  Jewish converts, 249
  in Jewish folklore, 210
  sexual abstinence in, 47–48
Circulatory disease, 232
Circumcision, 23, 24, 38, 223
Citron, 108–109
Civilization, Jewish degeneration and, 228–230
Claudication intermittente, 232–235
Commune (*kevutzah*), 291, 294
Consumerism, 340–341, 343–345
Conversion to Christianity, 249
Cordovero, Moses, 122, 123, 168
Cosmology, God's body in, 186–190
Covenant, 22, 23, 35
Cow theology, 183–184
Creation tradition, 23, 25–27, 50–54. *see also* Eden; Eve
Crown, 157, 158
Cultural contradictions, 17–19, 38

Dead Sea Scrolls, 21
Death
  and grotesque body, 69–70, 78–79
  martyrdom, 126–127, 185
  Shekhinah and, 168
Degeneration, 228–230, 284–289
Devil, 224
Disfiguration, 20, 21
Dismemberment, 73
Dodds, E. R., 192
Dolchstosslegende, 226
Donnolo, Shabbetai ben Abraham, 155–156
Douglas, Mary, 21–22
Dreams, 245–247
Dybbuk stories, 212

Eckstein, Emma, 246, 258, 260–263
Eden
  Christian and Jewish exegesis, 47–49
  divine blessing image, 60–63
  Enoch in, 54–55
  eviction from, 62
  joyous New Age and, 56, 59
  lesbian analysis, 364
  sexuality in, 11, 47–54
  temple attributes, 54–55, 63
  Tree of Knowledge, 108–109
Ein-Sof, 118
El'azar, Rabbi, 69–81, 86, 87–93
Elchasai, 153
Eleazar of Worms, 155, 157–161, 167
Elijah, 210
Enoch, 54–55, 151, 191
Eternal Jew, 255–257
Ethnography, 13
Eugenics, 230
Eve
  creation of, 50–54, 59
  lesbian analysis, 364
  niddah and, 103–106
  sexuality, 47, 49–54, 62
  tkhines for, 107–109
  women's atonement for, 102–106, 329
Evil, 129
Evil eye, 82–83, 89

Evolution, 244
Exile, 122–124, 170, 283
Exorcism, 212
Ezekiel, 20, 30, 35, 145, 297

Family life, Zionist ideology of, 290–291
Fano, Menahem Azariah de, 169–170
Fasting, 132–133
Fat, 70, 72, 73–74
Feet, 4–5, 12
  devil images, 224
  gender symbolism, 168
  genital associations, 145, 154, 164, 165, 169, 173
  of Jacob, 166–167
  Jewish military participation and, 224–228, 230
  neurology (claudication intermittente), 232–235
  as racial marker, 228–230, 236
  sexual euphemisms, 167
  washing, 169
  See also God's feet
Feminism, 7–8, 101
  American Jewish family life, 342, 344
  concepts of God, 33, 370
  gender roles and, 368
  lesbianism, 361–363
  in Palestinian Jewish settlements, 295–299
Feminization
  androgyny, 83–84
  of Arab, 284
  male menstruation, 254–255
  obesity and, 78
Fertility blessings, 23–24, 29, 48, 60. *See also* Procreation
Fishman, Ada, 295
Fiske, John, 339–340
Fliess, Wilhelm, 245, 246, 248, 252, 254, 258–263, 266
Flood, 23
Foetor Judaicus, 249–254
Folk culture, 204–205. *See also* Medieval Jewish folklore
Food, 117, 287, 318
Footstool, 146, 150, 152, 160, 162
Foreskin symbolism, 170
Foucault, Michel, 8
Free love, 284
Freud, Sigmund
  on cultural contradiction, 18
  hysteria cases, 233
  on male menstruation, 254
  nasal experiences, 245–247, 257–266
  sexual psychology, 252–253, 293
Freytag, Gustav, 248
Frustration, 287–288, 290

Galante, Abraham, 122
Gamliel, Rabbi Shim'on ben, 81
Garden of Eden, *see* Eden
Gender
  androgyny, 83–84
  evolution of, 244
  foot symbolism, 164–168
  of God, 10, 29, 32–35, 162, 370
  homorelationism, 369–370
  Jewish life and, 330, 354
  Kabbalistic representation of God, 119–120
  lesbian challenges, 362–363, 372–374
  niddah and, 316–317
  nose and, 261
  obesity and, 78
  odor and, 253–255
  public sphere and, 243–244
  of Torah, 154
  traditional role rigidity, 367–369
  See also Male dominance; Male/female complementarity; Sexuality; Women
Genealogy, 24, 25, 76–78
Genitals
  foot symbolism, 145, 154, 164, 165, 169, 173
  of God, 32–33
  nasal associations, 245, 248, 251, 252
  rabbinic traditions, 69, 75
German Pietists, 155–156, 160
Gerushin, 123–124
Gilgamesh, 58
Gnosiology, 244
Gnostic traditions, 127–136, 143, 155
God
  feminist concepts of, 370
  footstool of, 146, 150, 152, 160, 162
  gender of, 10, 29, 32–35, 162, 370

God, (continued)
lesbian image of, 370, 373
names of, 118, 159, 186
sexuality of, 32–35, 370
summoning of, 185
throne of, 28, 146, 161, 162, 188
visible encounters with, 30
God's body, 10–11
allegorical vs. literal descriptions, 185–186
anthropomorphic representations, 30–33
continuity of representational traditions, 143–144
cosmological descriptions, 186–190
as formless, 27–30
in *Hekhalot,* 151–153
Israel as part of, 157
in Kabbalah, 118–121, 155
linguistic problems, 31, 36–37
Lurianic cosmology, 128
man as image of, 26–27
measurement of, 151–152, 170, 183, 190–191
ragle Shekhinah idiom, 147
representational prohibitions, 27–28
scriptural ambiguities, 31–32
in *Shi'ur Qomah,* 151–154, 183–194
Torah and, 154
See also God's feet; *Shekhinah*
God's feet, 10, 12, 30, 143
biblical writings, 144–146, 156
divine judgement and, 144, 163
early mystical literature, 151–154
genital associations, 154
masculine symbolism, 164–165
medieval mystical literature, 155–162
messianic symbolism, 172
prophetic imagery, 170–171, 172
rabbinic theology, 146–151
Shekhina symbolism, 153, 156, 160, 167–169, 171
Golan, Shmuel, 300–301
Goldflam, Samuel, 234
Goodbye Columbus (Roth), 348–354
Gordon, Aharon David, 290, 299
Goslar, Hans, 287–289
Greco-Roman religion, 186–187
Greek Magical Papyri, 191
Grotesque body, 10, 69–93
Guttmann, M. J., 230

Haddlaqah, 102, 106–107
Haeckel, Ernst, 244, 251–252
Hallah tradition, 102, 103, 105, 106
Halutzim, 289–298
Hamadan, Joseph, 171–172
Happa'am, 50–51, 53
Harrison, Beverly, 372
Ha-Tzair, Hashomer, 293–295, 299, 300
Head of God, 157
Health, 5–6
"Jew's foot", 224–230
nervous diseases, 246, 255, 259–260, 286–287, 300
neurological disease, 230–235, 255
niddah and, 317–319
he-Hasid, Judah ben Samuel, 155, 156–157
Heine, Heinrich, 249
Hekhalot, 151–153, 191, 193
Hemorrhoids, 235
Herzl, Theodor, 265, 285, 288
Hess, Moses, 249
Hirschfield, Magnus, 283, 288, 293, 301
Hoffmann, Walter, 226
Hokhmah, 119–120
Hol, 206
Holiness, 21, 48, 54–55
Homorelationism, 369–370
Homosexuality, 164, 363, 369. *See also* Lesbianism
Honi, 192
Honor, 319–320
Horowitz, David, 298
Humor, 332–338, 347
Hysteria, 233

Idel, Moshe, 193
Image of God, 10, 26–27, 29, 31, 35–36. *See also* God's body
Imma, 119, 129, 132
Immortals, 206
Incest, 297–298, 299
Intermarriage, 287, 344
Intimate commune, 291, 294
Iranian myth, 205
Isaac, Simeon bar, 154

Ishma᾿el, Rabbi, 69, 74
Israel, as head of God, 157
Israelite religion
  bodily preoccupations, 20–26, 37–38
  body of God for, 27–33

Jabotinsky, Vladimir, 298
Jacob, 24, 84, 157–159, 165–166
Jastrowitz, M., 231
Jeremiah, 205
Jewish Agency, 311
Jewish American princess, 6, 332–337, 347–354
Jewish body stereotypes, 4–5
  construction of, 223
  ill health, 5–6
  male menstruation, 254–255
  military fitness and, 224–228, 230, 235
  nervous diseases, 246, 255, 259–260, 286–287, 300
  neurological disease, 230–235
  odor, 244–245, 249–254
  symbolic vs. physiognomic characterizations, 247
  urban life and, 228–230
  See also Feet; Nose stereotypes
Jewish identity
  body features and, 228–230
  genealogical vs. religious definition, 1–2
  niddah and, 312–313, 315–316
  nosology, 244
  racial differences, 223
Jewish mysticism, *see* Kabbalah
Joab, 213
Jokes, 332–336
Joy, 58
Jubilees, 53–54, 63
Judah, Rab, 57
Judaism
  cultural contradictions of, 17–19
  gender and, 330, 354
  positive sex traditions, 19–20
  "primitive" aspects, 3–4
  See also specific scriptures, traditions
Judgement, God's feet and, 144, 163

Kabbalah
  aspects of God in, 118–121, 143
  gerushin (exile) ritual, 123–124
  God's body in, 155
  God's feet in, 162–172
  Karo and, 124–127
  Luria and, 127–136
  mythic basis of, 143–144
  prophetic speech, 124, 125
  Safed community, 122
  sex rules, 134–135
  See also Shekhinah
Kallir, Eleazar, 153–154
Kanfe Yonah, 169–170
Karo, Joseph, 122, 124–127, 135
Kehilyateinu, 296, 298
Ketubot, 48, 57–60
Kevutzah, 291, 294
Kibbutz movement, 18, 300
Kingship, 28
Klein, Michael, 184

Lakish, Resh, 83–84, 89
Lavater, Johann Caspar, 247
Lesbianism, 7
  biological roles and, 368–369
  feminism and, 361–363
  God's image and, 370, 373
  Jewish tradition and, 363–372
  liberal Judaism and, 362
  male/female complementarity vs., 362–363, 372–374
  procreation and, 367, 373
  Yentl story and, 371
Levi, R. Joshua Ben, 146
Levi-Strauss, Claude, 18
Leviticus, 20–21
Liberal Judaism, 362, 368
Lichtheim, Anna, 263
Lilith, 205, 364
Linguistic dominance, 101
Lorde, Audre, 372–373
Luria, Isaac, 122, 126–136, 162, 169
Luatto, Moses Hayyim, 172

Mackenzie, John Noland, 252
Maggid Mesharim (Karo), 124–127
Maimonides, Moses, 204, 366
Male bonding, 369
Male dominance
  bourgeois political culture, 243–244
  Eve's sin and, 104, 329

Male dominance, (continued)
feminist challenges, 363
Hebrew language, 101
Israelite priesthood, 25
Jewish princess and, 347
niddah and, 314, 320–322
Male/female complementarity, 7
homorelationism, 369–370
in Jewish law, 364–367
lesbian challenges to, 362–363, 372–374
mythical traditions, 363–364
traditional rigidity of, 367–369
Marjorie Morningstar (Wouk), 348
Marriage, 11
creation myth and, 25
in Garden of Eden, 47, 49–54
with non-Jews, 287, 344
Zionist ideology, 283, 286–288
Martyrdom, 126–127, 185
Marx, K., 18
Masturbation, 205
Matriarchy, 296
Medieval Jewish folklore, 203–215
Alpha-Beth of Ben Sira, 205–206
body as protest in, 211–215
Christians in, 210
Dybbuk (possession) stories, 212–213
expressive concreteness of, 203
Joab story, 213–214
Rashi legend, 209–211
sex-based narrative conflicts, 207–208
sin and punishment, 208–209
spirit-body conflicts, 209–215
Meige, Henri, 255–256
Mekhilta' de-Rabbi Shim'on bar Yohai, 148–149
Mekhilta' de-Rabbi Yishma'el, 149
Menstruation, 20, 75
Edenic origins, 102, 104–105, 110
feminine identity and, 316–317
male nosebleeds as, 254–255, 261
odor, 253
Rabbi El'azar story, 71, 75
See also Niddah
Merkavah tradition, 158
Mesolelot, 365–366
Mesopotamian mythology, 36
Messiah, 145, 172
Messianic age, 135
Metatron, 151, 170
Middle class life, 341–347
Midrash
Edenic sexuality, 49–54
God's feet in, 146–151
See also Rabbinic traditions; *specific sources, topics*
Midrash ha-Gadol, 148
Milham, 206
Military, Jewish foot problems and, 224–228, 230, 235
Miqve, 314–315. *See also Niddah*
Mizvot, 101–106, 110–111
Moroccan women immigrants, 309–323
Mother
daughter interactions, 317
Jewish American stereotypes, 332, 338, 347
Kabbalistic representation of God, 119
Lurianic Kabbalah, 129, 132
Mourning, 56, 58
Musar, 101–102, 104–106, 110–111
Muskat, G., 228–229, 234
Mysticism, *see* Kabbalah

Nahman, R. Joshua ben, 158
Najara, Israel, 122
Nakedness, 32, 301
Names of God, 159, 186
Nebuchadnezzar, 205
Nervous diseases, 246, 255, 259–260, 286–287, 300
Neshamah, 120–121
Neurological disorders, 255, 285
New Age, 56–60
Niddah, 101, 309, 367
atonement for Eve's sin, 104–106
days of purity, 313–314
feminine identity and, 316–317
health and well-being and, 317–319
honor and, 319–320
Jewish identity and, 312–313, 315–316
Lurianic penalties, 133
Moroccan immigrant practices, 309–323
mother-daughter interactions, 317

Rabbi El'azar story, 71, 75
ritual bath (*miqve*), 314–315
sexuality and, 321
spousal relationships and, 314, 320–322
tkhines for, 107, 109, 110
in women's commandments, 101–102, 104–106, 110–111
Noah, 32
Nordau, Max, 5–6, 231–232, 251, 265, 285
Nordmann, H., 226
Nose stereotypes, 4–5, 12, 243–266
birthing symbolism, 261, 265–266
degeneration and, 251
Freud and, 245–247, 257–266
genital associations, 245, 248, 251, 252
German folk sayings, 248
male menstruation, 254, 261
racial marker, 247–248
See also Odor
Nosology, 244, 255

Obesity, 72, 74–75, 77, 78
Odor, 244–245, 249–254
degeneration and, 251–253
feminine, 251
gender identity and, 253–255
repression and, 258
Oral traditions, 203, 206
Orthodox Jews, 5
Ottoman Empire, 122

Palestine, Second and Third Aliyot, 289–298
Parzufim, 129, 130
Penis
circumcision rite, 23, 24, 38
foot symbolism, 154, 164
of God, 32–33, 119
nose size and, 248, 252
rabbinic traditions, 69, 75
Yesod symbolism, 171
See also Genitals
People of the Book, 1–3, 5, 7
Perversion, 252–253
Phallus, *see* Penis
Philo, 204
Phoenix, 206
Physical fitness, 231, 285–286
Physiognomy, 247. *See also* Feet; Nose stereotypes
Plaskow, Judith, 364, 372
Pleasure, 340
Political culture, male dominance of, 243–244
Popper, Marie, 289
Poppers, Meir, 169
Possession, 212–213
Power relationships, 321–322, 329–330
Pregnancy, 107, 373. *See also* Childbirth
Primordial Man, 119, 128–130, 134
Procreation
blessings, 23–24, 29, 48, 60
in creation myth, 25–26
cultural contradictions, 17
genealogy and, 24, 25
lesbians and, 367, 373
in Lurianic Kabbalism, 134
priesthood preoccupations, 24, 25, 33
rabbinic preoccupation, 76–78
as religious duty, 22–26, 47
spiritual filiation, 81, 85, 86–87, 93
Zionist ideology, 296, 297
See also Childbirth; Sexual intercourse
Professional status, 258
Prophecy, 124, 170–172
Psychosomatic illness, 212
Punishment, 208–209

Qumran, 21

Ra'aya Mehemna', 161–162
Rabbinic traditions, 143
Edenic sexuality, 49–54, 63
God's feet, 146–151
grotesque body, 10, 69–93
procreation, 76–78
Sabbath day sexuality, 56
Rabelais, 79
Race, 223, 228–230, 236, 244
Radner, Gilda, 337
Ragle Shekhinah, 147, 156
Rapoport, Eliahu, 300
Rashi, 51, 57, 209–211, 365

Regel, 164
Repression, 258
Reproduction, *see* Procreation
Revisionist Movement, 298
Rivers, Joan, 334
Rohrer, Joseph, 224
Rosh Hodesh, 368
Roth, Alfred, 227
Roth, Philip, 348–354
Ruth, 166–167, 364

Sabbath, sexual relations on, 55–56
Sacrifice, 21, 126–127
Safed, 118, 122, 127
Saint's body, 79
Samson, 298
Sandalphon, 169–170
Sandals, 169–170
Sarna, Nahum, 28
Savage in Judaism, The (Eilberg-Schwartz), 4, 8
Scholem, Gershom, 148, 160
Schopenhauer, Arthur, 250, 253
Schreber, Daniel Paul, 256–257
Scroll of Ahimaaz, 211
Second Aliya, 289–293, 302–303
Seder 'Eliyahu Zuta, 147
Seder tkhines u-vakoshes, 107–108
Sefer ha-Bahir, 155, 160–161
Sefer ha-Gematriyot, 150
Sefer ha-Hokhmah, 159, 167
Sefer ha-Komah, 186
Sefer Ha-Shi'ur, 186
Sefer mitsvas ha-noshim, 102, 104, 110
Sefer Tashaq, 171–172
Sefer Yesirah, 155
Sefirot, 11, 118–121, 129, 155, 163. *See also Shekhinah*
Self-affliction, 123–124, 131–133. *See also* Asceticism
Seth, 31, 37, 62
Sexology, 288, 293
Sexual frustration, 287–288, 290
Sexual intercourse
- adulterous fantasies, 82
- *Alpha-Beth of Ben Sira,* 205–206
- anti-normative folkloric encounters, 207–208
- foot washing euphemism, 169
- Kabbalistic rules, 134–135
- menstruation and, 71, 75
- as metaphor for God's covenant, 35
- mourning and, 56
- Sabbath and, 55–56

Sexuality, 11
- animals and, 29, 34
- child-rearing practices, 300–301
- in creation myth, 25–26
- cultural contradictions, 38
- in Garden of Eden, 11, 47–63
- of God, 32–35, 370
- Jewish American women, 329, 331–338
- in Jewish law, 364–367
- Jewish stereotypes, 288
- kibbutz movement, 300
- lesbian identity and, 361
- mother-daughter interactions, 317
- national ideals vs., 299
- neuroses and, 259–260
- new religious ethic, 372–373
- *niddah* and, 321
- odor and, 244–245, 251
- positive traditions of, 19–20
- power and, 329–330
- Second and Third Aliyot, 289–298
- *See also* Gender; Zionist erotic revolution

Sha'ar ha-Kavvanot, 169
Shatz, Zvi, 291–292, 294
Sheba, Queen of, 205, 206
Shefatia, Rabbi, 211
Shekhina
- death and, 168
- foot symbolism, 167–169, 171
- *gerushin* (exile) ritual, 123–124
- God's feet and, 146–149, 153, 156, 160
- Jacob and, 165–166
- Lurianic Kabbalah, 129, 133
- prophetic speaking, 124, 125
- proto-Kabbalistic descriptions, 159
- as throne, 162
- *Yesod* and, 171

Shi'ur Qomah, 10, 148, 151–154, 183–194
Sin, 121, 208–209
Singer, Isaac Bashevis, 371
Skin diseases, 20

Smell, *see* Odor
Sobel, Yehoshua, 303
Soll und Haben (Freytag), 248
Solnik, R. Benjamin Aaron, 102, 104, 106, 111
Solomon, 205, 206
Song of Songs, 147, 152, 298
Son of God, 145
Soul, 120–121, 129, 130, 132
Spanish exiles, 122
Spirit, in folk traditions, 206, 209–215
Spiritual filiation, 81, 85, 86–87, 93
Spirituality, 6, 20
Spiro, M., 18
Sport, 231, 285–286
Stereotypes, *see* Jewish body stereotypes
Stroumsa, Gedaliahu, 185
Sufi, 124
Syphilis, 232

Talmud
  grotesque body in, 69–93
  lesbian behavior in, 365
  wedding benedictions, 56–60
Tamar, 297–298
Targum, 51, 148, 158
Tarshish, 189
Tel Fekharyeh, 60
Temple, 54–55, 63, 150
Theophany, 144–146, 155–156
Theurgy, 121, 192–194
Third Aliya, 293–298
Throne of God, 28, 146, 158–162, 188
Tiferet, 120
Tiqqun, 129
Tkhines, 102–103, 106–111
Tobacco use, 235–236
Tree of Knowledge, 108–109
Trible, Phyllis, 34
Trumpeldor, Joseph, 291
Tsenerene, 108–109
Turner, Bryan, 340

Vascular disease, 232
Vidas, Elijah de, 121, 122
Vital, Hayyim, 122, 169, 173

Wandering Jew, 208, 255–257
Wandervogel, 293
Watchers, 54
Weakness, 5–6
Weapons, 85–86
Wedding rites, 56–60
Williams, Michael, 117
Women
  alterity of, 101
  American Jewish depictions, 329, 331–338, 347–354
  consumer culture, 340–341, 343–345
  creation of, 50–54, 59
  homorelationism, 369–370
  Jewish American princess, 6, 332–337, 347–354
  Jewish mother, 332, 338
  middle class life styles, 341–347
  odors, 251, 253
  power of, 329–330
  Zionism and, 289, 295–299
  See also Feminism; Lesbianism; *Niddah*
Women's Bible, 108
Women's commandments, 101–106, 110–111. *See also Niddah*
Wouk, Herman, 348

Yaari, Meir, 293–295, 298–300
Yakar, Rabbi Yaakov ben, 210
Yebamot, 51
"Yentl the Yeshiva Boy," (Singer), 371–372
Yesod, 171
Yiddish literature, 101–102, 104–106, 110–111
Yohanan, Rabbi, 69, 81–86, 88–90
Youth movements, 293, 300

Zeir, 129–130
Zeus, 188
Zionism
  family life, 290–291
  physical fitness and, 231, 285–286
  women and, 289, 295–299
  youth movements, 293, 300
Zionist erotic revolution, 6, 283–284
  child-rearing philosophy, 300–301
  cultural contradictions of, 18
  internal contradictions, 298–301
  marriage and, 286–287
  national goals and, 299

Zionist erotic revolution, (continued)
  polemic against degeneration, 284–289
  romantic failure, 301–303
  scientific approach, 288
  Second and Third Aliyot, 289–298
Zohar, 119–120
  God's feet in, 162–172
  manifestations of deity in, 119–120
  See also Kabbalah
Zoroaster, 205
Zo't happa'am, 50–51, 53

Printed in the United States
101759LV00003B/28/A

9 780791 411704